THE EPHESIAN CHRONICLES

VOLUME 1

THE PLANTING ACTS - 19

By

KEITH LANNON

Copyright © *Keith Lannon*, 2024

All Rights Reserved

This book is subject to the condition that no part of this book is to be reproduced, transmitted in any form or means; electronic or mechanical, stored in a retrieval system, photocopied, recorded, scanned, or otherwise. Any of these actions require the proper written permission of the author.

Unless indicated otherwise, Scripture quotations marked NKJV are taken from
The Holy Bible, New King James Version
Copyright 1979, 1980, 1982 by Thomas Nelson, Inc., publishers.

Scripture quotations marked NIV are from the Holy Bible, New International Version.
Copyright 1973, 1978, 1984, International Bible Society

Scripture quotations marked AMP are from the Amplified Bible.
Old Testament Copyright 1965, 1987 by the Zondervan Corporation.
The Amplified New Testament Copyright 1954, 1958, 1987 by the Lockman Foundation

Table of Contents

1. Annus Mirabilis The Premise Of These Pages......................1
2. "Go Into All The World..." But........................10
3. Wasn't The Time! Now's The Time!..............19
4. The Hand Of God In The Circumstances Of Life.................27
5. The Top Priority Build Team..............36
6. Baptism In The Holy Spirit The Biblical Norm..............41
7. Miraculous Impartation Acts 19:1-7..............62
8. Mentoring. Acts 19:6-9..............75
9. Modelling Ministry Acts 19:8-9..............82
10. Urgency, Necessity & Efficiency. (Acts 19:9-10)..............92
11. The Astonishing Everyday Routine For 3 Years...............104
12. The Ministry Of The Living Word..............111
13. PAUL'S DEFINITION OF WHAT CONSTITUTES "THE WORD OF GOD."..............117
14. Healing..............126
15. Deliverance (1) Basic Definition..............136
16. Deliverance (2) Beyond Casting Demons Out (Acts 19:12-19)..............149
17. Deliverance (3) The Practicalities Of Large-Scale Deliverance...............157
18. Paul A "Bond-Slave" "A Servant" (Acts 19:22. Acts 20:18-20)..............167
19. Mindsets That Precipitate The Miraculous – Introduction..............188
19 A. Mindsets That Precipitate The Miraculous. Number One: Taking It As A Given That Christianity Is Intrinsically Permeated With The Supernatural In Its DNA..............194
19 B. Mindsets That Precipitate The Miraculous. Number Two: Jesus Christ Never Commissioned Anybody To Preach, Without Also Commissioning Them To Heal The Sick, Cleanse The Lepers, Raise The Dead And Cast Out Demons...............201
19 C. Mindsets That Precipitate The Miraculous. Number Three: Start Perceiving The Miraculous As Normal In Christ..............208

19 D. Mindsets That Precipitate The Miraculous. Number Four: Holy Spirit Initiated Prophetic Ministry Is To Be Sought After As The Norm. 214

19 E. Mindsets That Precipitate The Miraculous. Number Five: If It Is In The Atonement, It Is For Everybody, And It Is For Now. 224

19 F. Mindsets That Precipitate The Miraculous. Number Six: Be Courageous And Speak Out The Rhema Prophetic Word................. 227

19 G. Mindsets That Precipitate The Miraculous. Number Seven: Holiness And Purity Of Life Is Not Optional. 233

20. Burning Their Bridges As Well As Their Books. Acts 19:13-20 238

21. Following In The Train Of His Triumph. 252

22. The Labour Pains Of The Transformation Of A National Culture. Acts 19:23-41 265

23. PAUL'S PERSECUTION, PRISON AND PRESSURE IN EPHESUS? 281

24. Paul The Prophet. 295

25. Paul Was Actually Converted By A Vision Of A Divine Visitation. (Acts 9:1-9; 22:5-11; 26:12-20).. 305

26. "Of Mice And Men!" "Of Paul And Persecution"! What's The Difference? 324

27. The Peak Of Transparency And Suffering. 350

28. FULLY PREACHED THE GOSPEL WHERE NO ONE HAD PREACHED BEFORE.. 376

29. The Lonely Walk From Troas To Assos. 384

31. The Miletus Good-Bye (Acts 20:17-21) 394

32. A BACKWARD LOOK AT THE BIG PICTURE AS PAUL LEAVES EPHESUS BEHIND?... 419

About The Author 428

1.

ANNUS MIRABILIS
THE PREMISE OF THESE PAGES.

To cut to the chase, I have uncovered, to my great joy, in the book of Acts, a biblical model of apostolic operation and evangelism that has frankly astounded me. The way I now perceive this "model" of ministry, this "Ultimativen Höhepunkt Beispiel" (Ultimate high achievement), is what I personally now refer to as (what it surely must be), "The Peak of Apostolic Ministry." There must be others out there who have read the Bible more often and with a deeper insight than I could ever dream of. However, I have to say, that in over half a century of reading and studying the Old and New Testaments, studying ascribed authorities and historians, listening to contemporary apostolic type men of God and bible teachers, I have never heard of, or perceived before what I am sharing in these pages.

I feel like some explorer ploughing across Africa, or the Atlantic in an attempt to fill in some huge blank space of the accepted maps of planet earth. I did not know there was a black space so large, and so basic in my understanding, that is, until I saw what I have tried to lay out in these pages. I feel like the man in the Crow's nest shouting loud and clear, "Land Ho!" while others on deck below scratch their heads shouting, "I can't see a single thing!" What I see is plainly, to my eyes at least, a huge continent, that to my understanding has not been seen or negotiated before.

I am referring to the Apostle Paul's, "Annus Mirabilis." It was actually more than one year, it was a period of three years or more where he peaked, but you know what I mean, I hope.

Many great men and women in history have experienced a period that could be referred to as their "Annus Mirabilis". The term was initially created, I believe, by historians and commentators describing Einstein's discoveries during his lifetime. "Annus," is Latin for, "year." "Mirabilis" means "outstanding," or "extraordinary". Indeed, Einstein's papers on Relativity are referred to by many physicists as, "The Annus Mirabilis papers." For Einstein, his peak year was 1905. The four articles he wrote in that year contributed substantially to the foundation of modern physics, creating a field of study and research presently known as quantum physics, changing views on space, time and matter. It was as if everything Einstein lived for and thought through was fully developed and presented to the world during the course of 1905. Thereafter he spent his life struggling to go beyond the content of those papers, whilst concurrently justifying them to the world. He lived 50 years more, after his Annus Mirabilis, and was fully acknowledged for his great genius throughout those years because of what he had seen and revealed to the world during 1905. As far as published papers and statements are concerned, he never surpassed his revelations of that year. We remember Einstein because of his life's production in 1905.

Sir Isaac Newton's Annus Mirabilis was 1666. Newton was born 1643. His revelations on calculus, gravity, motion and optics were received by the world, and scientists in particular, as something far beyond astounding. He revealed them all to the world in the year of the great fire of London at the age of 23. He lived another 61 years thereafter, but never exceeded his miracle year of 1666 in astonishing breakthroughs and discoveries of scientific thought.

Yet another example is Christopher Columbus. He strove and fought to be sponsored and released so that he could sail westward, and thereafter return home from the East. I remember learning at school that, "In fourteen hundred and ninety two, Columbus sailed the sea so blue." He enjoyed his Annus Mirabilis (which was actually much longer than a year), but yet again, the rest of his life was comparatively downhill after his discovery of the West Indies.

What is the nature of my discovery? Not that this is my Annus Mirabilis. I am talking about the Apostle Paul's greatest ever breakthrough.

I see Paul's mission in Acts 19, concluding with his speech to the Ephesian elders in Acts 20, as his ultimate Annus Mirabilis. For him it was a three year-plus period of astonishing "productivity," in a glorious intense extension of the Kingdom of God. I believe Paul's peak, his ultimate experience of the greatness of God's power and grace upon his life as an apostle, was the ministry he invested in Ephesus. I see all that went before as a learning curve leading and building up to his Ephesian Mission. These pages are intended to explain why I hold that conviction.

Saul of Tarsus was converted in Acts chapter 9 round about 35 to 36 AD. Authorities differ when trying to be exact re the date of the Damascus Road Christophany that turned a man who was systematically wanting to kill Christians, into the most powerful evangelist for Christ. We are not sure how long a time he spent in Arabia immediately after his conversion (Galatians 1:15 -17). That period, however, was undoubtedly a period spent seeking after God and gaining revelation on his newly given belief system and personal understanding of walking with Christ. He was not, for that period, "in ministry" per se, at least, not as far as we know. He, soon after, returned to even more "silent" years in his home town of Tarsus, leaving us utterly ignorant as to what he was doing during his stay there. This was a period that some scholars think was as long as 9 years (Acts 9:30 till Acts 11:25-26).

I have to throw in a remark for consideration here with an observation that shall be elucidated upon later, explaining how Paul's reminiscences in the letter we refer to as Second Corinthians, highlights many startling and shocking experiences that the book of Acts does not even hint at. My reason for entering that thought here is that these, possibly, "silent" nine years may not have been silent or static at all, but rather merely "unmentioned" in scripture. Any input on that issue must be pure conjecture. These are things we would all love to know, but alas are historically told nothing about their existence or chronological position in the life of Paul.

"Silent", or vociferously active, he was invited by Barnabas to leave Tarsus and join the ministry team in the church at Syrian Antioch. He was there for a few years before being sent out by the church via prophetic pronouncements.

Once he was prophetically set apart by the church in Antioch, along with Barnabas, and had set off for Cyprus, he was, geographically, a "flyer" (Acts 13:2-4). He seems, through the biblical text, to flit about freely enjoying – or better still - "enduring" - short evangelistic thrusts in many places. More often than not the Bible does not mention at all how long his stays were.

His first missional journey was something like three years long (Acts 13:4-14:26). In that period he stopped and preached at Salamis and Paphos, while crossing Cyprus, followed afterwards by a sea crossing to Attalia in Turkey, then travelling by land to Perga, Pisidian Antioch, Iconium, Lystra and Derbe. He then returned by exactly the same route, revisiting the converts made on the outward journey. No mention at all is made of the lengths of his stays in these places. We are, however, confident in asserting that those visits were short, sharp, brief and to the point in this first journey. This was a most remarkable baptism into winning Gentile converts to faith in Jesus Christ, and climbing the exponential "learning curve" on how to teach and handle gentile people pastorally, in the context of what were, to Paul, foreign cultures. He was here dealing with mostly non-Jewish people in various cultural contexts, each embedded with small (or sometimes large) Jewish contingents that were constantly decrying Saul, who, during that first mission had changed his name to Paul (a none-Jewish name). He had undoubtedly taken the leading role as the senior brother over Barnabas by the time they had completed their journey.

Paul's knowledge base of how to cope with gentile culture, together with learning how to handle the cross wiring of Jewish insistence of injecting more Judaism into his message, and how to move in the grace given to him as an apostle, was a long and difficult process of learning that was - necessary and vital for the far-flung future of the church. Many Jews at that time saw Christianity as a cultic off shoot from Judaism, while Paul's message insisted that Judaism was merely Christianity in gestation. Today I often hear the perplexed question of why it was so hard for Paul, and especially the church as a whole to become extricated from the Jewish grip on church beliefs and attitudes. One needs to remember, however, that at the beginning the church was well-nigh 100% Jewish, and it took a considerable amount of time for the church to be conceived of as something new, and not simply an extension of Judaistic practices.

A year or so later, after returning to base (i.e. Syrian Antioch), Paul's second missionary trip was with Silas (Acts 15:36 – 18:22). Again, in a period of between two to possibly four years, Paul visited other parts of Syria, then moved on through Cilicia, Lystra, Phrygia, Galatia, Troas, Philippi, Thessalonica, Berea and Athens. We have no particular idea as to how long Paul spent in these places, apart from the sure and certain knowledge that he spent two weeks only (three Sabbaths) in Thessalonica (Acts 17:2-10). Does this mean that two to three weeks was the norm? Any detailed answer, again, has to be pure conjecture. The text seems to suggest that each stop was a brief one, that is, until the apostle arrives at infamous Corinth.

Eighteen months at Corinth was (as far as we are told) the longest stretch he had, up to that point of time, stayed anywhere whilst on an evangelistic mission. We must state, also, that he stayed there purely on the specific instruction of Jesus Christ Himself, who literally appeared to him in order to reveal to him the needed to stay put, and reap a considerable harvest (Acts 18:9-11). The words of Jesus to Paul explicitly state that there was a huge number of prospective converts who lived in Corinth, waiting to be won over to the faith by his ministry during those immediately coming days.

It seems to this writer that something different had happened in heaven and on earth, and God's overseeing providence in Paul's life from those days in Corinth and onwards. The physical attacks on his person were less violent and ineffective in comparison to his previous experiences of mob rule. It was as if the motives and accusations of the demonically inspired mobs were sedated somewhat by God's grace and through the Roman proconsul in Corinth, who went by the name of Gallio. Or was it more "to the point" that by divine intervention Paul was being prepared for an evangelistic thrust, for which Corinth was but a precursor? One and a half years later, Paul was actually free to leave Corinth without being stoned, attacked, vilified or persecuted within that leaving process. I am not wanting to be trivial or light about this issue, but it was as if God had fully accredited Paul's status into being a "senior" Apostle of Christ, worthy to stay in a single province for such a time of church building, allowing him time to both found and build church (i.e., the people not any building) thoroughly. He was, after all, going to be ministering in Asia for a similar length of time to that in which Christ ministered in the Holy Land in the days of His flesh. It was to be a mission like no other before or since. A little bit more than three years. Ephesus and Asia were divinely intended to be ravaged by the gospel of Christ.

Paul left Corinth (after his 18 month mission) for Jerusalem. We are not told of any heavenly instruction, nor earthly persecution that caused him to leave. To our knowledge, he left calmly, at his own volition, in peace. It was so peaceful, in fact he took a couple of close friends with him. And after a brief stopover at the place called Ephesus, where he preached and debated in the Synagogues for a short undefined length of time, he was actually asked to return by the Jewish contingent in the Synagogue. Now that was a first! We read of that kind of Jewish response nowhere else. He left the city of Diana's temple promising to come back to speak to the Synagogue attendee's, only if God would allow him to (Acts 18:18-21).

After a brief, none eventful, coldly recorded visit to Jerusalem (suggesting that he was not too warmly welcomed), Paul set off on what is commonly referred to as his "Third Missionary Journey" (Acts 18:22-23). He went foraging in his unique evangelistic and church-building ministry, throughout Galatia, Phrygia and Asia and ultimately, in his western thrust, he turned up at Ephesus again.

As a vital, "By the way", it is important to note here that there are around 19 references to Asia in the New Testament, and it is assumed and confidently stated by all scholars and authorities on the subject, that the term very definitely refers to the Roman province which encapsulated the western section of the peninsula that we now refer to as Asia Minor. For those of you who are not au fait with historical geographical terminology, when reading the New Testament, just keep a mental note that when one reads, "Asia", it really means, "the western half of modern Turkey." That whole area was under Roman rule and designated as a governmental province referred to as "Asia." Ephesus was the capital city of that province.

Acts 19:10 says he was there for two years, although in Acts 20:31, Paul refers to his stay there as three years. Whatever the actual length of time and number of days, it was, as far as the book of Acts is concerned, his longest missionary effort in any one single place and was without doubt the most remarkable evangelistic mission since the Holy Spirit had fallen on the 120 in Acts chapter 2. Subtracting the first few months when he was debating in the synagogue (or synagogues), it is safe to assume that Paul had, at an absolute minimum period, somewhere around twenty months with a daily 5 hour "service", "debate" or, "meeting" at the school building of one Tyrannus. It is this period of ministry that I refer to as Paul's "Annus Mirabilis".

If time machines ever get to be invented in my life time, this is one mission in a passage and parcel of time that I would pay a lot to visit, remain in the midst of, and be part of.

Acts chapters 19 and 20 are typically, biblically, brief and scanty with their explanatory remarks, yet supernaturally and paradoxically (as always), full and comprehensive in their significance. This is, I believe, the record of Paul's later ministry that when understood and emulated by men of apostolic stature in our day, will undoubtedly change the world.

The mind boggles at the effort, the labour and the results as recorded. The secret of it all, I believe, was Paul's management of his ministry in the realm of the miraculous. It was his understanding of, and fame within the unseen universe of what, to most of us, is invisible that brought the great exploits to his hand. The power of God, in the wisdom given to him, gave the Apostle the right, to shout afterwards, with a cry of victory; "Ephesus is taken!" The city was truly taken for Christ. And so was the whole of Roman Asia.

The depth and totality of the work accomplished by Paul in Ephesus, as well as rippling throughout the whole of Asia, was such that we know and can see that in the last book of the Bible, it was acknowledged in heaven as a work that was especially significant amongst the entire world wide church at that time. I see it as if the entire life of Paul was a learning curve in lots of directions that led up to a period of ministry which by its divine shock and influence, changed the world. Paul had seen the sick healed before, but not on the scale of Ephesus. He had cast out demons before but seen nothing like the witches and wizards that were delivered in the city that was formerly known as, "the home of Diana of the Ephesians". He had pointed out people from the crowd before and ministered to them by the leading of the Spirit, but not as intensely as in Acts 19.

It was such an incredibly solid and comprehensive time of church building, that when the Lord Jesus gave John the apocalyptic prophecy of the book of Revelation, he only addressed the main seven church centres that were created and established by Paul's work in this particular mission, at this time. No other church, or area of churches was mentioned or acknowledged by the risen Christ as He stood amongst the candlesticks. In fact, no other candlesticks were referred to apart from those in Asia, the candlesticks that Paul himself had helped build during the mission in the real time of Acts chapter 19. The church of Jerusalem, Antioch, Alexandria or Rome are not as much as referred to. It was the seven churches of Asia, the churches founded in Paul's mission at Ephesus that was spoken of by the Saviour on Patmos. We are talking of serious culture and population impact with the gospel that is second to none in history, with a depth of foundation laying, and an awesome height of faith establishing, that I am convinced has been unparalleled since. We are examining a period of missionary work that had heaven's stamp of approval like none other.

Follow me through the divinely prepared situation of Paul's arrival at the capital and metropolis of Asia, the three years he laboured there, and the resulting outbreak of the Holy Spirit thereafter, and see if you agree with me, when I say that this section of scripture is the absolute peak of all known Apostolic ministry presented to us in scripture, as a model to follow.

2.

"GO INTO ALL THE WORLD..." BUT...

"Now when they had gone throughout Phrygia and the region of Galatia and were forbidden of the Holy Ghost to preach the word in Asia, after they were come to Mysia, they assayed to go into Bithynia: but the Spirit of Jesus suffered them not."

Acts 16:6-7 9 (KJV)

For a volume concerning an incredible evangelistic mission in the place called Ephesus, the very heart and capital city of Proconsular Asia, it may seem strange to start at the particular moment that God refused to allow the Apostle to enter Asia, never mind Ephesus. We do not read of such a thing anywhere else in the New Testament, so why here? What on earth is the significance of God's unwillingness to let them into Asia at this point?

We have to be talking of and referring to a Divine timing for Ephesus and its evangelisation. In the dimension of God's own modus operandi, and His predestined plans and foreknown circumstances, it would seem that the moment in real-time which Acts 16:6-7 refers to, was simply not Asia's moment. God's blueprint for the place was set for a later date. Sorry if it sounds a bit "Sunday school for the under 5's" simplistic, but looking at the big picture of this story, I have no other explanation.

God's plans and purposes all have their divinely appointed moment for being realised. Too early or too late could be catastrophic for some of the world's greatest ideas. We are told plainly in the biblical text, of the Spirit of God communicating his refusal about Asia, yet, we do not hear of any such communication concerning any other missional thrust anywhere in the New Testament. To be sure, we hear of circumstances that caused Paul to change his direction once or twice, but we are not told anywhere else that God refused them entry into any place. Neither are we informed of any other dream or vision that called them to go to any particular place, apart from the single dream of the man calling them to Macedonia. The book of Acts is explicit, Paul was "forbidden of the Holy Spirit to preach the word in Asia", and as they surveyed Bithynia for evangelistic purposes, it was not because of the lack of prayer support or finances that they, yet again, were turned away. It wasn't because people were not of a demographic that suggested they were not open to the gospel, or any other scientific model of "people type" readings of which we have plenty today. It says clearly; "the Spirit of Jesus suffered them not." To this writer, it is a simple inference, no matter how cryptic, that what was going to happen in Asia was going to be very special. God could foresee the very moment in time when Ephesus would receive the gospel, and how its influence would ripple to the edges of Asia, and no doubt beyond. So God took charge in a very singular and specific manner to ensure that the time was right for the window of opportunity for the Ephesian people, and the whole population of Asia.

Ephesus was not a place that was totally virgin to the gospel. There were people from Asia present on the day of Pentecost in Acts chapter two. Acts 2:5 in the King James translation states that there were devout Jewish worshippers, "out of every nation under heaven". Weymouth translated it as, "from every part of the world." Verse 9 actually states that there were people from "Asia". On top of that, as we will later see, a wife and husband ministry couple whose names were Priscilla and Aquila, together with a preacher named Apollos ministered there before Paul laid into the godlessness of what is, today, Western Turkey.

So, again we ponder, why were they forbidden at that moment of time? Christ had undoubtedly told the apostles to, "Go into all the world and preach the gospel" (Mark 16:15). Paul, of course, was not present to hear those words when they were first spoken. The Apostle had, however, from his conversion in Acts chapter 9 received, an apostolic call to travel the world and preach to gentile people as often and as best he could. Without being facetious, or trying to insult my readers, there is no way that call could have been fulfilled without him moving out into places where the gentiles dominated the demographic makeup. There was, as there always has been, more gentiles in the world than Jews. Here he was, doing that very thing to which he had been called of God. Yet he was somehow given the divine thumbs down on a substantial population area. An area and populace that was extremely influential on the world stage.

But why?

The Bible does not give us so much as a clue. Any suggestion put forward is pure hypothesis. Perhaps Macedonia, Athens and Corinth were more prepared in heart to be good soil for the seed of the gospel at that moment of time, because that is where he went next after been told to miss out Asia and Bithynia. Perhaps Paul wasn't yet prepared or ready for the labour and weight that was to be his when he was finally to minister in a way that would impact an entire sub-continent. Forasmuch as we are talking about one of the busiest and hardest working figures in scripture, what we later find out about his three years in Ephesus must have pushed Paul to an extreme limit physically, emotionally, mentally and spiritually. Perhaps he wasn't quite ready for such a heavy workload at the real-time moment of Acts 16:6-7. Extremely doubtful, but possible I suppose.

I do feel that because he had not ministered in any one place over long, Paul's training (and somehow the term, "training", seems utterly inappropriate when talking about the Apostle Paul), had not yet been completed.

What I personally consider as the best hypothesis for the Divine redirection away from Asia, is that the ultimate experience of "mission" that was to take place while headquartered in Ephesus via this chosen Apostle, known, at the time to which we are referring, only to God, needed what I shall only refer to as a, "preparatory run", giving Paul eighteen months in Corinth to see great fruit, and learn in practise what it takes to build a church from scratch to a solid and mighty establishment. Eighteen months to make a full despatch and unburdening of all he knew, and all he had, in Christ. Please understand what I am saying. I am not attempting to demean what went on in Corinth, referring to it as a "practice run". There is no such thing in the cause of evangelism, or the realm of the Spirit. But there are such things as learning curves in the entire vista of human linear existence. And no matter what had happened beforehand, what was ahead of him at Ephesus was to be the top of any learning curve he was ever to go through, short of martyrdom itself – not that Paul would have had a clue of his own future except for inner awareness of the Spirit's preparatory nudgings.

Having stated that thought, we cannot properly go any further to discover why Paul was refused entrance to Asia and Bithynia, apart from the overall cliché that would tell us, "God's Timing" had other ideas for the churches that were to be ultimately based at Asia, Ephesus, Smyrna, Laodicea, Philadelphia, Pergamum, Thyatira, Sardis and Colossae. Historical non biblical archaeological discoveries tell us that there were many more churches in Asia after Paul's experience there.

We can more positively assert some reasons that definitely were not the Divine motivation behind the redirecting of the Apostle. For instance, it was not that God did not care for the souls there. Were Asia and Bithynia therefore neglected by God because their lost state was to remain for another 2 years or so? Absolutely not! Not only was the peak of all Apostolic ministry that we know of, to take place in the heart of Asia and impact the entire province, we need to observe, also, that the first epistle of Peter is addressed to the strangers scattered throughout Pontus, Galatia, Cappadocia, Asia, and Bithynia. This suggests that Peter, later, covered this vast sub-continent himself with the gospel, and that Peter would indeed minister to those two provinces where Paul, at this first approach, was divinely denied access. God had no bias at all against Asia or Bithynia. We have the authority of Paul himself for saying that God would have all men to be saved, and to come to the knowledge of the truth. So! We pull down the very thought that there was any Divine neglect here concerning Ephesus and Asia.

I suppose the ultimate learning point of Acts 16:6 is the fact that a person can actually know and be informed of God's timing. We all need to see that often the secret to accomplishment is in doing the right thing at the right time. "Timing is everything," say experienced project workers. Solomon saw that, "He has made everything beautiful in its time" (Ecclesiastes 3:11). David's dynasty thrived because David's military leaders "understood the times and knew what Israel should do" (1 Chronicles 12:32). King Xerxes, the heathen king referred to in the book of Esther, understood this principle. Although he seems utterly deficient in moral character, he knew to surround himself "with the wise men who understood the times" (Esther 1:13). Asia needed the Gospel as desperately, if not more so, than some other places at the point of time in history. But this moment of Paul's first consideration of Asia was just not God's time.

We can also assert that "need", per se, on its own, does not constitute a call. Paul had just come from the east; they had been forbidden to go south or north, but they did not presume that the Lord was leading them to the west -- they waited on His specific directions. Oh, the need to observe Paul's logic, and his driven sensitivity to know the mind of God on all issues!

God has made it easy for us to understand His timing. He made it simple to discover His time by giving us the seasons of life. Everything in life has its season. There is a time for everything, and a season for every activity under heaven (Ecclesiastes 3:1). The four seasons of life are: Winter, spring, summer, and autumn. Each of these seasons demands peculiar action on life's issues. During the winter one needs to dream and plan in the long dark nights. Spring is planting season for seeds of life and achievement. Summer is for watering and cultivating and attending to growth. Autumn is for reaping, distributing and being generous. I am not referring to the twelve month Calendar when I talk like this. Please note that the four seasons, and the mode of their arrival that I am referring to, could be simultaneously upon us for various reasons. It may be spring for one dream, winter for one projects' creation, summer for a present activity, and autumn for another – all at the same time. Wisdom behoves us to know the seasons we walk in.

I read it somewhere that every great civilization and culture that is known for its human advancement and achievement, has enjoyed four distinct seasons because of its climate and their relationship to the equator. The great civilizations of Europe, Asia, and North America have enjoyed four seasons unlike some equatorial regions. What do the seasons have to do with their success? In Europe and Asia people were forced into their homes or shelters during the long nights in the cold winter season. There they had the opportunity to dream, plan, and envision the New Year and strategise. Yet in Central Africa, Australia, and Northern South America the climate is almost always hot and summer-like. As a result, these peoples never had the opportunity to be locked up in their homes over long dark evenings and nights to do nothing but dream. They were always outside enjoying the sunshine but never had the opportunity to accomplish anything great, because they never were forced to dream in long winter nights - and dream long.

Paul was susceptible to being taught about his seasons. He undoubtedly wanted to make gains in Asia and Ephesus for the kingdom of God. But he clearly perceived that the very moment that Acts 16:6 -7 refers to, was not the right time or season to press with any vision or dream for that geographic area.

To discuss the issue of God's timing always seemed dark, mystic and mysterious to me in my early days as a Christian. It was never an issue of gravity to Paul. In his letter to the church at Rome, he states clearly that he had oftentimes made plans to go there and minister, but up to that moment of him writing to them, he had been "hindered" (Romans 1:13). No deep explanation was felt needed. He planned to go to a certain place, and because of circumstances sometimes known, sometimes unknown, he did not always go where he wanted, when he wanted. Paul does not blame the devil, demons or the powers of darkness, and neither does he attribute it to the direction of God, excepting here in Acts 16: 6 where Luke states that it actually was God who was redirecting him.

A similar occasion arrived that is explained for us in 2 Corinthians. It would seem that at some point of his ministry in Ephesus ("Asia" in 2 Corinthians 1: 8), Paul's plan was to cross the Aegean Sea, visit the church at Corinth, travel up north to minister in the area we know as Northern Greece, that Paul knew as Macedonia, travel south again to visit Corinth and then move on. The apostle actually told them that this was his plan. But then he took a different route. Circumstances demanded it, and he did not feel bound to have followed his initial plan. His explanation is that he didn't fulfil plan "A" because of a disciplinary instruction that he had written in the letter we refer to as First Corinthians, that he wanted to leave them with time to enforce his instructions (2 Corinthians 1:23–2:11). But then he explains what happened when he took to plan "B" by going north to Troas before crossing the Aegean. He explains how a door of ministry was opened whilst he was waiting at Troas (2 Corinthians 2:12-13).

So the "opening of doors" to ministry, whatever that phrase meant to Paul, was an important indicator to him of where he was, and which way he had to go. I say "whatever the phrase meant to Paul", because I do not think it means what most people commonly take it to mean, i.e. a simple confluence of "right circumstances." I believe it was something seen, sensed or heard in the Spirit. However, in his own explanation in scripture, neither God nor the devil is blamed for his hindrance, nor does he enter into any religious jargon. He planned "A". He couldn't enact "A". So, a plan "B" was created. No problem. Statement made.

Concerning God's timing for certain things, I am reminded of an account shared by William Branham in his early days. The deepest principle of which may be the main reason for Acts 16:6-7. In the simplest of terms, Branham had a clear and open vision of someone who was very sick, on the point of death. In this vision, the person was sinking from life and had five people (friends and relatives) standing around their bed. In this revelation, Branham saw himself enter the room and pray for the dying invalid, who immediately arose completely healed. Having seen and remembered the oracle, he was shortly after called to pray for somebody who was dying. As he entered the house, he recognised both the room and the person in the bed as the same picture as he had seen in the afore mentioned unveiling (Branham had many visions daily, so this was not an isolated incident in his life.). There was a problem that stopped Branham praying for the lady in the bed however, a dear soul who was obviously fading from this life. There were only four people gathered around the bed. But, there were five spectators in his open vision. Branham courageously (in my view) said he couldn't pray until a fifth person arrived. "But nobody else is expected to visit," the people explained. "You must pray now, as she is about to pass away." Branham flatly refused, and told them he would sit and wait till person number five arrived. There was considerable discontent amongst the four that were present. (That is a Euphemism for people who were giving Branham a row.) An hour or two later a fifth person turned up, wearing the same attire that Branham had seen in his vision. At that moment he prayed for the person in the bed and the sick lady arose from the bed fully recovered.

What's my point of this Branham anecdote? Timing! In this account that involved seven people overall, there was a right moment for him to pray. That moment was when the divinely initiated vision had the choreography of people present and in the right position was seen in reality exactly as the vision facilitated Branham to see. I have no idea what would have happened if he had prayed before the fifth lady had arrived. But he was obedient to the heavenly vision he had received.

Perhaps all the personnel that were to be impacted in the Ephesian mission were not yet on scene for the drama to take place. Branham's vision involved a large house full of people. God's vision for Ephesus and Asia involved an entire sub-continent.

Whatever the nuts and bolts of the divine rationale were, Paul was told by God to bypass Asia, and in so doing, he would be bypassing Ephesus. He obeyed. Moving in the miraculous commonly and with seeming ease gives the untutored that Paul did things at his own whim, fancy and/or volition. The ease and commonness of such manifestations however is indicative of a vital motivation aspect of managing the miraculous. I am speaking of the motivation of having seen what God is doing and having heard what He is saying.

For now, Ephesus and Asia were a "no! no!"

3.

WASN'T THE TIME! NOW'S THE TIME!

"And he came to Ephesus"

Acts 18:19 (KJV)

Ephesus, around 54 AD, was like London is today, in as much as it was one of the largest cities created by mankind, a gigantic metropolis of its time, and extremely multi-cultural. It was like Bangkok is today, in as much as evil lifestyle and scary social "goings on" were commonplace. It was like Port au Prince in Haiti today, in as much as Black Magic and darkest witchcraft was rife, and multi religious syncretism was the norm.

The city authorities and the people of Ephesus did not have a clue what was being seeded in their home town when, amongst the throngs that were daily coming to and going from their city harbour, three particular persons came ashore off a boat from Cenchrea, early in the year 54 A.D (At least that is the date I am plumping for after much research). Amongst the masses, two men and a woman disembarked from their hired ship, possibly deep in spiritual conversation and interaction. A wife and husband that went by the names of Priscilla and Aquila, and a short, and most ungamely looking chap whom the couple referred to as Paul.

Little did anybody know that Ephesus was soon to emerge as the third capital city of the church world-wide, because of this man Paul. I mean, of course, third in chronology, not third in size. The church of Christ was, of course, birthed in Jerusalem (the first capital of the church), then, after the first persecution (See the end of Acts 7 and chapter 8), it would seem that the Christians who had left Jerusalem, "gossiping the Gospel" as they went, were more effective in the Syrian city of Antioch than anywhere else. The Bible leaves us with the distinct impression that the church in Antioch was the first place where a gentile constituent fully blended in with the Jewish Christians that had emigrated from Jerusalem, though, I am sure, not without the problematic situations that arise when differently principled cultures try to live together in harmony. Antioch thereafter, became the hub of the cutting edge of Christianity for a brief time. This was, what I am referring to as the second capital of Christianity. It was in this Antioch that followers of Christ were first referred to as "Christians".

Ephesus, however, though undoubtedly with a substantial Jewish and Judaistic element that already lived there, was the most cosmopolitan city in Asia. Paul's later impact in Ephesus, as recorded in Acts 19 and his own remarks as stated in Acts 20, rippled on throughout the entire province of Asia for a generation or two. Ephesus was to witness the fullest and most widespread development and manifestation of a non Judaistic presentation of the gospel of Jesus Christ ever seen in the days of the original apostles, resulting in a church that was more expressive of a gentile culture than Jewish. It became a major centre of Christian activity simply because of the size of the completed operation, and the entire Asian population that was influenced by the gospel because of that activity.

Ephesus, or what is left of it in the twenty first century, lies several miles inland and is a Ghost town of ruins and stones. However, in Paul's day it lay, at the very most, half a mile from the sea, possibly at the very sea front. Its harbour was, in those times, among the most sheltered and commodious in the Mediterranean, and would have been constantly thronged with vessels from every part of what was considered the "civilised world." The city lay at the junction of two great roads that were arterial to the whole of Asia, and commanded easy access to the whole interior sub-continent. Its population was multifarious and immense. Its markets, glittering with the produce of the world's art were the Vanity Fair of Asia. Imagine, in a first century setting, the largest and most varied shopping mall you can think of in cities like New York, London, Paris or Shanghai, and apart from the excessive population sizes of today, you have Ephesus well sketched. And Ephesus was no less cosmopolitan than it was vast in its spread, famous and infamous in its reputation, and wealthy in its industrial dealings.

Its kudos and attractiveness to world trade and religious cults was amplified also by the fact that it was also the seat of a Roman Proconsul, permanently resident in the city. Make no mistake, Ephesus was essentially Greek; but as with many cosmopolitan cities, the mixture of ever growing ethnic groups with differing cultures, belief systems, religions and practices was, much like London today, populated with more, "non-Londoners" than Caucasian English Londoners. Today third and fourth generations of families from all over the globe call themselves, "English", and pure "Londoners," (as, indeed, they truly are) and that would have been the status of many in this city of the goddess Diana. Ephesus was riddled with many cultish deistic influences, fostering superstitions and spiritual aberrations that made the place, religiously, something of a House of Horrors. Many of those houses of demonic fearfulness owed their efficient maintenance to the vested self-interest of various priestly bodies, and pontifical occultist personalities. This aspect of Ephesian life utterly debased the moral character of the people.

Just as the ancients abused the "holy" sanctuaries of European Cathedrals and churches in the dark ages, attracting as they did all the moral scum, cheats, debtors and murderers of society, who inevitably pauperised and degraded the entire vicinity, so did the attraction of wealthy Ephesus bring the robbing, cheating defrauding rogues of its time to its suburbs and centres. The vicinity of the great temple at Ephesus reeked with the congregated social, moral and spiritual pollutions of Asia and indeed the rest of this earthly cosmos. The vice, and evil of the district surrounding the temple of Diana was so inveterately dark and nasty, that one of its own philosophers declared that the whole Ephesian population deserved to be throttled, man by man for simply allowing it to be so, and for, seemingly, doing nothing about it.

Ephesus is the place that Paul was discussing when he later declared that, "a great door and effectual," had opened to him, accompanied by "many adversaries" (1 Corinthians 16:9). It is accepted as a matter of fact that Paul wrote First Corinthians in the midst of his labours in Ephesus.

Paul was probably bald headed when he first set foot in the precincts of Ephesus; that is extrapolating at this stage of his life he wasn't naturally bald. The book tells us that he had just had his head shaved for the purposes of a religious vow. So, surely, he could not have been naturally bald. He must have looked like a veteran soldier coming home from a war. His eyes were used to tears, he had said so himself once or twice (2 Corinthians 2:4. Acts 20:19 and 20:31). This man was used to adversity, refutation and harassment. The Lord Jesus Christ had promised Paul at the moment of his conversion that He would show him what great things he must suffer for his sake. This man knew what poverty was like, and affluence. However, all those exterior imposters were put aside for the intimate knowledge and relationship with Christ Himself. This man though reputedly small and insignificant in exterior form, was well known in the invisible world where God and angels, as well as Satan and his demons see more clearly as to who holds power in the temporal world. They saw Paul for who and what he truly was, a giant that walked intimately with Christ.

It was not only unbelieving pagans, or bigoted Jews that had persecuted and rejected Paul, but Christian people too. Make no error about the man whose missives comprise a huge section of the New Testament; throughout his lifetime he was deeply loved or extremely hated.

The working active principle of the anointing of the Holy Spirit that was uttered over the baby Christ, applies to anybody who carries an outrageously glorious anointing on their life, as did Paul. Luke 2:34 has the old man holding the Christ child in his arms and speaking God's word to Mary. "Behold, this child is set for the fall and rising again of many in Israel; and for a sign which shall be spoken against". Conclusions to draw from that prophetic word? The anointing divides! The anointing is loved or hated. The richer and deeper the anointing, the greater the division it creates. Many fall, and many rise also. The greater the man of God the greater the love or hate for him.

This man Paul is today understood to be the greatest "carrier" of the message of Christ, as well as the greatest manifestation of the power and grace that the message exudes, that has ever lived. He gathered friends who loved, trusted and admired him for the manner in which he fed their faith and nurtured their aspirations to holiness. He undoubtedly taught and tutored a considerable number of people. But his life and calling were unique. This man was physically not safe wherever he went. Some people actually followed him across Asia and Europe just to undo the message he had taught, the work he had wrought, as well as to get him killed so that he would not spread his message further. Neither from Jews, nor from Pagans, nor even from some Christians was he safe. He had suffered alike from lawless bandits, as well as the stately and outwardly sophisticated magistrates. He had been stoned by the simple provincials of Lystra. The Roman colonists at Philippi had beaten him. Perils among his own countrymen, we are aware, befell him in most places where he declared the power of the gospel. His degree of acceptance amongst the highest of the Apostles and church leaders, was never seen to be overwhelming, nor warm. But this man's heart was sold out for Christ in a manner that no depth of rejection, persecution, criticism or torture could stop. He was ever moving forward, and always pressing on into Christ. And so it says "He came to Ephesus" (Acts 18:19).

Paul was actually on the way to Jerusalem when he trod on Ephesian soil for the first time. He had no intention of staying long on this initial "stop over". He had just spent almost two years preaching, teaching and expanding God's kingdom in a place called Corinth. When I say that, I loosely hold the opinion, as stated above, that the "coming ashore" of this trio of God's children took place somewhere during 54AD, I hasten to add that no one is certain about when it actually took place. This "taster", this "testing the waters" of what Ephesus was about, and reaching out into the realm of the Spirit, asking God what He thought about Ephesus as a place of ministry, must have been swimming around his heart and mind during this brief respite in his travels. Only a few years before this moment, while Paul was doing all he could to spread the gospel on what we refer to as his, "Second Missionary Journey", God had actually forbidden him to even step into Asia. Now, without fuss or bother, without prophetic word or angelic counsel concerning the cancellation of the ban, "He came to Ephesus." If you, as a reader, are now expecting me to explain why that was, I am afraid you will be disappointed.

God has a time for everything. Millions of people just plod on ploughing their furrow of life regardless and probably ignorant of anything to do with "God's timing". On that second missionary journey, and his first visit to Corinth, he created a precedent when, for the first time in his Christian life he had endured the raving mob violence of his antagonists, and then, afterwards, he had enjoyed the luxury of being vindicated and encouraged by the Roman magistrate of Corinth no less.

This chief judicial magistrate of Corinth, a man called Gallio, had secured for Paul a period of time free of molestation after his early months of labour in that place. This judgement was the fulfilment of the promise that Christ Himself had given Paul in a visitation amid his early persecutions in Corinth. Paul must have considered himself in some sort of respite of such circumstances, and so availed himself of the comparative safety of ministering to, and building up of what is conjectured to be a church of many hundreds, possibly more, across Corinth and its environs. Some believe that there were thousands of converts. He left Corinth determined to revisit Jerusalem in time for the feast of Pentecost. He had not been there for round about three years at this point of time. We are not aware of why he "needed" to visit Jerusalem, although it is highly likely that he had collected something to give to the poor amongst the Jewish Christians that lived in the so-called, "holy City". Whatever the reason, I personally cannot help but think that he felt, every so often, the need and importance of maintaining as amicable contact and as close a relationship with the other Apostles as he could.

Although for us, in the twenty first century, when most preachers spend many sermons and lectures looking into the whys and wherefores of Paul's letters, and what he did in the book of Acts, it is clear to us that Paul was not so comprehensively adulated for his example and authority in his own life time. Paul obviously wanted to be in Jerusalem when church leaders would be there in their thickest numbers, some who were sympathetic to Paul's ministry and character, and some absolutely rejecting him and his teaching. Pentecost was several weeks away, and, as it was in Acts 2, when Jewish people from all over the world were present, he possibly wanted to make sure that he was not spoken against without being present, so he could give Christians the benefit of his own insight and perspective. This is my opinion. It would serve not only to allow him to give testimony of what God was doing amongst the gentiles, but the shaven head and his attendance at the feast would speak loud and clear to those Christians, and some of the church leaders, who claimed Paul held Judaism and its feasts in contempt. Such an act would show them that despite the cruelty and barbaric responses from synagogues wherever he had been, he was still, at heart, a loyal Jew.

So, in intention, Paul was only briefly touching base with the bulging population that was the heart of the business market and the religious world of the Goddess referred to as, "Diana," or "Artemis." He truly had his eye elsewhere – namely Jerusalem, when he first set foot upon Asian soil. He didn't stay long, but he must have chewed a few things over in his mind about the ripeness of Ephesus for a full blown attack for the kingdom of God. He may have been forbidden to come here years previous, but having landed in the heart of Asia for this stop over, he felt free to declare the gospel, or at least debate it, in the Ephesian synagogue (or synagogues). He was well received whilst in Ephesus on this occasion. No riots, no stoning! We are not even told of any dissenters amongst the Jews in the

Synagogues of the great Metropolis. He must have been asking Heavenly Father about His intentions for the place.

Paul's visit to the Jewish contingent, and nowhere else, suggests that there was no gathering of Christians, no church or Fellowship for him to identify with. His warm reception amongst the worshippers there may have given Paul the desire to return, but I do not feel confident at all to think that such an external superficial circumstance as the warmth of some Jewish people towards him was enough reason to deduce God's will for a return visit. Paul's spiritual level demands that his reasons to return or not to return would have nothing at all to do with the issue of whether he was loved or hated by the Ephesian Jewish quarter. The entire text of the book of Acts is a rock like foundation supporting what I am saying here.

So, with the same calm and undramatic manner in which he entered Ephesus harbour, Paul left. The spiritual black hole of Ephesus was left festering for just a little longer untouched. The 250,000 to 300,000 population of the city carried on in their business and lifestyle, the vast majority of them not having a clue of the divine Tsunami, the spiritual volcano that was about to sweep over them and their province several months after Paul had left Priscilla and Aquila alone in Ephesus.

The Synagogue attendees had asked him to return. His answer was that if God willed it, he would. We are here to say that God definitely willed it, and fully facilitated the return of His Apostle to the city of Ephesus in a manner that is doubtful that God ever facilitated anybody before.

4.

THE HAND OF GOD IN THE CIRCUMSTANCES OF LIFE.

"And after he had spent some time there, he departed, and went over all the country of Galatia and Phrygia in order, strengthening all the disciples."

Acts 18:23 (KJV)

"... Paul having passed through the upper coasts came to Ephesus..."

Acts 19:1(KJV)

The Bible does not by any means tell us everything that happened in the life of Paul. His own various statements in Second Corinthians lets us know that there were many "adventures" he went through that we are utterly ignorant of, apart from those remarks he makes.

For instance in the very opening chapter he says clearly, "For we do not want you to be ignorant, brethren, of our trouble which came to us in Asia: that we were burdened beyond measure, above strength, so that we despaired even of life. Yes, we had the sentence of death in ourselves that we should not trust in ourselves but in God who raises the dead" (2 Corinthians 1:8-9. NKJV. Scholars and Professors are almost unanimous in asserting that Paul's life threatening experience, to which he refers here, was during his ministry in Ephesus, that is, the very same period of evangelism that we are about to negotiate. But although we shall later discuss the riot that started in Ephesus among the Silversmiths in the latter parts of Acts 19, and although it was a major incident, we are nowhere given as much as an impression that Paul's life was in danger, or that he had grounds for thinking he was about to die. So, there was obviously some dire straits that Paul was in the midst of during "Mission to Ephesus" that is nowhere referred to apart from these desperate tones in 2 Corinthians 1.

As a general statement of his life's experience, chapter 4:8-11 of the same letter, refers to some shocking issues that affected him internally as well as physically. "We are **hard-pressed** on every side, yet not crushed; we are **perplexed**, but not in despair; **persecuted**, but not forsaken; **struck down**, but not destroyed— **always carrying about in the body the dying of the Lord Jesus**, that the life of Jesus also may be manifested in our body. For we who live are always **delivered to death** for Jesus' sake, that the life of Jesus also may be manifested in our mortal flesh" (NKJV. Bold face mine). Sounds desperate to my ears I have to say. "Hard-pressed on every side"! "Perplexed"! "Persecuted"! And don't forget, "Struck down." The point is that the written text seems to suggest that these were the experiences of "a normal day at the office", as it were. No wonder that there were those who considered Paul and his closest workers mad! (2 Corinthians 5:13).

There are accounts in Acts to which some of these descriptions could fit; but then we get to the sixth chapter of second Corinthians. From verses 4 through to verse 10, referring to his own experiences we discover things that add meat to what we have in Acts, as well as letting us in on stories that we are not made aware of anywhere else in the Bible. "But in all things we commend ourselves as ministers of God: **... in tribulations, in needs, in distresses, in stripes, in imprisonments, in tumults, in labours, in sleeplessness, in fastings**;... by honour **and dishonour, by evil report** and good report; as **deceivers**, and yet true; ... as **dying**, and behold we live; as **chastened**, and yet not killed" (NKJV. Bold face mine). 7: 5 states, "For indeed, when we came to Macedonia, our bodies had no rest, but **we were troubled on every side. Outside were conflicts, inside were fears**." We are not told what his trouble was on every side, nor what the conflicts and fear was about.

In the incredible eleventh chapter our sensibilities are assaulted again by a list of catastrophes that Paul had experienced in his life whilst ministering for Christ, catastrophes that leads us to believe that Acts merely informs us of the tip of a huge iceberg. From verse 23 to 33 we are shocked to discover that our beloved and treasured example of Christian living has – pardon the expression – been to hell and back many times. Quoting from the New King James, Paul defends himself against those "false Apostles" who belittle and deride him. The bold face words are those which are shocking and unaccounted for in Acts. I cannot imagine him writing without tears and deep emotion when he reasons: "Are they ministers of Christ?—I speak as a fool— I am more: in labours more abundant, **in stripes above measure, in prisons more frequently, in deaths often.** From the Jews **five times I received forty stripes minus one. Three times I was beaten with rods; once I was stoned; three times I was shipwrecked; a night and a day I have been in the deep; in journeys often, in perils of waters, in perils of robbers, in perils of my own countrymen, in perils of the Gentiles, in perils in the city, in perils in the wilderness, in perils in the sea, in perils among false brethren; in weariness and toil, in sleeplessness often, in hunger and thirst, in fastings often, in cold and nakedness** ... In Damascus the governor, under Aretas the king, was guarding the city of the Damascenes with a garrison, desiring to arrest me; but I was let down in a basket through a window in the wall, and escaped from his hands."

There are less than a handful of these experiences he refers to that are detailed in Acts, or possibly inferred. But what we have here is the proof that Acts is not a systematic history of Paul's exploits, but an account of some handpicked experiences, chosen by Luke for our benefit.

It makes me wonder about how Paul usually functioned in the process of evangelism throughout his life's ministry. To state my mind on the issue, I am strangely warmed to the thought that the strategy that we are about to examine for the province of Asia and

Ephesus was simply a larger version of what had happened in Corinth, and anywhere else he might have ministered that we do not know about.

Because of the biblical information that we have, we must conclude that although there are legends concerning the activities of all twelve of the original Apostles, Paul was the most aggressively evangelistic in the darkness of the gentile world of those days. We don't hear a lot about the whole twelve apostles after Acts 2, but here is the data for a starters if anybody out there wants to launch a project on the issue.

Peter died around 67 AD. One historical authority insists that both Peter and Paul were the founders of the church at Rome, and died in that city. I do not see how Paul could have founded the church there as he wrote his letter to the church at Rome before he ever entered its precincts, and that was as a prisoner of Rome. According to the early writers, Peter died at or about the same time with Paul, and Nero's mad persecution of Christians, AD 67 or 68. All the early church fathers and writers who discuss Peter's death insist that he was crucified. Origen says that Peter was, at his own request, crucified with his head downward. According to the tradition of him dying in Rome, and because of the addressees of his letters, it seems he travelled in similar area to Paul, but nowhere like as often. It is rather inconceivable that Peter travelled anything like as much as Paul.

Extra biblically, there are lots of documents that assert that John was the only one that died "peacefully". No dates are given, but it is guessed by various authorities that he died anytime between 90 AD right up to 120 AD. John also ministered in Asia after the days of Acts 19. He is reputed to have died on Patmos. But again, there is no evidence that his travelling was anything like as extensive as Paul's.

James the brother of the Apostle John and son of Zebedee was put to death by Herod Agrippa about a dozen years after Christ's resurrection. We know that for certain from Acts 12:1-2. He hardly travelled outside Jerusalem at all, as far as we know.

Andrew? A variety of traditions say he preached in Scythia, in Greece, in Asia Minor and Thrace. He is reported to have been crucified at Patrae in Achaia. Again, that is much less than Paul.

Matthew, it is reckoned by scholars, must have lived quite a few years after Pentecost, as he was the author of the Gospel of Matthew, which was written at least twenty years after the death of Christ. There is reason to believe that he stayed for fifteen years at Jerusalem, after which he went as missionary to the Persians, Parthians and Medes. That is well north of Jerusalem. However, there is a legend that he died a martyr in Ethiopia, way down south of the holy city. Well-travelled, Matthew must have been, but not on the scale of Paul.

According to tradition Phillip preached in Phrygia, and died at Hierapolis. It is now claimed that his tomb has been found.

The earlier traditions, as believed in the fourth century, say Thomas preached in Parthia or Persia, and was finally buried at Edessa. The later traditions carry him further east. His martyrdom whether in Persia or India, is said to have been by a lance

We know James Alphaeus lived at least five years after the death of Christ because of mentions in the Bible. According to tradition, he was thrown down from the temple by the scribes and Pharisees; he was then stoned, and his brains dashed out with a fuller's club.

According to tradition Thaddeus (aka Jude) taught in Armenia, Syria and Persia where he was martyred. Tradition tells us he was buried in Kara Kalisa, in what is now Iran.

Bartholomew and Simon the Canaanite are the two that absolutely nothing at all is known about. They don't even have any mythical legend about their mission, or where they went.

I assert, despite all the legends, Paul was the chief pioneer of the gospel in the gentile world, in the days of the original apostles. Paul was of special significance for the call of the church, travelling some 15,000 miles, at least, in his lifetime.

His missionary plans could not have been more practical. Even though we get the impression from Acts that it was often spontaneous, and just a simple matter of ploughing on Westward until the Holy Spirit gave words of direction, it is surely correct to talk of Paul's, "Missionary Strategy." When his journeys are thought on while one has a copy of "The Acts of the Apostles" in one hand, and an Atlas in the other, one cannot but get a picture of systematic and repetitive movement. It is so systematic, so based on the principle of serving an end, so planned in advance for the swiftest and most extensive spreading of the gospel, one cannot fail to see a wilful and deliberate plan which must have lain at the base of all his movements.

But it was not, and could not have been Paul himself who did the planning, but the Lord he served. An immediate example of this is the instance earlier referred to of the dream/vision at Troas, through which Paul, seemingly without a personal thought, or a reflective, prevaricating hesitation, concluded that he was called to Macedonia and thereafter Greece (Acts 16:8-11), so that then, on the ground of Divine revelation, not the East, but the West should be made the chief theatre of the sowing of the gospel seed. Paul was bound for, what Erich Sauer refers to as, "Japhetic Europe and the Western peoples in general." Paul had planned a certain direction, but "the Spirit of Jesus suffered it not" (Acts 16:6-7, twice). Paul kept in step with the divinely communicated program. So, even though we speak of "Paul's Evangelistic Strategy," it is the strategy of Christ to which we refer, not Paul himself. It was the strategy not of the ambassador, but of the Sender. It was the plotting and timing not of the herald, but of the Lord who gave the herald his message. Christ was the Captain, Paul was the privately owned soldier. Christ was the Directive Coordinator, Paul the explorer. It was the Heir of all things who was in charge. The co-heir simply submitted and complied.

To these outward stamps of his evangelistic trailblazing, must be added the inward characteristics of the evangelist himself. Have you noticed how Paul was an evangelist firstly to the harbours and seaports? It's true! If one makes a study of the large anchorages Paul landed at, and checks out their strategic geographical significance, the student cannot but be struck that Paul's bridgeheads were to be found where the sea winds blew, and in the trading and passenger routes of the Mediterranean, especially around the Aegean waters with its multifarious boatyards which dot its shorelines. It was in these waters and their vicinity that lay some great commercial harbourages. There, or at least in the neighbourhood of these ports, lay the great commercial docks of Troas, then Thessalonica, followed by Athens, and to nearby Corinth, and finally the place of our present meditations, Ephesus. Note that even Syrian Antioch had a harbour at Seleucia, and Rome had its own port at a place called Ostia.

Whether Paul was simply, passively accepting where he was as God's will, or whether it was a conscious move of his under the hand of God, there were always advantages to these Harbour landings.

Greek was the major lingua franca of the majority of Rome's conquered nations. Because it was the bridging language of the time, this meant that Greek had spread far more widely in harbour cities than in the rest of the world that was more inland. For this pioneering preacher/teacher, the time swallowing, all consuming hindrance of learning languages was thereby factored out of the operation as conveniently as wiping a dirty plate. Because of this fact, the gospel could advance with incredible speed westward through the nations.

Similarly, when the apostle had founded a church base in a port, the gospel could spread more quickly from seaport churches than those lying more inland. Sea travelling businessmen, day trippers to harbours, general seafarers, and other world commuters who, during a stopover in any sea haven were changed by the gospel, could on their own account, as they journeyed further out, or on their return home, always be fresh pioneers of the saving message in ever new lands and regions of the world. The widespread knowledge of Greek facilitated the perpetual repetition of the gospel message wherever there was somebody just arriving, or just departing. By this modus operandi the number of "testimonials", preachers, missionaries and Bible teachers, and ports reached by them, increased exponentially, and were added to the workers and lands reached by the strategic sowing of the apostle Paul. It also simplified the commissioning and sending out of the narrower circle of his fellow-labourers.

Also, seaports could be reached more easily than the provincial cities far inland. By sea one made quicker and safer progress than by road. Even though Roman roads were indeed famously well-built, travel by land was still slower than sea travel, and more often than not quite dangerous. This remark is vindicated by Paul's own statement, "in perils from rivers, in perils from robbers" (2 Cor.11: 26). Pliny the Elder wrote that one could travel from Spain to Ostia (Rome's harbour) in four days, and from Africa in two. He tells us also, that there was a daily commuters ship that plied the "Alexandria - Asia Minor" route.

Paul was utterly non-intimidated by the huge cities of his time. In fact he purposefully planned to plant the gospel in the great cities of Greek culture. This is exactly what Antioch, Troas, Philippi, Thessalonica, Athens, Corinth, and Ephesus were. This is why he yearned to preach in Rome, the mother of all capital cities.

To Paul, in his particular commission, it was given to him "to proclaim the unsearchable riches of Christ among the nations" (Ephesians 3: 8; Colossians1: 25, 27; 1 Timothy 2:7; 2 Timothy1: 11). This is undoubtedly why many scholars and Christian intellectuals tell me that, in Ephesians 3:8, the statement, "to me (Gk. emoi) was this favour given to preach unto the Gentiles," was stressed and made emphatic, being placed at the beginning of the sentence. By this one extreme distinctive, Paul was harmoniously differentiated from the apostles to the circumcision (Galatians2:7-10; Acts 15).

As an incredibly gifted pioneer for Christ, it was his ministry and life to introduce the message of salvation into ever further lands. He went primarily to regions where the gospel had not been heard before (Romans 15: 20). The carrying of the gospel further inland, in the regions where he had worked in the ports, was left to those newly-won believers who emerged as preachers and church leaders. His own task was to form centres of grace, power and light, in his building of missionary-minded local churches, in those larger "chief" cities (that were mostly sea-ports). Thus Philippi was the "chief city" in Macedonia (Acts 16:12), Corinth that of Achaia, Athens the chief intellectual centre of Greece, Ephesus the chief city of Asia, Rome that of the whole world. From these "Headquarter churches," if you will, the gospel was to permeate their surrounding district (1 Thessalonians 1:8).

Once such a centre had been birthed, established and was functioning, it seems that the man from Tarsus moved on – until he came to Ephesus. Generally, however, once the centre was built, and the message was being spread, in those circumstance, Paul would declare that he had "no more room" (Romans 15:23), though hundreds of thousands of unsaved lived in the area. In such a scenario he would declare that in that place there, he had "fully proclaimed the gospel of Christ" (Romans15:19). Anything else would be wrong to him, as if he was, "building on another man's foundation" (Romans15: 20).

Having said all that, he actually approached Ephesus from the hinterlands of Asia. He visited the churches through Phrygia and Galatia, and then having followed, as it were, the northern borders of Asia, came down south towards Ephesus itself.

His mission to Ephesus would be to fish for men. On his journey betwixt Jerusalem and Ephesus he was not only fishing, but keeping the aquarium. I cannot help but wonder if he had any spiritual presentiment at all of what was about to take place.

5.

THE TOP PRIORITY BUILD TEAM

"... Paul having passed through the upper coasts came to Ephesus: and finding certain disciples, He said unto them..."

Acts 19:1b-2a (NKJV)

Original, primitive apostolic evangelism had its set priorities. When Paul finally returned to Ephesus, the first thing he did was hugely significant. We are not sure whether it was a spontaneous "accident" that he met a dozen men who were serious about following God, or whether he arrived in the Ephesian suburbs hungrily looking for some men who were already, to some degree, discipled for Christ. Certainly, after reading the text of those first few verses of Acts chapter 19, it does sound like a "spur of the moment" thing in Paul's mind, but a circumstantially predetermined incident in the mind of the Almighty. What I call a "God moment".

Thirty plus years after Acts chapter two real-time, there were Christian "disciples" scattered all over the map. Some leading others. Some looking for leadership. There were those that returned home to their gentile country, after hearing nobody but John the Baptist. There were those who would have circulated having heard the Lord Jesus in "the days of his flesh," but knowing little of His death and resurrection. There were also those who travelled abroad having been present at the feast of Pentecost, as described in Acts chapter 2.

The account in Acts 19 explains to us that before the apostle addressed any of the unsaved in Ephesus, God Himself had decided that he needed to meet these men, the number of whom, the scripture mysteriously says, was "about twelve". "About...?" Surely it was twelve, or it wasn't? One cannot really have an approximation with such a small number, can one?

Paul "bumped into", or "sought out" a nucleus of believers who had within themselves a desire for growth, and to be used in evangelism. These men would receive ministry input from Paul that would facilitate them being helped to achieve their maximum potential in God. Their spiritual experience was catapulted forward by their submission to the God given apostolic anointing that sat on the life of the apostle to the gentiles. Paul was aware that the impartation of his anointing to others, could pierce through the darkness of the society in whatever culture they lived. These existing disciples were found by God's providence. Paul stepped forward to minister.

Throughout the Bible, the Apostles are seen to be functioning at least in pairs, and often in teams. It is clear throughout the book of Acts that Paul did not function at his best when left to work alone. He seems to be in a kind of strange morass when by himself ministering. Paul served best when he was active in tandem or in team. I am on safe ground in asserting that Paul was always the man in charge of those teams. Because of what Paul says and does with his fellow workers, I also conclude that the entire twelve original apostles had the same modus operandi. Apostles rarely, if ever, prefer to work alone. (I am using present tense for what is, to this writer, a self-evident truth, that what Apostles were and how they moved in the days of Acts 19, is how present day Apostles will be moving also.) Jesus didn't send workers out alone, and neither should we. Jesus sent each one out in good company. He sent them out in two's (Mark 6:7).

The lesson gained by reading Acts and the epistles is that part of the apostolic anointing is to gift the gathering of a body of disciples, educate them in God, and also to impart to them whatever can be imparted in the Spirit, and put them to work as an extended team. Paul's first step when he entered the environs of the city of Ephesus was to gather whatever disciples he bumped into who were already there. Only "about twelve" are mentioned. From these twelve he formed a radical apostolic team that together built one of the greatest churches in history, with strong autonomous satellites all around the same provincial spiritual honey pot.

Gathering these disciples together was putting, first things first.

But something was not quite right amongst these twelve disciples. Paul had discerned that they were men of faith, justified and zealous for God in a true Jewish understanding of Yahweh. Not that the scripture gives us the slightest clue as to whether any of the twelve were Jewish, Gentile, black or white. But the discernment of Paul told him that these people despite a faulty content to their faith, were open hearted and teachable.

With the presupposed understanding that Paul was in Ephesus when he wrote 1 Corinthians, we know that Priscilla and Aquila are mentioned as being part of the team whilst Paul was in Ephesus. Trophimus and Tychicus, possibly both Ephesians, worked with Paul when he left Ephesus (Acts 20:4). Could they have been members of the twelve mentioned at the commencement of Acts 19? Epanatus was probably an Ephesian also, as most manuscripts say he was of the "first fruits of Asia," and he later travelled to Rome (Romans 16:5 American Standard Version, Moffatt translation, Montgomery Centenary version, and the Weymouth translation.). We are informed that Timothy and Titus were ministers with, and companions to Paul for at least part of the mission to Ephesus. Philemon seems to have been in Ephesus when he met Paul. Paul made such an impression on Philemon's slave, Onesimus, that for a time, Onesimus ran away from Philemon and Colossae and joined Paul. Paul sent Onesimus back to his master from Ephesus to Colossae; a journey of circa 115 miles. It seems that Apphia, Archippus and Epaphras came from Colossae also (See Philemon 2 and Colossians 4:12). I mention all these people wondering who, if any, were part of the twelve that he met in Acts 19:1-7

A true disciple is a person that lives according to the Word of God to the best of their understanding. Jesus described a disciple as one who "abides in His Word" (John 8:31). Disciples love the Word, are lifelong students and doers of the Word, and are spiritually hungry. They always remain teachable (2 Timothy 2:15; James 1:22). They know the Word of God and the ways of God. There are many believers in the world, but oh so few disciples. These men, the scripture tells us, were all disciples.

Notice that Paul asked these disciples if they had received the Holy Ghost since they believed in Christ. Their response was revealing. They said they had never heard of the baptism of the Holy Ghost.

At this point in Paul's life he is a seasoned apostle of grace. Many years had passed since he was first sent out from Antioch. Because of the warfare against his own life and ministry, Paul was aware that these disciples needed to be baptised in the Holy Ghost. He knew by experience that just as he was perpetually tested and harassed from Jews mocking and deriding his message, disciples that were linked with Paul would get the same treatment as he always did.

When Jesus formed His revolutionary team before His ascension back into heaven, he directed them to wait for the promise of the Holy Spirit. (Acts 1:8). Notice Jesus said you would receive power after and not before. Apostles are fathers of the faith, and never ignore the spiritual condition of their team members. Apostolic team members need the baptism of the Holy Spirit with the evidence of speaking in other tongues and prophecy. The baptism in the Holy Spirit is all about power. (Acts 19:6).

It was all that they needed at that moment, and was to be a facilitator of future growth and capacity to believe in the majestic and magnificent mission to Ephesus, that was to end up as a Mission to the whole of Asia.

These twelve men would never be the same again, and would end up being part and parcel of the Holy Spirit invasion of Ephesus and the surrounding population. The impartation to these "about twelve" men, and their friendship and allegiance to Paul was clearly part of the substance of the gift of God and the management of the miraculous that was carried by them all over the coming three years.

6.

BAPTISM IN THE HOLY SPIRIT THE BIBLICAL NORM.

The Old Testament prophets had hold of a stream of revelation concerning the Holy Spirit. It was a river of understanding that Paul explains as one of the major planks of what was promised to Abraham (Galatians 3:14). For instance, Joel foresaw God pouring out the Holy Spirit on "all flesh." He qualifies it by saying that a time was on the horizon where sons and daughters would prophesy, young men would see visions and old men would dream dreams. Servants and handmaids also would receive the impact of this outpouring. It's there in Joel 2:28-30 as plain as language could make it. Both genders, all classes, all flesh. It was something that the prophets themselves had never seen nor experienced in any of their respective generations or histories.

The Old Testament faith experience was a Holy Spirit "visitation" culture (Judges 3:10. 6:34. 11:29. 13:25. 14:6. 14:19. 15:14.). The Spirit would come upon men in order to fulfill a task, and then withdraw from them. What the prophets were envisioning was a time when the norm would be a Holy Spirit "permanent anointing" culture. The abiding, falling upon and remaining of the Holy Spirit would start with Messiah, and then be poured out on the receiving believer (Isaiah 32:15-17. 59:21. Ezekiel 39:29. Zechariah 12:10). They saw the time where the Spirit of God would descend upon people - and remain. It was stated literally as the outpouring of the Spirit of God (Isaiah 32:15-17), and was promised metaphorically as water (Isaiah 12:3. 35:7. 41:18. 44:3. 49:10) and fire (Isaiah 10:17. 29:16. 30:30. 66:15-16. Ezekiel 1:4. Zechariah 2:5. Malachi 3:2).

They could not have been talking of justification by faith, they already had that. Abraham believed God and it was counted to him as righteousness. Nobody has ever been made right before God by means other than faith. From Adam and all the way through time to the point when Jesus told Nicodemus "You must be born of the Spirit." It did not start there. Every man of God throughout the Old Testament was made such by faith. Even Moses – the man who gave us the Law. And yet, the New Testament tells us clearly that the promise of the Father, that is the Spirit of Promise that Paul explains was promised to Abraham and his seed (Christ) was not received in the days of the Old Testament. This outpouring was to be something never seen or experienced before.

Paul saw that this promise was not only given to Abraham, who never received it in his pre-resurrection life, but it was given to his seed, i.e. Christ Himself (Galatians 3:16. 3:19. Isaiah 11:1-2. 42:1. 61:1). John the Baptist saw this also. He was told by God Himself that the one upon whom he saw the Holy Spirit descend and remain, that man was Messiah (John 1:33). And as the New Testament believer is "in Christ," it is the inheritance of every person in Christ to have the Spirit of God descend upon them and remain.

I repeat, this cannot possibly refer to conversion. Yes, of course, to be converted is to be born of the Spirit. But why do we assume that Old Testament believers entered into faith without the breath of the Spirit. OK! OK! OK! So they did not know the language. So, it would seem that they weren't even conscious in the early days of the Old Testament of who the person of the Spirit of God was. So the revelation of the Old Testament does not put the imperative in their "present experience" of being in relationship with the Spirit.

The descending of the Spirit upon the believer just as He came down upon Christ, is part of the Christian's inheritance (John 1:33. Acts 10:38). We are not talking of the conversion experience, glorious and "of the Spirit" though that is. We have *access to the grace* wherein we stand through justification by faith in Christ. The truth of the Spirit *within us* is not to be confused with promise of the Spirit *upon us*. Does anybody actually think that the perfect sinless humility and holiness of Christ was not in touch with the indwelling Spirit of God within Him?

Note that the perfect communion that existed between God's only begotten Son and His Father in heaven could not be activated into ministry until the perfection of Messiah had been immersed in the Holy Spirit – who also was sent from heaven.

So! If Christ never preached, healed, delivered or prophesied before He had been anointed by the Spirit, what kind of insanity causes us to even play with the idea that we can minister without the same. To say, "Jesus needed it and I don't," is ludicrous. To suggest that as the Spirit was poured out on the world in Acts chapter 2, therefore every born-again believer has the same baptism, or anointing makes wonderful glass case theology, but is hideously unsupported by what we see in the Christian world.

The experience of the baptism in the Spirit was so fundamental and vital to the way Jesus saw the reality of winning the world, He actually commanded the disciples not to even start until they had received the promise of the Father, the baptism of the Spirit, the enduement of power. Baptism in the Spirit is all about power and evangelism.

No Christian should be left to live their life without the Baptism in the Holy Spirit. From the very mouth of Christ, before He returned to heaven, came the command for the disciples to stay in Jerusalem – i.e. no preaching, no healing, no casting out demons, until they were baptised in the Holy Spirit. That was the priority that Jesus Christ placed on Holy Spirit baptism. Dare we teach a lesser imperative?

The nature of the Baptism of the Holy Spirit is not left to human conjecture or doctrinal fancy in any way whatsoever in the Bible. It is defined in a way that leaves me often times aghast in how it is missed or fogged over. One needs help to misunderstand it.

Matthew 3:11. Mark 1:8. Luke 3:16. John 1:33.

The fact that it is, from God's perspective, a truth to be understood and experienced by all believers is made clear by John the Baptist's declaration, "I indeed baptize you with water to repentance, but he that cometh after me is mightier than I whose shoes I am not worthy to bear. He will baptize you with the Holy Ghost and with fire" (Matthew 3:11. Mark 1:8. Luke 3:16. John 1:33). The entire point of the Baptist's ministry was to lead people into repentance, and then water baptism as a sign of that repentance. Repentance and the dipping of the repentant in the Jordan was the entire thrust of John's ministry, and it was not just for a few. Repentance was for all, as was the immersion into water for all who had repented of their sin. The point John was making was, that what he did with water, Christ would do with the Holy Spirit. His self-evident presupposition was that, the baptism in the Holy Spirit was to be the norm that the Messiah would seek to give to all believers, just as baptism into water was the norm under his own ministry.

I repeat again: Jesus Christ Himself did no miracle, gathered no disciples, and preached no sermon until the Holy Spirit had fallen on Him. In fact, the Holy Spirit not only descended seemingly in a physical form, but landed on Him, and, *"remained,"* according to the Baptist. Jesus left the Jordan driven by the Spirit, and returned to society after the temptation in the wilderness "in the power of the Holy Spirit". Hebrews tells us that He offered Himself through the eternal Spirit, and even in His resurrected body, He spoke through the Holy Spirit to the disciples before He returned to heaven. So even the resurrected Christ was speaking under the power of the same Spirit He received at his water baptism in the Jordan (Acts 1:2).

This is the reason that this writer refuses to accept any of the apocryphal, non-biblical stories and legends of Jesus performing miracles before his baptism in the Jordan. I have no doubt He could have, but He definitely was silent until His time had come, and He had been "immersed" both in water and the Holy Spirit.

Ministry of the miraculous without the power of the Spirit is a call too high for mankind to aspire to. If Christ could not set about fulfilling His Messianic call until the Holy Spirit descended upon Him, how on earth can anybody else on the planet even imagine that they can emulate Him, without the same immersion into the Spirit of God?

So Paul's opening question to the "about twelve" men in Ephesus, hungry for God, is ""Did you receive the Holy Spirit when you believed?" (Acts 19:1-3 NKJV). This has to be one of the most important questions asked in the context of the baptism in the Holy Spirit. Why? Nearly all biblical scholars and evangelical churches in the world would assert that one cannot be brought to faith without the work of the Holy Spirit. Entering into faith is being "born of the Spirit." So if these men were born again of the Spirit of God, and they must have been if this mature, seasoned Apostle of Christ didn't instruct them how to be saved but asks this question straight off, why would they be asked if they had received the Holy Spirit? The only answer could be that receiving the Holy Spirit is not the same as the biblical teaching on being born of the Spirit. Only the born again can receive the baptism in the Holy Spirit

To emphasize this, before moving on, even though these twelve men had an incomplete understanding of the faith, having only heard and responded to John the Baptist, and then obviously didn't stay around to hear and see Jesus in the days of His flesh, their faith must have been a saving faith. If they were saved they must have been saved by the Spirit's work even if their belief system was deficient in any way, and therefore, being "born of the Spirit," they must have had the Spirit of God dwelling within them.

Why did Paul ask them if they had received the Holy Spirit since they believed, if being born of the Spirit and the baptism of the Holy Spirit are synonymous, as many non-charismatic, and non-Pentecostal Christians would teach?

It is this writer's absolute conviction that no one should rightly be ministering the gospel without being baptised in the Holy Spirit, and that every Pastor and church leader should be concerned about any committed, professing Christian in their church who is not baptised in the Holy Spirit, or in the process of seeking that baptism. Holy Spirit baptism is the New Testament norm.

Holding such a conviction, I feel that I cannot in all conscience write about how Paul would not let these twelve move on with God and become part of his team to take Ephesus for Christ without them being baptised in the Holy Spirit, without a full and robust statement concerning my rationale that substantiates this belief.

When John the Baptist was questioned, by the Pharisee's and Sadducee's messengers from Jerusalem, he gave an answer that is recorded in all four Gospels with only slight differences. This suggests to me that it was a repeated phrase that John used often. It is a startling and often neglected statement.

Matthew 3:11 (NKJV) quotes it as, "I indeed baptize you with water unto repentance, but He who is coming after me is mightier than I, whose sandals I am not worthy to carry. He will baptize you with the Holy Spirit and fire." Luke 3:16 (NKJV) states it similarly as, "I indeed baptize you with water; but One mightier than I is coming, whose sandal strap I am not worthy to loose. He will baptise you with the Holy Spirit and fire." Mark makes it briefer with, "I indeed baptise you with water, but He will baptize you with the Holy Spirit". Mark 1:8 (NKJV). The Apostle John reports it as if he overheard John the Baptist actually quoting what God the Father had said to him: "I did not know Him, but He who sent me to baptise with water said to me, 'Upon whom you see the Spirit descending, and remaining on Him, this is He who baptises with the Holy Spirit.'"

"I immerse in water." "He will immerse in the Holy Spirit." That's what John the Baptist taught the people. It was not about holiness per se, but about power (And please do not imagine by that statement that

I am even inferring that the Baptist did not teach holiness, or was himself holy). The "fire" undoubtedly refers to the cleansing delivering power of the Holy Spirit. The Spirit who is Holy can hardly hob nob with sin in the heart and leave it as it is. On repentance, it was John's mission to dip in water. The water was not the act of repentance. The act of repentance was internal to the human heart, the dipping was an external corollary administered by John to the person repenting, moving in conjunction and unity with John's word. Once Christ had returned to heaven, it was His mission to baptise His church, one and all, in the Holy Spirit. The baptism in the Holy Spirit was not, in itself, an act of repentance. Repentance, however, would qualify the believer as a candidate for the baptism in the Holy Spirit. The act of immersing a Christian believer in the Holy Spirit is performed by Christ upon the human frame of the believer. It was to be a fundamental ingredient in the soteriological work of God in redeeming His people.

Every believer needs to be baptised in the Holy Spirit and with fire.

Matthew 3:13-17.   Mark 1:9-11.   Luke 3:21-22.   John 1:32-34.

The experience of Christ when He was baptised, is again fully exposed to us through the writings of all four evangelists. The Spirit descended upon Jesus and led Him into the desert. After His forty days temptation, He returned in the "power of the Spirit." (Matthew 3:13-17. Mark 1:9-11. Luke 3:21-22. John 1:32-34.). From that moment on, the ministry of Christ, we understand, was completely manifested in "the power of the Holy Spirit." It all started with the anointing of the Holy Spirit at the Jordan River.

John 7:37-39.   (John20:22-23)

In John 7:37-39, Jesus said, "If any man thirst, let him come to me and drink, and out of his inmost being will flow rivers of living water." He was undoubtedly referring to the inner thirst for the Holy

Spirit Himself and the things of God. John's gospel actually informs us that Christ was referring to the outpouring of the Holy Spirit that would not take place until Christ was risen, ascended, and glorified. Then He Himself would pour out the Holy Spirit.

In reference to what He said in John 7, He referred to the human experience as being received by drinking from Him, and then being sustained by the rivers of living water flowing from one's innermost parts. In John 4 Jesus referred to the process of salvation as being started by asking Jesus for a drink. One mouthful of "salvation" from Christ would become a well within, said the Master. After having received the cup that led to the well of salvation within, Jesus in John 7 talked of a drink that is subsequent to salvation that leads to rivers flowing out of the believer's innermost being.

However, John 7 is clear that what Jesus was talking about could not happen until He was glorified. It could not happen as stated in John 7 until Christ was glorified and sitting on the right hand of the Father.(See also John 14:12-17. 15:26. 16:7-15.).

Acts 1:4-5.

After the resurrection, and before Jesus had ascended to heaven, He said something that is remarkably missed by many preachers. "Acts 1:4-5 read, "And being assembled together with them, He commanded them not to depart from Jerusalem, but to wait for the Promise of the Father, "which," He said, "you have heard from me; for John truly baptised with water, but you shall be baptised with the Holy Spirit not many days from now."

What is it that is remarkably missed?

Firstly: Jesus commanded them to wait for the baptism in the Holy Spirit. It was not advice, or counsel. This was a command from Heaven, as the resurrected Christ spoke in the power of the Spirit.

Secondly: What they would be waiting for was the promise of the Father. This cryptically meant that what they were waiting for was for everybody who was converted. How do we know that? Because when it finally arrived, Peter in his apologetics for the experience pointed to what Joel had predicted, that God would pour out His Spirit upon all flesh. To be consistent with all of scripture, it could only mean all flesh that was "in Christ."

Thirdly; Christ initially told them what they were waiting for, and the fact that up in heaven it was referred to as "the Promise of the Father." But then he immediately speaks more direct and less cryptically; "You shall be baptised with the Holy Spirit not many days from now."

If it was a "federal" outpouring, i.e. an experience that does not have to be repeated because Acts 2 was the entrance of the Spirit into the church, meaning that the rest of the Christian world would straightway receive the same on conversion whether they are aware of it or not, one can discount everything I say in this chapter of the book.

If, however, it was an infusion that every single born again Christian who ever lives qualifies to have as a replicate experience for the replicate need, we need to be concerned about those who have not received it. It is this writer's conviction that what happened in Acts 2:4 is for everybody who believes. It is the inheritance of every child of God. It is not a doctrinal hobby horse to peddle, it is a biblically exemplified practical requirement to facilitate the full character of Christ in healing the sick, casting out devils and raising the dead.

Acts 2:1-4

What exactly happened in Acts 2:4? There was the sound of a rushing wind. That was God's doing. There were seen, tongues as of fire upon the heads of the one hundred and twenty that were present. Again that was a sovereign act of God. The believers present all spoke with other tongues, i.e. languages that none of them intellectually knew. That was an act of God working together with the submission of the believers. Every Christian present received the tongue of flame as well as the tongue of language. I leave the significance of that fact for the reader to deduce. There were foreigners within earshot of the outpouring who heard their own language being spoken. Their understanding of what was being spoken amazed them because these folks spoke so many current foreign languages. On top of this incredible experience, the entire 120 believers were knocked for six – in other words were somewhat departed from the normal religious stance of serious Jews in the middle of such an important Jewish feast. The audience actually thought that the 120 were drunk. This suggests that there was laughing and, perhaps even staggering going on. Peter stood up to explain that none of them were drunk, but what they were spectators to was the fulfilment of Joel 2:28-32.

Such was the biblical qualification of the Apostle Peter to their experience that we cannot but conclude, that this was indeed the Baptism in the Holy Spirit. "They were all filled with the Holy Spirit and began to speak with other tongues." One needs to be filled with the Holy Spirit in order to be baptised in the Holy Spirit. But the filling in itself does not necessarily mean the baptism.

How did this thing happen? Peter explains that, "Therefore (Jesus) being exalted to the right hand of God, and having received from the Father the promise of the Holy Spirit, He poured out this which you now see and hear" (Acts 2:33). John the Baptist said that Jesus would baptise with the Holy Spirit, and here in Acts 2:33 Peter confirms the same. Therefore, what we see in Acts chapter 2 is the baptism in the Holy Spirit.

Biblically the tongues of fire were not seen again (although I have heard of others receiving flames of fire on their heads anecdotally). The rushing mighty wind was not noticed again. But when the Bible explains what happened concerning the baptism in the Holy Spirit, tongues, prophecy and/or something *observable* is always mentioned. If Peter's inspired sermon is to be examined as a true and prophetic statement, we also have to conclude that what happened to the 120 in

Acts 2, is what God wants to do with every soul who believes in Christ. The baptism in the Holy Ghost is therefore the norm for all Christians everywhere.

Acts 8:5-19

The next time the baptism is referred to in the book of Acts is in chapter 8. The chapter is about Philip the evangelist going to Samaria to preach the gospel. It says he went to "preach Christ." This signifies the purity of his message. He simply declared who and what Jesus Christ is. It states that the multitudes, with one accord, heeded the things spoken of by Phillip. They must have remembered the wonderful 3 days that Christ spent with them 2 or 3 years earlier (John 4). But verse 6 informs us that it wasn't simply the preaching that caused faith to rise – faith that converted the people, but that they saw and heard testimonies of miracles. Unclean spirits came out of people, demons were making loud screams as they were expelled. They also saw the miracles of healing that were done in the name of Christ. Conversion to Christ is a wonderful joyful thing, and there was great joy in the city of Samaria. The gospel is undoubtedly something to see as well as something to listen to. New Testament evangelism to the unchurched includes miraculous healings and the casting out of demons.

New Testament evangelism that precipitates healing and deliverance is defined as "preaching Christ". One does indeed need help to misunderstand the biblical truths explained here.

When the apostles in Jerusalem heard of the wonderful things that were happening in Samaria, they sent Peter and John to see the people and to learn how non-Jewish people were responding to walking with Christ. There was, however, a situation common to all converts in Samaria that the Bible explains as if it was a strange anomaly. It says of Peter and John that, "they ... prayed for them that they might receive the Holy Spirit. For as yet He had fallen upon none of them. They had only been baptised in the name of the Lord Jesus. Then they laid hands on them, and they received the Holy Spirit."

But hold on! If they saw the miracles and heard about Christ and believed, they **MUST** have been "born of the Spirit." So the new born Samaritan Christians must have had the Spirit of God indwelling them. So…what was missing?

The text in Acts 8 now reveals to us that the baptism in the Holy Spirit has other Euphemisms, such as "The Holy Spirit falling on them," and "receiving the Holy Spirit."

Neither tongues nor prophecy are mentioned in the text, however, Simon Magus was so impressed with what he *saw* when Peter and John prayed for them to receive the Holy Spirit, that he offered them money to be able to impart the gift in the same way. He was severely spoken to by Peter because of Simon's lack of insight and personal selfishness. Simple, elementary extrapolation from every section of scripture where the baptism in the Holy Spirit is referred to leads to the unalterable conclusion that Simon Magus *saw* and *heard* some manifestation of the Spirit in one way or another – otherwise why would he offer money to be able to "do" what Peter and John "did." The more needful question is: "What did Simon Magus see?" We are not told in Acts 8, yet to be consistent with what we read in Acts 2, Acts 10 and 11 and Acts 19 we cannot but soundly extrapolate that what he saw was people speaking in tongues and/or prophesying. Something took place that told Simon Magus that Peter and John by prayer and the laying on of hands imparted something wonderful to the Samaritan converts.

Most importantly, it seems that Peter and John, together, took it for granted that people who had not been baptised in the Holy Spirit *should have been*. There is utterly no remark about Philip's ministry lacking in any way whatsoever. No reason is given to explain the phenomenon. The two apostolic pillars prayed for all Samaritan converts to receive their baptism in the Holy Spirit. They laid hands on them, prayed and they received.

The inference is made by this report that New Testament evangelists, in bringing people to Christ, had not completed and fully delivered the message until people had been healed, demons cast out, people received the message, and were baptised in the Holy Spirit – and not necessarily in that order.

Acts 9:17-19

Acts 9 is the next stage in the biblical revelation of the baptism in the Holy Spirit. Saul of Tarsus was famously converted on the Damascus Road. So bright was the revelation of Christ, Saul was blinded. He was unable to see with his physical eyes, but saw more of God in 3 days of being physically blind, than he had in his entire life up to that point with perfect vision. In his blindness he saw a vision of a man called Ananias coming to him to lay hands on him for him to receive his sight and for him also to be "filled with the Holy Spirit." It happened, literally as he had seen it.

The scripture states that he was filled with the Spirit after Ananias had prayed. Again, neither tongues nor prophecy, nor any other manifestation is referred to. It is the opinion of this writer, and many Pentecostal theologians, that although no tongues are mentioned, the Holy Spirit in fact did fall on Saul.

The conclusion is not such a random sounding one when one reads in 1 Corinthians 14:18, "I thank my God, I speak with tongues more than you all." Ananias states that he was there not just for Paul to regain his sight, but that he "might be filled with the Spirit". That is the same phrase as is used in Acts chapter two when the initial baptism in the Spirit was received.

It is this writer's opinion that wherever in the New Testament the phrase "filled with the Spirit" is used it is referring to either the baptism in the Holy Spirit, with the manifestation of speaking in tongues, or prophecy after a Christian has been baptised in the Spirit.

Note that we learn by the experience of Saul of Tarsus that it is legitimate in God's economy of things, that "non-apostolic" hands may be anointed to impart the baptism in the Holy Spirit.

Acts 10:44-48   Acts 11:15-18

The next biblical reference to the baptism in the Holy Spirit, continuing in chronological order through the book of Acts, is contained in the account of Peter's visit to the house of Cornelius in Acts 10:44-48, and his explanation of what happened in his report to the other apostles as contained in Acts 11:15–18. Peter was invited by Cornelius to visit him, and instructed by the Holy Spirit to respond favourably to the invite immediately. Peter started to preach to Cornelius and his household and was interrupted, literally, by God as he spoke. The household of Cornelius *all* started to speak in tongues.

Acts 10:44 states that the "Holy Spirit fell" on the people whilst Peter was preaching. From this we learn that laying on of hands by a minister, or apostle is unnecessary. From this we also are taught that the baptism in the Holy Spirit is a work done by God Himself. Human hands are not necessary.

Both Peter and his entourage were taken aback for these people who were speaking in tongues were utterly non-Jewish and uncircumcised. No surprise is mentioned when the half gentile Samaritan's were baptised in the Spirit, but here with full blown Roman gentiles speaking in tongues, the apostolic eyebrows were raised.

Peter concluded that the speaking in tongues proved that these people were already converted to Christ. This is the biblical verse that becomes the ground for stating that the baptism in the Holy Spirit is an experience that is subsequent to the experience of conversion. It might be given in the same moment of conversion, but definitely not before. For the few people I have met in my life who claim they were baptised in the Holy Spirit before they were converted, I answer that whether you knew it or not, you were converted when you first spoke in tongues by the Holy Spirit. One must be converted before the Spirit is received. Peter said, "... God gave them the like gift as he did unto us, who believed on the Lord Jesus Christ..." Believe in Christ first. Receive the Holy Spirit subsequently.

The terminology of Peter used to explain the experience of Cornelius and his household are several. "The Holy Ghost fell on them." On them, "was poured out the gift of the Holy Ghost." They "received the Holy Ghost." Peter describes it thus: "Then remembered I the word of the Lord, how that he said, John indeed baptised with water; but ye shall be baptised with the Holy Ghost." "Could it be plainer?" I ask.

Another insight is gained as we meditate on our conclusions so far. Water baptism, before or after the baptism in the Holy Spirit is neither here nor there. In Acts 2 Peter's preached sequence was: Repent and believe – be baptised in water – receive the Holy Spirit. In Acts 8 the people repented and believed, and had to wait until Peter and John arrived before they were baptised in the Holy Spirit. In Acts 9 we are not 100% clear. However, it seems to this writer, on the grounds of the words of Ananias, that Saul had believed, then after prayer, was filled with the Holy Spirit (i.e. the baptism in the Holy Spirit euphemistically) and then baptised in water. Acts chapter 10 was the same as Acts 9. They people present were all obviously in faith and soundly converted. Peter saw them baptised in the Holy Spirit. To correct the situation he stated that they should be immediately baptised in water.

If there was any doubt concerning the conversion of these gentile believers at the home of Cornelius, the manifested baptism in the Holy Spirit resolved the problem. The baptism of the Holy Spirit resolves many issues in the kingdom of God, and throughout the church. In fact

I would declare that it is His absence that often times creates the problems.

Acts 19:1-7

And so we arrive at Acts 19. We are back in Ephesus. Paul met about a dozen disciples. What is his first and primary apostolic concern for them? Are they reading scripture often? Are they praying daily? Are they in Christian meetings often? None of these were even on his agenda. His first question to them, in fact his opening line of greeting it seems was, "Have you received the Holy Ghost since ye believed?" Could any question be more significant?

First question surely indicates first priority! First remark clearly indicates what's most important! First enquiry definitely suggests what has apostolic weight and precedence. If you are not converted, the first apostolic line is, "Believe on the Lord Jesus Christ and you will be saved." If you are a Christian, the first apostolic line is, "Have you received the Holy Ghost since ye believed?" That is as plain and as straight as I can make it, because that is as straight as it is presented in scripture.

So we find: There were believers in the world in Paul's day, just as there are in our day, who are soundly saved, and may even consider themselves true disciples. (In fact the scripture says that these twelve *were* true disciples) but are ***NOT*** baptised in the Holy Spirit. Just as the Samaritan converts were an anomaly to Peter and John that was easily and soon corrected by the laying on of hands, so were these twelve disciples in Ephesus a spiritual anomaly. It is not a sin not to be baptised in the Holy Spirit. There is no superiority to be even considered in those who are baptised in the Holy Spirit. It is nobody's fault when a Christian is not baptised in the Holy Spirit. The answer is to seek God Himself in order to receive the baptism in the Spirit.

Paul was obviously not willing to have these twelve in his ministry team unless and until they were baptised in the Holy Spirit. Otherwise it would not have been so deftly written by Luke.

1 Corinthians 12 and 14

Because of what is written in First Corinthians concerning Tongues, prophecy and the gifts of the Spirit in general, I feel it necessary to explain a little. Things like, "Do all speak in tongues?" have led many to embrace the status quo for those who are not baptised in the Holy Spirit. Context desperately needs to be maintained in one's understanding.

1. It was extremely common in church meetings to have the gifts of the Spirit exercised. Why should Corinth be unique?

2. The Holy Spirit gives these gifts severally as He will (1 Corinthians 12: 7-10).

3. I believe that one generally requires people to be baptised in the Holy Spirit before one can properly exercise the gifts of the Spirit as listed in 1 Corinthians 12.

4. The fact that the impression is given that all in the church of Corinth were eager to use the gifts, suggests that the entire church was already baptised in the Holy Spirit. To state it from another angle; the baptism in the Holy Spirit is the norm for church members as well as ministering personnel.

5. In the exercise of the gifts, people tended to specialise in one or two of the manifestations of the Spirit. It is in that context that the apostle wrote, "Do all speak with tongues?" I say this because I have met people who claim to be baptised in the Holy Spirit yet have never spoken in other tongues. These people have all unanimously used 1 Corinthians 12:30 to "defensively" justify their claim. Without sounding too dogmatic, I inwardly reject such a claim. Biblically I believe there has to be tongues or prophecy that explains to all and any that are present, and gives assurance to the recipient, that God has indeed baptised them in the Holy Spirit.

6. When praying in tongues, it is clear that a person is speaking to God in mysteries (1 Corinthians 14:2). Many liken the use of

praying in tongues to the groaning in prayer referred to in Romans 8:23 and even in 2 Corinthians 5:2-4. As a prayer weapon, Romans 8 justifies its use in prayer as we do not know how to pray or what to say.

7. When one prays in tongues, one's human spirit is praying (1 Corinthians 14:14). The fact that Paul says in that verse that the mind is "unfruitful" does not mean it is useless in the exercise. He who speaks in tongues edifies himself says 1 Corinthians 14:4. That is probably in that context that Paul says he spoke with tongues more than them all (1 Corinthians 14:18).

8. Those that are especially effective when using tongues, be it in prayer, bringing a word that requires interpretation seem to have some kind of proper office or function. 1 Corinthians 12:28 reads, "And in the church God has appointed first of all apostles, second prophets, third teachers, then workers of miracles, also those having gifts of healing, those able to help others, those with gifts of administration, and those speaking in different kinds of tongues." I confess I need light on that one.

9. So, although there may have been some who, when using the gifts of the Holy Spirit in the context of church life did not speak in tongues, the precursor to their use of the gifts, whatever those gifts might be, was that the person concerned was baptised in the Holy Spirit.

10. To demonstrate that a person is baptised in the Holy Spirit, they must have spoken in tongues or prophesied.

It is in the context of number 10, with Christians that are already baptised in the Holy Spirit, that he says he wishes that they would all speak in tongues in the use of the gifts (1 Corinthians 14:5).

The context of 1 Corinthians 12 and 14 as justification for whether or not speaking in tongues should be the norm throughout the Church of Christ is a fallacy. The baptism of the Holy Spirit is one issue that needs to be taught as a believer's privilege, and the promise of the Father. To baptise the believer in the Holy Spirit was one of the purposes that Christ came to gift us with.

But having stated all that about the baptism being for the whole church, we move on to a completely different subject, namely the gifts of the Holy Spirit in church life. Here we have a "some do" and a "some don't". "Not all do this" and "Not all do that". Be wise, be careful, and make sure all is done to edify the people. In fact it's a whole raft of wise advice that is needed when such spiritual gifts are privileged to be used amongst us. This writer believes that the baptism in the Holy Spirit is for every Christian, and should be "received" as the gift it is, just as salvation is received.

It is on the basis of what I say above, that we are all encouraged to prophesy, in the context of spiritual gifts, not in the context of being a prophet - that is something utterly different.

Those Christians that speak and pray in tongues are encouraged to ask God for the interpretation of what they are saying (1 Corinthians 14:13).

Tongues is a positive sign to unbelievers present in the church gathering (1 Corinthians 14:22).

With the basic understanding that the receiving of the baptism of the Holy Spirit is an act of God wanting to pour out His Spirit upon the entire church of Christ worldwide, we have the sound biblical reason why Pentecostal people quote Ephesians 1:13 "You were marked in him with a seal, the promised Holy Spirit" (NIV), or as it says in the King James Bible "after that ye believed, ye were sealed with that holy Spirit of promise, Which is the earnest of our inheritance until the redemption of the purchased possession, unto the praise of his glory"(Ephesians 1:13b-14), as referring to the baptism in the Holy Spirit.

It is also the reason why the gift of speaking in tongues is assumed by Pentecostal people when Jude 20 says, "But you beloved, building up yourselves on your most holy faith, praying in the Holy Ghost," is understood as referring to praying with the human spirit, in the Holy Spirit, i.e. tongues.

We have lengthily bared our souls as to the entire raft of truths and significances of the baptism in the Holy Spirit to make a point. We have said all that to say this: Every Christian needs to be baptised in the Holy Spirit, especially those who are church leaders and/or full time Christian workers. The world is too dark and too assertive in its darkness for Christians to minister without the power of the Holy Spirit that is endued from on high upon those baptised in the Holy Spirit.

Without qualification, the first issue on Paul's heart when he met twelve good disciples and true, was to see them immersed in the Spirit. The proof of such an inward work of grace was the outward sign of speaking with tongues, and/or prophecy.

In the immediate context of those opening verses of Acts 19, we believe that this is the New Testament biblical pattern for building ministry personnel and apostolic teams. All ministering team members should be filled with the Holy Ghost to be properly effective. For those who claim to have been ministering for years without the baptism, I merely respond with, "But how much more could you have accomplished with the promise of the Father in your life?"

Remember, we are making notes while watching the Apostle Paul commence a work that will ultimately be the most incredibly effective mission ever seen. It is my contention that Paul's apostolic model for Ephesus, is the ultimate model for successful evangelism. I believe that the pressure from worldly and demonic influences is intense, and that it is unwise to attempt to handle the extreme pressure and opposition to the Gospel without Jesus' Dunamis (Greek word for "power". The word from which we have "dynamite") to witness, that is, the Holy Spirit himself.

Having laid hands on the twelve, Paul then sought to take them further in God.

7.

MIRACULOUS IMPARTATION
ACTS 19:1-7

The issue of impartation both in the Bible, and in my own personal experience, is the point where things that look and seem totally natural, almost trivial in its external, physical, and visual processes, are actually utterly transcendent and supernatural in what takes place. I suppose it starts off in scripture where Isaac passes on the blessing of his father Abraham to Jacob (Genesis 27). It was not just an eastern way of how to pass on the inheritance, this was a divine impartation that announced that the blessings given to Abraham and Isaac were now being endowed into the life of Jacob. It was a father laying his hands on one of his sons, but it was giving Jacob all that God had given Abraham. We are talking of things unseen as well as the tangibly seen.

Jacob blessing his own sons and Grandsons is also a phenomena to normal western thinking, even, so called, "Christian Thinking." The importance of impartation is seen in the crucial moment of Jacob crossing his hands to his grandsons, and Joseph attempting to correct him (Genesis 48:14-20). These graphic moments in Genesis are part and parcel of the biblical introduction to something that is so important, sometimes vital, yet is pooh-poohed by many Christians. It is an action, a prayer, a wilful giving of a fellow human being who has been blessed in some way that actually, in reality, passes on the blessing concerned, to another recipient.

To put it in the plainest of terms, the bible teaches that there are some gifts, even some characteristics, some intuitive blessings of God that under His leading and initiation, can be quite literally given to somebody else by some sort of action that commonly looks artificially symbolic to the untutored. What I am saying here is denigrated and even ridiculed by some Christians, with questions like; "What if the person isn't worthy of the imparted blessing?" (Is anybody "worthy"?). "How can we be sure it was God's will for a blessing to be imparted?" "Isn't this putting into human hands something that is totally God's responsibility and ability?" To these kind of questions, my answer is to see it modelled in scripture first of all, and then listen to testimonies of where it has happened.

Impartation of the nature I refer to is more common than many give credit to. I am not talking of things intellectually learned. That is natural enough. I am talking of things that are literally given from heaven. I was brought up by my grandfather, and in his later years, whenever I would call to see him, as I hugged him to say my farewell, he would always take a ten-pound note out of his pocket, and stuff it into my jacket pocket. In so doing, he gave me something that belonged to him, something that was part of him and his wealth. As I left, something that was his, was now mine. He had imparted to me something of his own. In this illustration I am being so physical as to talk about money. But, in the reality of my relationship with my Grandad, it was truly something far beyond money. There was a continued bonding in his action toward me, a prolonging of the relationship I had had with him throughout my entire life. Just as the physical currency passed from his pocket to mine, there was a "love currency" that was tangibly passed from his heart to mine. I received that "love currency" with grateful relish.

In acts 19 and those first seven verses, Paul, undoubtedly imparted something of himself to these twelve men. I feel sure one of these twelve was Epaphras who founded the church at Colossae, I believe, during Paul's mission in Ephesus. Epaphras went to Colossae and evangelised the place, so that when Paul wrote to the Colossian church he was extremely confident of what had been preached there because of the degree he had imparted of himself to the man.

In Romans 1, Paul explains how he wanted to go to Rome in order to "impart some spiritual gift" to the church that already existed there.

For years I understood that to mean that Paul simply wanted to preach to them and impart something of his understanding into what it means to live in the grace of God. After all, his understanding of things spiritual was more than profound. Now, having seen, in my travels and experience, how Godly men of stature and authority have tangibly passed on to others something of the gift of the Holy Spirit that was rich in their lives, I understand Romans 1:11 in a totally different vein.

There were gifts that Paul imparted to Timothy through prophecy and the laying on of hands. Paul encourages Timothy to keep those prophetic words in the fore front of his mind to inspire him in the midst of life's battles. That is that, by faith, Timothy was to remember how things that were intrinsic to Paul's gifting and authority, had been given to Timothy by the laying on of the apostle's own hands.

The English Dictionary defines, "impartation," and, "to impart," as Firstly, "to communicate (information); relate. Secondly, to give or bestow, especially some abstract quality: to impart wisdom." Plain enough! The word used in the Greek New Testament is, μεταδίδωμι, transliterated as "metadidomi", phonetically spelt as "met-ad-id'-o-mee". It means, simply, "to offer by way of change. One offers so that a change of ownership is produced. One shares; sometimes merely: One imparts, bestows." In short, one shares and one gives of something that is birthed in the Holy Spirit – that is what spiritual impartation is all about.

I am speaking like a geek, to make the point that there is no theological skulduggery here. We are simply using a commonly spoken word, but using it in the realm of the Spirit and things that are invisible yet intrinsically and practically tangible in their manifestation.

Biblical examples of impartation of spiritual life, or gifts are quite plentiful. It is my conviction that Paul imparted the gifts and aspects of authority of his apostolic ministry to those twelve disciples that he met on entry to the borders of Ephesus (Acts 19:6). I believe that the apostle taught his new team of twelve the power of apostolic impartation, by he himself imparting as much to them when he taught them as he did by laying hands on them. He found twelve godly disciples of John the Baptist who were deficient in the body of truth that they believed, and were deficient in the power and illumination of the Holy Spirit that they had not heard of. After Paul prayed there was a release of the Holy Spirit on these men of faith and commitment, and they began to speak in other tongues and prophesy. That moment of ministry in itself would have been a self-evident impartation of the anointing of the Holy Spirit that was upon the apostle falling on the twelve. These twelve carried on working with, and following Paul with the view of imitating him. When he later stopped speaking in the synagogue and had decided to hold daily meetings in the school of Tyrannus, the disciples were still with him. They received much from Paul's impartation. Apostolic ministry is a ministry of rich impartation. (Romans 1:11). That is what it was all about. They are master builders of something that is "deepest" in the realm of the Spirit, and in the kingdom of God.

I worked for three years in Lagos, Nigeria with a very powerfully anointed African pastor, the late Prophet T.B. Joshua. The gift of God on his life was so tangible that I witnessed several times a literal "giving" of a spiritual anointing and gift to various people. It was done so plainly, so publicly, and so immediately visibly effective that I was astonished at the directness. I had always believed in the principle of impartation, but not so simple and instant as what I am about to recount.

There was a team of ministers that this pastor had around the church. I was one of that team. It was one Sunday evening, while he was praying for a huge number of sick people, that something happened that seemed to me to be utterly spontaneous. Although the ministry team had been imparted to by the pastor in issues of healing and deliverance, he had explained once or twice that God had not released him to impart the gift of prophecy to anybody. He is known as a "prophet" per se, and I have many memories of the most incredible prophetic words for people in his ministry, words that were always immediately vindicated and corroborated as true. On this particular day he stopped for a moment and grabbed the nearest microphone. He announced to the congregation of many thousands, that God had told him that now is the time to release prophecy to someone. One of the team that was stood nearest to him was called to his side. Whether it was because he was the nearest, or whether the choice of this person came with the heavenly communication, I have utterly no idea. The young minister he chose, I shall refer to as "A". The pastor cum prophet took hold of "A's" hand, and simply cried out, "In the mighty name of Jesus Christ." No other words left his lips. He held tightly on to "A's" hand for something like 30 – 40 seconds while "A" wriggled violently and then fell to the floor, still wriggling. After a few moments "A" stopped moving and lay still on the floor. At this point I need to say that of all the dozen or so junior ministers and pastors in the church, "A" was possibly the most unclear in his normal speech. I have to say, without meaning to insult "A," that he was definitely not the most intelligent amongst us all, and was generally quite a retiring and quiet person, excepting when it came to praying for people that were ill. The prophet let go of "A"'s hand, and retired to his office. "A" was simply left alone to carry on praying for the extremely long prayer line. "A" continued praying for people as he always had done, however, he was now ministering personal prophecy to the people he prayed for. During the rest of that prayer line, he delivered five or six profoundly complex personal prophecies to individuals and couples that were revealing, healing, and delivering as he spoke them. Every prophetic word he gave was later confirmed, revealing the power and exactness of what "A" had said to them. That is impartation. Each one ministered to thanked God and were drawn to Christ. Each person to whom "A" had prophesied was astounded that he could know the contents of what "A" had spoken.

In my travels and interaction throughout my four decades plus as a Christian, I have met and listened intently to ministers who move in the prophetic. I know clearly from what I have learned and heard from prophetic people, as well as those that are known as "prophets" that many of them spent years, if not decades, seeking God and "working their anointing" to increase and improve their prophetic gift. Yet, apart from the pastor himself, I have never heard anybody else anywhere in the world prophesy so clearly into the depths of people's lives as I heard "A" minister that day. In one single moment of impartation "A" entered into an anointing that many had prayed for over many years.

I am aware of others who live under this pastor's mentoring and impartation at this very moment as I write that have also been translated into the same dimension as "prophetic" ministers, if not "prophets" in their own right.

The principle of impartation is simple enough for a child to understand. However, what I am talking about here is something so profound in the realm of the Holy Spirit that it is denigrated by many as "unsound theology". What happened that day started with a man who had been given to the church as a prophet, who has a rich and deep weight of anointing in that area, in fact it is an anointing of such weight that it is undoubtedly tangible to many who even walk by him? He had, at that moment (or so it seemed to me), heard from heaven to impart the gift. His response was immediate. In exactly the same manner in which my grandfather stuffed money into my pocket, so the prophetic gift was stuffed into the spiritual pocket of "A" in exactly the same manner. The result was instant. The analogy of my grandfather giving me money actually falls short in the reality of spiritual impartation. My grandfather was ten pounds the poorer when he imparted his gift to me. The pastor I worked with in Nigeria, if anything, seemed to me to be richer in his prophetic gifting afterwards than he was previously. It seemed to me that as he "gave it away", what he had increased.

Character can never be imparted. Experience and spiritual stature cannot be imparted. I am convinced that the main reason some Christians deny the reality of true impartation is obviously with the thought that whatever can be imparted could or can be misused, abused, or even neglected. A man who has the ability and authority to impart could do so arbitrarily. The wrong person may be imparted to.

There are obviously limits to what can be given. But what exactly are those limits? Impartation from an apostle, even the apostle Paul, could not and will not turn the person imparted to, into an apostle. There are different levels and various kinds of impartation. Some levels of impartation are permanent, and some are temporary. Some are utterly dependent on the person imparting, and occasionally, the character of the recipient is almost irrelevant.

The more I look into the life and ministry of the Apostle Paul, especially as I approach what went on in Ephesus, the more I see his heart to give away of himself those things God had placed within him. He lived to see others effectively trained in matters to do with God; in issues of doctrine, in affairs to do with spiritual insight, and in concerns of ministering in the Holy Spirit. For example, listen to the heart he carried when he said: "For I long to see you, that I may impart unto you some spiritual gift, to the end ye may be established; that is, that I may be comforted together with you by the mutual faith both of you and me" (Romans 1:11-12,KJV). Paul's desire was to help others to rise in effective ministry through all that God had given to him. He learned that he could pass on through impartation blessings and giftings of God that would release others into the fullness of God, and a profound awareness of the Holy Spirit in all they did. When we speak of impartation we mean the ability to give unto others that which God has given to us ... either sovereignly, or through other anointed vessels (messengers) of God. Impartation has to do with the giving and receiving of spiritual gifts, blessings, healing, baptism in the Holy Spirit, etc., for the work of the ministry. It is the transference of these "gifts" from one man or woman of God to another, classically through the laying on of hands, but in actuality through many different ways. In impartation there is an invisible flowing of spiritual ability from one to the other. That invisible flowing goes from the spirit and heart of the imparter through the arms and hands into the spirit and heart of the one receiving.

In Numbers 11, we are told that the burden of Leadership was becoming too heavy on Moses' life. When he asked God about this, His response was to get Moses to gather together 70 men of the Elders of Israel (Numbers 11:16-17). God actually promised to take of the spirit that was upon Moses and impart it to the 70 elders, so they could share in and carry the burden that Moses was carrying (Numbers 11:24-25). God Himself imparted of the Spirit from Moses to the 70 Elders. When that happened they began to prophesy - something they had never done before. That impartation enabled them to take on greater responsibility to support Moses, to minister to the people and to release the Holy Spirit out of their lives to bless others. There was a transferring from one (Moses) to others (the seventy), so the one receiving could function much more like the one doing the imparting or transferring. We do not, however, read anywhere that Moses suffered loss in any way because of this transference, or better, impartation.

The reality of the impartation was sealed and noted when the seventy began to prophesy.

It has been my privilege to observe once or twice in my life some of the great pioneers of the Pentecostal movement in the United Kingdom. I remember one particular time hearing the great John Nelson Parr preach in Bethshan Tabernacle in Manchester, England. He was in his eighties. I am talking about 1968-9 shortly before his passing. He preached passionately as if we were all lost and about to go to hell. He made an appeal and about a dozen or so people when forward. It was an amazing sight as nearly all the people who had gone forward to be converted were obviously totally unchurched. Mr Parr asked them if they knew what the baptism in the Holy Spirit was. From my seat in the middle of the church I saw the entire line shaking their heads. Mr Parr then came down to them and touched each one of them on the forehead in turn. To each person he simply shouted, "Receive the Holy Spirit in the Name of Jesus!" Each one of the line immediately spoke in tongues very loudly and for quite some time. Some of them knelt, some of them lay prostrate on their backs, one of them jumped up and down waving his arms. Not one of them knew what was to come when Mr Parr came down to pray for them. That was impartation in the realm of the Spirit. They received by faith and the Holy Spirit did the rest.

I remember this experience whenever I read of the two of the seventy that were not present for Moses to lay hands on them. The camp. They had no idea what was going on with Moses, yet they still received the anointing from the impartation and started prophesying in the camp.

The Lord Jesus sent out the twelve in pairs, and later the seventy. They were sent to preach, heal the sick, cleanse the lepers and raise the dead. How on earth were the twelve and the seventy learners supposed to get on with a job that hitherto could only have been done by Christ Himself? The answer is plainly given in scripture. Matthew 10:1 states that, "Jesus called his twelve disciples to him and gave them authority to drive out impure spirits and to heal every disease and sickness." Verses 7 to 8 follow up this impartation of authority by filling in the details. "These twelve, Jesus sent out with the following instructions: ... "As you go, proclaim this message, 'The kingdom of heaven has come near." Heal the sick, raise the dead and cleanse those who have leprosy, drive out demons. Freely you have received; freely give." The process of impartation is wonderfully exemplified here, by Christ Himself, and the model is set in place for all time.

It is important to note that the authority given by Christ to the twelve (and later to the seventy) was nothing to do with the intrinsic state of those disciples, even as repentant sinners. The impartation was absolutely nothing to do with the character or spirituality, or the morality and faith of the recipients. How can I be so certain to make such a dogmatic assertion? Simply because one of those imparted to, was a man called Judas Iscariot. That was a man that Christ referred to as "a devil". Yet he also went with a partner in discipleship to preach, heal and deliver the demoniacs.

It is my understanding that impartation of this nature requires an uncommon weight of anointing, power and authority. This is the kind of impartation that was extended to my friend "A" as referred to above. The impartation from the African pastor I was working with was of a similar nature to what the Lord Jesus gave here in the gospels. How do I know that? Firstly because this writer was one of those that were imparted to. Secondly, because the pastor concerned explained it to be so.

When the Holy Spirit came in Acts chapter two the anointing of authority and power was of a different nature to that which they had received in the days prior to the crucifixion from the mouth of Christ Himself. The anointing received at Pentecost was a permanent issue. This anointing depended on their heart condition, their walk with God, and their own character. It was their very own anointing, poured out by Christ when He sent the Holy Spirit from Heaven.

What we are reading in Acts 19:1-7 is this very principle. Paul at Ephesus was not only able to instruct believers into a deeper revelation of understanding, imparting wisdom and insight as he taught, but he was also able to impart through the laying on of hands, and by interaction with the twelve, something of that deeper dimension of the Spirit. After they were water baptized he laid hands on them (Acts 19:1-7). Through impartation by the laying on of hands, those believers were released into a dynamic new dimension of the Holy Spirit, including the gift of prophecy.

We need to see in our generation way beyond the empty religiosity and law keeping morality that dominates so much Christianity. We need to take hold of the fact that, there is an incredibly deep purpose in the earth that is of God's mind and intention. We cannot judge what God is like by what we see in Christianity generally. It is an essential necessity of life that not only Christians, but the unsaved person on the street who sees God through weak, wishy washy human beings that are unsure of their gender, their belief systems, their bible and their church, have to be presented with a more spiritual, authoritative, empowered group of people that are called Christians. We need to dig deep, and bore a hole even, through the hard crust of ordinary, natural Christianity (as if there was ever such a thing) that allows us into the white hot, glorious presence of Jesus Christ. We need to allow the very impartation of His heart to overwhelm and subsume ours, and then touch others. It takes more than a couple of weekly, hour long services, where the sermon is "tip toeing" around people's sensitivities to keep them happy. We need to ask Heavenly Father, if He will change us by an impartation of the Spirit of God in the mighty name of Jesus Christ. Nothing else will do. Anything short of what we are seeing of Paul, in Ephesus, is "sub normal Christianity."

Impartation takes place when the Word of God is actually received into the core of our being. Impartation requires a certain strength and depth of reception of divine truth for any transformation to take place. We will be judged in the presence of God by how much we have been changed into the image of Christ, and nothing else. The burden of New Testament ministry is definitely NOT just to scatter seed on all sorts of ground. The battle of New Testament ministry is to see fruit. One plants, another waters, but fruit comes by the preaching and teaching of the Gospel, as presented in the bible.

We all desire to see the church growing and thriving and our lives to be full and rich with the blessings of God, but we fail to count the cost of true spiritual impartation. Many need mentors to lead and impart to them. My conviction is that there are men and women of God out there who are ripe to mentor and impart to others, but have nobody under them to impart to.

Paul was a giant. He imparted traits of giant hood into those that would allow him to get close. Paul's first task in Ephesus was to gain some good brothers who were godly and hungry enough to be referred to as disciples, minister to them being baptised in the Holy Spirit, and then imparted to by spending time and sharing himself with them.

Finally, one of the greatest modern stories of impartation I know of. This is an extract from the book entitled, "Holy Ghost Evangelism" written by Reinhard Bonnke with George Canty. It was written in a section of the book entitled "The Great Commission to Each Generation" This extract is Evangelist Bonnke talking:

Passing on the Flame.

"In 1961, at just 21 years of age, I completed my studies at the Bible College of Wales in Swansea, the UK. I could go home to North Germany. The route took me via London. My train was not due to leave until the evening, so I spent the time doing some sight-seeing. I went where I pleased, and somehow wandered on to the nice avenues of Clapham, South London. Then, on one pleasant road, I saw in front of me a notice on the panel – "GEORGE JEFFREYS." I had just read a book by this evangelist and could hardly think I had chanced upon the very house where the same man might be. George Jeffreys came out of the Welsh Revival and, with his brother Stephen, introduce the flame of the full Gospel message publicly to the people of Britain. His work shook cities, and tens of thousands saw mighty miracles. He planted not only churches, but an entire movement. Here was a man worthy of the name of apostle. Eagerly I ventured up the path to the door and rang the bell. A lady appeared and I asked, "Is this the George Jeffreys who founded the Elim Pentecostal Church?" The reply, to my delight, affirmed my hopes. "Could I please see Mr Jeffreys?" The reply was a firm "That is not possible." But then that deep Welsh musical voice that is said to have held thousands spellbound with its authority, spoke from inside, "Let him come in." Thrilled, I entered, and there was George Jeffreys, looking to me like a man of 90, but then 72.

"What do you want?" were his words to me. I introduced myself and then we talked about the work of God. Suddenly the great man fell on his knees, pulling me down with him, and started to bless me. The power of the Holy Spirit entered that room. The anointing began to flow, and like Aaron's oil seemed to run over my head and "down to the skirts of my robes," so to speak. I left the house dazed. Four weeks later, like Elijah, George Jeffreys had been taken to glory. He died soon after I saw him. But I knew I had picked up something from this former Holy Ghost, fire-brand evangelist. I am sure the Holy Spirit had arranged my meeting with him. How else was it possible that I should stumble upon this one house in a city of ten million people when George Jeffreys wasn't even on my mind?

"Whatever this happy event did for me, one thing I can claim – seeing this man made me understand that we build on the people who went before."

If a man of the calibre of George Jeffreys could pass on something so tangible and powerful, think of what the Apostle Paul could do with twelve men under his tutoring and mentorship for two years.

8.

MENTORING.
ACTS 19:6-9

"When Paul placed his hands on them, the Holy Spirit came on them, and they spoke in tongues and prophesied. There were about twelve men in all. Paul entered the synagogue and spoke boldly there for three months, arguing persuasively about the kingdom of God. But some of them became obstinate; they refused to believe and publicly maligned the Way. So Paul left them. He took the disciples with him and had discussions daily in the lecture hall of Tyrannus"

. **Acts 19:6-9**

Paul found these twelve disciples, ministered to them, to bring them to the baptism in the Holy Spirit, after which they undoubtedly stayed with him. They were his students, his protégés, they were his ministry team of helps and aides, with a view to becoming whatever they would develop into. After three months of preaching in the synagogue in Ephesus, he left the Jewish congregation of Judaists, and, "took the disciples with him." It is agreed by all writers, scholars, preachers and commentators that "disciples" here is referring to the "disciples" as referred to in Acts 19:1. A reading in all English version leads to no other conclusion.

So these twelve were hooked up with Paul in a very essential and vital relationship. Paul was a father to these children, a master to these servants and a mentor to these protégés. He was a personal tutor to bring these children to full maturity in Christ. One cannot be a Christ-like mentor without spending a lot of time with those being mentored. Mentoring means to personally develop those being mentored in whatever field, work, calling or activity the relationship is required to further. It is simply where someone who is more advanced and richly endowed in whatever it takes to be successful in the field to which they are being mentored, is pouring into the heart and life of the mentored a practical "hands on" course of tuition for the mentored to develope, and hopefully, ultimately surpass the mentor in skill and effectiveness. True mentoring cannot be done remotely, or by reading books (although books may be a part of modern mentoring processes).

True mentoring is not just being there when questions are asked. In fact it is more likely for the mentor to be asking the questions. Mentoring is about an ongoing, ever deepening relationship of learning and growth, dialogue, debate and challenge. A mentor is a master teacher in one's life. That is what Paul was to these twelve. It is wise counsel to move towards anyone who increases one's life, and to move away from anybody who decreases one's life. That is why these twelve stuck with Paul. Within that Mentor-protégé relationship one needs to draw on Gods resources so that one's life becomes better not bitter. By that I mean that having a human mentor, makes it easier to lean on them too much, depend on them more than is correct, or blame them when things go wrong. This is why Paul's protégé's were faithful to the end. They stayed with him through the thick and thin of the tumultuous days in Ephesus. Both Paul and his protégé's were successful in all the dimensions that we human beings look for success in. Always remember that success is a collection of relationships. This collection of relationships between Paul and the twelve was incredibly successful for all concerned. It was a God thing.

These twelve stayed with Paul through the thick and thin of the Ephesian mission that was imminently about to explode into being at the end of the real time of Acts 19:7. Two believers are better than one, especially when they are one. Twelve believers are better than two, especially when they are one. When one moves with the wise, one becomes wise. Paul was wisest of the wise. If one of them could chase a thousand, and two of them could chase ten thousand. Think of the exponential maths and logic of twelve men together with the apostle Paul, all baptised and filled with the Holy Spirit and battling in Christ's name on the front line of evangelism and church building,

Paul headquartered in Ephesus, and the twelve evangelising all over Asia. And that is exactly what happened.

I believe that the western cult of individualism makes Christians in the west afraid of submitting to anybody as a mentor in the way that these men sat at the feet of Paul.

"Mentoring" is an ongoing process that always involves communication, and should be highly intensive relationship based. A mentor is anybody capable of growing and increasing one's life. Just as Paul was doing, emulating Christ Himself, with the twelve. One needs to choose their friends, and especially their mentor with great care, you may become what they are. There were twelve potential "Apostle Paul Mark 2's" in the offing, hanging around the mighty apostle. Paul was the prototype. These twelve were production models. They respected him, listened to him, and studied him. His life was such that he could boldly, humbly, yet accurately say to them, "Follow me, as I follow Christ." He, or she, who wants to be respected in life, must first respect the power above them, both human and divine. The rate of growth, and the depth of fellowship between the thirteen men must have caused speedy development and powerful manifestation.

Jesus Christ never attempted to succeed alone. For that very reason, neither did Paul. Neither should you. Neither did these twelve. Christ put a huge amount of time and effort into reproducing Himself in His disciples. One's mentor may be older or younger than one's self. A mentor may be of a different race. A mentor may be of a different culture. When I lived in Lagos the senior pastor that I was working with was a father cum mentor to me. He called me "Papa" because I was older than him. I called him "Papa" because he was where I wanted to be in God. I am white, he is black. I am English by domicile and culture, he is totally Nigerian in every dimension. I was in my late fifties, he was in his early forties. The externals are utterly irrelevant. I made sure I sat at his feet. Just make sure you sit at your mentor's feet.

These twelve that sat with Paul had chosen a mentor whom they trusted was being led by God each day. They were wise. We must do the same. Success begins with someone. Success begins somewhere. Success has to do with challenge. To become an overcomer, one needs an obstacle to overcome. The greater the obstacle, the greater the power of the overcomer. Overcomers start with mentors that have already overcome.

Paul undoubtedly had to instil true doctrine into the twelve disciples, to reprove them from time to time, to give them instruction in the righteousness of faith, and to correct them. He would have corrected them to form them into a straight and true arrow. Correction makes a leader. He who wishes to be great, must first respect great men. Great men correct things around them. Correction makes a bright future possible. Listen to the words of your mentor. Words are the bridge to your future, your mentor's words, more so.

Show me your mentor, and I will predict your future.

But, like these twelve, you must give both Jesus, and your mentor, time! The results are working themselves out, slowly but surely. Some slower than others. There must be seed-time and summertime, before the autumnal reaping of a harvest. By the successful and faithful implementation of all these means, the follower of today will be the leader of tomorrow. The handful of people today can be as many as a nation in the future. Find your leader and follow, and I do not just refer to the Lord Christ Himself. Plan your strategy of following. God honours people who plan. Jesus planned. He knew what He was born for. He planned for tomorrow, knowing where it would end in this life, and how it would begin with resurrection life. Jesus planned for tomorrow. Jesus Christ was a "tomorrow thinker". Be a tomorrow thinker, and have no fear. Your developed gift will make room for you to meet great men.

Because of his insight and application to the principles of following Christ, Paul was the first person to say, "I am seated in

Heavenly places with Christ." "But Paul, you are walking here with me on planet earth, breathing in the same fresh air!" But Paul was seeing things from God's perspective, i.e. the heavenly point of view. Hear, believe and confess the heavenly point of view on your life. Beware of good intentioned people around you giving advice from a human or natural point of view. Watch, make notes and emulate your mentor. Do not be anxious. If he is a godly and Christ-like mentor, you will never lose your individuality or character. In fact you will find yourself more quickly. Great men, simply have great habits. Emulate them. Always understand, however, that nobody knows you better than yourself. Follow and be patient. Patience is the power that forces deception to reveal itself. Oh how painful to have deception reveal itself to you. And this is especially true when the deception is found to be within yourself. Conscious, wilful faithfulness will banish deception from your presence.

Give yourself to the cause, along with your mentor. Live a life of investment, not expenditure. Be a giver not a taker. These twelve men stayed with Paul in the midst of heartache, trouble and great stress. Their minds had to manage the stress that their mentor entered into. Mind management is the first priority of the overcomer. Solid spiritual mind management in the midst of crisis is the Christ-like way of doing things. One's input to mind management determines one's output of same. That is a principle of the universe. We all reap what we sow. Sowing one's life into the Kingdom of God will reap something of eternal weight and glory. Emulating a mentor that has gone further than you will carry you further than him.

Whatever these twelve were actually doing in Ephesus, as Acts 19:1-7 came to pass, is not known. Yet, they were there at the right place, at the right time, to meet the right man, with the right attitude. God had prepared those to receive Paul, because they were at the place of their divine assignment set in concrete before the foundation of the world. Paul gave them on the job training by daily demonstration. Surely this developed to some delegation at times in the Ephesian "headquarters" and then led to their being sent out to replicate Ephesus in places like Colossae, Smyrna, Thyatira, Heiropolis, Laodicea, Pergamos, Sardis and Philadelphia. That would have been exactly the modus operandi of the Lord Jesus and His disciples. The mentor of all mentors, was copied by Paul and the same number of disciples in almost the same time frame.

There is yet another insight that their mentor Paul, activated towards them. When he met the twelve, the body of truth they were committed to and were carrying was incomplete. Their doctrine, however, did not make them incomplete as believers. The truth they believed was incomplete, but their faith made them complete, and so Paul could ask them outright, "Did you receive the Holy Spirit since you believed?" They responded in faith to what they knew, but what they knew was incomplete though it was indeed the truth (Acts 19:1-5). My conclusion is that there is no such thing as an incomplete Christian believer. Just as John prepared the way, and many submitted to his teaching, it seems neither Apollos, nor the twelve ever went any further than John for several years. Their doctrine was incomplete, but their faith made them complete. They thought the way was complete in John, while John himself had declared that he was only a preparer of the way. It is my conviction that there are many in this world who have prepared the way to meet God, but then, having met God in preparation, they have not sought more truth for the fulfilment for which they were prepared. Any alleged conversion that does not leave the believer totally committed to God is incomplete, imperfect and therefore questionable, no matter how much truth has been delivered. But these twelve with their incomplete body of truth and tenets of faith were, indeed, soundly in the kingdom. Remember Cornelius? Here was yet another incomplete body of faith, until Peter preached.

The need of the day, especially for the younger element of the twenty first century western world is mentors. There are Christians, young and old, screaming out for mentors. There are potential mentors out there in the world, screaming out for protégés to lead. God make us all sensitive to our calling in life, and our roles in that call.

Mentoring, therefore is a concept practiced by Jesus with the twelve. The apostles copied the Master. Mentoring is therefore an apostolic concept. It was the means by which Paul took Ephesus. It was an integral factor to Paul's management of the miraculous.

9.
MODELLING MINISTRY
ACTS 19:8-9

"Paul entered the synagogue and spoke boldly there for three months, arguing persuasively about the kingdom of God. But some of them became obstinate; they refused to believe and publicly maligned the Way. So Paul left them."

Acts 19:8-9 (Today's NIV)

A Christian preaching the full uncompromising undiluted Gospel in a fundamentalist Synagogue shows great courage. To speak in that context "boldly," just once, shows divine enabling. To preach boldly in such a place for 3 months is downright remarkable. Twelve weeks with possibly three or four official meetings per week, and goodness knows how many opportunities for discussion and debate, which is very much the Jewish manner of study and development, must have exercised even the mighty apostle to the gentiles. For a mentor, or father figure to function in this way with his protégé's and children spectating, making mental notes for the future, and perhaps even entering into the debating fray themselves, must have been the most wonderful course of study and learning that any Christian could undertake. Paul was undoubtedly a "role model" par excellence. Next to walking with the Lord Himself for three years, walking with Paul in Ephesus for the same amount of time must have been a phenomena.

Imagine on the twenty first century Curriculum statement: "Module #37. To study, make notes, and emulate Mentor while he models a demonstration of boldness in his ability to preach, teach and debate the Gospel to a hostile and vitriolic group of religious people. This module will take three months to complete". That is exactly what happened in Acts 19:7-9. Grace for spiritual boldness and gracious persistence is an apostolic trait. And the Apostle Paul trained by example.

It was in such an amazingly God given, God created environment that Paul and his twelve found themselves. The entire team took hold of the chance to see and hear Paul speaking boldly in the synagogue challenging and attempting to sway his listeners. Make no mistake, the purity of God's power on Paul gave expression to his apostolic boldness manifesting itself during spiritual conflict. The Holy Spirit loves boldness. Without boldness in this sort of context the Holy Spirit cannot reveal His power. To be bold shows a readiness to take risks and face danger.

It is fascinating to note that Luke tells us that Paul taught about "the Kingdom of God". This confuses some. The kingdom of God infers that it was the full blown gospel as he preached everywhere, with a slightly different emphasis. There is only one gospel. But like any priceless diamond, the gospel message can be slightly turned to reveal a completely different facet of colour. In a nutshell the preaching of the Kingdom of God is simply an appeal to an audience or listener to wilfully become subject to the great King. The Great King is He who is named as the "King over all Kings," in the book of Revelation. We are talking, of course, of our Lord and Saviour Jesus Christ. There will be a future reign of Christ on Earth which is referred to as the Kingdom of God. This was a key factor in the understanding of scripture believing Jews.

There is the rule of Christ in the hearts of believers now, which is described in Hebrews as tasting "the powers of the world to come". This is of course, that part of the rule of God's Kingdom in our own hearts when we are in a most deliberate and sanctified manner subjected to Him completely. It is in this capacity that Christ stated, "The Kingdom of God is within you." The life of all Christians should be incipiently, ever increasingly Kingdom factored. Christians living in the Spirit, are virtually living in the future. Kingdom living is referring strictly to the rule of the King. The Kingdom of God is anywhere where the rule of Christ is impacting. In theological theory, the Kingdom of God should have the same borders and parameters as the Church of God. Unfortunately history shows the extremely pathetic history of many "church" centred actions, deliberations and pontifications, which were as far from the Kingdom of God as the East is from the West. The Kingdom of God has to be truly the manifestation of God, or it just is not the Kingdom. The kingdom of God includes the true church. The church as we see it is not always synonymous with the kingdom of God. So sad, but absolutely true.

Certainly Paul must have spoken of the death, burial and resurrection of Christ and the atoning blood. I would flatly reject any thought that he did anything else. But the emphasis in his preaching, in talking to a Jewish audience, tended toward the emphasis of the rule of the Great King in His Great Kingdom. The Scripture says he spoke boldly about the Kingdom of God. The message of the Kingdom of God is establishing as much as is possible the reign of the King of the Kingdom of God on earth through faith in Christ. Apostolic grace is a visible almost tangible factor in some men. True, biblical, apostolic evangelism is the proclamation of the Kingdom of God in the fullness of its blessings and promises, which we also call, 'salvation'.

Paul did what Jesus did. He may not have done it to the same degree as Christ, but he emulated the Saviour inasmuch as he did more than "preach the Kingdom". Paul demonstrated that the Kingdom was here and ready to be accessed by demonstration of the rule of the King's will. He displayed its tangible reality in our time space world with the very 'signs of the Kingdom' that proved Christ was present, doing what He does best, i.e. save, heal, deliver and sanctify human lives. Paul, like Jesus, gave evidence in the public place that the Kingdom he was talking about had come. It was (and still is) in the "here" and the "now". We shall see as we read on through Acts 19 and 20 that Paul fulfilled his role as Christ's ambassador in a much more literal way than many Christian leaders think of today.

1 John 3:8b states that "The Son of God appeared for this purpose, to destroy the works of the devil" (NASB). So it is hardly a challenging concept to understand that Christ inevitably came into collision with those areas where the prince of darkness, the devil himself, was ruling. The signs of the Kingdom were evidences that the devil was being forced to retreat. In fact, where he did not want to retreat he was literally thrown out wherever Christ was. As it was, so it is. Where Christ is, the prince of this world is literally retreating before the advance of the King. As Jesus explained it at one point of time, once the strong man has been overpowered by the Stronger One, his possessions can be taken from him (Matthew 12:29; Luke 11:22).

Hebrews 2:14 and 15 teaches us that "... since the children share in flesh and blood, He Himself likewise also partook of the same, that through death He might render powerless him who had the power of death, that is, the devil, and might free those who through fear of death were subject to slavery all their lives." So, again, it seems a logical outcome from such a statement we understand in retrospect that Christ's authority over death was being exercised as He ministered to people's death situations. The work of nullifying totally the devil's rule over death itself was not completed until Christ committed Himself to the Father with His last breath (thus defeating death's authority while on this side of the grave), descending into hell and snatching the absolute authority of death and hell (the keys), and removing all the righteous dead who had died before that date from Sheol and lifting them to God's presence. He also rose from the dead making the devil's lease as the "authority over death" over and done with. The raising from the dead of Jairus's daughter, the widow's son at Nain, and Lazarus were merely hors deouvres to the main course of His defeat of death. The widow's son, Jairus's daughter and Lazarus would all, of course, have died again at a later date. But Christ, in the days of His flesh, conquered death and incipient death (that is sickness) by His every action in healing and freeing the people. It was the plain, straightforward sign that the King had arrived. His rule was omnipotent. And those three and a bit years prior to His crucifiction were just a small taster of what is to follow when David's Greater Son sits on David's throne when He returns to earth.

This is the Gospel of the Kingdom. It's all about the King.

I would passionately desire to have a copy of Paul's sermon notes (if he indeed used any) for those three months of debating and preaching and refuting in the Synagogue. As a New Testament Bible preacher, I have the 27 books of the NT to link with the OT to seek out the direction that Kingdom preaching must have gone. Paul had only the Old Testament in the light of God's revelation. How glorious! In His light, we see light.

To preach the Kingdom of God requires boldness for the simple reason that in the Jewish context of exchanging views with orthodox people and their Rabbi's the entire conversation would revolve around answering one Question. "If you are telling us, Paul, that the King and the Kingdom have arrived, what are the signs of the presence of this Kingdom? Show us this Kingdom? Where is this Kingdom?" Did Paul know how to answer this? Is the sky blue? Even in debate, Paul would have undoubtedly moved towards demonstration of the things he was declaring.

The first *sign* of the presence of the Kingdom of course is the very consciousness and manifestation of the presence of the King. Jesus shall one day reign on earth, "where e'er the sun." In that day He shall reign whether received or not. But now when He reigns when submitted to by any human heart, and there he is present (Luke 17:21). He is there where two or three are gathered in His name (Matthew 18:20). Where He is, the Kingdom is. Paul was declaring the Kingdom with twelve committed disciples present in the Synagogue. There must have been an impact with Christ's presence through the power that was given in the baptism of the Holy Spirit.

With Paul's own presence, there was also Paul's own declaration that the Kingdom was not only future but present. They could see he was an intelligent man, and that he previously had a rabbinical status amongst his people. A Jew so well learned could not declare the presence of the Kingdom without a full declaration that the King had already been present amongst mankind. In short, there was no gospel of the Kingdom to proclaim unless Christ, the Great King, had arrived. Paul must have explained how Christ declared, when He had come, that the passage we refer to as Isaiah 61:1-4, was talking about Him (Luke 4:18-19). Paul must have explained that Christ's answer to the last minute doubts by John the Baptist were met with Him quoting from Isaiah 35:4-8 (Luke 7:22) declaring all the works and fruits of Messiah's presence among men. In Paul's preaching of the Kingdom, he would be pointing to the Kingdom itself, but primarily to the King.

So from Isaiah 35, we have further biblically designated signs of the presence of the King and the coming of the Kingdom. Verses 4-9 in the Complete Jewish Bible screams joyfully to us:

4Say to the fainthearted, "Be strong and unafraid!

Here is your God; he will come with vengeance:

with God's retribution he will come and save you."

5Then the eyes of the blind will be opened,

and the ears of the deaf will be unstopped;

6then the lame man will leap like a deer,

and the mute person's tongue will sing.

For in the desert, springs will burst forth,

streams of water in the 'Aravah;

7 the sandy mirage will become a pool,

the thirsty ground springs of water.

The haunts where jackals lie down will become

a marsh filled with reeds and papyrus.

⁸A highway will be there, a way,

called the Way of Holiness.

The unclean will not pass over it,

but it will be for those whom he guides —

fools will not stray along it.

⁹ No lion or other beast of prey

will be there, travelling on it.

They will not be found there., but the redeemed will go there. **(Isaiah 35:4-9 Complete Jewish Bible).**

The "fainthearted" becoming strong and unafraid shows us conversion and the new birth. It reveals character change. Springs bursting forth from the desert, and streams in the valleys is talking of life from the dead. The "sandy mirage" becoming "a pool" in reality, means the substance of many a dream will become tangible. Whenever people 'turn to God from idols, to serve the living and true God' (1 Thessalonians 1:9-10), an encounter has taken place in which the spell of idols, whether traditional, or modern, whether literal idols or twenty first century icons, has been broken. Wherever demonic forces have strongholds they are broken in the presence of the King. The power of God is intrinsic to and inherent in the Gospel message itself (Romans 1:16), and people who turn to Christ, who have been rescued from darkness to light and from the power of Satan to God (Acts 26:18) are said to have 'tasted ... the powers of the age to come' (Hebrews 6:5). Paul would have undoubtedly challenged them with the Kingdom and the King as described in Isaiah 35.

But, going further with Isaiah 35, when the King who is God comes, there will be healing and ...wait for it...miracles in nature and the animal world. "The eyes of the blind will be opened . . . the ears of the deaf will be unstopped . . . the lame man will leap like a deer, and the mute person's tongue will sing." He will leave a trail of healing, joy and redemption behind Him when He comes. What a message to the Jews about the King who rules in the Kingdom of God.

In nature? "In the desert, springs will burst forth, streams of water in the 'Aravah; the sandy mirage will become a pool, the thirsty ground springs of water". So where there was dryness and barrenness in nature will be transformed also. Paul would explain that the literal fulfilment was tasted with drops of living water when he stilled one storm with a word, walked on the wild water of another great rain, and fed five thousand with a few bits and pieces of food, amongst other things like changing water into wine.

The animal world? "The haunts where jackals lie down will become a marsh filled with reeds and papyrus". "No lion or other beast of prey will be there, travelling on it." The conduct of the animal kingdom, it seems will be subject to the tranquillity of those who are joined to this Great King. This King was amongst the wild animals in the desert (Mark 1:13) when the angels ministered to Him. Healing and nature miracles were common place when He came in His first Advent. His second advent will smite the globe with the glory of His presence. All my Christian friends and ministers agree that these were not only signs pointing to the reality of the Kingdom's arrival, but also anticipations of what will happen in the final Kingdom from which all disease, hunger, disorder, and death will be banished forever. Paul would have been authoritative on these issues. He would declare with great conviction that God is still free and powerful, and performs miracles today, especially in front line evangelism situations where the Kingdom is violently advancing into enemy-held territory, as was Paul when he entered into Ephesus.

Another aspect of the King in His Kingdom is in the language that declared, "He has sent me to bind up and heal the broken hearted, to proclaim liberty to the [physical and spiritual] captives and the opening of the prison and of the eyes to those who are bound" (Isaiah

61:1 Amplified Bible). Isaiah is here talking about casting the devil down, and throwing him out, that is, out of this world, out of people's lives, and out of their circumstances. When we see Jesus quoting Isaiah as referring to Himself, we have to own up that another sign of the Kingdom is casting out the devil, and or demons wherever they are found to be interfering with people's lives. Whatever your flavour of Christianity calls it, it is part of the manifestation of the King and His Kingdom. Exorcism! Deliverance! Expulsion! Dispossession, even Ejection! Purification! A "casting out!" There are many titles given to this kind of ministry. If Christ was confronted by so many demons, and so many kinds, my conviction is that, generally speaking, western Christianity is blind to what is really going on in the lives of people. It is a biblically based conviction of mine that there are more demons interfering with people's lives than we see cast out. It is serious issue. I will refer more to this when we see the incredible dealings that Paul had when he was battling in Ephesus against satanic powers. I believe that there are certainly evil, invisible, personal intelligences under the command of the devil that are present more than we discern in everyday life in the western world in the twenty first century. Demonization, and influence, internal, external and circumstantial is a real and terrible condition that more live in than we Christians would like to own up to. Deliverance, freedom, expulsion or exorcism is possible only in an encounter of faith and power in which the name of Jesus is invoked and prevails. We shall look at this in later pages.

Yet another sign of the Kingdom that Paul definitely believed and is seen in the scripture in Isaiah 53, is the horrible thought of the Great King of the Kingdom of God suffering. If it was necessary for the King to suffer in order to enter into His glory. Indeed, he surely has left us an example that we should follow in his steps (1 Peter 2:21). Suffering for the sake of righteousness, and for us, simply for the sake of Jesus - and to bear such suffering courageously and in purity is a clear sign to all who perpetrate such evils against Christians, or just spectate while it takes place, that we are part of the Kingdom of the Great King (Philippians 1:28-29; cf. 2 Thessalonians 1:5).

The aspects of Kingdom preaching that I have mentioned above are only my own thoughts based on the grounds of various things that both Christ and Paul are said to have declared. I merely need to express that the declaration of the Kingdom of God was neither different from nor contrary to the truths contained in the message that Paul refers to when he said to the Corinthians, "I determined to know nothing among you, save Jesus Christ and Him crucified." It is different aspects of the same message that we are referring to.

The twelve disciples Paul found in Ephesus would have listened to Paul declaring these kind of truths to the Jewish people at the Synagogue and would have seen the ultimate in New Testament ministry being modelled. The manner, mode and pitch of Paul's vocal delivery of the message was all part and parcel of his management of the miraculous.

10.

URGENCY, NECESSITY & EFFICIENCY.
(ACTS 19:9-10)

"But when some were hardened and did not believe, but spoke evil of the Way before the multitude, he departed from them and withdrew the disciples, reasoning daily in the school of Tyrannus. And this continued for two years, so that all who dwelt in Asia heard the word of the Lord Jesus, both Jews and Greeks."

Acts 19:9-10 (NKJV)

The plot thickens. Having been asked to return by the Jewish Synagogue congregation at the end of Paul's original brief stopover in Ephesus (Acts 18:19), Paul has been true to his word, and returned by God's guidance to the very same synagogue. However, after three months of further discussions with Paul, some of the Jewish congregation had heard enough. We often harangue the Jewish synagogues in Acts unjustly, saying they were simply, "against Christ". I am sure it was often true. Key to the Jewish rejection of the gospel message were certain words that Paul used, and teachings he asserted that the Jews just could not cope with.

Paul taught in Ephesus (as he would have taught everywhere) that both Jews and gentiles have equal access to God Almighty through Christ. I am convinced that he would have preached it everywhere, but I refer to the Ephesians here because this very same issue is noted in what we refer to as "Paul's letter to the Ephesians." The placing of gentiles on the same footing as Jewish people in the context of God's saving grace was unacceptable to most Jews who did not have an open mind at all on the issue. We need to understand that Paul was not preaching anything at all being wrong *per se* with Judaism. He was preaching that the Messiah they longed for had come in the person of

Jesus of Nazareth. Paul believed in the same God that was worshiped throughout Judaea and the Diaspora by all Jewish worshippers. He used the very same Scriptures they used and taught the very same things out of the Torah and the Prophets. Paul was obviously, visibly Jewish. When he was among Jews, he lived as a Jew and was comfortable with that (1 Corinthians 9:20). But added to the conceptual problem of the equality of the gentiles in the far reaching appeal of the declaration of the Kingdom of God, some of them just did not believe what Paul was saying. To them, such a concept inferred that Israel had ceased to be "God's chosen people." Whatever the rationale that caused offence in the Synagogue at Ephesus, some of the worshippers were so hardened and offended in their heart against the apostolic preaching that they stood up and spoke evil of "the Way." That means they slandered Paul's doctrine and Christian people, as well as Paul's use of the Old Testament to explain his understanding of Christ and who He is.

Perhaps, Paul could have heard their contrary opinions, and continued on with the debates and remained there, if the negative responses were private, or even if they were open minded enough to keep on asking him to explain more. However, some of them spoke evil from the platform, i.e "Before the multitude." How easy it is to hide behind position, podium and the public when one wants to illogically and without continued discussion or objectivity, deride someone. Having impacted the congregation considerably (I am assuming that the word "multitude" means not only the Jews within the community of the Synagogue, but those out on the streets also who did not attend but were in the Jewish circle of things), Paul "withdrew the disciples," suggesting that the twelve were now well and truly part of Paul's ministry team and protégés, and they all left the synagogue to continue the outreach meetings elsewhere.

This fall-out and separation with the Synagogue, as an institution, is shown to have been fully justified as the textual account continues in Acts 19. Paul just carries on, in the presence of both Jews as well as Greeks, whatever course of studies, lectures, monologues or debates that had been going on in the Jewish home base. It sounds productive enough with the first line of explanatory description, "reasoning daily in the school of Tyrannus".

"Reasoning," means intelligent and challenging communication. Sermons! One to ones! Debates! Yes! Debates! And also, arguements. Martin Lloyd Jones defined preaching as, "Logic on fire." It is the logic of the Gospel when delivered in the power of the Holy Spirit that changes people and will change the world. When the Spirit of God carries the message of the Gospel to the receptive human heart, it doesn't necessarily need to be heavy and theologically sticky. The man with divine revelation is never at the mercy of the man with academic study behind his message, no matter how simple the revelation is. Revelation of God and His Word, is what saves people and changes the direction of their lives.

"Reasoning Daily...," gives me a slight problem. "Daily," to me suggests meetings that were conducted seven days a week. Paul was incredibly loosed from the law. We know that his stepping out of the synagogue facilitated more regular meetings, and more hours of work. But, every single day? It was probably three or four times a week that the synagogue was open for devotion and debate, but now the whole evangelistic fervour went up a couple of gears. "Everyday meetings" would take a heavy toll on anybody's physical constitution. The "Reasoning," would drain him of nervous and mental energy. Just being available for ministry in a public meeting for five hours of every day would drain any man both physically and emotionally. Billy Graham lost a huge amount of weight when he spent 6 weeks preaching nearly every night to huge crowds in London in 1954. And he did not have the heavy schedule that Paul had "daily" for 2-3 years in Ephesus.

Paul was, "Reasoning *daily* in the school of Tyrannus". What kind of school are we talking about here? And who was Tyrannus?

It was probably a private school run by a man named Tyrannus, and either this Tyrannus had got converted and was happy for Paul to use his building, or, perhaps Paul simply rented his building because it was available. The word used for school in non-biblical original Greek (σχολείο) scholío meant "leisure." It seems, after some researching around, that in Paul's day discussions and debates were usually conducted during "leisure time." In the process of time the language of the Greeks changed, and the word finally came to refer to a group of persons meeting for the purpose of having discussions with the intention of learning, or the place where such a meeting was held. Schools, during Paul's time, should be thought of as something similar to modern day literary gatherings, book clubs, debating classes and philosophy groups, or something similar. There are a considerable amount of remains in the ruins of what was ancient Ephesus, but no titles, no signage boards and nothing inscribed to even infer that any of them happen to be "The School of Tyrannus" has yet been discovered. Ah! It would be gloriously fascinating if the place was ever identified. I would love to know the size of the place from which Paul ministered day after day and masterminded a strategy that took a whole subcontinent.

Concerning the Tyrannus here mentioned, nothing more is known with certainty. The name is, however, connected with one or two interesting coincidences that are suggestive of something. Like its Latin equivalent, "Rex," it was not uncommon among the class of slaves or freedmen. It is found in the Columbarium of the household of Livia on the Appian Way, and as belonging to one who is described as a Medicus or physician. Both names and professions in this class were very commonly hereditary, and the hypothesis is that this Tyrannus was also a physician, and that as such he may have known Luke, or possibly may have been among the Jews whom the decree of Claudius (Act 18:2) had driven from Rome. If there is any factual content of this hypothesis it would mean that Tyrannus shared the same fate as Aquila and Priscilla, and so the theory fits in with and explains the facts as recorded in Acts. An unconverted teacher of philosophy or rhetoric was not likely to have lent his class room to a preacher of the new faith.

But here we have something extremely fascinating and illuminating. There is an ancient text that adds information at the end of Acts 19:9, saying that Paul taught "in the school of Tyrannus from the fifth hour to the tenth." It is a text that is in book form, as opposed to a scroll, and the manuscript we refer to is known as "Codex Bezae Cantabrigiensis" or "manuscript D Syriac (Western text)". The fifth hour is 11.00am. The tenth hour is 4.00pm. There are about seven or eight translations in English that have this addition at the bottom of the page in small print, but not in the main columns to be read out in public. The only English translation that has been bold enough to have put it in the main text (howbeit in italics) is the Amplified Bible, and they have the hours strangely changed to "10.00am through to 3.00pm". Why the hour difference than is generally understood? This writer has no solution or answer to the question. Some think that those five hours were the hottest parts of the day where most folks would have a siesta (something that does not ring true to this writer), and some believe that those five hours of the day were the part of the day when people were expected to be conducting leisure activities and not work. During those hours men pursued their hobbies, they rested, or they took part in great discussions in a lecture hall or school, as it were. Now *that* sounds logical.

Perhaps Paul took the school of Tyrannus simply for its size.

Authorities rationalise the whole scenario claiming that the School of Tyrannus most likely held conventional, normal school classes in the mornings when sunlight was bright, and the heat was minimal, facilitating human activity and study. It might possibly be something connected to Paul's statement in Acts 20:34 where Paul says, "You yourselves know that these hands have provided for my necessities, and for those who were with me" (Acts 20:34). So, Paul possibly worked his trade as a tentmaker in the mornings, to provide for not only himself but also for "those who were with him", and then taught at Tyrannus's school in the afternoons, when it was empty as most of Ephesus conceivably pursued their hobbies and fancies, and then as we shall see later, the apostle spent the rest of his day visiting the homes of people and ministering to them.

Not wanting to get too pedantic or pseudo academic on this, but it is possible to make the case that this could have been Paul's normal procedure upon leaving or being expelled from the synagogue of any city. A case could be made to suggest that he normally used a large residence, offered by one of his more prominent and wealthy disciples, or he rented an establishment whereby he could reason and debate with people. In Philippi, for instance, Paul worked from Lydia's home (Acts 16:14-15). In Thessalonica, it seems he operated from Jason's home (Acts 17:5-9). In Athens he used the marketplace and the Areopagus, probably because the few believers there may not have owned a suitable place for public discussion, or if they did, didn't offer it for Paul's use. However, when he arrived at Corinth, he used the residence of Justus (Acts 18:4-7), which had a common wall with the local synagogue there.

All these places were used by Paul to discuss freely, anything and everything which pertained to the Scriptures. In the synagogue one could do this, but only to a point. Once it was considered offensive, the Gospel could not be preached there as the synagogue leadership would not allow him to speak. It seems to this writer, after considerable research and enquiry that Jesus could be preached as long as the gentiles were not equally accepted alongside the Jews in the salvation process. Once the Jews understood they had to philosophically "share" favoured status with God with any gentile that believed, Paul's teaching was no longer welcome. The synagogues in Judea did not hinder the Gospel, as long as their traditions were not brought into question. Saying one was justified by faith in Jesus, but still practicing the Jewish tradition, never really brought those traditions into question. It was simply the way all religious Jews lived, even the Jewish Christians at first.

So….during what we may refer to as the hours of leisure for the Ephesian population, Paul was preaching, debating and discussing the Word of God, and seeing a glorious demonstration of the Holy Spirit. The apostle, it would seem, used the school building during these five hours for gaining the largest audience possible, affording him the morning hours to actually work at his own trade.

We also know that due to his lectures at the school of Tyrannus, Paul gained many contacts with officials in Ephesus that proved to be helpful to him later. Acts 19:31 states, "even some of the officials of the province, friends of Paul, sent him a message begging him not to venture into the theatre." If the whole of Asia was to hear the word during these days of ministry at the school, there must have been some people of influence who would have helped to fan the flame of evangelistic fervour in the city, and beyond.

In the urgency of the hour, and the pressure that all evangelists feel to touch base with as many people as possible we have here an amazing observation to make, with a few challenging extrapolations. Follow my logic as I meditate on a few facts:

- Paul conducted a five hour "Church Meeting," or "Religious Gathering," or whatever one prefers to call it, every day of the week. In modern times we can hardly see beyond the five day week, and the bug bearer of the Jewish Sabbath could deflect us to a six day week. But in heathen, mostly gentile Ephesus, I suspect that "everyday" means just that – "every day." So we are envisaging 35 hours of ministry in the context of a church type gathering every day for 2 to 3 years. Acts 19:10 tells us he was using the School of Tyrannus for two years. Acts 20:31 has Paul saying he never ceased his work, day or night for three years. It suggests that after two years they left the school building, and thereafter some other modus operandi was initiated that we are not informed of. Or: perhaps Paul was out of circulation for a year – like "in prison." We shall raise that issue later.

- Five hours a day is 35 "in church" ministry hours, per week. 365 days of 5 hour church services in a year means 1,825 hours a year in ministry in what modern Christianity refers to as "evangelistic meetings". Over two years we have Paul ministering 3,650 hours within the four walls of a church, or in this instance, inside a school room.

- I am assuming something that to this writer is blatantly self-evident, that Paul's ministry was extremely productive and utterly none-religious and had the highest impact possible. I am saying this on the grounds that after this mission, the whole of Asia had heard the word.

- I then questioned myself about what happens in the average church today. Sunday morning services of a couple of hours (Many are less than that). Sunday evening services of between 90 minutes to two hours (There is a trend in the UK where many churches do not even hold evening services). Midweek services usually consist of a prayer meeting, and some sort of Bible ministry. We shall say three hours. So we are talking of the average modern church holding seven hours of church based gatherings in the ordinary course of a week. I would respectfully request that my readers do not reject what I am saying if you have more hours than this in your fellowship. We are talking of a mean of seven hours a week in church ministry. That's about 364 hours a year in church services.

- Mathematically it would take just over five years for people in the west to have had as much time under the ministry of prayer and the word in western churches as Paul had in a single year in Ephesus. Please understand that in no way whatsoever am I even suggesting that we have 5-hour services for the sake of it. God help us! I promise my readers that I also have been in some churches in the UK where 30 minutes is more than enough. However I have also been in many services that have lasted over eight hours and it was too short. Why? It is all to do with what is being said, and what is happening during the time spent in the church meeting. When people are being healed, saved and set free from the deepest of darkness's, I promise you, nobody wants to go home.

- There is also the issue that the gentile heathen mind needs to be repeatedly and in a concentrated manner disabused of world views, attitudes and concepts believed, as well as issues of character. Some people vitally need 35 hours a week of the power of God being ministered to them.

- In one church I have attended there was nothing but a ninety minute Sunday morning service and a home group meeting every two weeks of about 2 hours or so. That averages out at 2 and a half hours per week. That is 130 hours a year in church type gatherings. That means that the church to which I am referring would take just over 14 years to receive as much ministry as the Ephesians received from Paul. On top of that, 14 years ministry from some men would seem like 140 years because of the lack of impact and lack of fruit. There is in this world that dismal truth of something I refer to as a "Common Message." That is, bible explanations that though legally and strictly speaking are as sound as a pound, nevertheless, in some uncanny way kill faith, dull the brain, and hardly encourages anybody. There is also an "Uncommon Message." This is what Paul delivered. He was no "peddler of the word," but a man who delivered Christ in all His fullness to the people in a manner that captivated his audiences and sprouted immediate saving faith.

Just imagine the effort invested, the energy expended, the time in preparation, the contacts made, the preaching and teaching that was necessary to consolidate the converts and necessary to renew the occultists that had been set free. Imagine the explanatory sessions demanded by people who were absent from the meetings, but received healing from handkerchiefs that had touched Paul's body. The entire concept of biblical teaching, and ministry in the power of the Holy

Spirit takes on an incredibly fuller meaning than is ever even considered in the majority of churches in the world today.

With no internet, no advertising, no newsprint, in two years the whole of Asia (i.e. today's Western Turkey) heard the word of God. Word of mouth is always the best advert for such evangelistic efforts. The testimonies of the saved, healed and delivered are like fresh water to the thirsty masses. People need to be given something to tell their friends, neighbours and acquaintances about. This was the self-evident fruit of Paul's management of the miraculous.

A miracle is not an end in itself but a means to an end, which is the salvation of people's souls. It is a saying of many preachers that, "Miracles and healings are the "dinner gong" for the Kingdom of heaven." They are signs and wonders that God's Kingdom has arrived and that Christ is risen. The gospel message is a message that screams at its recipients, "After you have received your miracle, follow Jesus," as per Mark 10:52. The problem is that many are invited to follow Christ having received nothing but a sermon, and often it is a dead sermon as well.

This peak of apostolic ministry it would seem, occurred in a school lecture room of a size we are not even told of. Five hours a day for two years Paul preached, prayed, cast out, confronted, refuted, taught and established the most phenomenal move of God in history. Paul was in the most literal and tangible sense a "Holy Spirit Carrier." With urgency, clarity and with Godly sincerity, Paul gave Christ to the masses. God confirmed the message with signs following the preaching. Ephesus was taken for the Kingdom of God. Ephesus was taken for Christ. There were miracles, healings, deliverances and astonishing demonstrations of the Holy Spirit. It was God.

Ministry must come through the Holy Spirit's anointing and the personal spiritual overflow of the one ministering. Management of the miraculous such as this comes from efficient and Godly mind management of the one ministering. Therefore mind management is clearly the first priority of the overcomer. Mind management just has to be the very topmost priority in a successful management of the miraculous.

What is ministered should be concepts and mind matter that initiates and creates faith, thereafter it focuses faith and brings results. The power of the Lord is always present to heal. The Word that heals, however is not always delivered. The word and the Spirit together bring the miracles. "Jesus Christ heals you now" must be authoritatively decreed in the power and grace of the Holy Spirit for the truth of that word to be manifest. Paul ministered faith, and the fruits of faith were seen in the lives of the people. Paul assumed a responsibility for the management of the miraculous in the development of the relationship he had with the Holy Spirit. That relationship with God and the Word, through the Holy Spirit is open to us all.

The whole two or three years spent in Ephesus showed a mature and incredibly responsible management of the realm of the miraculous, the manifestation of the miraculous, and the fruit of the miraculous. It all needed to be assessed, explained, not only before, but during and after the manifestation of the miracle. Many today can hardly manage the message well enough, never mind the miracles that emanate from when the message is properly delivered.

Acts also clues us in to the fact that Paul did not only share the good news in the lecture hall of Tyrannus, but he also went "from house to house," and, "with tears," as per Acts 20:31, "you know that I have not hesitated to preach anything that would be helpful to you but have taught you publicly and from house to house…So be on your guard! Remember that for three years I have never stopped warning each of you night and day with tears."

Whatever went on in those 5 hour gatherings at the school of Tyrannus was exciting enough for people to tell the story of what they saw, heard and experienced. Whatever stories they heard, sermons they learned, ideas of faith that they saw, it was gossiped and spread around.

This school room, or rooms, this forum for the gospel message was probably the greatest use of time and space being used for the Kingdom of God ever. It was very much part of Paul's management of the miraculous.

Paul's activity demonstrated a peak in urgency to take Ephesus and the province. His activity and plan proved the urgency of his heart. The final results manifested the efficiency of his time in the Mission to Ephesus.

11.

THE ASTONISHING EVERYDAY ROUTINE FOR 3 YEARS.

"He departed from them and withdrew the disciples, reasoning daily in the school of Tyrannus. And this continued for two years..."

Acts 19: 9b-10a (NKJV)

"You know, from the first day that I came to Asia, in what manner I always lived among you,"

Acts 20:17 (NKJV)

"How I kept back nothing that was helpful, but proclaimed it to you, and taught you publicly and from house to house, testifying to Jews, and also to Greeks."

Acts 20:20-21a (NKJV)

"Remember that for three years I did not cease to warn everyone night and day with tears."

Acts 20:31b (NKJV)

"Yes, you yourselves know that these hands have provided for my necessities, and for those who were with me."

Acts 20:34 (NKJV)

So the screenplay is written. The choreography of Paul's daily work is etched. We have all the notes that assist us to understand Paul's "normal day at the Ephesian Office." We, quite literally, have Paul's routine to think on. We know for certain, from Acts' chapters 19 and

20 what Paul did for the 3 years he ministered in Ephesus. It is amazing enough that we know exactly what he got up to everyday, however, the content of his days is even more astonishing.

I am not being legalistic, and because of the biblical statements, we are tempted so to be. However, the picture I gain from Acts 19 is that Paul gained to his support and assistance a dozen (or so) men of faith, as he entered Ephesus for a second time, and while tutoring them in the faith, preached at the Synagogues for three months. I am not 100% sure what that means time wise during those 90 days or so, but from what I have read and studied about those times, it suggests to me that there might have been two services every Saturday in the synagogues in Ephesus that Paul attended and spoke at, and possibly a couple of meetings cum debates during the week. After three months (approximately 13 Sabbaths) Paul had gained some believers but had also gained many maligners of "the Way", that is, critics of Christianity in general. So he went to a school building known as, "The school of Tyrannus" and preached and ministered, every day, in such a manner that the whole of Asia heard the word in the space of about two years. If you have a passion to see God move in this generation, I gladly excuse you to reach for the oxygen mouthpieces before I continue. What on earth was Paul doing? Two years? The whole of Asia? From a single school room? And we must not forget his "about twelve" apprentices as well.

Every day for two years! That means 730 days minimum, Paul preached and ministered the miraculous. Can you imagine! The Bible tells us that there were "unusual" miracles done by Paul. Sadly we live in a day where Christians hardly know the difference between the "usual" miracle and the "unusual." Here in the west, apart from a few small pockets we do not have any "usual" or "ordinary" miracles. That is because most Christian people in the west have never seen a miracle. Period.

So! Let's run through and restate what we understand to be taking place in Ephesus in Acts 19. Potentially, 730 services in 730 consecutive days. That's a smack in the face for the philosophy that says it is immoral and illogical to reach an area via Church meetings. If a church has one service a week (like many in the UK do), that means Paul ministered as much in two years as those churches receive in fourteen(14) years. Chew on that one! Added to this, having been, for a time, part of a ministry team in a church where healings and miracles were (and still are) many and frequent (almost daily), this writer would randomly suggest that the meetings in Ephesus would need to be several hours long. The mental and spiritual stimulus, combined with the visual aids of healings, miracles, prophecy and deliverance, would create an atmosphere where folks would not want to go home, and where some even complain that an eight hour service is too short. We have also noted in this context that some manuscripts state, as the Amplified Bible inserts in italics, that Paul's meetings were between 10.00am and 3.00pm. Sounds about right to me. If we compare that to a "Ninety Minute Service Once a Week Church," we have the startling statement that in 2 years Paul had as much ministry time preaching and healing, prophesying and delivering in Ephesus as some modern churches have in 42 years plus. (?) 'Nuff said.

Not that I am in anyway suggesting longer services for their own sake. Never! I have been in some 90 minute services and left the building thinking it was 80 minutes too long. But I have to say also, that I have been in quite a few services (not in the UK) that started at 8.00 am on the Sunday morning and finished round about 6.00pm the same evening, leaving both the congregation, as well as myself, bitterly disappointed because the meeting finished too early. What's the difference? The whole package of the preaching of the Word, Healing and testimonies of healing, deliverance and testimonies of the freedom, and personal prophecy and confirmations of its correctness. Or, to be absolutely frank, it is the glorious manifestation of the wonder of Jesus Christ and the outpouring of the Holy Spirit. Friends, there is preaching....and there is preaching. There is praying for the sick people... and there is healing. There is the gentle prophetic breeze of prophetic words of encouragement, and then there is the Tsunami of true biblical personal prophecy – and not just personal prophecy.

In a first century environment that was filled with superstition, black magic, witchcraft and murder, overlaid with rich and deep tones of fanatical idolatry and false religion, as well as a dash of legalistic Judaism and a sprinkling of rank atheism, I cannot possibly imagine that singing "Blessed Assurance" and "Abide with Me," and then listening to a nice tidy 3 point sermon on the tenets of evangelical Christianity could change the face of a continent in the space of 2 years. (Come to think of it, that first century environment sounds the same as the twenty first century environment! Oops! I walked into that one didn't I?).

Before anybody writes to correct me, I am well aware that when the Bible talks of Asia it does not mean the entire continent of Asia as we refer to it. It was still a huge area of land that heard the word from Paul's two years in Ephesus. Asia in the days of the book of Acts was the majority of Turkey and a bit more.

Back to the subject at hand, we are talking of a church gathering for several hours of the supernatural workings of the Holy Spirit, interspersed with incredibly inspired explanations as to what was happening before their eyes, and why. They also heard a graphic portrayal of Christ's life, death, burial and resurrection being absolutely branded with fire in the hearts and minds of all those that were present. I have tasted the very same under another man's ministry. I believe Paul did exactly the same in Ephesus, only to an even greater degree than what I have tasted.

A church that is built with plain speech sermons and the power of God, not only sees the tide of a fallen world turn around, but in itself it becomes part of the wave that "tsunami's" the local geography with the Word of God.

Christianity is bigger than we see it in the West. We have Americans thinking that we are too small minded in the UK. We have many Christians in the UK refusing to listen to American preachers because too many of them look and sound like second hand car salesman when viewed in the context of English culture. We have the leadership of the State Church in the UK unable to make a clear and concise statement on euthanasia, abortion and homosexual - so called - marriages, and we wonder why folks do not listen. Paul just knew Christ.

New Testament Christianity took the whole issue of God and His relationship to man out of the high intellectual strata, and down into the low practicalities of life. It ceased to be a cerebral adventure of concepts and ideas of the Divine, and became a discussion of, "How does this blind man see?" And "How does that crippled woman now walk?" It took the whole "God-talk" out of ethereal prognostications, and into the practical reality of changed lives. The Apostle Paul in Ephesus was only a smaller scale of Jesus of Nazareth in Judaea, when looking at healing, deliverance and prophecy.

The daily routine for two years after he ceased ministering at the Synagogue was a five hour session of preaching, debating, praying for the sick and casting out demons. It is my conviction also that he ministered in prophecy to people. But as this is not explicit in the particular verses we are looking at the moment I shall explain that aspect of ministry in the context of other verses later. Was it 10 till 3, or was it 11 till 4? Whatever, we suggest that there were five hours out of every day for two years ministering from a school room. "Daily!" "For two years!" That is what the scripture says. It would be rational to suggest that Paul may possibly have had a day off, here or there, but it definitely is not so stated.

The next part of his passionate and effective routine was plain and simple: secular work. "You yourselves know that these hands have provided for my necessities, and for those who were with me." From other verses concerning Paul's trade as a tent maker, we can only assume that his tent trade was so significantly successful that he was paying the expenses for his entire team. Whether that was merely the twelve disciples from Acts 19:1-7 or other members of the team like Timothy, I have no idea. We are just not told. What we are told is that he worked at a trade that kept him and others, while he lived at Ephesus. It seems that he worked like that from the first day he arrived there. "You know, *from the first day* that I came to Asia, in what manner I always lived among you," The example for others to follow was truly astounding.

Finally we are aware also of how Paul taught, preached, shared and testified wherever he was in Ephesus all through this period. "I kept back nothing that was helpful, but proclaimed it to you, and taught you publicly and from house to house, testifying to Jews, and also to Greeks." So where did he fit this into his daily routine? It would seem that if he wasn't working on his tents, or ministering at the school of Tyrannus for five hours of the day, he was busy ministering to people in the comfort of their own homes. He declares that he held nothing back that was profitable for them. That would mean everything we have in the New Testament from his hand and more. It would also seem that here in Ephesus he was utterly freed from the bondage of Jewish legalists persecuting him and stirring up trouble. For he may have gone to a Jewish household here, and to a Greek (gentile) house there. No friction! No riot! Freedom of movement, and freedom to minister. Was this just five in the evening when such visitations were made, to coincide with High Tea or supper? I jest, of course! He said to them all afterwards that they needed to, "Remember that for three years I did not cease to warn everyone night and day with tears." Day and night! Convenient or not convenient! In season or out of season! House to House! "To warn everyone!" We are talking here of prophecy, and not just the warnings of the Gospel message.

Three aspects of activity that utterly filled his life for three years in Ephesus. 1. Tent making. 2. Public ministry for a set time of five hours every day. 3. House to house. The pressure on the apostle physically, mentally and spiritually must have been utterly phenomenal.

The remark of visiting both Jews and gentiles is also very significant. Paul had learnt well how to minister to the racial and cultural mish-mash in Antioch. Paul was here demonstrating in the most practical and down to earth manner that he himself was free of any racial elitism or superiority. He was utterly innocent of any kind of religious, racial or cultural prejudice. At last we have it stated as clearly as could be, that in the very practice of his ministry, the wall between Jew and gentile was broken down and non-existent. The textual content for this observation is tiny. The principle we see is galactic in importance. However, it seems to be stated in his testimony to the Ephesian elders to make a specific point. He ministered from the multi ethnic school of Tyrannus to Jews and gentiles, he went from house to house, to both Jews and gentiles.

It is tragically unfortunate that I have heard, in my own life time, Christian people say that they love Christ, yet refuse to worship in multi-ethnic settings. I have seen it. I have heard it. Any apostolic team must set the strongest possible guard on themselves to keep them all from partiality, favouritism and discrimination whether it is race, religious background, and any other kind of labelling that may keep them from delivering the full gospel of Christ to all people.

In the midst of this hectic, pressured, work load of a routine, the miraculous seems to have been common, plentiful and society changing. His self-appointed, Holy Spirit driven, working day was as much an integral part of Paul's management of the miraculous as was his preaching and praying.

12.

THE MINISTRY OF THE LIVING WORD

"But when some were becoming hardened and disobedient, speaking evil of the Way before the people, he withdrew from them and took away the disciples, reasoning daily in the school of Tyrannus. This took place for two years, so that all who lived in Asia heard the word of the Lord, both Jews and Greeks."

Acts 19:9-10 (NASB)

"So mightily grew the word of the Lord and prevailed."

Acts 19:20 (ASB)

The Word of God! If one was to ask a hundred preaches to define the preaching of the Word, one would undoubtedly have more than a hundred opinions. How on earth can it be defined? To preach the Word is to present to an audience, be it one or many, as full and as clear introduction and description of Jesus Christ who was crucified, died, buried, risen ascended and glorified, and is totally desiring to be the God and friend of all, if only people would believe it. End of story! Period! That is, for this writer, the definition of preaching the Word. It isn't *per se* an explanation, or a presentation of academic abstract concepts. It is a declaration of truth. Preaching does not necessarily mean the formal understanding of traditional Christianity that is constituted by a man standing up and without interruption is allowed to speak for a period of time, long or short. It is a communication of certain truths that if believed will change the inner person's will and desire. To believe is a choice. To disbelieve is a choice. Faith is a free will option. Unbelief also is something decided upon. The declaration of truth is the communication of knowledge. That knowledge can be accepted or rejected. The Bible declares that the very declaration of the truth, when believed, is in itself the very communication of the power of God to that believing person that saves the soul. It is the active belief in the biblical truth that is declared that communicates God's salvation to the human soul. "The preaching of the cross is, to them that perish, foolishness. But to us who are being saved it is the power of God." Paul said once, "I am not ashamed of the Gospel because it is the power of God to them that believe." The message has all of God's power embedded in its full and bold declaration.

The word of God, when preached, bears the fruit of what is declared when it is believed. "Jesus Christ died for you!" That statement is the crux of the gospel. When He was here, in the days of His flesh, He healed people's sickness, He set them free from demonic bondages and setbacks, He even went so far as to raise some that had died, back to life again, as if they had died before their time. If He did that before His death and resurrection, how much more is He willing to do it after rising again out from among the dead?

Because the facts of the Word of God are, in themselves, an incredible series of statements against life's status quo, it is always more convincing when the word is spoken with the same attitude that God has against sin, sickness, demons and life's hardship. To facilitate that very thing, Christ forbad the first twelve apostles to preach until they were endued with power from on high through the Baptism in the Holy Spirit as demonstrated in Acts chapter 2. It was not a suggestion, but a command. "Gathering them together, He commanded them not to leave Jerusalem, but to wait for what the Father had promised, "Which," He said, "you heard of from Me; for John baptized with water, but you will be baptized with the Holy Spirit not many days from now" (Acts 1:4-5 NASB). And when they were baptised thus, the upper room that had become their secret hiding place, became a platform from which to speak to thousands of people. The whimpering, Christ denying, child fearing Peter, was immediately metamorphisized into a wild, giant, dangerous prophet of God that was not to be messed with. The Word, spoken with love and power is almost irresistible. To the God seeker it is nothing but irresistible. When it is declared in the same manner that Christ spoke with, people stop and think, simply because God Himself is speaking to them. That is the declaration of the true Word. The Word of God is not hindered because it is a man speaking it, it is enhanced and made authentic and genuine. It is God Himself that chose the foolishness of preaching.

When the true word is communicated, and believed there is an impact in the life of the one believing. That belief, brings Christ into the choreography of the believer's life. Once Christ has "entered stage right," anything that is positive, healing and beneficial could happen. And my experience is that what takes place is not only what is consciously believed for, but occasionally totally beyond what is believed for. The belief is placed in the heart of people by God Himself. For the heart, to believe is, in and of itself, an act of God's own kindness and grace. It is God's initiative once the heart and mind is opened by the wilful choosing to believe the Word of God. The wonderful permeation of the Spirit of Christ in the heart of the believer changes all things. It means that when He, the Holy Spirit, is allowed free reign, all heaven breaks loose within the physical, mental and spiritual framework of the believer, as well as the believers circumstances, surroundings and history. To say that the whole experience is somewhat glorious is a profound understatement.

It is as if Luke, when writing this account, saw and understood that all that was happening was so godly, heavenly and Christ-like that he did not want to taint it by saying, "Paul said," "Paul did," or "Paul prayed." The debates "took place for 2 years". "All who lived in Asia heard the word of the Lord, both Jews and Greeks". It does not say, "All in Asia heard Paul." The spirit of the whole thing here in verse 10, as well as the later verses re healing and deliverance, seem to remove Paul from the equation. Oh! How wise is that! My own understanding of mentoring, teaching, and developing protégés, suggests that somewhere along the line, Paul would step back and let the student demonstrate to the master how well he has learned and developed. So, of course, we have to put in the soup of our thoughts, that some of the, "about twelve" disciples, and/or Timothy, or others ministered from time to time. Perhaps, Paul's attitude and demeanour towards Luke was a kind of insistence that Luke was not to write it as if Paul was the prima face cause of the widespread knowledge of the Word, the extensive healing of sicknesses, and the commonplace experience of people being freed from demonic interference. It was God that did it, and all the glory was to go to Him.

The fact of the matter is, that, as per usual, the extreme brevity of the biblical text, when properly thought over, reveals an entire interlinear galaxy of presuppositions that must be true, though unwritten. For instance, it must be true, that in the first century AD, for an entire subcontinent to have heard the word of God, there must have been a great many believers, hundreds of thousands, perhaps over a million. My point being that people who attended the school of Tyrannus to hear Paul, and who did not believe the message, are hardly likely to hit the streets and make the message they didn't believe a hot topic of conversation. For the whole of Asia to have heard the word, it must be true, logically, that the word of God was believed by the many that lived in Asia. One "authority" reckons that there must have been a million and a half people that lived in Asia at that time (I have no clue how demographic expertise functions to result in such a remark), and if that is true, there must have been an awful lot of believers "gossiping the gospel" to bring about 1,500,000 hearers of the word, even if they did not all believe.

Jumping ahead a little we have to bring Acts 19:20 into this picture, where the word of God is likened to a living thing. "So mightily grew the word of God and prevailed." That's the American Standard Bible. The New ASB so wonderfully focussing on the tenses of many biblical statements has it as, "So the word of the Lord was growing mightily and prevailing." In plain language the whole verbal repetition of the message of Christ that was heard at the school of Tyrannus, was being repeated, discussed and debated all over Asia, and being believed by many. I would like to suggest that in the vast majority of all cases a message could only be believed as long as it was presented by somebody that believed it. That status was in a constant state of increase and growth in the volume of repetition, and the numbers that were believing the message. The use of the word, "Mightily" also suggests that there were visible manifestations of the truth of the word. The only manifestations that Acts 19 and 20 offer us, is that there were many converts, many healings, and many people set free from demonic bondages. This thing in Ephesus was truly as big in Asia as it was in heaven. Asia was shaken. Ephesus was taken.

This point of Luke's narrative is not a unique description of the word "growing." It is declared three times throughout the book of Acts. Chapter 6:7 states; "And the word of God increased; and the number of the disciples multiplied in Jerusalem greatly; and a great company of the priests were obedient to the faith." In the midst of faith, and unity amongst a seemingly ever growing number of believers who were living in community, the word of God increased, expanded, and became more influential on the culture of where those believers resided. That increase crossed religious, racial and every prejudicial barrier that it is possible to think of. And at the point of history that Acts 6 is discussing, the church had not spread outside of Jerusalem.

In Acts 12:24 it says simply, "But the word of God grew and multiplied." Again the word, the message, the substance of the subject of apostolic declarations is spoken of as a living, growing thing. It "grew," meaning it was believed more purposefully, more strongly and more intelligently, and continued on in that state of growth. It "multiplied," meaning, in a very obvious way, that the number of people who believed it was continually increasing.

In order for the Word of God to grow it must have been planted and rooted, as per Christ's parable in Matthew 13 of the parable of the sower. The seed is the word of God. Via Paul's anointing, planted it was, or it could not have grown. Proof of the true planting of the word, is the opposition that grew in an attempt to thwart its progress. Growth of the word always arouses opposition; but where the Word grows with inward vitality it ever prevails over outward opposition. No other proof of power in the ministry of God's word will equal that which is seen in its practical effect upon our hearers' lives towards purity and Godliness.

The power of the Holy Spirit in the lives of those that minister, imparted to those who believe, is a fundamental condition for the word to grow in a believer's heart in the face of opposition. Without this there can be no life, and therefore no growth.

The Word of God is intrinsically miraculous. When it is handled and ministered properly it becomes, possibly, the most important aspect of the very management of the miraculous. It definitely becomes the most significant factor in the changing of the lives of those that believe it. It isn't even that the miraculous has to be emphasized and hyped in order to bring the miraculous into being. The reliable, convincing declaration of the whole arc of biblical truth concerning the authority of Christ over all circumstances of life, when properly presented, will take root and bring forth the fruit that the seed was sent for. It is in this very context that Isaiah 55:11 becomes activated, when it informs us that Almighty Yahweh says, "So shall my word be that goes forth out of my mouth: it shall not return unto me void, but it shall accomplish that which I please, and it shall prosper in the thing whereto I sent it."

Possibly the greatest weapon of mass reconstruction of life in the management of the miraculous, is the ministry of the Word, and how it is handled. And Paul was a master builder.

13.

PAUL'S DEFINITION OF WHAT CONSTITUTES "THE WORD OF GOD."

"...all the Jews and Greeks who lived in the province of Asia heard the word of the Lord."

Acts 19:10

An absolutely vital issue in the ministry and management of the miraculous is the actual contents of the message that is declared, alongside which the miraculous takes place. Jesus Christ did not talk of healing as an optional extra that may be included or excluded as individual preachers desire. "They shall lay hands on the sick and they shall recover" (Mark 16:18), is what Christ said. It was not given as an optional extra and cannot possibly be soundly interpreted as such. Healing the sick, we have to add, was alongside things like speaking in tongues and casting out demons. It is all part of fulfilling the Great Commission to reach the world. It definitely is not that healing, the baptism of the Spirit and deliverance were to be the "strange doctrines" as envisaged and received by Cessationist Evangelicals. It was the norm with Jesus to move in the miraculous, and it was part of His commission for the church to follow in His footsteps. The entire statement of the Saviour is comprehensive and clear. The miraculous manifests itself as an integral part of the message presented that is assuming the full biblical message is declared. The Bible does not so much as give us an explicit systematic theology of healing (although there is a profound theology of healing implied and embedded throughout both testaments), but gives us more a series of, "Just go and do it," statements that we are to fulfil, always remembering that it is He that does the healing and the delivering, not us.

Miracles are not an "add on" for those who are "more zealously inclined," or more, "extreme" in their belief system. Not wishing to insult the intelligence of my readers, but in Mark 16:18 there is a presupposition that the minister of the word must create a forum where his (or her) hands are laid upon those that are sick in order for them to recover. Things like the laying on of hands do not happen by accident. "Oops! I am sorry sir! My hands just laid themselves upon you quite involuntarily, and I am so happy that you accidentally were healed of your terminal disease!" It self-evidently does not happen like that. It is to be a wilful, planned and choreographed act of the laying on of hands.

Healing the sick is not intended to shock and surprise us. It may take the recipient of the miracle by surprise when someone like Paul shouts at you, "Stand up on your feet," but that surprise was greatly softened because Paul saw by divine communication that the man had faith to be healed (Acts 14:10). Howbeit it would have been a pleasantly traumatic shock for the rest of the audience, raising their faith to a new high. Healing the sick, and/or laying on of hands is done by wilful intent of those that minister the word of God.

The message of the gospel of Jesus Christ has in its full declaration the answer to all fundamental issues of life, and when preached under the anointing and direct power of the Holy Spirit it imparts faith to the listeners who start believing and taking hold of those very things that are promised within the gospel message. The gospel results are for "now" for the scripture lays down the plumb line that, "Today is the day of salvation (i.e. Healing, deliverance, and salvation)" (2 Corinthians 6:2). The gospel message contains many glorious promises that are embedded in both Testaments, promises given by God Himself, and "Every promise that God ever made is "Yes" in Christ and "Amen!" in Him" (2 Corinthians 1:20). The gospel of Christ, the message of the Kingdom of God, is intrinsically the power of God that brings saving, healing, deliverance and signs and wonders, from the realm of a mental understanding to spiritual apprehending, and from spiritual apprehending to physical manifestation.

The telling of the message is intrinsically the release of the power of God (Romans 1:16). The open heart and mind believes the facts of the gospel as an absolute spiritual truth. It is the hearing of faith that receives the miraculous (Galatians 3:2 and 3:5).

When the sick, the sad, the sorrowful and the sinful hear the message it brings to their consciousness their dreams of being clean, healed, free and known by God Himself, as well as the glory of knowing Him. The listener to the gospel, the recipient of the message of the kingdom, goes from step to step, from, "It could never happen," to, "It has happened in Christ," onwards to, "It could happen to me," moving to, "It will happen to me," and finally climaxing in, "It has happened to me."

The very spoken message of the Kingdom of God" has inbuilt into its fullness the concept that, when believed, heals the body as well as transforms the soul. The truths of salvation, healing, deliverance and indeed everything to do with the miraculous are securely embedded in the message that is verbally delivered, that is, when the message is *fully* delivered.

The scripture says that when the apostles went preaching, the signs and wonders followed alongside the message (Mark 16:20). I know that the famous King James translation says, "These signs shall follow them that believe," but the Greek word translated, "follow," is "Parakoloutheo", and where "para" occurs in this word, it means, "alongside of." The miracles accompanied the message, and were manifested alongside the preaching. It is unintelligent to conceive of preaching a gospel where the means of healing, freedom and cleansing take place without actually declaring within the context of the message that Christ is the healer, deliverer and Saviour of all of mankind, and "for you as an individual – whoever you may be." For people to receive faith to be saved, healed and delivered, they must have the message affirmed to be from a Personal God to the individual person who is listening.

So what was the message that Paul preached in Ephesus? By reading Acts chapters 19 and 20 we have a skeletal, yet comprehensive outline of what Paul was delivering every day in the School of Tyrannus. I do not mean that Paul preached the same message every day, of course. I do mean, however, that no matter how little or how much content there was in his delivery every day, there was always enough for folks to come to Christ, come to faith, receive healing and be delivered, every day.

The message was "The Kingdom of God" (Acts 20:25). Paul does not say that he preached "about" the kingdom of God, but that he had been, "preaching the kingdom of God," whilst he was living amongst them. That is the overall umbrella label of all he delivered to the Ephesians; The Kingdom of God.

But what are the constituent truths that pertain to preaching the Kingdom of God? Paul explains that he had been declaring that people should have, "Repentance toward God," and, "Faith towards our Lord Jesus Christ."(Acts 20:21). Once that repentance and faith had been exercised a person becomes connected with God (as per what happened in Acts 2 on the day of Pentecost, Acts 8 in Samaria and Acts 10 in the house of Cornelius – although whether Cornelius was actually converted before Peter arrived is wonderfully debatable). Old sins are forgiven. Old habits are broken. It is only people's minds and understanding that have to catch up with what has happened to them in their human spirit, in the Holy Spirit via that repentance and faith. When a person has faith they are part of those who are the "called out" ones, i.e. the church - the Ecclesia (Acts 20:28). Paul explains to the Ephesian elders how God Himself has purchased the Ecclesia to be under His ownership. What was the means or the cost of the purchase? It was made "by His blood (Acts 20:28)." This states clearly, no matter how cryptically, that Jesus Christ was Himself God incarnate. Christ's blood was indeed God's blood, and that blood purchased the believing souls who had repented towards God, and had faith towards the Lord Jesus Christ.

On arriving in Ephesus, the first question posed to the, "about twelve," disciples, was, "Have you received the Holy Spirit since you believed?" (Acts 19:1-2) In the context of the whole book of Acts, this line of scripture reveals along with others that after conversion there is the baptism of the Spirit, a "second blessing" if you will, that brings all three persons of the Godhead into the fray of human salvation. From this we understand that by believers having repentance towards God, and faith in our Lord Jesus Christ, there is a need to also "receive" the Holy Spirit. There are people who have turned to Christ who have not received the Holy Spirit (Acts 8:14-17). This is a vital truth in the body of reality that comprises the warp and woof of the biblical teaching of the kingdom of God. Obviously being "born of the Spirit" is a different experience from "receiving the Holy Spirit." We also learn by Paul's initial question in Acts 19:2, that life needs to be lived within the parameters and direction of the level of belief a person has in the promises of God, including those uttered by John the Baptist.

Combing through those first verses of Acts 19, we cannot escape that after repentance and faith comes the rite of water baptism. Paul laid hands on them in order to receive the Holy Spirit, and the reception of the gift of the Spirit was validated and verified by the speaking in tongues and prophecy. It's all in Acts 19:1-6. This is all part of the message of the Kingdom of God. This is what the scriptures teach as the normal Christian experience.

The need to be mentored and imparted to is also shown to us by the fact that these disciples stayed with Paul and were tutored in the faith. Mentoring is a biblical concept that is somewhat neglected in a western individualistic culture that spawns independence without wise external human guidance.

The manifestation of the disciples' speaking in tongues and prophesying is also validation of the supernatural gifts of the Spirit in Kingdom life. Those who have no experience of the baptism in the Holy Spirit are often compelled to teach that what took place in Acts

2 was federal for the body of Christ, meaning that "the Spirit was now given in the earth," and therefore nobody needs to receive a similar experience ever again. That idea is obviously contradicted by scripture itself because of what took place in Acts 8, Acts 10-11 and Acts 19. This leaves us with most non-charismatic evangelicals covering the issue with Cessationist ideas, i.e. that the miracles stopped with the death of the apostle's and the completion of the canon. It is this writer's absolute conviction that New Testament Christianity in all its parameters is exactly the same for today. The baptism in the Holy Spirit, once received, opens the door to a whole range of supernatural gifts as explained in 1 Corinthians 12 and 14. It facilitates prayer, spiritual warfare, hearing words directly from God and self-edification.

The gifts of the Spirit are absolutely no indication of the character or spiritual stature of the recipient, but nevertheless indicate what should be the norm in the Christian life of (a): Listening to what the Holy Spirit is saying in the "now." Paul himself indicates this along with other prophetic people who were hearing the same as Paul as in Acts 20:23. And (b): Being led by the Holy Spirit, which again, we assert that Paul was setting the bench mark for in Acts 16:6-7 and in 20:22. All these aspects of the spiritual life are part and parcel of the preaching, teaching and exemplifying life in the Kingdom of God.

Because of the nature of the world that we live in, the word of the Kingdom needs to be boldly declared, especially in the midst of unbelieving people. Bravery and courage are both in the very DNA of practical biblical faith (Acts 19:8).

Even though Acts chapters 19 and 20 give us a strong skeletal indication of what it means to declare the Kingdom of God, there is much more to it than these bullet point headings that we are here listing from these two chapters, as Paul's letter to the Ephesians clearly reveals. Paul himself explains that New Covenant preaching should cover the whole will of God (Acts 20:27), and hold back nothing that is beneficial to the believer (Acts 20:20). There needs to be a pressing of the audience to respond and believe the gospel message of the Kingdom of God (Acts 20:21).

This kind of preaching and teaching should cause great glory to be given to Christ, even from those that don't believe (Acts19:17). Note that good biblical preaching gives people something to *see* as well as *hear* (Acts 8:6). But that kind of honour to Christ was not given just through Paul's preaching, but by the awe inspiring manifestations of healing and deliverance. What Paul did in the process of casting out demons set a "trend" for Jewish exorcists to copy, even though they did not know Christ. This would not have happened, I believe, if Paul had not made deliverance seem "easy" and "clean cut." It is important to note that even though Paul's ministry of deliverance was admired and emulated by many, nobody is on record as exalting Paul as the source of power, or the "great man of faith." It was the name of Jesus that the people exalted through his impact on Ephesian society.

Acts 19:11-12 reveals that healings, miracles and deliverances were effectual not only in his presence but away from his presence, by cloths and sweat cloths. This "preaching of the kingdom" was as God intended it to be. Paul was doing what Jesus did. Jesus did it by His own intrinsic purity and faith in His Father and by the power of the Holy Spirit. Paul achieved the same results simply by aligning himself with the concept of being Christ's bond-slave, contemporaneously with being His ambassador.

By this ministerial lifestyle of Paul, mentoring, imparting to some and modelling ministry to a team of disciples that, were obviously eager learners, the whole of Asia's Jews and Greeks heard the word of the Lord. That same word of the Lord grew mightily and prevailed (Acts 19:20). The statement that the word of God, "prevailed," cannot mean anything but that it was believed upon and impacted society throughout the Roman province of Asia, what we would refer to these days as Western Turkey. There simply must have been some demonstration of the power of the word in that process of the message "prevailing."

In the context of the church, the Holy Spirit appoints pastors, overseers and elders to shepherd the people (Acts 20:28). These people watch over the flock (that is the church and those seeking God), and as far as Ephesus was concerned, all their elders were present as the sermon from Paul was delivered in Acts 20.

In the context of the hearing of, as well as the demonstration of the word, the minister of the gospel, in this case Paul, was heavily involved in spiritual warfare to a degree I have only ever known with one minister that I have met in my life. How do I know this? We know it to be true when demons exclaim, "Jesus I know and Paul I know" (Acts 19:15). This means that in the stark reality of the realm of the spirit, Paul was known by Satan and his demonic hordes. This statement must be the ultimate definition of a man who is forceful and extremely effective in extending the Kingdom of God, and the downfall of the kingdom of Satan. It is undoubtedly this, the deepest of all personal relationships with Christ that made him the fear of hell, as well as making him the mighty deliverer and the master church builder.

The prophetic insight gained by the intimacy the apostle enjoyed with the living Christ, as well as the sensitive ear he had to the Holy Spirit gave him the sure and certain knowledge that wolves in sheep's clothing would arise and tear the Ephesian Christians apart. Not physically, but in their understanding of God, His plan, His purpose and His word. This glorious outpouring of truth, grace and power through God's word was about to be twisted and distorted by demonic means, even using some of those leaders whom he was addressing at that moment (Acts 20:30). He had ministered to them with tears and deep, heartfelt, spiritually motivated emotions and was about to be reduced to tears again as he said a final good-bye to them.

Paul did the most powerful thing he knew, he commended them all to God and His word (Acts 20:32). This was not just a passive leaving of the people, but an active prayer and commitment to God giving them grace to walk in the truth and hold fast to the gospel of the Kingdom of God as he had delivered it.

14.

HEALING

"Now God worked unusual miracles by the hands of Paul, so that even handkerchiefs or aprons were brought from his body to the sick, and the diseases left them and the evil spirits went out of them."

Acts 19:11-12 (NKJV)

God made man a complete person. It is true man has a body, a soul and a spirit. It is also true that God does not save only one part of man. The whole person is the recipient of the package of salvation when the gospel message is received and believed. The human spirit is instantly rebirthed, renewed and complete. The soul (the mind, the volitional parts of humankind and the emotions) is in the process of being renewed in one's mind and is in the process of the growing process of faith and obedience in Christ. This is the renewing of the mind. The body is also quickened, and should be reinvigorated with energy and health. There is no record of Christ accepting sickness as the status quo for anybody. We only have records of him removing sickness from those who came to him with sickness. Knowing Christ precipitates the bringing of healing for the entire person. I am aware of how we may hear evangelical Christians praying for, "souls." "Lord give us souls! Above all things Lord, save souls!" I hear it, and I concur with what is meant by the praying of it. But, as with a lot of evangelical jargon in the twenty first century, what is said is not strictly biblical, although what the heart means surely is. God never saves just, "souls." God saves people. People are body, soul and spirit, i.e. a whole and complete being.

The gospel of Christ is supernatural. The entire being of man, once in Christ, is in the process of being utterly healed, and is always a candidate for any supernatural healing that the believer has not "yet" received. I believe scripture teaches us that this is so. Our understanding and grasp of what this means will either give us more and more of Christ's grace and power in our lives, or it will place a glass ceiling on our faith, telling us that to believe for more is impractical, a little extreme, and ultimately "not sound" biblical teaching. I wish to challenge any glass ceiling that evangelical readers of these pages may have had placed over their lives, especially in respect of healing and wholeness. Nowhere in the gospels, or in Acts did Jesus Christ do "half a job" and leave it unfinished. He did not say, "I am the Lord that heals you sometimes," or I am the Lord that heals some of your diseases."

To declare that the Bible is inspired by God, and then to deny that healing, deliverance, prophecy or the Baptism in the Holy Spirit has ceased since biblical times I personally find both an intellectual and academic obscenity, and an affront to every other biblical truth that can be soundly declared. To tell people who have faith in Christ, that He does not heal today is a serious denial to the integrity of scripture, and a hilarious joke to atheists and agnostics that jump with both feet through any logistical loophole Christians give them.

Cessationists are people who believe, amongst other things, that miracles have ceased. This writer considers Cessationism a total embarrassment to Christianity, and a heretical perspective of the character of God, and the gospel message that Christ gave us to preach.

Supernatural healing for the body, the soul and the human spirit are all intrinsic to the generally acknowledged Good News of Jesus Christ. There is more space taken in the gospels explaining the healing and the deliverance ministry of Christ than there is to His sermons. Healing was so much part of normal church life that it was birthed with preaching together with demonstrations of healing (Acts 2:43). Healing was therefore foundational to the nature and structure of the church.

It is inferred that healing was commonplace by Peter's answer to the crippled man in Acts 3:6. Church prayer meetings were asking for healing miracles to abound (Acts 4:29-30). It was what the prayer meeting was all about i.e miracles that came out of the preaching. Healings were multifarious through the apostles. There were healing lines and great numbers of people looking for healing filling the streets. The power and anointing that rested on Peter was great enough for his shadow to heal the people as he simply walked by (Acts 5:12-15). That kind of anointing was upon him through the baptism in the Spirit that he received in Acts 2. People came for healing from all the towns around Jerusalem, bringing their sick loved ones for that shadow of Peter to fall on them. The Bible clearly states that they brought those that were sick in body, and those that were tormented by demons, and *all* of them were healed (Acts 5:16). All? Yes! "All," is exactly what is says, in Greek, Aramaic, Latin and any other language that I can find it translated to.

It is self-evident that understanding of the dynamics of the miraculous and the anointing, and faith that works in the realm of the miraculous, was commonplace. Stephen, a deacon (i.e: a non-ministerial person) in the church at Jerusalem, on street mission, was accompanied by the miraculous (Acts 6:8). Philip on "Mission Samaria" healed the sick and cast out demons as a simple matter of course (Acts 8:6-8). The Christian man in Damascus whose name was Ananias never questioned the concept of the miraculous when instructed to minister and manage the miraculous with Saul of Tarsus. Ananias' problem was with what he had heard about Saul, but as far as praying for a man to receive his sight, that was seen as a simple little task in his mentality (Acts 9:10-18). Peter's travelling ministry evinced miraculous healings (Acts 9:32). Peter raised the dead as well as healed the sick (Acts 9:36-42).

There's more! Paul healed the sick on his front line missions to the gentiles in various places, as well as moving comfortably in the miraculous in other directions other than healing. The man, who was later to take Ephesus for Christ, spoke words that struck Bar-Jesus, a sorcerer in Cyprus, blind for attempting to keep somebody from the faith (Acts 13:6-11). Paul in his management of the miraculous, through the Holy Spirit, performed signs and wonders at the place called Iconium (Acts 14:3). He spoke healing to a man lame from birth at Lystra (Acts 14:8-10). In a different direction, although by the same Spirit, Paul survived being stoned in Lystra (Acts 14:19-20). Now that was miraculous! He healed a young demonised girl by deliverance at Philippi, after she followed him and interfered with his preaching (Acts 16:16-18). When Paul arrived at Thessalonica, there seems to have been miraculous manifestations (1 Thessalonians 1:4-5) even though they are not mentioned in Acts. So here, we stumble across the seed thought that breeds the question: How many miracles were managed in Paul's travels that are simply not even mentioned in the book of Acts? All the above happened prior to Paul arriving at Ephesus during Acts 19 and 20.

Further still, Paul refers to more miracles in his letters that also, are not referred to in Acts, as in Romans 15:18-19. The miraculous is strongly inferred in 1 Corinthians 2:4-5, and the fact that the church he founded in Corinth seemed to relish much of the gifts of the Spirit, amongst which were healing, miracles, faith and discernment of spirits, suggests that the Corinthian church "Scholars" were only moving in the direction that was exemplified by their "Teacher." Galatians 3:1-5 is a glorious piece of logic where the miracles that were wrought in Galatia (which, again, are not mentioned in Acts) were used to explain how that Christianity, is a matter of faith and the reception of the Holy Spirit, before good deeds or works. The greatness of God's power given to the believer that is like "the same mighty power that raised Christ from the dead," (Ephesian 1:19) certainly infers something in the direction of the manifestation of the miraculous. The fact that miracles *per se* are not directly referred to in Ephesians, the very place where there seems to have been outstanding miracles, should also let us know that Paul "talked down" the amount of miraculous manifestations in his ministry. Perhaps I should add a rider there and say that he doesn't talk of the miracles in his ministry like modern apostolic and evangelistic figures do. It is the firm conviction of this writer that here in Ephesus, the anointing to heal and deliver that sat on Paul's life was at its' peak.

The extraordinary miracles that took place in Ephesus, I believe, is also self-evidently informing us that the volume of miracles was glorious enough, but the manner of some of the healings was extraordinary. I do not believe there were but a few "extraordinary" miracles only. The extraordinary miracles were simply the icing on a large cake of "ordinary" miracles.

The gospel, without the demonstration of the Spirit is not the full gospel. Preacher's called by God are sworn to tell, "The truth, the whole truth, and nothing but the truth." Yet many preach without as much as a thought to this aspect of ministry. There are sick people who cannot listen properly to the gospel because of the pain they endure. There are demons and sicknesses that prevent people from listening properly with focus. Jesus Christ came to set all these people free. I speak from deep experience whilst working with other men of God.

Healing is normal to Jesus Christ. As air is available for breathing, so healing is present when the power of the Lord is present. And when the full gospel is preached Jesus Christ is present to perform the promises of the gospel to all who believe. What is in desperate shortage is the know-how and the wisdom to manage the miraculous and create forums where it can and does take place. Healing lines, and meetings where prophecy and deliverance can function in church meetings within western Christianity are as rare as common sense and genius.

If somebody claims to deliver the Word of God without all the constituents of repentance, faith, salvation, deliverance and healing and prophetic demonstration in that Word, it is not the true Word of God, nor can it be. The whole arc of biblical truth was in Paul's delivery. Signs and wonders following the preaching of the word is the norm, and anything short of that is subnormal, a deviation from what Christ told the apostles to do. The word must be declared in a manner that prepares the way for healing, and healing in *all* its manifestations. The Word declared is simply presenting Jesus Christ the complete Saviour of mankind to an audience. Jesus Christ Himself accompanies the message - that was His promise. Jesus Christ is the total and complete, wilfully intending Healer to all issues of life.

It has to be made clear to people that as far as God in Heaven is concerned, relative to Jesus dying on the cross, healing is not a big deal at all. If God gave something so incredibly precious and glorious in the very person of Christ, it does not need a degree in logic to discern that the healing, that millions of people are crying for, is of less value compared to Him who died and rose again. If you want proof of that statement, read Paul's logic when he wrote, "If God spared not His only son, but gave Him up for us all, how shall He not also with him freely give us all things. (Romans 8:32).

"God worked ... miracles by the hands of Paul." It is the will of God to heal the sick. It is the will of God to heal them now. So the issue of management of the miraculous is wrapped up in how and when Paul's hands are used in the healing process.

"God worked unusual miracles by the hands of Paul." As for me, I would like to see the usual miracles and the ordinary miracles preparatory to breaking through into the unusual and the extraordinary.

"... So that even handkerchiefs or aprons were brought from his body to the sick." Sweat clothes, and aprons used by Paul were impacted by the power of God and the anointing that rested upon him. This piece of information has two effects on those who do not believe that God heals today. They either relegate it to a strange and marvellous "one off" that happened whilst Paul was in Ephesus, never to be repeated again, or they attach it as a one liner to nice and tidy three point sermons that the influence of Paul was "rather incredible."

Then if they hear that anybody on the planet tries to emulate the same, "they are obviously people who are, "in deception," "possessed of a demon," or are simply, "unsound.""

I believe that the acid test is what happens to the people who receive the sweat cloths and/or aprons, or their modern equivalents, as well as the body of truth that the person who sends those items declares.

Let me add as well that if it was reported that the results of the prayer cloths or handkerchiefs being sent were non-existent, it still would not leave me free to say that they were deceived, possessed or unsound. Christ's life was an example to us, as well as a substitutionary sacrifice. Paul's ministry is also an example, a bench mark – if you will. If one attempted to move in the same dimension with right and good motives and falls flat on their face, I say, "God bless you! Get up and try again!" Touch not the Lord's anointed! If a person is believed by some to be "anointed," and by others, not to be "anointed," wisdom suggests that it is best to keep "shtumm" and let God be the judge. It is to Him and Him alone that we all stand or fall.

Paul gave his aprons and sweat cloths. Why would he do such a thing? He was aware that, by the anointing of the Holy Spirit that rested upon him, and by the application of faith of both himself and the people concerned, healing and deliverance could be ministered "by proxy" in the human sense - but it was always God who performed the healing. Distance is not a barrier. Whether it be by the faith of those that took the cloths to the sick persons, or the faith of the sick people themselves, or both of them in combination together with Paul is not explained. But the apostle himself made the initial suggestion and gave the cloths to be used in this manner. This writer, for one, does not doubt for an instance that the offer would not have been made on the strength of a whim, or a moment's fancy. It was faith in action. The whole operation would have been awe inspiring if it had happened once. But by the choice of Luke's language one can but deduce that it happened on a regular basis through the wilful choice of Paul to use the items he did.

The fact that men of God do the same today and are ridiculed and belittled by Christian leaders for their action is a statement at the desperate low ebb tide that Christianity has receded to in the western world.

When the cloths were placed on the bodies of those that were sick and demonised the truth came out. Diseases responded to the anointing that was on the items, and left. Further still, active, malignant, demonic life forms were aware of what the cloths were, somehow. They left in the presence of the cloths, as if Paul was himself present commanding them to leave. Demons do not leave easily, that is why we are encouraged to cast them out, drive them out and expel them. The entire process was activated when demonised people came in contact with Paul's personal possessions. For those who are not aware of what "the anointing" is, or experienced in ministering deliverance, to make any remark of criticism to men of God that use this means of ministry at all, is to reveal ignorance of a rare but very profound nature.

When the gospel is preached in its glorious fullness, it lifts people to a place of faith. Repentance becomes a free and natural response, and the whole attitude of the recipient of that faith, facilitates the Lord Jesus stepping out of the invisible, the spiritual, the mental and the "irrelevant" into this time, space world and to do what He does best. Sicknesses whether they be mild and time related, or incurable and terminal, flee in the presence of the well-received Christ. Hang ups, problems, be they mental, spiritual or physical, that are part and parcel of demonic infestation in a human beings life or circumstance have to leave when addressed. Freedom, joy and new life is unleashed with divine power on all who receive, believe and walk in that newness. Most sicknesses and demonic infestations need prayer for healing or exorcism. However, I do know people who were freed from both illness and demons without direct prayer, but simply by exercising their saving faith.

Anybody on the planet can receive. It takes character and persistence to maintain what has been received. And, even the incredible means of maintaining such gifts are integral with the full package of what we refer to as, the "Gospel."

Management of the miraculous in the context of Christ healing people and delivering them needs to be astutely studied, watched, and experienced by ministers in their all-round management of the miraculous. Mind management must be the first priority of the overcomer. Mind management in the realm of the miraculous needs to be attended to astutely. That spiritual and mental attack on the biblical whys and wherefores of the miraculous is a mandatory concept in the renewing of the mind in the context of seeking to have a credible ministry in management of the miraculous.

All this happened ubiquitously while Paul was ministering in the school of Tyrannus without any adulation being given to Paul, by the writer of Acts. That fact, also, in and of itself, is a major issue in management of the miraculous. A miracle is not an end in itself but a means to an end, which is the salvation of people's lives and souls. Ministerial adulation utterly defeats that end. Wilful propagation in the current of modern advertising that leads to adulation of the minister of the miraculous is woefully self-defeating.

To sum up, the point is that divine healing is the supernatural power of God bringing health to the human body. Healing is a perpetual wilful desire embedded in God's pleasure. Genuine desire on the part of the seeker, plus God's ability in the life of the one ministering, brings healing of all dimensions. Healing and forgiveness are gifts from God, which are to be received by faith. They are all for, "whosoever will" (Revelation 22:17). Healing belongs to you. It is a gift; it is yours. Healing of the temporal body, however, is for the goal of your eternal salvation. Healing, salvation and all of God's blessings have been paid for and are offered freely. I encourage all readers to increase their knowledge of God's Word, because in it is healing, in it is deliverance, in it is blessing. Never forsake the concept that it is always God's will to heal those who seek His healing

15.

DELIVERANCE
(1) BASIC DEFINITION

".. Handkerchiefs or aprons were even carried from his (Paul's) body to the sick, and the diseases left them and the evil spirits went out. But also some of the Jewish exorcists, who went from place to place, attempted to name over those who had the evil spirits the name of the Lord Jesus, saying, "I adjure you by Jesus whom Paul preaches." Seven sons of one Sceva, a Jewish chief priest, were doing this. And the evil spirit answered and said to them, "I recognize Jesus, and I know about Paul, but who are you?" and the man, in whom was the evil spirit, leaped on them and subdued all of them and overpowered them, so that they fled out of that house naked and wounded. This became known to all, both Jews and Greeks, who lived in Ephesus; and fear fell upon them all and the name of the Lord Jesus was being magnified. Many also of those who had believed kept coming, confessing and disclosing their practices. And many of those who practiced magic brought their books together and began burning them in the sight of everyone; and they counted up the price of them and found it fifty thousand pieces of silver."

(Acts 19: 12 – 19 NASB)

If I were to ask you what the first miracle of Jesus was, you would probably say it was when He turned the water into wine in John 2. That miracle, undoubtedly, historically, and chronologically was the first miracle Christ performed in history, the apostle John says so. Mark (1:21-28) and Luke (4:31-37), however had more in mind than historical chronology when they listed what they perceived to be the first and primary miracle that Jesus performed, that needed to be chronicled in their respective gospels. As far as they were concerned something incredible took place when Jesus was interrupted in His preaching by a man crying out one morning in Synagogue. He then cast the interrupting demon out of a person. This was the first time the Bible tells us so clearly and explicitly about what I am here referring to as "deliverance." In fact it is so crystal clear, we seriously need help to misunderstand it. It all happened in the synagogue in Capernaum.

- There was a human being with a demon spirit that was actually residing within him. Where did it live? In his heart? His mind? Which part of his body? We are not told. How did it get there? Was he born with it? If not, what did he do to allow it in? What other symptoms apart from disrupting Christ's sermon, did the man have that showed people he had a demon? Whatever the answers to these questions were, we need to just note at this point of time that there was a demon malignantly, secretly, present amongst them, as they worshipped.

- The suggestion is that the demon had been there for some time, not struggling against, nor fighting in the man's efforts to attend church - or synagogue as it was at this time. The demon knew he was safe every week in this church context because nobody knew about him or about demons in general, about their influence or the way they obstructed people's lives. The demonic entities thrive on the ignorance and unbelief of people in general. A demon is an evil, mischievous, yet malignant spirit. Demons do not have the kudos of evil or the weight of power that Hollywood would try to teach us.

- The evil spirit within the man knew the anointing of God was in the room (i.e. The Spirit of God resting in the heart and life of another person). The anointing upon Jesus was an anointing without measure. If you will, it was an anointing that no other could ever receive - the ultimate infusion of the Holy Spirit into a human life. The perfect, sinless man walking under the influence and power of the perfect Holy Spirit, with perfect communication from one to the other. Jesus said He only did what He saw His

Father do and said what He heard His Father say. And what He did and what He said was all under the guidance and power of the Holy Spirit. Demon Spirits are conscious when the power of God is present. Many human spirits are so ignorant of the demonic that they consider it just a sickness or a person's idiosyncrasies when it sometimes is a demonic force. Christ was present in the power of the Holy Spirit. The demon spirit knew this, and was impacted not only by Messiah's presence, but greatly by His preaching and teaching. None of the people, nor the church leaders were aware exactly who was present. Some were accepting what Christ said, some were no doubt rejecting Him and His words. The power of the Spirit embedded in the declared word of God has power to save and heal. Human beings could accept or reject, believe or deny what Jesus Christ was saying. However, the demon could not so choose.

- The demon could not stay still nor silent in such an environment. Note that it makes no difference how many people present are ignorant of demons and their modus operandi, it only takes one person in the Holy Spirit, and with the insight to see and to know, and the demon surfaces. One may ask of the demon, "Why scream and reveal yourself? You were safer when hidden in the poor man's psyche and silent." It would be like asking a fallen soldier in the Crimea war who was having his leg amputated with a saw and no anaesthetic, "Young man, why are you screaming?" The self-indulged settlement of the demon spirit in the life of his host was profoundly disturbed by the presence of God, the power of God and the word of God, as well as being fully aware that Jesus knew who and what He was and why He had come.

- The man in whom the demon was residing may have been a pleasant chap. He was probably part and parcel of the church/synagogue family. The presence of the demon in no way interfered with his hearts faith in God, but would have played havoc with his health, his mind, his understanding, and his volitional choices. The demon was hiding within the man's psyche and his entire human make-up. The man might not have even been aware that the demon was there within him. The demon was "in hiding," and would occasionally "surface" within the man's relational activity to cause the man to do something, probably habitually, against his normal characteristic self. The man might have even been saying to himself whilst the spirit was troubling him, "Why did I say that?" or, "Why did I do that?" There might even have been times when somebody would have asked him why he did this, or said that, and he might not have even known he had said it. The man could have felt comfortable and inspired listening to Jesus preach and teach. Something inside him, however, was deeply distressed at the visit of the person from Nazareth. Like a human being sat in a room that is on fire, or a fish that had always lived in the darkness of the sea 5 miles deep being brought to the surface and the day light, the demon began to wriggle, or whatever the parallel response is of a demon in the realm of the spirit. The demon was exposed by the light of the Son of God and was therefore out of his normal dark habitat. He was in a strange and torturous place where the malignancy of his evil was suffering – like a polar bear being left in a sweltering tropical forest. It just didn't feel normal to be there.

- The anxiety of the demon, in the presence of Christ, became the anxiety of the man in whose life the demon was living. The sweat or discomfort that would have swept over the man, would have been noticed by others, as well as his body language and breathing. It is possible the man knew nothing of it. Demons have a certain amount of insight simply because they are spirits, dealing with human spirits, and here, they were confronted by the very Spirit of God. That is why they know how to hide within. Demons can manipulate people very well, especially those who do not even know they themselves are spirit, or those who deny they themselves are spiritual beings. The spiritually minded Christian should be aware of the dimension he is in. There is deep, deeper and deepest in the concept of being spiritually minded. This is why the preaching and teaching of the word of God should constantly exhort believers to put on the new man and press into more of God.

- The demon, who was troubled because he sensed the power of God in the room, had a voice and spoke beyond the choice of the man whose body he was dwelling within. It might not have even been the man's normal voice that people heard. My experience would suggest that the man's face may or may not be contorted, but would definitely not look like his normal self-whilst the demon "surfaced" and spoke. The unclean spirit did the speaking while the victim was not only ignorant of the fact that his mouth was talking, but was probably in a state of "blackout". I don't know what phrase they would use in psychiatric circles for something like this, but the man was "unconscious," yet awake and moving while the demon spoke through him. When asked, later, he would undoubtedly not know what he had said under the influence of the demon spirit. Like some science fiction concept, there were two intelligent entities within the same body. The human entity was at home as his creator intended him to be. But the trespasser was illegally squatting, and there were moments where he could shut the proper owner out of the proceedings, and take over the helm of the ship. This is more common than is widely understood, and more tormenting for the victim trespassed against than human language can express.

- The spirit had hitherto been comfortable when in a religious service, because the deeper his victim got into the teachings of his church/synagogue, the safer he thought he was, and the better developed was the hiding place he had created for himself. Nobody had known he was there, apart from those who were sharp enough to know that the victim occasionally did things that were way out of character to his normal activity. There were times when this man was doing some hideous things, and he was hardly aware he had done it, if people hadn't told him. It is a strange mysterious world when one is demonised.

- To disbelieve in the very existence of demons when it actually is one renders true and accurate diagnosis a hideous impossibility. To render a psychological prognosis, or to prescribe psychiatric treatment when it is actually a demonic issue that is at hand complicates the issue further in the west. If a man has some illness that is caused by demonic infestation, and a western doctor prescribes medicine or even surgery, the demon's presence is not interfered with, and there is a probability of his evil being simply redirected to another part of the patient's being, be it physical, emotional, psychological or spiritual.

- It was the spirit's fear, discomfort, and dare I say, pain that caused him not to stay in his hiding place. He could have stayed silent, and maintained his ease and his "human host" in perpetuity until he died, whereupon it would conceivably move in to some surviving loved one or confidante of the demised victim. But the anointing was painful for a demon to be around. He knew he was discovered. As a creature of the dark screams when pure light is focussed on him, and in the consciousness of discovery and his complete vulnerability to the power and word of God, this demon being cried out as if in a spasm of agony. I have seen it many times. It is as if the demon spirit itself is, for want of a better word, a "misfit" in a normal human body. It is as if the malignant spirit does not have the wherewithal to control a human body or mind and act normally.

- The spirit knew he was absolutely subject to Christ, and that whatever was to happen now, Christ would not make him welcome. The people present and the scribes and/or teachers who led the services there, just did not know this, and were sat their confident in their choices of accepting or rejecting what this man Jesus was saying. Never could they have conceived of any creature having such a response to the truths and the belief system that they held as fundamentalist Jews. Not that the term, "fundamentalist" had been thought of at that time. Such is the nature of sin that man's pride may, and often does, argue about submission to Christ, and the very authority of His person. Mankind can deny the power and presence of God. Neither angels or demons can ignorantly be in the presence of God's power.

- I would say, that at this moment, the demon spirit was the only one in the room who was aware of who Christ was. And if you were to say to me, "On a point of order! What about the disciples, whoever it was that was present with Jesus at the time?" I would answer that even they did not at this time know exactly who it was that they were following, not in the full and comprehensive theological way that this demon spirit knew it. He knew who Christ was on a higher level than any University Theology lecturer could know.

- The spirit knew Jesus was "the Holy One of God." That language lets us know, that the demons were fully conscious and aware that God in the flesh had entered the room, and they knew that to parley was futile. It was "Emergency Code Red" time for any being from hell.

- The greater the anointing of the Holy Spirit, the more powerful the presence, the quicker the demon will answer. The evil spirit literally had to come out of hiding in the presence of the anointed one. He could do nothing else. Without any consideration to the feelings or dignity of the man who was hosting this hideous demonic force, he cries out, manically.

- "Leave us alone..." the voice cried. Oops! They have given something away there! There is more than one of them. It wasn't an "it." It was a "them." It wasn't a "me." It was an, "us."

- "What business do we have with each other?" was the demonic continuation. By the very nature of the demon's existence, the anointing of God challenges them by direct command, or by indirect words of God. Jesus, as yet, had not spoken directly to the demon, but it had taken personal offence that whatever Christ was talking about, was against hell. The demons were aware that heaven was invading planet earth. The evil powers knew clearly that the power of God was manifesting to add to heaven's human population, and to plunder hell's property. The devils know that Jesus came to expel them. The demons were aware that Messiah had come to put a halt to the demonic trespassing on humanity. For this purpose was the Son of God manifest: to destroy the works of the evil one.

- Note Christ had simply preached and taught. Whatever the content of the teaching had been, it had dislodged the demons from their comfort zone, thrown them out of bed, and the things were exposed. The spirit, or spirits, wanted to be left alone in their hiding place. They were crying out like spoilt brats who were about to be told to leave the nursery, get out and never come back.

- "I know who you are!" This suggests that the many had a single spokesman.

- "I know who you are!" He did as well. He was absolutely fully compus mentus about the divine personage who was in the synagogue with them. One demon was now speaking for however many demons there were within the victims life. This is a normal thing. Many demons; one strong man leader. Sometimes they talk en bloc as a group; sometimes it is the leader that vocalises. Sometimes it is correct to just call it "a spirit." Sometimes it is sound to refer to, "them." It is not important. But it's a fact. It is not always multiple spirits that are infesting a person, but often it is.

- "Have you come to destroy us?" This is a fear the inhabitants of hell carry around with them as a natural facet of their existence. The plain answer, of course, would have been a loud and clear, "YES!" The scripture tells us that, "For this purpose was the Son of God manifest, to destroy the works of the evil one (1 John 3:8). But Christ was not about to waste breath, energy and words to such a malignant little being.

- Demon power knows that its interference with mankind is one day to be brought to an end. These evil malignant intelligent life forms in the synagogue this day thought their time had come. The question was voiced as an immature and manic one. Such is the nature of those spirits in this man

- Note that once the demons had chosen to come out of hiding, they were uncivil, confrontational, and as street language would have it today, "in yer face!"

- Jesus had other priorities, and was not to suffer distraction longer than was necessary, although He knew full well that faith would rise amongst the people when the demons were silenced and expelled. So: "Be quiet, and come out of him!" was the severe and unbending command of the Son of God. Obviously, Jesus did not want the demon to talk in the midst of the service, not because of any legalistic law concerning the issue, but simply so that, for this, the first time ever to our knowledge, the people would learn what demons were, and how they had to flee when God's word was used against them. They were told to be silent, and they were.

- "Come out of him!" It was not a mental condition, although I am sure that psychiatric people would detect a mental condition of some kind in a demonised person. Jesus attacked the victim's state at its very root. He commanded the malignant beings "Out!" Demons do not, cannot, and will not hang around when told to do something, under the anointing of the Holy Spirit.

- These demons from hell would not, and could not stay. By the finger of God Christ rid the man of his demonic infestation and was healed instantly and restored to normalcy. Such was their grip and permeation of the man's being, they threw him to the ground as they left. Mark says that, "throwing him into convulsions, the unclean spirit cried out with a loud voice and left the man." So now, the demon in charge, or as Jesus referred to his kind once - "the strong man", the leader of the pack was screaming for them.

- Luke tells us that even though the demon threw the man down on the ground, he did him no harm. The man stood up healed, and sound in every possible way.

- The people were amazed! Why? Because they had never heard of such a thing before. This was breaking new ground for mankind. It was one small word from Jesus. It was one giant step for the kingdom of God. For the first time ever, as far as we know, a human being, in whom and upon whom the Spirit of God was comfortably residing and abiding had spoken to a demon from hell without fuss or incantation, and sent him packing. This was the dawn of a new dimension for the people of God.

- This was a vindication to the truths and the power that they talked about every week in the synagogue when they discussed the biblical accounts of God's dealing with mankind from Adam till their present moment.

- Messiah had arrived, and the Kingdom of God had been manifested amongst them. See how the power of God causes amazement. The manifestation of God in the earth causes faith to rise. The word of God happening amongst the people creates useful and faith building conversations, debates and discussions. It nourishes faith. That's part of its ongoing benefits. Mark says that people were saying, "What's this?" Luke say's they started discussions off by exclaiming, "What is this message? For with authority and power He commands the unclean spirits and they come out." The people were talking about Jesus in terms of power, grace, authority, and the rule of God. The word of God was magnified and started to grow amongst the people.

- The power of God brought a state of amazement to the recipients of that power and grace, as well as to the spectators who were witnesses to that power and grace being ministered. The power of God brought fame to Christ. The power of God brought money to the cause. The power of God opened some doors, and closed others. The power of God resounded for miles around. And this account, according to Mark and Luke, is exactly where it started.

- Jesus Christ actually stated that, "If I with the finger of God cast out devils, no doubt the kingdom of God is come upon you" (Luke 11:20). Deliverance is the children's bread, freedom belongs to mankind, and God's ministers and disciples need to feed the people with that bread today. It is by these means (amongst others, of course) that Paul took Ephesus. It was a key armament in Paul's management of the miraculous. Let us be clear that Jesus taught that when unclean, vexing, harassing, tormenting or demonizing spirits are cast out of people, the Kingdom of God is being manifested. It is insipient millennial blessings. We are tasting the power of the world to come. We are eating now as a delicacy, what will be daily fare in Christ's millennial reign. Wholeness and freedom is ours.

- Jesus, the Word incarnate, was anointed by the Holy Spirit. The Holy Spirit came upon Jesus and stayed there. He was moved by the Holy Spirit throughout His entire life. Like Jesus, we too need the Holy Spirit in exactly the same way.

- It was the presence of the Holy Spirit, and Jesus living in the power of the Holy Spirit, that effected the deliverance of that first miracle in Mark and Luke.

- Jesus said the Holy Ghost was a gift from the Father. He told his disciples prior to His return to heaven, that they "should not depart from Jerusalem but wait for the promise of the Father. For John truly baptized with water but ye shall be baptized with the Holy Ghost not many days hence" (Acts 1:4-5). We understand that Jesus may have said that to some 500 people. Some listened, some didn't. Only 120 were in Jerusalem on the day that Jesus baptized them with the Holy Spirit. For those that gathered together on that day, to them gave He power.

- Uncommon blessing, such as this, catapults people into faith and joy. We understand why, on the day we are referring to, deliverance ministry was rare, in fact as far as the simple manner in which Christ commanded, it was unheard of before that moment. But in the church of Christ in the twenty first century, it should be an assumed grace that church leaders, and Christians in general, walk in.

- The waiting believers in Acts 1 and 2, and the others that were later baptized with the Holy Ghost with the evidence of speaking in other tongues (Acts 2:1-8; 8:14-18; 10:45-46; 19:5-6), to them was given power to tread on serpents and over all the power of the wicked one. They wasted no time confronting devils and casting out unclean spirits.

"There came also a multitude out of the cities round about unto Jerusalem, bringing sick folks, and them which were vexed with unclean spirits: and they were healed everyone". (Acts 5:16).

Philip went to Samaria. "And the people with one accord gave heed unto those things which Philip spoke, hearing and seeing the miracles which he did. For unclean spirits, crying with loud voice, came out of many that were possessed with them: and many taken with palsies, and that were lame, were healed. And there was great joy in that city."(Acts 8:6-8)

And here we have in Ephesus with Paul: "So that from his body were brought unto the sick handkerchiefs or aprons, and the diseases departed from them, and the evil spirits went out of them" (Acts 19:12).

People need help. Where will they find it? This man was already going to church, listening to the preacher and meditating on the Word, but still he was demonized by an unclean spirit. Going to church, reading the bible alone is not enough. People need an encounter with Holy Spirit power and anointing.

The bottom line is this: The anointing on the words of Christ caused this unclean devil to manifest. When it manifested Christ did not ignore it, He told it to shut up and come out. The act of deliverance was fulfilled in a public place. Today thousands need the same kind of deliverance from unclean spirits. Would we know a demon spirit if we encountered one? The significance of what we are saying here shall be enlarged on in our next pages.

16.

DELIVERANCE
(2) BEYOND CASTING DEMONS OUT
(ACTS 19:12-19)

".. Handkerchiefs or aprons were even carried from his (Paul's) body to the sick, and the diseases left them and the evil spirits went out. But also some of the Jewish exorcists, who went from place to place, attempted to name over those who had the evil spirits the name of the Lord Jesus, saying, "I adjure you by Jesus whom Paul preaches." Seven sons of one Sceva, a Jewish chief priest, were doing this. And the evil spirit answered and said to them, "I recognize Jesus, and I know about Paul, but who are you?" and the man, in whom was the evil spirit, leaped on them and subdued all of them and overpowered them, so that they fled out of that house naked and wounded. This became known to all, both Jews and Greeks, who lived in Ephesus; and fear fell upon them all and the name of the Lord Jesus was being magnified. Many also of those who had believed kept coming, confessing and disclosing their practices. And many of those who practiced magic brought their books together and began burning them in the sight of everyone; and they counted up the price of them and found it fifty thousand pieces of silver."

Acts 19: 12 – 19 (NASB)

Let's go back to Noah for a moment! You and I know the full story, from beginning to end. The end of the story is that Noah and his three sons, with their respective wives, were all safe and sound in the huge ark that they had built whilst the rest of the population of the world were under water. The reality was, of course, that during that 120 years that it took Noah to build the ark, the population of the world was already "under water" and perishing i.e. the spiritual reality is that the devil had drowned them all in their sin before the water arose to physically take them. The end of the story simply made a physical reality what was already a factual scenario. For 120 years, the eight that were saved through the ark were already saved and being saved through their faith. There were probably other righteous people, like Methuselah (who I am assuming walked in faith like his father Enoch) who died immediately prior to the deluge and the opening of the great deep that resulted in what I believe to have been a global flood. Life went on, people were married and given in marriage, eating, sleeping, walking and laughing their way through life, but the consequences and state of mind of the masses had already precipitated the flood before a drop of water was seen. That is why Noah could have built his ark in a desert. The fact that would be seen in the future flood was already a fact of life as far as Noah was concerned, even though the physical flood was still a thing of the future.

It is the same today and has always been the same. Isaiah 25: 6-9 gives us an insight into the same scenario as at present, only using a different analogy to explain the situation. Allow me to quote the scripture and explain as we read:

"And in this mountain shall the Lord of hosts make unto all people a feast of fat things, a feast of wines on the lees, of fat things full of marrow, of wines on the lees well refined." **(Isaiah 25 :6).** I believe Isaiah is here talking of Calvary and the atoning work of Christ. He was probably referring to Zion as a whole. That is the mountain upon which Jerusalem was built. In Christ is the feast of fat things full of marrow, that is, health giving nutrients, and wine on the lees well refined.

"And he will destroy in this mountain the face of the covering cast over all people, and the veil that is spread over all nations." **(Isaiah 25:7).** There is, "the face of the covering cast over all people." Isaiah has an absolutely global insight to how people live and breathe, and what motivates them and/or limits and controls them. "He (that is Christ) will destroy ... the veil that is spread over all nations." One

cannot be anything but struck by the vivid image created by Isaiah's words. According to the prophet the entire world is held under, "the face of the covering," and, "the veil that is spread." My Hebrew interlinear phrases the two statements as, "the faces of the wrap, the one wrapping over all peoples," and, "the blanket, the one blanketing over all the nations." The "wrap" and the "blanket," have always been there since the fall of Adam. It is still there today. The apostle John states with crystal clarity, "the whole world lies in the wicked one" (1 John 5:19).

The graphic language used to illustrate the status quo of humanity and the world is seriously stunning. The "wrap" and, the "blanket." The NIV has it as, the, "shroud" and, the "sheet." The NLT has, "The cloud of gloom, the shadow of death. . . that hangs over the earth." The Holman translation pushes the envelope even further in descriptive language and refers to the, "burial shroud, the shroud over all the peoples, the sheet covering all the nations." The ISV refers to the "burial shroud that enfolds." God's Word translation talks of, "The veil of grief... and the mask covering all nations." The only other variation I can find is the Douay-Rheims Bible which refers to the same as a "web."

The concept of spiritual veils that prevent normal vision and understanding are common throughout the bible. Abraham could not see the ram until he raised his knife to Isaac. Hagar could not see the water that would save her son and herself until the Angel of the Lord opened her eyes. 2 Corinthians 3:15-16 talks of the veil that hides the truth of the gospel from Israel as a people, a veil that is removed as people turn to Christ.

Christian's are alien to this world, just as Jesus declared, "My kingdom is not of this world." Christians are citizens of heaven. Christians are, to create another analogy, people of "the ark", as opposed to people "in the water". Noah was really of a future cosmos, where every trace of the world prior to the flood was erased.

This world is run, organised and directed by the devil. The Bible is as clear on this issue as anything. In the gospel of John, especially in the eighth chapter, the Lord Jesus is confronted by people who Jesus explained, "are of your father, the devil." The devil is the thief that Christ spoke of in John 10, who came to, "Kill, steal and destroy." When these scribes, Pharisees and Sadducee's accosted Christ, the Lord was actually arguing with demonically inspired strongholds in the minds of these people's mind sets. He was, quite literally, confronting demons in their own natural world. When the Jewish religious leaders were provoking the crowd to scream, "Crucify Him! Crucify Him!" it was a demonic manifestation of hate, prejudice and godlessness.

So why didn't Christ just cast the demons out?

I am sure there will be the theologically minded readers who would quickly reply that it was in the plan of God for Christ to die. "It pleased the Lord to bruise Him." So the question of, "Why didn't Christ cast the demons out of the crowd," is nullified by an easy answer. The point I am making, however, is that there are some manifestations of pure evil that cannot be cast out, apart from confronting it with truth. Demons who secrete themselves in the human psyche where unconfessed sin and iniquity exist, or once existed, are different. And let me quickly add, that once a demon has entered a person, there are times when faith and commitment to Christ leaves the infestation of demons in a deeper hiding place, even though that person may be walking in faith and obedience to God's word. The woman in Luke 13 whom Jesus declared to be a "Daughter of Abraham," meaning that she was a woman of faith, had a demon secreted in her being somewhere that had doubled her over for eighteen years. From this we understand that believers can have demonic issues. Even when all sin is confessed and dealt with.

It is the opinion of this writer that the majority of Christian's long term problems are demonically related.

Verses 8 and 9 of Isaiah 25 confirm to us that these verses are talking of the removal of the death shroud and the covering veil that suffocates the whole world, by the cross of Christ. What Christ achieved on Calvary will be fully and totally manifest when He returns to reign on earth on David's throne. The second advent of Jesus Christ will bring the entire issue of deliverance to a glorious totality of freedom for all in the resurrection, and even those who will not be part of the resurrection in the millennium. But until that time, the cloud, the shroud, the web, or whatever other analogies there are in scripture, is removed bit by bit by the gospel message and through the power of God in the declaration of Christ crucified, the healing of people in the "mighty name of Jesus Christ," the casting out of demons, and the prophetic word. All these manifestations of God pierce the darkness of the death shroud that covers the earth, and bring light into the world. These statements of God's grace rip open the shroud and allow the people to see Christ Himself as the answer to their eternal as well as temporal needs. It brings down the webs that entangle mankind and allow the demonic spider-like movements of evil to communicate their iniquity to the hearts and minds of the masses.

In Acts 19, the remarks that Luke makes about the Word of God being heard by all the people that lived in Asia (19:10), and then, how the word of God grew mightily and prevailed (19:20) are both a preface to, and a coda after, his remarks of demons being cast out, sicknesses fleeing, and witches and wizards burning their bridges when they burned their books of spells and incantations.

The Bible refers to the world, the flesh and the devil. The devil is plainly the personal enemy of Christ. The devil works through the flesh and the fleshly mind of people to build the Christless world, as it is, that is under his rule and domination. There are mind sets, philosophies and world-views that cannot tolerate the presence of God, all over the globe. Not one of us is exempt from falling foul of demonically inspired thought processes, no matter how deeply we are entrenched in the scriptures and the Spirit. Unless you are perfect in thought, philosophy and understanding, you need setting free from something more. The Christian is swimming against the Tide, and paddling upwards in the midst of a vertical waterfall. The Christian, like Paul, needs to progress with more force and strength than the flow of liquid evil that seeks to control us all and bring us down. The whole direction of the planet, is contrary to God the Father. I believe it was Watchman Nee's book, "Love Not The World," that said, "The world, the flesh and the devil, stand in opposition to the three divine persons. The flesh is ranged against the Holy Spirit as Paraclete, Satan himself against Christ Jesus as Lord, and the world against the Father as Creator."

My overall point here is that deliverance ministry, one to one, is undoubtedly the casting out of demons, and healing the sick. But deliverance ministry is also the declaration of every truth that is helpful to the salvation of mankind, and is needed to be widely declared and believed to remove the shroud from a person, a family, an area, a nation, and, one day, the whole world. Gospel preaching is intended to be the removal of the grave clothes that enshrouds people's lives. The more bible truth illumines the minds of those that believe, the more the shroud is removed, the web is broken down, the light breaks through the darkness and people are translated from the kingdom of darkness into the kingdom of God's dear Son. Deliverance, by definition, is to be absolutely freed from the hands of the devil, or circumstances that militate towards killing, stealing from and destroying people's lives. The Christian message is a message of deliverance.

Personal deliverance. Individual healings. Prophetic words that change lives for the better as they bring healing and deliverance, as well as preaching, are all tools and weapons to free a lost and bound world. The gospel is the power of God to those that believe. For these miraculous things to happen, the message itself must be presented by a credible, believable witness who can demonstrate the miracle of deliverance to those that hear him or her, and fill in the blanks of understanding with the new divine logic that needs to steamroller into oblivion the old way of thinking. And when I talk of a credible, believable witness, I do not only mean credible and believable to man, but credible and believable to angels, demons and God Himself. This credibility in heavenly places is why the demons cried out, "Jesus we know and Paul we know." Oh to be famous in the invisible world of the spirit.

If any person be in Christ, they are a new creation. The daily experience of the deliverance of Christ, which is diametrically opposed to the world views and the mentalities of the world we live in, needs to be fed with strong truths and insight that strive to take huge steps towards completely removing the shroud that smothers and interferes with people eyes physically, mentally and spiritually. Solid, ongoing mind nourishing truth, removes the cloud over people.

This is, by far, the biggest part of the management of the miraculous.

Anybody can, and millions have, received the gift of salvation, healing, deliverance and understanding. It is the maintenance of what is received that is an even larger issue. Having opened the door to the truth, those truths that save and keep a believer developing on a regular and daily basis need engrafting into the mindset, philosophy and world view of the Christian mind. The biblical truth needs to become a part of the recipient's mindset.

The word of God in its fullness and power, presented with signs and wonders that demonstrate the truth of what is being said, is the overarching secret to apostolic management of the miraculous.

I believe that it is a different rank of satanic being that permeates human life on a different level that dominated the belief systems and attitudes of the scribes and Pharisees, as they still dominate the world at large in every generation. Yes, there are demons that need to be expelled, but the human mind needs a different kind of warfare where imaginations and everything that opposes God and His truth are thrown down by bringing every thought captive to Christ through solid, thorough, teaching and preaching of biblical truth (2 Corinthians 10:3-5).

17.

DELIVERANCE (3) THE PRACTICALITIES OF LARGE-SCALE DELIVERANCE.

".. Handkerchiefs or aprons were even carried from his (Paul's) body to the sick, and the diseases left them and the evil spirits went out. But also some of the Jewish exorcists, who went from place to place, attempted to name over those who had the evil spirits the name of the Lord Jesus, saying, "I adjure you by Jesus whom Paul preaches." Seven sons of one Sceva, a Jewish chief priest, were doing this. And the evil spirit answered and said to them, "I recognize Jesus, and I know about Paul, but who are you?" and the man, in whom was the evil spirit, leaped on them and subdued all of them and overpowered them, so that they fled out of that house naked and wounded. This became known to all, both Jews and Greeks, who lived in Ephesus; and fear fell upon them all and the name of the Lord Jesus was being magnified. Many also of those who had believed kept coming, confessing and disclosing their practices. And many of those who practiced magic brought their books together and began burning them in the sight of everyone; and they counted up the price of them and found it fifty thousand pieces of silver."

Acts 19: 12 – 19 (NASB)

I spent a very special part of my life working as a member of the ministry team of what was possibly the most dynamic healing, prophetic and deliverance ministry in the world at that time. That is this writer's opinion anyway. I was with a widely known pastor/prophet in Africa. It was one of the greatest learning curves of my life. This man had been based at the same church in the same location for twenty plus years. That makes a statement in itself. This pastor/prophet has now passed on.

What I witnessed, learned and observed there was the nearest thing to Paul in Ephesus that I can imagine. Regular numerous meetings each week. Prayer lines documented by written details in the church archives and video recorded details of almost everything the prophet ever said and done in public. Testimonies, rife with the supernatural. Deliverance of individuals in the sight of the whole congregation that must have been something like twenty thousand or so on a normal Sunday. I was in the thick of it for about three years. I loved every minute of it. And what I learned there I am about to use as a suggested template for what I believe must have been happening in Ephesus for Paul's two to three years there. I want my readers to be aware that what I am saying here is solidly based on experience, even though some observations and remarks are not stated in scripture. Some of the practical logistics are self-evident.

I am not going to systematically go through everything I experienced in Africa, but I am going to write with my bible open on my desk at Acts chapters 19 and 20, and write what I see with my mind's eye as I read.

Firstly, the length of the church services is an issue (Acts 19:9 Amplified Bible). Here in the west some churches refuse to hold meetings that are longer than 60 or 90 minutes. We are given to understand that Paul had the School of Tyrannus open to him for five hours a day. I have to wonder whether it could have been longer. For prayer lines in Lagos, sometimes, of over 200 people, the time needed to pray for them, and hear their testimonies, deliver prophetic words to people, and allow them to confirm the truth and accuracy of what has been spoken over them, and finally to cast out the demons of those that needed deliverance, can take around five hours of the day.

On top of that, undoubtedly there would have been some kind of corporate prayer for those who are sick but were not in the prayer line.

We must not forget the preached word either that was fitted in to this sort of church programme every week. I have personally experienced, as have the thousands who attend this pastor's meetings regularly, services that started somewhere around 8-00am and with everything that was going on, the service was still alive till around 4 or 5 in the afternoon. The latest I remember was just after 8-0clock in the evening. We are talking of thousands attending, popping out for a quick lunch on the church campus not wanting to miss anything that God was doing. Many hours in church services that the majority of the people considered too short, only because they were seeing the power of God in action.

The word of God grew, multiplied and prevailed (Acts 19:10. Acts 19:20). Because of the nature of this African pastor's pastoral and prophetic ministry, his sermons were utterly revelatory. I cannot but hold the conviction that Paul's preaching and teaching must have been the same, only more so. In Lagos this pastor's teaching went beyond what we would call normal. What he delivered by way of preaching was uncommon, as opposed to common gospel preaching. I have heard many visitors from western type churches say that at first hearing, the sermons were too simple. Many of them would later return and say that although when the addresses were heard they seemed so much like a young child's Sunday School lesson, nevertheless they had never stopped thinking about the lesson's content since they had heard it. This makes the anecdotal self-evident point that the man with revelation is never at the mercy of the man who merely has academic insight. Revelation built on orthodox Christian truth was the secret to winning thousands to the kingdom. This African pastor was totally orthodox in his belief system and teaching. I have never met anybody who has attended the church he pastored say anything different. I have heard many criticise him who had never been to hear him or meet him. I know these things because of debates and discussions I have had with many Nigerian pastors.

Acts tells us that the whole of Asia heard the word (Acts 19:10). The same syndrome has worked with the preaching, teaching and signs and wonders done in Lagos. The news that God was saving, healing and delivering people in huge numbers brought folks from all over the world to Lagos. Many African states especially have masses suffering with unspeakable diseases that have no GP's (Doctors), no National Health System, no hospital within many miles, and no natural hope of recovery. There are times when some of the most shocking and abominable sicknesses that Africans had contracted, had been left to develope because of advice and practices of witch doctors and so called "ogbanjes" ("agents of satan."). Having sought out as many means as possible and failed, as a last resort, being told that they are near to death, and/or incurable, they heard about the ministry in Ikotun Egbe in Lagos where the "incurables" were "cured", and those that were near to death receive resurrection. People came, sometimes, from hundreds and even thousands of miles away across Africa seeking healing and restoration, knowing full well that they were to meet with Christ.

Paul must have had a healing line (Acts 19:11-12). Either that, or he spent hours calling out the healings from the platform. When Paul says he ministered in "the demonstration of the Spirit" (1 Corinthians 2:4-5), the word "to demonstrate," in Greek, means literally, "to point out." Whether prayer line, or prophetic pointing out for the healings, there must have been a forum at some point of the service for healing to take place, for demons to be cast out, and for prophecies to be shared. This takes time, organisation and incredible precision by the minister and his team. And Paul had a team.

Paul had his, "about twelve," as his team along with Timothy and Erastus, who were "two of his helpers" (Acts 19:9, 19:22). My African mentor constantly stated that if it wasn't for the organising team, and the administration department that coached the crowds, the perfect order of the hugely attended services would be a shambles. Team is a very practical, but huge issue in the context of biblical evangelism.

No matter how much arranging and organisation there is, and there has to be lots, the people who were burning their occult books in

Ephesus, along with the secrets of the magical arts and the occult, were undoubtedly witches and wizards (Acts 19:18-19).

Not wanting to insult the readers intelligence, but Witches and Wizards do not attend church services with the intention of coming out for prayer. The vast majority of them come to kill or curse the minister or members of his team (John 10:10). The only witches or wizards that I ever saw in a prayer line, were those who had life threatening diseases to which they knew no cure, or an ulterior motive to tap into the power they see at work (Acts 8:9-24). These witch doctors that were commonly prophetically discovered in prayer lines, were mostly stricken ill by the demons they were serving and subject to. They entered the prayer line claiming to be Christians from other churches. Countless Muslims did the same, attending the prayer line giving westernised Christian names to impress people that they were something that they definitely were not. It was not that the senior pastor/prophet wouldn't pray for them because they were not Christians. That simply would never happen. He would pray for anybody who asked for prayer regardless of their state or position, their religious beliefs or lack of them. Prophetically, as far as I ever saw, he always knew when people were lying about themselves. My point is, that there had to be some forum, as well as some spontaneous space in the course of the service, where these kind of people that were sat in the midst of the congregation could be called out, sometimes called out by name, and then healed, delivered or prophesied to. Some of the manifestations were formally asked for by people. Some were in need of being called out because they were frightened or ashamed to reveal their problem. As in Lagos, it must surely have been in Ephesus.

I observed also, that the generals of the occult, the witches and the wizards, only turned up because they had been losing support because of what my mentoring pastor was doing in the realm of deliverance and healing. Some of them explained afterwards that they were being reduced to poverty and being made unimportant in their country villages because too many had been to hear him preach, and/or be prayed for by him, and then they came home free from the diseases and curses that they had put on people, testifying to anybody who would hear them. That is exactly how I believe the word of God grew and multiplied, and mightily prevailed in Asia, for this is how the word has spread throughout southern Nigeria. Word of mouth from people who have tasted the power of God to set them free has intrinsic power. I believe the same thing happened in Ephesus where many were turning to Christ because of what was seen and heard of the gospel (Acts 19:17-19) and discussed and gossiped out on the streets.

What am I saying? The big people in occult circles, those that were made rich by the occult and held huge influence over many people, would only brave exposing themselves to the ministry of the senior pastor where I was working when they were desperately losing their livelihood and practice, or even their own lives. Paul must have delivered a lot of people, cast out hundreds of demons, to have the "big boys" attend his meetings, and finally get set free themselves, whether they came looking for freedom, or not. The manifestation of the power of God creates awe, injects faith, and sets the adrenalin running in the joy of all the congregants present. To say the excitement is real in such circumstances is a huge understatement.

The book of Acts tells us that these witches and wizards made public confessions concerning their evil deeds (Acts 19:18). Having, myself heard many witches and wizards (probably into three figures) make confession and full explanations of their lives in the occult, I assert that the educational value of hearing how they operated and what their goals were, was priceless. In the realm of the spirit I believe these people, at the height of their evil, were going far deeper in the occult and the devil, than most Christians ever dare to do with Christ. Thankfully they came under the influence of a man who had gone deeper, if not deepest with the Saviour.

In Acts they burned their books (Acts 19:19-20), in Lagos I witnessed animals used for occult purpose screeching as the utensils and tools of witch doctors were burned and the demons in the animals fled. The burning of the books, and their complete confession in public, was very much an integral part of their deliverance in the Acts narrative. The same was practiced in Lagos, only instead of books, it was charms and amulets that needed destroying.

I always observed and remembered ever so clearly, 100% of the time, that when witches, wizards and ogbanjes were delivered, they walked around with an air of unspeakable peace and tranquillity immediately after the act of deliverance. It was visibly astonishing to see. Wild uncontrollable men and women, became quiet, serene and lovely Christian people as Christ took control of their lives.

The build-up of deliverance after deliverance, finally attracting the witches and wizards to come and try and stop the pastor, had a similar syndrome with the glorious phenomena of healing. The more that received healing, the more it was talked about, and the more people came with worse and ever worse diseases. I always had conflicting thoughts about this way of things. I sometimes thought that the devil was sending sicknesses that were more and more incurable to tempt the pastor and the anointing on his life. Other times I perceived it as part of the development of his anointing, and how it just elevated his authority to handle the abominable sicknesses that I saw with my own eyes. I personally never saw anybody walk away unhealed. That is my true testimony. I am witness to the fact that skin complaints that even revealed the bones beneath, were healed with two or three days, after the pain left immediately after prayer. Some skin diseases were so sensitive that people had been living almost stark naked for years because they couldn't bear to have clothes touch them. I saw people in this condition immediately being free from pain, and being completely normalised within days. I saw growths and tumours that defy description, healed. I witnessed cancerous growths literally liquefy before my eyes. When things like this are happening on a very regular basis, is it any wonder that people don't want to go home even after several hours of this kind of apostolic church.

I say these things to make three points. Firstly, the constant exercising and working of the anointing on a person's life increases the dependability and strength of that anointing, in whatever dimension that anointing might be. Secondly, if lack of modern medical means, and the preponderance of occult practitioners leads to such monstrous manifestations of sickness in modern day Africa, why should it not have been exactly the same in Ephesus in the first century, in precisely the same circumstances? Thirdly, there must have been lots and lots of, "ordinary" miracles before the "extraordinary" miracles started to manifest. The daily pounding against the gates of hell started at one level and escalated as my two to three years progressed. After all, this was war. The enemy upped the ante until he was aware he had lost the confrontation.

Acts 19 gives more space to the process of deliverance and its impact on the Asian and Ephesian population than any other aspect of Paul's mission (Deliverance explained from Acts 19:11-20). The demons were not cast out in a private room away from the crowds. It was not perceived as the Cinderella of the ministry process, but a major plank of the truth of the power of the gospel and the authority of Jesus Christ. Deliverance is truly the bread and butter of the ministry, not the extreme icing on a cake that can only be eaten by a few. There are more demonic issues in people's lives, saved and unsaved, than we acknowledge. In the west we turn blind eyes to things demonic and substitute counselling for the ministry of the miraculous. God help us and take us to where such ministry becomes commonplace. God grant us both His power and His authority.

Paul was copied (Acts 19:13). Jewish exorcists attended Paul's meetings at the school of Tyrannus to see how he did it, and then went out to do the same things themselves. The astonishing thing was that prior to Christ casting out demons with a word, such ministry was unthinkable. Mantras and biblical quotes, incense and prayer were commonly used to exorcise both homes and people. Paul, in the power of the Holy Spirit, and in the authority of Christ cast them out simply by his word. So the seven sons of Sceva tried the same. It is amazing to note, that for a certain length of time, it worked. The fact that it says, "One day," suggests that they had done it many times previous with total success. It was a demonic quoted response that brought the fear of the Lord.

Just as Paul was emulated in ministry, so is the man of God I was with in Nigeria. His phrases, his manner of stretching out his hand, his custom of sometimes just touching the person in the prayer line without a word being spoken, and the resultant incredible success of seeing folks healed has led to many pastors worldwide to pray in the same way, with the same language, and the same bodily manner. Right or wrong, good or bad, of God or not, I have no judgement. I merely make the observation that as it was with Paul, so it was with this man of God in Ikotun Egbe in Lagos.

It seems that the astonishing thing about the time the sons of Sceva were stripped and sent running was the fact that the demon cried out, "Jesus I know, and Paul I know" (Acts 19:15). The words would have left people breathless at the thought of, "Who is this man called Paul, that even the demons know him?" Yet again, the same things happened in Lagos, and the biblical account parallels what I have seen and heard in Africa. Demons acknowledging the authority of Christ through a man of God, and saying so, is, as far as I am aware, a totally unknown and unheard of feature on the landscape of western Christianity.

Yet in the midst of this, it wasn't Paul's name that was glorified, but the name of Jesus Christ (Acts 19:17). This aspect, yet again, is mirrored in what I myself have experienced. I have memories of seeing my past mentor in Lagos turn away from people who have so much as hinted that it was he who had healed them. "You blaspheme me in order to shame me!" I have heard him say, as he has turned his back on people just to make the point. "I am not the Healer. Jesus Christ is the Healer." This was a daily statement heard around the huge fellowship in Africa. Whenever an extraordinarily spectacular miracle took place, like a blind person instantly seeing, I would observe him disappear for a few moments so that the excitement would not centre on him, and the worship group would be asked to sing a particularly Christ glorifying song. It was my conviction that because of Acts 19:17, my mentor and friend followed the example modelled by the apostle Paul.

"In this way, the word of the Lord grew mightily and prevailed." "In this way?" In what way? The way of deliverance, and healing the sick. There is much more I could say, but I have stated enough to create a word picture of what I believe things were like in the days of Paul's mission to take Ephesus for Christ. It was a daily manifestation of the power of God, with biblical teaching that supported what they were seeing. In fact, the scripture puts it the other way around stating, "Signs and wonders followed the preaching of the word." (Mark 16:20).

I have written this chapter because I was not present in Ephesus, but I have played a part, no matter how brief or trivial, with a man of God that moved in a manner, no matter how much more reduced, similar to Paul. I suppose that orthodoxy demands that I subscribe to the view that Paul's anointing was greater than anybody who has moved in healing, deliverance and prophecy since. That would mean that Paul's venturing into those areas excelled what I have seen. Perhaps I am understating, therefore, what I think it was like in Ephesus.

All I know is, that as a result of this kind of ministry, ex witchdoctors are now men of God leading churches. People who were dying of Aids are now completely whole and healed and some of them travelling far and wide with their testimony. There is a church that I know, more than any other I have been a part of, that is built on the power of God, and not in the wisdom of men. And all these things scream at me about what was happening in Ephesus while Paul was there.

18.

PAUL A "BOND-SLAVE" "A SERVANT" (ACTS 19:22. ACTS 20:18-20)

"After these things were ended, Paul purposed in the spirit, when he had passed through Macedonia and Achaia to go to Jerusalem, saying, after I have been there, I must also see Rome. So he sent into Macedonia two of them that ministered to him, Timothy and Erastus; but he stayed in Asia for a season"

(Acts 19:21-22).

[My thesis in this chapter is simple. Paul was baptised in the Holy Spirit and was utterly submitted to Jesus Christ. Having received the anointing of the Spirit, he lived a life that maintained the power that was given him through that baptism. The fullness of the baptism is generally understated and under rated in many Pentecostal circles. Because precious few walk in the fullness as received, they live a life beneath their true privilege. The attitude of "bond-slave" to Christ meant that the relationship between Christ and Paul had expressions that were purely from God's activity and manifestation, however at the same time, Paul's own character and personality in relationships was obvious. The ultimate example of a man in Christ, his attitude to God, ministry and people is seen in the biblical biography of Paul.

There is no "superior" attitude about the apostle. He did not have a special clique that surrounded him yet he attracted friends and loyal friendship not at all demanding respect or position. The grace on him in one manner was obviously unique. The authority he had in the realm of the Spirit, and insight into God's dealings was such that 2,000 years later the church of Christ is still searching the full depth of meanings in what he thought and wrote. He did not surround himself with unlearned youth to dominate and rule. Yes, of course, he must have had some youth with him, those to whom he could pass on the baton for the next generation. However he had married couples, professional people, like doctors around him. He had people who are referred to as being part of a "household," suggesting that the majority of his team and travelling companions were mature both in life skills and in Christ. He was meek and gentle with people, and people surrounded him. His gregarious nature and the full depth of his relationship with so many, informs us that Paul did not need to be some withdrawn "hermit" kind of man in order to fulfil his call and be what God had called him to be. It is my conviction that his friends and relationship circle was part of the secret of his dynamism. That is why this is an important part of his commitment to Christ, and a vital dimension of his activity in the realm of the supernatural and his management of the miraculous.]

Paul called himself a "Bond-Servant of Jesus Christ" in Romans 1:1. The Greek word is famously "doulos." There were slaves of different privileges and levels, but "doulos" was the lowest of the low. A doulos was simply owned by another as a horse or a cart would be, and utterly without rights. A person who owned a doulos could kill their slave, mame them and/or abuse them, and no one in Roman society would even blink. The person that was a doulos was almost non-human when it came to rights or privileges. All the historians of Paul's era, as well as through the ages assert that in the Roman Empire at this time, there were more slaves than free men in the population. Twenty-first century human rights organisations would have had a field day if they were transposed to the first century when the apostles were alive.

The incredible point about Paul referring to himself as a slave of Christ, is that he was so by an absolute choice of free will. He had of his own volition, joyfully, as an act of faith, chosen to be, "not his own." It was a wilful surrender of his right to be his own person. I know all truth loving evangelicals and Pentecostals preach and teach about being Christ's doulos, but Paul took its meaning to a level rarely emulated, or even understood.

This writer believes that this choice, this choosing to deny himself in such a basic way, was a result of his being baptised in the Holy Spirit, and thereafter was continually being filled with the same Spirit. The anointing that had come upon him to lead others into the baptism of the Holy Spirit (Acts 19:1-6), left him fully open and ready to sell all he was for Christ. It is because of Paul's explained and demonstrated Modus Operandi in his Epistles and in the Acts of the Apostles, that I see the Holy Spirit Baptism as a must for all and any practising Christians. The sole reason given for the baptism into the Holy Spirit is power for witnessing for the living and resurrected Christ. The true baptism experience of the Holy Spirit does not leave a person's spirit free to choose as they previously did *per se*. Unless the Spirit of God is in any way restrained within a person's processes of choosing, the Spirit of God runs riotously free in a human life that is surrendered to God and has their human spirit immersed on an ongoing and permanent basis in the Holy Spirit. And this is exactly how Paul lived his life.

It is Christ that baptises the believer in the Holy Spirit. Because it is Christ's baptism, it is a wholly divine enabling and empowering of the believer to live the Christ like life. It is this writer's opinion that baptism in the Holy Spirit is the highest and sublimest evidence of Christ's power and goodness in a believer's life. When God's power comes upon the believer as it did on the disciples on the day of Pentecost, everything about that receiving believer will be affected by the depth of intimacy now realised in the Holy Spirit in their immersion in Him.

God's anointing came upon Paul when he was baptised in the Holy Spirit, just as it does with all who are similarly baptised. Anointing is performed by God Himself. Holy Spirit Anointing is, in the realm of the spirit, what anointing with oil is in the physical. When Samuel poured an entire rams horn filled with oil the young shepherd boy, it would have soaked David from head to toe and made his clothes and body smell of that fragrant oil for days, if not longer. When God anoints a man or a woman to a calling or gift, it simply becomes part of that person's reason for living. The anointing breaks the yoke, and that is what New Testament ministry is all about, i.e. breaking the yokes that proliferate in people's lives. The manifestation of the power of the Holy Spirit that goes beyond the preaching of the gospel, and heals the sick, cleanses the lepers, and grants the power of deliverance as well as prophetic insight, is the veritable seal of authenticity in Christ, and authority in the Spirit. It is Paul that says "Be healed!" but it is God embodied in the anointing that does the healing. It is Paul that says to the demons, "Out in the name of Jesus!" It is the anointing that flows with Paul's words that facilitates Christ's expulsion of the demon. It is the anointing of God that supplies the prophetic insight, as God relates intimately to the one anointed. It is Paul that speaks the prophecy, seemingly, to the unlearned, picking the thought out of the air.

But anointing is not just for Peter, Paul and other apostolic figures. The baptism in the Holy Spirit is the anointing. Christians need to work and exercise that anointing to discover if there is a particular gift embedded in the anointing that rests on them through their baptism. In this way, a Christian is to be under the influence and control of the Holy Spirit in the same way that a drunkard is under the control and influence of alcohol and liquor. It is dominant, but unseen. When a believer receives the Holy Spirit, a sense of security, blessing and victory will permeate one's being and impact beyond the grave. As alcohol causes one to lose their presence of mind, so the Holy Spirit works the opposite way and sharpens the human sensibilities and understanding. Anointing, carried and manifested in a person possessed of Christ-like character is absolutely everything. When one receives the Holy Spirit, the joy and peace the scriptures so often speak about will become a reality in one's life.

Any believer can receive the baptism in the Holy Spirit, in fact, millions have, but it takes character to maintain the full impact of that gift. The baptism in the Holy Spirit is about power, it is not so much about character. Submission and obedience to the word breeds character. Jesus said to the twelve that they were clean through the word He had given them. The seeds of character were there in that word, but no power to walk in that cleansed state. When Christ-like character receives the baptism in the Holy Spirit, we have in skeletal form what the apostle Paul had. My observation of Christian circles is that power without character results in fringe extremism that attracts inappropriate behaviour, and is unsustainable for sound church life. Character without the power, leads to a very straight-jacketed brand of Christianity that rationalises the miraculous in the Bible into symbols and signs. It solidifies into Pharisaic legalism. Power, however, married to character, leads to authentic and authoritative Christianity. That is where the bulk of the New Testament church was. A man, or woman, with the power of the Holy Spirit indwelling together with the ever developing character of Christ will rise to leadership as sure as cream rises to the top of the milk. This was clearly where Paul was.

Paul had the baptism and the power that we are talking of, the character and the wisdom that we are referring to, and he worked the anointing that was given him unceasingly until it was part of his very nature. Whatever the nature of a person's anointing is, it needs working at, tweaking, improving and perfecting. Peter fed Christ's sheep in Acts chapters two and three, but that gift had not been honed, and the anointing had not been worked. He was an incredible overcomer because of his revelling in the impact of the cleansing of Christ, the ongoing power of his testimony, and the veritable truth that he was conscious of, and that he loved not his life in the face of death. He didn't invite death. He wasn't foolishly wanting death to come. But he was fanatically wanting to live like Christ and obey everything he received from heaven. He was aware that to live a life like Christ, would cause him to have to die a death like Christ. That concept did not shake his conviction, nor cause him to waver in his obedience.

Because of his deliberately chosen "Slave – Master" relationship with Christ, Paul not only loved company and friendship, but was loved by many that joined his company, and gained many friends who actively drew close to him.

My thesis about Paul's period in Ephesus being the utter peak of apostolic ministry as presented in the Bible, includes this aspect of Paul's serving. He was often surrounded by people in the midst of the incredible outbreak and manifestation of the power of God in Ephesus, and the ripples that soaked the entire Roman Province of Asia. It is my belief that, apart from a short period during the 2-3 years he was in Ephesus, he was surrounded by men and women to whom he ministered continually simply be making himself a spectacle and example of Holy Spirit living.

As the days, weeks and months progressed, the word of God kept on growing in its reception. The numbers of those who came to faith went "through the roof." Power healings and the miraculous power of Christ was seen by more and more, and many of the wicked and degenerate of Ephesus and its surrounds became new creatures in Christ.

Grasp the picture. We have a word image that is built up on the grounds of the plain statements of scripture, and my belief that Paul's stay in Ephesus was the mountain peak of Paul's ministry, as well as the most maximised achievement of apostolic ministry overall. We are seeing the apostle to the gentiles conducting his tent making occupation and, in so doing, making enough money to feed and look after those that were "with him" (Acts 20:34). Readers might be somewhat astonished by the time we finish this section of our thoughts, to see how many companions Paul had with him whilst he was in Ephesus. We also understand from the book of Acts that he was holding at least a 5 hour "service" every day in the school of Tyrannus (Acts 19:9 Amplified Bible). I put "service," in quotation marks deliberately, as I venture to suggest that with, discussions, debates, deliverance, prophecy and healing occurring on a regular basis, if not daily, to think of a 5 hour service as most westerners conceive of a church service, is absolutely as far as the east is from the west, from what went on in the school of Tyrannus.

There was also Paul's daily venturing out into the homes of both Jews and gentiles sharing truth and grace with all that would allow him to. The context of Acts 20, suggests that those visits were to converts who were already believers, but undoubtedly, as is the norm, even today, he would be meeting unbelievers of all shapes and hues in those homes. There must have been those who wanted to meet him for good reasons or bad. Paul was definitely famous (or in the eyes of some, infamous) at this period of time. The whole of Asia heard the Word while Paul was there. His networking skills must have attracted thousands of the equivalent of modern Facebook friends, meaning, people who met him just so they could tell others that they knew Paul from Tarsus.

What was this man? Superman? Driven? Workaholic? Or, was he just living the normal Christian life, as it is, when lived in the fullness of the power of the Holy Spirit? I am sure many will merely fob off this challenging thought that I raise, with the old cliché, "Well! It was different with Paul. He was a chosen vessel, with a very special calling!" I feel sure that the second sentence is a truth absolute. The first statement however is, frankly, "cowardice in the face of the enemy." Paul had a 24 hour day and a seven day week like the rest of us. On the basis of what I have read from some commentator's, it is vaguely possible that I have now lived life longer than the time Paul spent in his mortal coil. On the basis that I have spent my life fighting issues of laziness, and a dreaded inner compulsion that screams to me, "Why do it today, if it can wait till tomorrow?" I cannot help but assert, no matter how much it crucifies and condemns me, that Paul's experience is what we should consider the norm. Details of his Christian life in scripture are intended to inspire us to emulation, and not spectate merely, in awe as we grasp the greatness of what he achieved. The whole issue of God's motive in giving us the Bible is to read it and say, I need to be like Paul, or anybody else that we read of who is virtuous. Christ, of course, is the ultimate bench mark for us to emulate and strive towards.

It sounds a little ludicrous, knowing that Paul was making tents, ministering the word in power, and visiting homes every day, to ask another strange question, but I want to know: What else did he do whilst in Ephesus? And: If he did anything else, how on earth can we know it? How did he fit it in his schedule? I know typewriters and high rise office blocks had not yet been conceived of in Paul's day, but surely with an operation that was impacting so many, he must have had something that was equivalent to an office in his day, or had "admin' staff" around him.

Paul did lots of other stuff while he was turning Ephesus and the whole of Asia to Christ. He still had those twelve disciples to tutor, so he was running what we would today, call a "Bible College," as well as a "Tent Making Company," and a very active "Evangelistic Association". I have to add that I am sure it was nothing like any Bible College that I or my readers know about. On top of all this, he definitely wrote one lengthy letter to the church at Corinth. And in days where computers and word processors were sheer science-fiction, as were pens and a smooth plain writing pad, the sixteen chapters of first Corinthians, written by quill on rough parchment was not exactly like the few moments it takes to send a text message around the world from a mobile phone. It must have taken several days, possibly weeks to write what we refer to as, "Paul's First letter to the Corinthians," given the previously stated facts of his normal daily routine.

All academic authorities are absolutely certain that First Corinthians was written in the midst of Paul's mission to Asia, from Ephesus. It doesn't take a degree in research to know this, simply because it says so in the letter itself (1 Cor 16:8). Paul was clearly at Ephesus as he was writing to say, "A great door and effective work, has been opened to me" (1 Cor 16:9). Our point for mentioning First Corinthians is that there are insights given to us concerning who came to visit Paul briefly and who came to stay, who left Ephesus and who was helping Paul, what letters were written, and what letters were received, during those days of Acts 19. Some of these issues are made clear by other scriptures also. We shall take note as to their significance.

Let me just throw in at this juncture, one more matter. Even though some things are settled unequivocally, some other issues are theorised as settled, but, for us, today, not one hundred percent certain. I am specifically thinking of the fascinating perspective that is fast becoming the accepted academic point of view, that some of Paul's "prison letters," that have hitherto usually been considered to have been written very late in Paul's life, whilst he was imprisoned in Rome, are now being understood to have been written whilst imprisoned in Ephesus. It is mainly the conclusions of a scholar named Helmut Koester that are the driving force behind this new acceptance. But those that give his idea support make a very strong case

"But," you cry, "Acts does not mention Paul being imprisoned whilst in Ephesus! So how can this be?"

I have earlier noted, in these pages, how obvious it is, that there are lots of occurrences and situations that the apostle's Paul and Peter went through, and referred to in their epistles which are just not in Acts or anywhere else. The book of Acts tells us the things that Luke was told. I take it as simply read, that Luke's account is scanty and brief, with possibly lots of stories and catastrophe's, in Paul's life especially, just not mentioned.

Paul's letters to the Philippian church, and his notelet to his friend Philemon in Colossae, head the list of those pieces of scripture now considered to have been written from Paul's Ephesian prison. I personally have to add that I cannot see how Philemon could have been written from Ephesus, without adding the Colossian letter to the list, whether it was written from prison or not. Those two letters were undoubtedly despatched together.

By taking note of some of the personal intimations of friendships, and the comings and goings from that single epistle that was definitely written from Ephesus (First Corinthians), and those others that are *now* being considered to have been written from Ephesus, we should be able to sketch a picture of how many people sat around Paul's supper table, or Mission board room, at the end of any particular day during his time in Ephesus.

So where do we start?

First of all we understand that Paul entered Ephesus with both Timothy and Erastus. Although it is not specifically stated that they were there at the start of Acts 19, Timothy is seen as Paul's most constant and consistent protégé, and as he is mentioned as being sent off to Macedonia together with Erastus from Ephesus (Acts 19:22), we conclude that they were with him from the start of the time in Acts 19. By default, we affirm that at the entry into Asia, Paul's evangelistic band numbered possibly three, i.e. Paul, Timothy and Erastus.

As he entered the suburbs of Ephesus, at the beginning of Acts 19, there were those disciples of John the Baptist that Paul encountered. They seem to have, thereafter, accompanied Paul during the entire two to three years in this great outreach. These twelve (or so) zealous, spiritual men, successful candidates for baptism in both water and the Holy Spirit, accompanied Paul during those opening three months in the synagogue. It actually says that Paul took "the disciples" with him (Acts 19:9). This phrase, say some, refers to all the converts Paul had hitherto made in the Synagogue. However, it could not refer to such a large crowd when, in Acts 19:30 Luke tells us that it was "the disciples," that stopped Paul from taking the platform in the midst of the Silversmith's riot. It seems that this dozen or so men, had influence with Paul, such was the relationship he had gained with them as a father in Christ. Nor could the term refer to the entire church gathering when, in Acts 20:1 Paul called "the disciples" to him, in order to say "Farewell!" This writer is convinced that the word "disciples," when used in the narrative of Acts 19, concerning Ephesus and the Ephesian church, refers to those men Paul met in Acts 19: 1-6. So I extrapolate that there was at least Paul and fourteen others as the mission began to gain momentum.

Then there were the married couple Aquila and Priscilla. Early Christian tradition insists that they were part of the 70 that Christ sent out ministering. So they were a mature, stable couple. Paul had met them in Corinth and accompanied them on his first visit to Ephesus (Acts 18:18). They lived, worked and travelled with Paul for a period. This couple tutored Apollos, the preacher who was mighty in the scriptures, teaching him some sound doctrine before he went off to ply his God given anointing in the church at Corinth. They seem to have lived in Ephesus up to the time when Paul wrote to the Roman church, when they were at that time living in the great capital (Romans 16:3-4). We know for certain they were in Ephesus with Paul because of 1 Corinthians 16:19. (See also Acts 18:2-3. Acts 18:18-19. Acts 18:26. And 2 Timothy 4:19.). They were in Ephesus no doubt two leading Christians in the church as it was when Paul turned up in Acts 19:1. So right at the commencement of the mission, we are now understanding that Paul had a team of around sixteen people around him. Aquila and his wife were so committed to Paul that they risked their lives for the great apostle. It says so in Romans 16. For that reason I say that they must have been in Paul's inner circle.

Anymore?

The first convert in any mission is prone to become closely attached to the team and the workers. And would you believe it, Romans 16:5 tells us who the first convert was in the province of Asia. I suppose that it could possibly have been a soul-winning venture prior to Paul's entrance into Ephesus, within the borders of Asia, however, the fact that, after the whole of Asia hearing the word of God, Paul still remembers Epenetus (spelt differently in different versions) and refers to him as a, "dear friend," as well as "the first convert in Asia," is greatly indicative as to the relationship Paul and he had built up whilst the apostle was in Ephesus. I know that this does not necessarily mean that Epenetus actually stayed with Paul, but I am including him in the team of companions that surrounded the apostle during these relevant days, because of the relationship stated in Romans. So now, by our reckoning, Paul, potentially, had the possibility of seventeen in his Holy Spirit mission team.

Another man who was there to support and stand by Paul, whilst he went through the trials and stresses of building the church in Ephesus, was Onesiphorus. I think I would have loved this man if I had met him. 2 Timothy 1:16-18 tells us quite a bit about his character. Onesiphorus refreshed Paul quite often. Whether that refreshment was food and drink, or prayer and encouragement, Onesiphorus was a man who Paul could count on. On top of that he was not ashamed to visit Paul in prison and identify with Paul whilst he was in chains. Seemingly he arrived in Rome while Paul was imprisoned there – or was Paul referring to the time he was imprisoned in Ephesus? Whichever city it was, Onesiphorus went looking for Paul, to find out where it was that the authorities had put him. Yes, indeed, if I can in the corner of my thoughts identify with Paul, Onesiphorus would be way up near the top of my favourite people. In 2 Timothy 1:17 Paul prays for this brother's eternal blessing, and then says something to Timothy that has always startled me. "You know very well how much he helped me in Ephesus." Wow! Onesiphorus, it seems, was a minister par excellence in Ephesus! We are all called either to serve a people, or a person. Onesiphorus, whatever else he did, was called to minister to Paul. He was one of the great sources of blessing Paul had enjoyed, especially whilst he was in Ephesus. We therefore declare that number eighteen in the circle, is the lovely brother, Onesiphorus. I have to also scratch my head pondering whether or not he was one of the "about twelve" in Acts 19:1-6.

We are aware from what is said at the end of Acts 18 and the beginning of Acts 19 that Apollos, the rising star in the preaching world at that time, was wowing the believers in Corinth as Paul entered Ephesus. He was obviously a great inspirational character and preacher. It is the opinion of some that it was he that wrote the letter to the Hebrews. When the members of the Corinthian church problematically started breaking off into "fan club" sort of cliques, along with those who supported Paul and those that supported Peter, there was also those that supported Apollos. He was therefore, obviously, very well received in Corinth, held in esteem that matched Peter and Paul. He must have returned to Ephesus some time during Paul's mission. We are not told when. He was there, however, in the room whilst Paul was writing the line that we refer to as 1 Corinthians 16:12. Paul wrote that he was encouraging Apollos to return to Corinth with the three men from Corinth who were returning there with the letter that we refer to as 1 Corinthians. Apollos, however, did not want to go back at that moment. And no wonder! I think I would have wanted to stay in Ephesus at that time, to hear, study and learn from Paul's ministry, especially as he was moving so much in divine power as he was in Ephesus. So for our team registration for the Ephesian Mission, Apollos was definitely Paul's nineteenth team member in Ephesus. I am impressed also very much by the fact that Paul had not the slightest tinge of jealousy to Apollos being praised for his silver tongue.

Number twenty on the Paul's list of confidantes was a man called Sosthenes. I feel I am on safe ground including him in the list of board members as he and Paul actually wrote First Corinthians together, and First Corinthians was written in Ephesus. In the midst of the pressures of life with Paul making tents, building Christians up in their faith, holding 5 hour daily meetings and visiting people every day, somewhere, at some time, Paul sat down with this fellow Sosthenes and wrote the forty sixth book of the Bible (1 Corinthians 1:1). Whether Sosthenes was simply the amanuensis that wrote as Paul dictated, or whether he made any contribution to the substance of the letter, we will probably never know. I suggest that to play such a role, even if he was only present because of his writing skills, demands the extrapolation that this man was amongst those that were running the mission in Ephesus. Was Sosthenes an Ephesian? Was he one of the twelve perhaps, that Paul came across in Acts 19:1-6? Is it at all possible that he could have been the same Sosthenes who was once leader of the Synagogue in Corinth (Acts 18:12-17)? If he was, it would mean that having been beaten up by his own people for not having a proper charge to bring against Paul whilst the apostle was in Corinth, he later was converted and became a close associate and brother in Christ with the man he once tried to get Gallio to execute. It is a fascinating exploratory thought. Most academics reckon that the Acts 18 story is too extreme for the man in 1 Corinthians 1:1 to be the same. I have no idea what the truth is, but I would not be surprised at all if it was the same man.

And, we are not finished yet!

Numbers twenty one and two to add to our register are Gaius and Aristarchus, both from Macedonia. These two Christian men were so dominant in the group that when the silversmith's held their riot, in an effort to express their anger, and in Paul's absence, they grabbed these two as a token of their spite towards Paul (Acts 19:28- 31). For this, I believe that these were two important men, in association with Paul. In an attempt to see them released from any danger, it was at that very moment when Gaius and Aristarchus were being dragged into the theatre that Paul stepped forward and was about to confront the frenzied masses. "The disciples," however, stopped Paul from making himself known. Paul was obviously no coward, but for the sake of his mortal safety, the twelve, or members of the twelve disciples held Paul back. Paul's day had not yet come.

This character Gaius is a very interesting man in Paul's life. Firstly, according to 1 Corinthians 1:14, Gaius was one of the few that Paul actually baptised in water, along with another man called Crispus. Although baptised in the context of Corinth, Acts 20:4-6 gives me the impression that "Gaius from Derbe," accompanying Paul, was the same man as is mentioned in Acts19:29. Romans tells us that Paul was staying with Gaius while he wrote the letter to the Christians in the Roman capital (16:23). If it wasn't for the fact that the academics reckon 3 John was written so far in the future from Acts 19, I, personally, would be tempted to assert that the church leader that the Apostle John names as Gaius, in 3 John 1 was the same person that we are talking about here. Very interesting, to be sure. However, Gaius of Macedonia was definitely a leading light in Paul's travelling evangelistic team.

Aristarchus the Macedonian was from Thessalonica in Macedonia (Acts 27:2). Acts 20:4 tells us he was travelling with Paul later, as the apostle was moving from Greece back to Asia. Colossians 4:10 and Philemon 24 actually tell us that Aristarchus was a fellow prisoner with Paul (in Rome? Or Ephesus?). For that reason I include him in Paul's inner circle here in Ephesus.

Paul and a team of twenty two is definite and cannot be argued with. But there were possibly more.

If the idea of Paul being imprisoned in Ephesus is a sound one, and if Colossians was written from an Ephesian cell and not a Roman cell we have further discoveries.

Paul did not visit Colossae. Epaphras was the evangelist cum-pastor who founded the body of believers in a city that was about a hundred miles due East of Ephesus. If the premise we are discussing is a factual one, it would make sense that Epaphras would have been seconded out from Ephesus from the midst of the main mission, and started a similar church plant in Colossae. Again I ponder: Was Epaphras one of the twelve baptised in the Holy Spirit in Acts 19:1-6? Any answer is pure speculation. However, going along, tentatively with this accepted scenario, I would suggest that Epaphras was therefore, possibly team member twenty-three. Epaphras being there in Colossae, and Paul's ownership of the fatherhood of their faith (see Col 1:24-25. 2:1-2) suggests a much more appropriate and relevant ground for Paul to explain how he had sent Epaphras to them from the same province, as he was still in Ephesus, though in prison. The thought of a man from distant Rome who supposedly was an isolated prisoner in a Roman dungeon who was somehow identifying with people he had never seen and had no part with, has often stretched my mind as not credible.

Colossians 4:7-9 talks of Tychicus being sent to Colossae to minister to them. This man, says Paul, was a faithful minister of Christ. Again I say, if the premise of Colossians being written from Ephesus is correct, I would add Tychicus to the circle of friends with Paul. We now have a group of Paul and twenty four others.

Aristarchus was in prison with Paul when Colossians was written, and Mark (John-Mark) the cousin of Barnabas was, or so it seems, visiting them in their cell. Paul tells them to receive Mark if he turned up at Colossae, yet he was present with Paul as he wrote. Perhaps his going to Colossae had not yet been decided upon, but was being discussed (Col 4:10). That is questionably, yet reasonably, number twenty five in the list of lodgers with Paul.

There follows a trio of names of folks who were with him, who were either prisoners, or at least visiting Paul and identifying with his chains. A man whose name was Jesus whose alias was Justus a Jewish believer was present. Luke who wrote Acts and the gospel that bears his name, and Demas were also there. Demas unfortunately deserted Paul at a later date. Whether that means that he also deserted his faith we are not told. All these names are also added as sending their greetings to Philemon in the brief letter that bears his name. This would suggest that over and above the twenty two "definites" who were part of Paul's gang, we have a total of twenty eight names of folks who were part of Paul's life whilst in Ephesus. The last six are premised on a scenario that is quickly becoming the accepted fact, i.e. that Colossians and Philemon were written from Ephesus.

In the midst of all these people coming, going, staying and sharing with Paul we have three more to add to the list. These three were definitely not part of Paul's team in Ephesus, but there is a good chance that they became part of Paul's team whilst he was in Corinth.

It was anything between a year and three years since Paul had left Corinth having founded the church there in an eighteen month mission. Apollos had been preaching and teaching for a while. Problems had arisen within the interaction of all the believers. My opinion is that even though the problems arose whilst Apollos was there in Corinth, he did not have the wisdom, understanding or authority to correct them. Chloe, a Corinthian Christian lady who obviously carried some weight in the church, wrote a letter explaining what all the problematic issues were. She then sent three men, Stephanus, Fortunatus and Achaicus undoubtedly on the same boat ticket as Apollos, to Ephesus, to get Paul's response (1 Cor 1:11. 1 Cor 7:1. 1 Cor 16:17.). I always think of the trust that Paul placed in Chloe to respond as he did.

In addition to all these things, Paul talks in 1 Corinthians of being in deep hardship. The apostle pictures in 1 Corinthians 4:9-13 a harassing, negative, grinding scenario around himself as a present situation. He explains how he and his team were "like men condemned to die in the arena." He says that, "to this very hour we go hungry and thirsty, in rags and are brutally treated." It definitely reads like he was explaining how things were at that particular moment. This is undoubtedly one of the statements that helps to secure the idea that Paul was in prison for a while during his stay in Ephesus. Acts 20:34 informs us that he worked hard to make money to feed his team, and to help the poor. Yet here in the one letter that we know for certain he wrote from Ephesus he is talking of extreme hardship. A spell in prison seems to be a logical answer.

The idea of a prison stay in Ephesus has not been accepted by scholars previous to the last twenty years or so, simply because of lack of textual "evidence." Within the biblical evidence we have certain knowledge that Paul was imprisoned in Rome. Apart from the brief stay in a Philippian jail we are not informed of any other period of imprisonment apart from those after he had appealed to Caesar. If any of my readers has ever visited the ruins of Ephesus, you will know very well that the guided tour takes you to a brick structure which they claim is the site of the prison in which Paul was kept for a brief while.

On top of this we have the cryptic, "I fought with wild beasts in Ephesus," in 1 Corinthians 15:32, as well as the statement that is more ominous than cryptic, "There are many who oppose me" (1 Corinthians 16:9). There is also the cry from the first chapter of 2 Corinthians when Paul is explaining what happened whilst he was in Ephesus.

"We do not want you to be uninformed, brothers, about the hardships we suffered in the province of Asia. We were under great pressure, far beyond our ability to endure, so that we despaired even of life. Indeed, in our hearts we felt the sentence of death. But this happened that we might not rely on ourselves but on God, who raises the dead. He has delivered us from such a deadly peril, and he will deliver us" **(2 Cor 1:8-10).**

If indeed Philippians was written from Ephesus, the case for prison becomes, if it is possible, even starker.

"Now I want you to know, brothers, that what has happened to me has really served to advance the gospel. As a result, it has become clear throughout the whole palace guard and to everyone else that I am in chains for Christ. Because of my chains, most of the brothers in the Lord have been encouraged to speak the word of God more courageously and fearlessly" **(Philippians 1:12-14).**

A period of imprisonment whilst in Ephesus, seems to supply quite a few answers.

Never a dull moment when one is a bond-slave of Jesus Christ.

The point of these thoughts is the impact of Paul on these people, and their impact on him whilst the heavenly visitation to Ephesus and Asia was going on. Human relationships and the way they are conducted are all part and parcel of the whole character and person. Paul's management of the miraculous shows an acute awareness of being sensitive to the horizontal relationships of the humankind, as well as vertical relationships of the heavenly kind.

I wonder how and when Paul achieved time for himself. I wonder how his mind, body and spirit handled the continuous strain of the daily routine in Ephesus. I am amazed at the thought that this imprisonment and hardship was part and parcel of his brief experience for him whilst in Ephesus.

The entire context of carrying an apostolic ministry for Jesus Christ and the image of such a role that I have held for many years dissipates into nothingness as I see more and more clearly a man who was freed in mind and spirit, yet heavily oppressed by the responsibility of error and misconduct in the churches he had brought to birth, the training of his friends, as well as the work that he wanted to complete while he was there.

Ephesus was not the only potato on his plate, even though he seems to have put more hours each week into building the church there than any minister or pastor I know has ever worked. The energy he worked with was as much a miracle to be managed as the healing of the sick or the casting out of demons (Colossians 1:28-29).

LIST OF PAUL'S TEAM / BOARD / TRAVELLING COMPANIONS WHILST HE WAS IN EPHESUS

Paul Himself.	
Timothy	Definite
Erastus of Corinth (Acts 19:22)	Definite
The "about twelve" Disciples (Acts 19:1-6)	Definite
Aquila (Acts 18:18-19) of Pontus	Definite
Priscilla (Acts 18:18-19) of Rome	Definite

Epenetus of Ephesus? (Romans 16:5)	Definite
Onesiphorus of Iconium (2 Timothy 1:16-18)	Definite
Apollos of Alexandria (1 Cor 16:12)	Definite
Sosthenes. Ephesian. (1 Corinthians 1:1)	Definite
Gaius of Macedonia (Acts 19:29)	Definite
Aristarchus of Thessalonica (Acts 19:29)	Definite
Epaphras ministered in Colossae (Col 4:12)	Possible
Tychicus of Ephesus (Acts 20:4. Col 4:7-9))	Possible
Mark relative of Barnabas (Col 4:10)	Possible
Jesus aka Justus (Col 4:11)	Possible
Luke the physician (Col 4:12)	Possible
Demas (Col 4:12)	Possible
Stephanus of Corinth (1 Cor 16:15)	Briefly
Fortunatus of Corinth (1 Cor 16:17)	Briefly
Achaicus of Corinth (1 Corinthians 16:17)	Briefly
Onesimus (Col 4:9) returned to Philemon.	Briefly and
Nymphas of Laodicea (Col 4:15) Ephesus?	Met Paul in
Philemon of Colossae (Philemon) in Ephesus?	Met Paul
Apphia of Colossae (Philemon 2) Ephesus?	Met Paul in

Asians, possibly Ephesian who later defected from Paul:

Alexander of Asia (1 Tim 1:20)

Hymenaeus of Asia (2 Tim 2:17)

Hermogenes of Asia (2 Tim 1:15)

Phygellus of Asia (2 Tim 1:15)

Philetus of Asia (2 Tim 2:17)

19.

MINDSETS THAT PRECIPITATE THE MIRACULOUS – INTRODUCTION.

Many ministers and preachers that I have met in my lifetime have a particular emphasis in the overall context of a full biblical message. What I mean by this, is that even though they are totally orthodox and have a good and sound knowledge of the whole arc of gospel truth, there is often one, or perhaps two emphases that they major on as a particular burden, or a truth that particularly challenges or inspires them. I have heard some claim that God spoke to them concerning their particular emphasis. I have heard some say that they just "love" the subject that they talk about. Period. I have also heard others that are in denial about their preference. One itinerant minister I am thinking of in particular, when I have heard him speak, always starts by saying, "I have sought God with deep intensity, asking Him what I should minister on tonight." And then commences to speak on exactly the same subject that he always speaks about. I don't have a problem with any emphasis a man assumes, as long as it is biblical and true to the balance of scripture.

I know some perfectly sound Bible teachers who spend their entire life teaching and preaching about the second coming of Christ. They preach the whole arc of truth, yet from their burden and heart, all of the Christian life is seen under the shadow of the return of Christ to the earth. They will talk of repentance and life in the Spirit and many other things. They are however, always seen under the umbrella of the Second Advent. There are those that emphasize prayer, spiritual warfare, leadership, prophecy and many other aspects of biblical truth. There are those that emphasize prosperity and faith.

Some of these ministers may be criticised and attacked for their particular emphasis and push. This is because if one happens to have a biblical emphasis that is not agreed with by the majority, the emphasis that preachers make, becomes the only focus of their detractors. Yet when responded to with an open heart, like the Berean Christians who were, "more noble," in the sight of God, the entire umbrella of these people is perfectly sound and Godly.

By the very nature of a Godly person spending much time of mind and spirit in a particular field of truth, they tend to talk of issues encompassing their emphasis that the general body of Christ has not even heard of, never mind entered into. This can lead to misunderstanding and even disdain from some.

This does not mean that we must accept every emphasis that is made by every preacher. Not at all! The Bible alone should seriously determine what is orthodox and what is not. Shallow thinking, however, and purely academic study which, by its very nature, causes the student to nearly always run along doctrinal rails that have been set down for many generations post biblical, inhibits free thought on the infallible book. When Peter, for instance, challenged what was considered orthodoxy in Acts chapter 10, what he saw and thought and acted on was absolutely consistent with God, the Bible and what the Spirit had revealed to him. But for a time, the body of Christ in general, and even the other eleven apostles believed the new emphasis of Peter (i.e. going to, sharing with, and even living with a gentile) was unsound.

I believe in the infallibility of scripture. I also believe that there are depths of biblical truth that have either been neglected or lost through the centuries and need to be rediscovered. Human experience is like water and runs as quickly as it can to its lowest possible level so that it can rest and settle. But there are more underground rivers with wells that access them that have been blocked.

We need to have independent minds that cling tenaciously to the principle of examining all things in the light of scripture AND in the light that the Holy Spirit gives. The Psalmist said as he was addressing God, "In your light, we see light." And that is how it should be. Unfortunately what happens mostly is that we see the light of scripture, in the light of the theology books and pastors that we read and listen to regularly.

Christianity is a thing of the Holy Spirit. The whole experience of knowing Christ, walking with Christ and developing our own belief system has to be understood and carried out on His terms. God should be running this thing called the church. When He runs it, and dictates the agenda, the kingdom of God is beginning to break out. But that is not always the modus operandi of Christian people.

We thank God for the giants of previous generations. We believe that the scriptures of both the Old and New Testament are the absolute bench mark of what and how we believe concerning orthodox Christianity. There have been since the completion of the canon many giants of the faith who influenced not only their own generation, but every generation since. Luther, Calvin, Wesley and others. I believe it is because some of these historical giants were so profound in their grasp of what they believed when they set down their theology in writing. Since then, millions of Christians have read and understood their belief system, but nevertheless hold their teachings in their minds only, and not in the spirits. I am not suggesting that people are not saved who cling to the teaching of these people. God forbid! What I am suggesting is that having come to faith, the Spirit of God urges them to understand more, and rather than do it the long hard way of reading scripture and seeking God about it, they take the generally accepted philosophy of "standing on the shoulders of giants that have gone before," and learn the statements of these giants in their head, and not so much in their spirits. This is no statement against the Luther's, Calvin's and Wesley's and their ilk. How great were these men! However with new biblical revelation that has come to the church world-wide since their day, there are clearly chapter headings in Systematic Theology books that clearly need additional caveats, or even brand new chapters.

In the context of modern western living, Christian activities like the church looking after the sick, elderly, the poor and needy have been forgotten with the rationale that states, "the Government does those things". The New Testament practice of ministers casting out demons, cleansing people of "incurable" diseases, healing the sick, and generally, by quietly getting on with those things, gaining a high profile that impacts the society in which they are based because of those tangible and beneficial activities, have been neglected and, in some circles, verily, trashed. The theology and mindset that is commonly labelled as "Cessationist" is to my mind a total escapist thought pattern, hiding in an academic cubby hole that is so unreasonable that those that hold such a view have reduced Christianity to nothing but an intellectual, manmade and man led organisation, wherein God is just talked about but never seen or properly negotiated with. The likes of the great Reformation giants being received as perfect and complete in their theologies leads many to refuse to accept what Pentecostals and charismatics walk in. It is a puzzlement and a shame.

I do not in any way wish to say anything against the emphases majored on by any man or ministry. There are many gifts in ministry and practice, but there is only One Lord that authorises those gifts, One Saviour that opened heaven so that such gifts could be given to men, and there is only one Holy Spirit that administrates and works upon men, making those gives effectual and authentic.

Some of my friends tell me that this volume is the emphasis of all I am and think. I am not sure I agree. I believe I have several emphases.

Paul, it seems had no such "single" or even a "double" emphasis. He wrote more than half of the New Testament and his thoughts and teachings have been pondered over for two millennia. His emphasis was a comprehensive "whole" of all that is orthodox in the faith and of the Spirit. In my belief system, Paul is the most complete minister of the Gospel. His emphases are the emphases of God Himself. I believe that.

Paul moved in the miraculous often. To facilitate moving in the miraculous, bringing to people personal prophecy, deliverance and healing, and even the raising of the dead, it is evident that the Apostle held certain, what I refer to as, "Faith Mindsets" that facilitated such activity in the supernatural. These mindsets, sadly, are normally considered utterly radical in many Christian circles today, and even heretical by some. However, I believe I am being soundly logical, and showing childlike obedience to the mentality of the Bible, when I suggest that we need to emulate and absorb Paul's mindsets to have Paul's impact. On this very issue, I would go further and declare that Paul's mindsets were obviously mindsets of the Lord Jesus Christ Himself. If we desire to do what Jesus did, we need to live like Jesus lived. If we wish to live like Jesus lived we absolutely are required to think as Jesus thought. There is absolutely no way I can claim insight into all of Paul's thoughts in this direction of course, but I do believe I am in the grasp of a few crumbs that have fallen from the table that Paul has laid out for us in the scriptures. Those tiny crumbs feed me well.

The approach of Jesus to the miraculous is a phenomena in itself. It obviously was not a shock to Him when he first changed the water into wine. It was premeditated, calmly and rationally approached, with practical instructions of how to bring the miracle into physical manifestation. And, in that first instance, only those that were physically active in the administration of the miracle (the water pourers), and His mother, had any idea what had happened. Take note that the miracles of Christ were not always so secret. Far from it. But the general mindset, as Jesus administered the miraculous, and/or spoke the miraculous into being, has to be searched out. From the attitude and mental processes of Christ, it is clear to see that Paul emulated Christ in many ways, including this aspect of the management of the miraculous.

Faith should build into itself mindsets that feed it and free it into blossom and greater growth. Faith needs feeding. All truth feeds a person's faith. But there are certain truths that reach so deep into the psyche, and cut so profoundly into the status quo of one's life, that they need to be mentally chewed on and spiritually masticated until it becomes the engrafted word of truth to our souls. There is stuff in the bible that we have to wrestle with in order to have it engrafted into our being.

In the following few chapters of our observations of how Ephesus and Asia was taken for Christ by Paul, we shall look at a few of these mindsets. I will never claim I know all these biblical hooks on which to hang my convictions, and I am always searching for greater insight. But these are what I refer to as "Mandatory Mindsets for the sustained Management of the miraculous." We are desperately seeking God for truths that will impact ministers and ministry, to the point that they will be regularly seeing the power of God that is present to heal and confirm the Word that is preached.

We first need to teach ourselves how to step into the miraculous, in order for us to have miracles at all to manage. God give us grace to firmly take hold of this issue and confront it with open spirits and minds, as God Himself has opened His heaven.

19 A.

MINDSETS THAT PRECIPITATE THE MIRACULOUS.

NUMBER ONE: TAKING IT AS A GIVEN THAT CHRISTIANITY IS INTRINSICALLY PERMEATED WITH THE SUPERNATURAL IN ITS DNA.

Christianity is inherently and intrinsically supernatural. Even cursory thought has to concede this point. It was conceived in the supernatural. The whole concept of the Christian faith was foretold and prefigured in the realm of the spirit, or what is commonly referred to as, "the supernatural." So much so, that many "scholars" of recent generations thought the Old Testament too downright accurate and true to have been written before Christ – because, if the Jewish Bible (the Old Testament) was truly written before Christ, they would have had to 'fess up that much of the canon, especially the prophecies with the details of the crucifixion were supernaturally inspired. The whole message is built on the fact that Christ was born of a virgin, conceived by the Holy Spirit, and that God became flesh in the person of Jesus Christ. One, plainly, just cannot get around this truth without some consideration. Denying it, if one wishes to, is the only way around it, and to deny that, according to the Apostle John, is to put you beyond the parameters of the definition of a true Christian (1 John 4:2-3). The awesome wonder is that the Christian faith is explained in such a way in the New Testament that the Hebrew Jewish scriptures do not need to be altered or interfered with in any way whatsoever to substantiate and validate the claims of Christ, or Christianity itself. The New Testament does not have any adaptations of the Hebrew Scriptures. Any accurate translation of the Hebrew Bible will do – Christians refer to it as "The Old Testament". The Old Testament has downright supernatural ramifications for its future as well as ours.

Christ lived a totally sinless life, healed the sick, cleansed the lepers, raised the dead and claimed absolute deity of His own person. We are trying to define the historical account that, as we highlight these truths, is to be noted as one supernatural, factual event after another.

The most vital creed of Christianity is simply a list of historical events, prophetically introduced, miraculously conceived, supernaturally expressed in the life of Christ Himself, and thereafter evidenced openly in the disciples, later called apostles, and then in the church as a whole.

The passion of Christ, His suffering, crucifiction, death and burial seem natural enough when glanced at without research or forethought. However, when reading through the words and actions of Jesus, as remembered by those that have left us with the four Gospels, we are traumatised to realise that not only did the Old Testament foresee the very details of what happened in Christ's passion, but that Christ Himself seemed to know what, how, why and when His death was going to be. Death, hell and the grave didn't sneak up and steal Him away as they have for millions, if not billions of people before and since. He went to meet these unnatural monsters on His own devised terms and not theirs. He declared clearly, "I have power to lay down my life, and I have power to take it up again" (John 10: 17-18). And that is exactly what He did!

But what these pages are to immerse our thoughts in, is the wonderful truth that the gloriously divine manifestation of the miraculous power and grace of God, was not only marinated in the bundle of life that was Christ's, but is dispersed and sprinkled over the life of all Christian believers.

I can see many raising their hands responding with, "But I have not ever seen the miraculous!" or, "I have only seen such things once or twice in my 40, 50, 60 years as a Christian." I would quickly reply with, "One's experience or lack of it is not in any way the criteria for determining the truth of the intentions of God." The teaching of scripture is the final benchmark of practice and belief, and it is that truth I am pointing to.

The church itself was birthed in the miraculous. There was a gust of wind from a supernatural source; tongues that looked like fire that were seen by all, languages spoken clearly that were utterly unknown to all that spoke them, verified by thousands of hearers from varied peoples and nations. There were one hundred and twenty people who were talking in different languages on that day. Sixteen ethnic groups are referred to in the body of listeners, and the scripture tells us that every person present heard the works of God extolled in their own language (Acts 2:6). The settled, traditional obedient Jewish and non-Jewish adherents to, what we would refer to as Judaism were dumbfounded. We are told that on that first day, with the wind, the fire and the tongues, three thousand people added to their deep set traditions and beliefs in the Old Testament, and their expectation of the coming Messiah, the reality that Jesus of Nazareth was He for whom they were looking and anxiously waiting. The tin was opened and the contents could not be returned to the tidy container of Judaistic tradition. God was out on the streets.

But it did not end there.

We have people healed through the hands, the prayers, the pronouncements and the ministry of the Apostles (Acts chapter 3. Acts 9:32-35). There were, publicly and clearly, supernatural goings on. We have these disciples of Christ who were cowardly hiding, and even denying that they knew Christ at the time of His Passion, looking death straight in the eye via those that had the power to have them executed, and telling them as if they were Sunday School beginners that Christ was Lord and Messiah, as well as accusing them of His murder. Supernatural? We then have a prayer meeting where the building in which the church prayed, literally shook with the power that they were asking for (Acts 4:31). We have people dropping dead for attempting to deceive the apostles and defraud God, saying that they had happily given all, when they had hidden some of their fortune (Acts 5:1-11). We have the paradox of thousands of people getting converted and joining these "Jesus People", and thousands also simply afraid to get physically near to them in case something "supernatural" might happen against them (Acts 5:13). We have "many signs and wonders" done by the hands of the Apostles (Acts 5:12). We are told that the water table of faith and expectancy was so high that people brought their sick relatives and family and positioned them so that the very shadow of Peter would fall on them as he passed. This shadow was to facilitate them being healed – and they were (Acts 5:15).

Next, this ministry of the supernatural was extended to not only the twelve, but beyond. Stephen and Philip, two of the newly appointed "non-ministerial" members, saw the miraculous in their "lay-mans" ministry just as the apostles did (Acts 6:8, Acts 8:6). When people embraced the Christian faith in Samaria, for some reason that we are not told about, the new Samaritan Christians did not "receive the Holy Spirit." What? Nothing supernatural at conversion? So Peter and John went over to Samaria, laid their hands on the new Christians, and the Samaritans also received what the apostles had received, which logically could only be the tongues and prophecy that were present in Acts 2 (Acts 8:15-16). We have angels directing forums of evangelism (Acts 8:26). We have the Holy Spirit whisking preachers away from one place and allowing them to reappear in another place miles away, in order to carry on with their mission. "Beam me aboard Scotty!" But this was divinely supernatural, not Sci-fi. (Acts 8:39-40).

But it doesn't end there either. We have miraculous visions of Christ (Acts 9:3 -7), and miraculous predictive visions of what ministers would do, before they did them (Acts 9:10-16). We have the raising of the dead (Acts 9:36 -42). We have visions that were radical in their concept speaking to ministers and cryptically teaching them how to handle certain situations before they were to encounter them

(Acts 10 and 11). Again we have the Holy Spirit falling on people facilitating them to be speaking in other tongues and prophesying (Acts 10:44-46). This "tongues phenomena" was obviously the normal experience throughout the church. The church had established "prophets" by the time of Acts 11:27, and prophecy by its very nature is supernatural - or it just isn't prophecy, is it?

As well as people being martyred for Christ (Acts 7:59-60. Acts 12:2) and supernaturally seeing Christ waiting to receive them in heaven, there were those who were miraculously delivered from the prospect of death. Imprisoned Peter, the night before his planned execution was released from his cell by an angel, as were all the apostles earlier (Acts 5:19. Acts 12:7-11).

We get to Acts 13, and we hear that Saul of Tarsus (the Apostle Paul) and Barnabas did not commence any missionary because of their "training", or because they felt "called," but because the Holy Spirit spoke through a prophet (or prophets) telling them that they should "Go!" While preaching and seeing people converted to faith in Christ (something that most Christians would refer to as miraculously supernatural in itself), miracles were performed by the supernatural workings of the Holy Spirit through the Apostle's (Acts 13:9-12.14:8-10.). While Paul and Silas were busily evangelising they had supernatural visitations and dreams telling them where to go and where not to go (Acts 16:6-10). The whole being and enterprise of the church of Jesus Christ seems to have been immersed into the world of the Spirit. They were truly naturally supernatural, and supernaturally natural. We see demons cast out when required (Acts 16:17-18), earthquakes taking place that would seem to be solely for the purpose of releasing the preachers from prison (Acts 16:25-31). There are more miraculous signs and supernatural dealings all the way through Acts.

In the nineteenth chapter of Acts we have, as far as the biblical account is concerned, what I consider to be the peak of Paul's ministry which was 3 years preaching and teaching in Ephesus where the complete arc of truth and New Testament evangelistic ministry was exemplified in Paul's activities there. People being saved, healed, delivered from demons, and prophetic outpourings that changed the entire face of Asia.

This whole historical trawl, that I have only half glanced at, is for no other reason than to make the point that the miraculous is the New Testament norm. Cryptically expressed, the supernatural should be natural to the Christian. Christianity is naturally supernatural.

This writer has the absolute conviction that what is normal to the activity of the Holy Spirit in the name of Jesus Christ, is often perceived as miraculous by the non-Christian. It also is troublesome to the rationale and theology of many Christians to say these things in a western nation where the manifestation of the miraculous in Christ's name is a comparative rarity when seen against the scriptural model of the book of Acts.

I am aware that some of the moments I have listed above had a considerable time gap between them. I am fully aware that the book of Acts covers something like 30 years or more of history. But that fact does not dilute in any way the point that I am making. Jesus Christ gave the great commission to the church with the idea of doing exactly what He did in His life time, which was to make a traumatic confrontation with sin, sickness, demons, death, the grave, hell and all its accoutrements and supporters. That confrontation could not be done without the enduement and impartation of the power of the Holy Spirit and the delegated authority of God Almighty Himself in the mighty name of Jesus Christ. Because of the state of the world and people's lives and entanglements in the twenty first century, there are millions who need the miraculous intervention of faith in Jesus Christ and His liberating word. That is the call to ministry.

I need, finally, to repeat that I am under no illusion that all these supernatural issues listed above were all happening at every hour of every day. I quickly understood in my early days of bible reading, that the time line in the book of Acts and the biography of Paul is stretched much further than a cursory read informs us. The Apostle Paul was not saved on the Monday and then elevated to apostolic status by the following weekend. There were many years of preparation in the history of Paul's life. Years of preparation is what many in this generation don't want to go through.

In the same way as Paul's life consuming preparation, there were months and sometimes years between the occurrences of some of these miracles listed above. The Christian life is not simply a series of miracles, it is a daily routine of character building and obedience to God's word. But to those whose life's situation demands a miracle to resolve some awful issues that inhibits them moving forward, their miracle is the dinner gong to being saved through faith in Jesus Christ. The world is sick, hurting and dying, and millions of Christians, as well as non-Christians, need a miracle that only God can give them. It is not a matter of being unrealistic about "expecting a miracle every day". But if ministers are interfacing with the world at large they will meet people "every day" that need a miracle. Ministers of Christ need to be in "miracle mode" for those that are beyond the pale of verbal advisory resolution.

Predicted, exemplified, birthed and sustained by the miraculous, New Testament ministry worked on the basis of the bar being much higher than it is today. If this generation is to be saved, it must see proof that Jesus Christ is the same yesterday, today and forever. Christ imparting that miraculous power is one of the great proofs required.

19 B.

MINDSETS THAT PRECIPITATE THE MIRACULOUS.

NUMBER TWO: JESUS CHRIST NEVER COMMISSIONED ANYBODY TO PREACH, WITHOUT ALSO COMMISSIONING THEM TO HEAL THE SICK, CLEANSE THE LEPERS, RAISE THE DEAD AND CAST OUT DEMONS.

In a nutshell, the fact is, Jesus Christ never commissioned anybody to preach without also commissioning them to heal the sick, cleanse the lepers and raise the dead in the same breath.

That single truth is an indictment of where Christianity is, in general, today. No! I do not think it means that every preacher in the world should be praying for the sick with every single sermon he preaches. But it does mean praying for the sick whenever the sick are present and seeking healing. And in Britain today, there is every indication that praying for sick people when they are present, will almost definitely mean praying for the sick with every sermon. It also logically infers that by the biblical criteria, if a man or woman claims to be called to ministry, the whole idea of healing the sick is wrapped up solidly in the Heavenly Magna Carta of that call. The entire world is sick in body, soul and spirit, and Jesus Christ is the answer to all those fundamental issues of life.

When I first shared this revelation with my wife, she asked me two questions immediately. "Does that mean that those that don't exercise a ministry of healing are NOT called?" I stayed silent. Her second question was: "Or does it mean they are called but disobedient?" My answer was, that as faith comes by hearing, and hearing by the Word of God, it mostly suggests that the statement at the top of the page would be radical "breaking news" to many preachers and ministers in the world. Yes, there are some preachers currently, to whom the teaching of Christ healing sick and diseased people today would be new and radical. My statement above leads to my declaration that if any reader of this page is called to preach, I feel absolutely confident in stating that, on biblical grounds, you are also called to pray for the sick and see them healed. Refute me if you can, biblically!

My declaration is based on several passages of the Bible. The underlined sections below are those that particularly make the point I am stating.

1. Matthew 10:1 - 8 states:

"Jesus called his twelve disciples to him and gave them authority to drive out impure spirits and to heal every disease and sickness. These are the names of the twelve apostles: first, Simon (who is called Peter) and his brother Andrew; James son of Zebedee, and his brother John; Philip and Bartholomew; Thomas and Matthew the tax collector; James son of Alphaeus, and Thaddaeus; Simon the Zealot and Judas Iscariot, who betrayed him. These twelve Jesus sent out with the following instructions: "Do not go among the Gentiles or enter any town of the Samaritans. Go rather to the lost sheep of Israel. As you go, proclaim this message: 'The kingdom of heaven has come near.' Heal the sick, raise the dead, and cleanse those who have leprosy, drive out demons. Freely you have received; freely give."

What we have is Christ sending out the twelve to preach. In sending them to declare the Good News, He gave them the authority over impure spirits (i.e. to drive out demons), as well as over every disease and sickness (Heal the sick),to raise the dead (the ultimate result of all sickness), and to cleanse those that had leprosy (i.e. incurable diseases). Could it be plainer? Preaching and healing are conjoined twins in the mind of Christ it would seem. What is the point of declaring, "The kingdom of God has come," if that kingdom cannot me manifested in their lives?

2. Mark 6: 7 - 13.

Mark's emphasis is slightly different with another perspective. Mark is the Gospel of the Servant, and so remarks a little more on the manner of the servant's presentation and preparation.

"Calling the Twelve to him, he began to send them out two by two and gave them authority over impure spirits. These were his instructions: "Take nothing for the journey except a staff—no bread, no bag, no money in your belts. Wear sandals but not an extra shirt. Whenever you enter a house, stay there until you leave that town. And if any place will not welcome you or listen to you, leave that place and shake the dust off your feet as a testimony against them." They went out and preached that people should repent. They drove out many demons and anointed many sick people with oil and healed them".

We still see clearly the commission for deliverance (i.e. casting out impure spirits). Note also that even though Mark does not recite Jesus commissioning the twelve to "heal the sick," he still records that they emulated the Saviour and did so. We have here a second record of Jesus commissioning, what we would refer to as, the manifestation of the miraculous, that is: miracles performed by God Himself through the hands of the disciples, along with, in the same breath, the commission to preach.

3. Luke 10: 1 - 17.

At a later date, Jesus sent out 70, or 72 disciples (dependant on what translation one reads). This is important to our thinking, because there are many who errantly say that miracles were imparted by the gift of Christ only to the twelve disciples, who became the first twelve apostles.

Far beyond the twelve, Jesus addressed them; *"After this the Lord appointed seventy-two others and sent them two by two ahead of him to every town and place where he was about to go. He told them, "The harvest is plentiful, but the workers are few. Ask the Lord of the harvest, therefore, to send out workers into his harvest field. Go! I am sending you out like lambs among wolves. Do not take a purse or bag or sandals; and do not greet anyone on the road. When you enter a house, first say, 'Peace to this house.' If someone who promotes peace is there, your peace will rest on them; if not, it will return to you. Stay there, eating and drinking whatever they give you, for the worker deserves his wages. Do not move around from house to house. When you enter a town and are welcomed, eat what is offered to you. Heal the sick who are there and tell them, 'The kingdom of God has come near to you.' But when you enter a town and are not welcomed, go into its streets and say, 'Even the dust of your town we wipe from our feet as a warning to you. Yet be sure of this: The kingdom of God has come near.' I tell you, it will be more bearable on that day for Sodom than for that town. Woe to you, Chorazin! Woe to you, Bethsaida! For if the miracles that were performed in you had been performed in Tyre and Sidon, they would have repented long ago, sitting in sackcloth and ashes. But it will be more bearable for Tyre and Sidon at the judgment than for you. And you, Capernaum, will you be lifted to the heavens? No, you will go down to Hades. Whoever listens to you listens to me; whoever rejects you rejects me; but whoever rejects me rejects him who sent me." The seventy-two returned with joy and said, "Lord, even the demons submit to us in your name."*

I have quoted the entire section to make a point. It is clear that the 72 are 72 "others," i.e. the twelve disciples were not included. Christ sent the 72 over and above the twelve. This tells us that in the days of His flesh, there was a certain point of time when there were 84 men, visiting the villages in Israel (or Judea as it was called in Christ's day) in 42 couples, preaching and healing the sick, casting out demons and.... if they did not raise the dead, we know He had given them authority to do that very thing. He sent them to heal the sick, to preach, and to build relationship with whoever they stayed with. They came back, surprised that even the demons were subject to them, so that also must have been part of their commission. It should be added as a "by the way" that they were not to stay where they were not wanted.

These instances mentioned above were all episodes in the gospel days of Christ before the crucifiction. But what about after the resurrection and the Great Commission.

4. Matthew 28:18 - 20

"Then Jesus came to them and said, "All authority in heaven and on earth has been given to me. Therefore go and make disciples of all nations, baptizing them in the name of the Father and of the Son and of the Holy Spirit, and teaching them to obey everything I have commanded you. And surely I am with you always, to the very end of the age."

At the very end of Matthew's Gospel the risen Christ leaves the apostles with what is generally known as the Great Commission. In the commission to make disciples, He says that the apostles must be diligent in, "teaching them to obey everything I have commanded you". What had He commanded them to do? From the passages of scripture we have listed above, the answer must include, preaching the Gospel, healing the sick, cleansing the lepers, casting out demons and raising the dead.

If Church leaders had been obedient, each generation would have been instructed to do exactly the same as Christ had originally told the twelve.

5. Mark 16: 15 – 20

The Great Commission is referred to in Mark's Gospel also, yet it tells us in a different manner.

"He said to them, "Go into all the world and preach the gospel to all creation. Whoever believes and is baptized will be saved, but whoever does not believe will be condemned. And these signs will accompany those who believe: In my name they will drive out

demons; they will speak in new tongues; they will pick up snakes with their hands; and when they drink deadly poison, it will not hurt them at all; they will place their hands on sick people, and they will get well." After the Lord Jesus had spoken to them, he was taken up into heaven and he sat at the right hand of God. Then the disciples went out and preached everywhere, and the Lord worked with them and confirmed his word by the signs that accompanied it."

Again we have the commission to drive out demons, and placing their hands on the sick and seeing them recover. There is also the issue of speaking in tongues, picking up poisonous snakes, and drinking deadly poison when murderous malice is aimed at them, and their being impervious to venom and poison of any kind. We are talking not only of Kingdom aggression of Light and goodness and healing, but Kingdom defence against malice and hate, and murder attempts.

This is a plain instruction and Commission of the tools for evangelism. To all who are called to minister. I say we are clearly called to be managers of the miraculous.

6.　*Luke 24:45 to 53*

"Then he opened their minds so they could understand the Scriptures. He told them, "This is what is written: The Messiah will suffer and rise from the dead on the third day, and repentance for the forgiveness of sins will be preached in his name to all nations, beginning at Jerusalem. You are witnesses of these things. I am going to send you what my Father has promised; but stay in the city until you have been clothed with power from on high." When he had led them out to the vicinity of Bethany, he lifted up his hands and blessed them. While he was blessing them, he left them and was taken up into heaven. Then they worshipped him and returned to Jerusalem with great joy. And they stayed continually at the temple, praising God".

Luke has a different approach, but ultimately says the same thing as Matthew and Mark. How can I say that? Because Luke wrote volume two of the Gospel of Luke, namely, the book we call "Acts of the Apostles." When the Holy Spirit came upon the God Seekers in the upper room in Acts chapter 2 the whole of heaven's miraculous power was released to those who received this mighty Baptism in the Holy Spirit and fire. Peter, Paul, Stephen and Phillip! All have some vestige of their ministry and activity recorded in the book of Acts. The miraculous followed them all. The exercise of "performing miracles" was given to apostles and non-apostles alike. It was conjoined with the necessity of preaching.

Our conclusion from these plain and straight forward thoughts, is that the ministry of healing the sick, casting out demons, cleansing lepers and even raising the dead was a demand embedded in the warp and woof of Christ's commission. This truth needs to be absorbed. The western mind needs to marinade itself in such truths.

I am aware that the general mindset of Christians in the west is harassed and besieged by the philosophies of an unbelieving culture, but for God to raise up wild, giant, dangerous prophets in this humanistic cultural context is a desperate imperative.

19 C.

MINDSETS THAT PRECIPITATE THE MIRACULOUS.

NUMBER THREE: START PERCEIVING THE MIRACULOUS AS NORMAL IN CHRIST.

There is a need for Christian leaders to stop seeing the miraculous as some Holy Grail to strive for, instead of a wonderful Heavenly gift to simply receive and be thankful for (Mark 16:20). The whole issue of the miraculous is about seeing something that simply could not be of human origin (John 9:25). If a man is healed of HIV/AIDS or the inability to walk, or if a blind man can see after prayer, or demons are cast out of people's lives, or even if a man prophecies something that could not possibly be manufactured or manipulated, people will have to say, "That is God!" Don't get me wrong on this. I am definitely *not* suggesting that at the sight of the miraculous everybody will leap into the kingdom of God and be saved. That does not happen, and it never has (Matt 11:21. Luke 10:13).

The miraculous takes Christianity out of the realm of logic, book learning, and reasoning of the five senses, and elevates the whole thing into awe and wonder while people discuss God in a different light and from a totally different perspective (Mark 2:12).

I had an Auntie and Uncle (now deceased) who attended some of George Jeffreys' meetings in London at the Kensington Temple Church Centre many years ago. They told me several times that they went with a neighbour who had been crippled and in a wheel chair for many years. They told me, always in an animated and excited fashion, how they stood next to their neighbour whilst Mr Jeffreys laid hands on her head and prayed for her. They told me how the wheelchair was vibrating, and almost bouncing as he prayed. They acted out the moment when their neighbour leapt out of the wheelchair and started trotting as she never had done for years. They told me boldly and clearly, as if they were evangelists themselves, "Jesus Christ healed her when the power of God came upon her." They affirmed how their neighbour died of pneumonia or something 20 years later, but was in full health and mobility until Pneumonia attacked and took her, so glorious was her healing. "Oh!" says I, on each occasion they recounted the story, "You must have been so strong in faith when you became a Christian?" "Oh no!" was their repeated answer. "Christianity is alright for some, but not for us!"

In my mind I believe that some evil force or something blinded my Aunt Agnes and Uncle Harold from seeing the light that was dazzling their eyes. Yet whenever I gave my testimony, or shared anything of the gospel, they always talked "spiritual" talk, about the power of God, and God's grace working in people's life. They couldn't argue against it. However, they simply rejected it.

My point is that Western Christianity is full of logic, good preachers, good singers, good ministers that can teach and build churches into bodies of people that are strong in their assurance of salvation and evangelical fervour. All these things are good and right and healthy. These things, when seen from God's perspective, can be done in the power of the Spirit and under the grace of the Lord Jesus Christ. But, these things can also be done by people with natural character gifting, and have nothing to do with God.

Even though I never heard Billy Graham preach about the supernatural, nevertheless I believe he was a gift to the church worldwide and had a supernatural anointing on his preaching. The world, however, simply put his success down to him being a man with the "gift of the gab." Give the world a chance and they will put preaching, praying, singing, conversion, testimonies of a changed life, and answers to prayer, down to human ability, natural circumstance and/or coincidence. By doing this Christianity is kept in the domain of worldly empirical logic and the exploration of the revelation of Christ never ascends beyond the academic and pragmatic.

Many denominations will not allow people into the ministry without some academic theological achievement that can be put on the Church notice board. And let me make it clear, this writer is in no way against book learning, study, and theological training. But If we merely win the lost by fantastically intricate debating techniques and skill, all we bring to birth are Christians that have an entry into the kingdom by worldly, academic, logical points of learning. Christianity is very logical. Most Christians grow by gaining their own experiential points of logic as they progress. It's called Bible teaching.

But Christianity is more than that. Christianity, to be biblical and apostolic, must have the supernatural manifestations of the Holy Spirit as a foundational expression of God, to demonstrate that Jesus Christ is alive and is the same yesterday, today and forever. If billions of this generation are to believe, they must see proof that Jesus Christ is unchanged from the modus operandi he utilised in the gospels (John 4:48).

The atheistic and agnostic arguement would be hard put to keep the discussion, and hold the opinions they do, if the healing power of God was seen regularly and in a manner that was published by the healed instead of the minister whose prayers precipitated the healing. Apostles, prophets, evangelists, teachers and pastors are never healers, they are ministers. Some carry an anointing that brings healing. Some occasionally enter the realm of faith in a manner that brings the supernatural into being. Some are Holy Spirit "carriers" in some direction or other where the miraculous can happen, almost without them knowing. I have sat under some evangelists and teachers where their sermon has been interrupted and then closed altogether because people were being healed and delivered while the person was preaching.

I saw at one meeting many years ago, one high profile preacher just fall to his knees and cry, seconds before the corner of the auditorium, where the people in wheelchairs were, just erupted in shouts of praise as several of them (not all) simply stood to their feet and started running around. Almost concurrently to that happening, the corner where a woman was translating into sign language what the preacher was saying to thirty or forty deaf people, erupted with noise and shouts and cries while many of them (not all) could suddenly hear perfectly well. Later the preacher said he had nothing to do with it, and explained how he broke down and cried as he saw a visible cloud descend on the two corners. Nobody else in the auditorium claimed to have seen the cloud, but sure enough, when they rerun the video of the moment it had occurred, it was clearly seen that the preacher looked to the two corners followed by an expression of shock and an outburst of tears. The miracle of modern technology allowed us to witness a man who was actually in the act of "seeing the invisible."

What's my point? My point is that the manifestation of the miraculous stops endless discussions about the existence of God, and "Why do people suffer?" evolution, and, "Did Jesus really die?" - and lifts it into, "How did this man walk?" and "How did this deaf man get his hearing?" It might not guarantee conversion, but it guarantees people's souls being confronted by the reality of the power of God and the living Christ. This sort of thing needs to be sought after. It is part of the package of the ministerial calling. It is, indeed, the inheritance of the believer.

The miraculous is part and parcel of the gospel message. Neither Jesus nor Paul seemed to have the slightest worry that somebody might be healed and not get converted. Neither the Saviour nor his apostle's needed to tag on to healing the sick a warning saying, "You must guarantee that you know how to get saved, as well as healed." They were not concerned about people believing for healing and "seemingly not being bothered" about the saving of their soul. To be sure both Christ and the apostles were always ready to preach when the opportunity arose, as every minister of Christ should be. The Acts

3 sermon, however, was more to the spectators than the man who was healed. The Gospel message is the power of God that brings salvation. If whilst the message of the power of God is being preached, that very same power of God is manifest, why should it need qualifying? The difference between theoretical learning, and practical application is a western concept, it is neither a Jewish nor an eastern mindset. True biblical theological concepts are simply to be acted upon. They are to be believed and practiced, not believed and debated.

We should preach with the wallpaper of our thinking expectant of the miraculous. The miracles are a verification of the message that the minister of Christ is preaching the authentic word of God. The Word of God is miraculous, and we should handle it and declare it for what it is, otherwise we are open to the indictment of being, "pedlars of the word."

Many Christians in western culture, when they hear talk like this, start off on the, "We had better be very cautious of lying wonders," or, "counterfeits of the devil." Of course we should! But why do people who have never ever seen a miracle seem to be the ones that always come up with this kind of response. If we preach truth, with confidence and assurance, we are surely expecting the Spirit of God to sanction the truth that is being preached.

Signs and wonders should follow the preaching of the word. When the word is undiluted and uncompromising, there must be the element of the miraculous, healing, deliverance, prophecy and God making ways where there previously were no known ways in people's lives. It should not be perceived as something so high and lofty that a standard of holiness we have never seen before, or a repentant spirit that we have never witnessed, must first take place before it happens. And let nobody conclude from that remark that this writer does not believe in repentance or holiness. The miraculous is entered into by faith. Faith does not require Godly character to be effective. Faith in Christ and His power imputes holiness to the person exercising the faith, but Christ like character does not happen, it is built. Faith should be lived in to build character. But it is faith, not character, that grasps the miraculous.

Godliness of outlook and mentality does not just happen it is built. Galatians 3 tells us that the miraculous takes place because of the hearing of faith. That is what is needed to take us into the realm of the miraculous. It must be seen as normalcy. The minister of the miraculous must be received as the rule, not the exception. The expectation for healing must be in the routine expression of the minister's life, not the special moment of glory - glorious though it is. Deliverance must be absolutely seen to be the divine bread for all God's children, not the special diet for a few. Prophetic utterances that reveal the innermost secrets of people's hearts and sets them free must be held as the bread and butter of New Testament ministry. Oh dear Lord! Pour out your Spirit upon us.

"A normal day at the office?" Exactly! I do not mean to be blasé or light when it takes place. Some things that happen every day in a commercial office are absolutely vital for the running of the company, and no matter how many times a day a payment is received, or a bill is sent out, or a contract is considered, it is of grave importance and treated with total sobriety every time it is dealt with. So must the miraculous ministry of the Holy Spirit be treated.

Obviously there will be those who are more fluid and lucid in the exercise of one or more, or even all these manifestations of the Spirit amongst the apostles, prophets, evangelists, pastors and teachers and beyond. The plain belief and expectation for the miraculous to happen in the here and the now in our own time-space world is a definite necessity of a mindset to help precipitate a continuous and sustainable ministry of the miraculous.

19 D.

MINDSETS THAT PRECIPITATE THE MIRACULOUS.

NUMBER FOUR: HOLY SPIRIT INITIATED PROPHETIC MINISTRY IS TO BE SOUGHT AFTER AS THE NORM.

I am sure readers have understood my carefully chosen language when I am discussing, "Management of the Miraculous." I am assuming a life of ministry when, like the apostle Paul, the miraculous has become common place. I do not mean that anybody should ever be blasé about healing, deliverance or prophecy. God forbid! That's why attitudes and responses need to be "managed." Mind management is the first priority of the overcomer. But seeing such glorious acts of God in such great profusion means that the heart needs guarding like never before.

Ministers are called of God because God has put something within them and upon them that when properly developed and managed will change many lives. The call to minister presupposes that a person's life is in a place where not only the ministering servants themselves are established in the faith, but they have a gift, an anointing, and a heart to establish others in the same faith in one way or another. As God enables the minister to function as such by His Spirit, so the act of ministry is to be performed by the push and direction of the same Spirit.

The point of all New Testament ministry is to impart faith and whatever gifts the minister has been given, as well as to build Christ into people's lives. The call is to utilise those God given Holy Spirit empowered gifts to the benefit of all who are being ministered to. Yes! The minister must ensure that whatever is spoken is truth, as unadulterated and as potent as he can make it. But the constant issue after that is not what is being ministered, but what is being received by the listener. Paul said that the Galatian Christians received their miracles by "the hearing of faith" and not primarily by the preaching of the same (Galatians 3:2 and 3:5). The imperative is transcendent of how well prepared the minister is, as to how much of his ministry was empowered by the Spirit of God. Beyond feeding the minds of those ministered to (and make no mistake the mind of all Christians needs constant feeding and changing by the logic of the scriptures) there is the priority of the Spirit of God in the heart of the minister reaching, touching and impacting the spirit of those being ministered to. The declaration of and/or the teaching of God's word must impart faith.

Faith comes to people by the ministry of the word. Faith comes by hearing (Romans 10:17). Faith that was not there, or if it was, faith that was sat in a comfort zone of non-activity, needs to be aroused and brought into activity by the preaching of the word. "Faith comes by hearing and hearing." Truth requires declaring over and over again until faith surfaces into action and moves the one being ministered to into a stance of faith and confidence in what God has said. Faith comes by hearing and hearing by what? By the word of God. The declaration and explanation of God's word should be aimed at imparting faith. Paul says in Galatians 3:2-5, as a, "by the way," while talking on another subject, that the miracles that occurred amongst the Galatian Christians while Paul was there preaching, came by "the hearing of faith," or in plainer, more modern English, the miracles were received by the people believing what they heard. This suggests that the carrot of the results of faith must have been presented to the people for them to believe that they could receive a miracle. One must believe one can be healed and/or delivered before one enters into that freedom. One cannot merely inform people of a few dry facts, and expect the miraculous. I have heard sermons that were supposed to be the "ministry of the word," yet they depressed me and caused me to withdraw. The word of God is to elevate and dignify people to the degree that it causes them to have faith for the miraculous. The gospel is intrinsically the seed that carries the power of God that brings salvation, healing, deliverance and a raft of other benefits. The gospel is good.

The minister of the word requires something in the guts, solidly and securely buried in the depth of the human spirit, that wings the concepts of the words spoken into an equally deep recess in the spirits of the listeners and bursts out into practical, active faith. This is the norm that I am talking about, not just the irregular break out from tradition, or things that are left to the high profile evangelists.

True New Testament Ministry needs to be manifested out of the overflow of the Holy Spirit in the human spirit of the one ministering. If it doesn't flow like a river out of the minister's innermost being the entire concept of "ministry" is limited. At best it is reduced to a kind of testimony of things learned by the minister, at worst it becomes "mind to mind" instead of "spirit to spirit." The manifestation of the Holy Spirit is the biblical prerequisite, before, during or after the preaching of the word, which is the very thing that qualifies it to be categorised as New Testament ministry. Christianity is a thing of the Spirit (both divine and human) that has the miraculous embedded in its DNA. When preaching is in the Holy Spirit and imparted by a heart flowing in the Holy Spirit, it is possible for a person ministering the word of God to know, by hearing the voice of the Holy Spirit, what is going on in a the life of a person or persons in the audience and be able to speak into their life. The mightiest men of God that I have known to move in this process as a "normal day at the office," do it in a relaxed and easy manner that could only be described as "naturally supernatural," or, "supernaturally natural." (I have never been one hundred percent certain of which way round is most appropriate.)

I have heard lots of preachers decry those Christians who are, "seeking various experiences that they have heard that somebody else has had." Such an accusation was thrown at me once. I was accused of simply seeking an, "experience," with God, and that it was a sign of immaturity to be in pursuit of such a thing. My answer was that I do not want an experience *per se*, but I do hunger to be the man that has such a relationship with God that he can minister "experiences" to others. By "experiences," I mean being saved, healed, delivered, baptised in the Holy Spirit and then established in the faith. I would call that legitimate experience seeking. I insist it to be so. I do not in any way seek it for myself, but I desperately want to give those, "experiences," to those that need it. I believe that there are people who attend churches every week, all over the world, who desperately need an experience of the miraculous. Millions have gone home from their church every week for prolonged periods of time not having received their miracle and having to fight their spiritual battles on a front that the local church of Jesus Christ should have removed from them. Normal church ministry should be so comprehensive that it makes all para church organisations obsolete.

I know too many Christians that live with crippling diseases of body and mind that utterly inhibit their service for God. That is, in itself, a fact of life that all ministers of the gospel must be ready to meet. But what I find distressing is that many Christians, having lived so long with disabling diseases, sicknesses or general mental and spiritual debilities that they do not even fight to be whole because ministers have not encouraged them to seek healing. Healing of every dimension and degree is absolutely intrinsic to the message of the gospel. Some even excuse the situation and live with sickness believing that God is teaching them some kind of profound lesson. I personally find that almost criminal. Jesus Christ is the answer to all fundamental issues of life, and must be presented as such by the preachers and teachers of God's word. Sickness is insipient death, it binds and destroys people's self-esteem, confidence and ability. Jesus Christ Himself said that the thief, i.e. Satan, comes to rob, kill and destroy, and that He came to give us life more abundantly. We must not confuse the two. Sickness is part of the curse.

So boldness and active co-operation with the Holy Spirit, allowing Him to direct the ministry of healing, deliverance and prophecy. It is under the anointing of life by the rhema "now" word spoken in the Holy Spirit, that makes one particular healing, deliverance or prophetic word create desolation and havoc in the kingdom of darkness and win many for Christ. God wants all healed, but there is always a key moment in most churches or evangelistic thrusts, that seems to break the doors of hell down, and bring the torrents of the Holy Spirit in. It takes courage, boldness, and sensitivity, along with the tangible anointing of the Holy Spirit to enter into such moments as God intended it.

As an instance, there is Acts 14:8-12. The apostle Paul arrived in a town called Lystra in what is today known as Turkey. Paul was preaching. While delivering the word of God, there was a crippled man, in the crowd, listening intently. Paul noticed the man even while he spoke, and knew he had faith to be healed. The apostle looked at the man intently and then shouted to the man, suggesting that he was at the back of a considerable crowd of people, "Stand up on your feet!" At which the man arose. It was so impressive to the crowd that some of those that were not listening, thought that Paul and his companion were Greek Gods come down amongst them. What's the point? The point is that within these verses and this story we have a biblical definition of New Testament ministry.

- Paul was speaking, i.e. preaching. He was declaring truth that caused a crippled man who had never walked in his life, to believe that he could walk. How was such a thing possible if Paul was not declaring with deep conviction, truths that could construct a faith that contradicted a life's time experience? The Word was not depressive, but releasing. The words were from Paul's spirit, filled with the Holy Spirit, aimed at the human spirits of those that were listening. It impacted a man that knew how to be nothing else but a cripple.

- The sermon was obviously constructed about meeting the needs of people that were lost in terrible conditions. Can we perceive how incredibly powerful and pointed the sermon must have been to bring a crippled man to even have hope that he could walk. The sermon was a declaration of Christ's all sufficient power to meet all needs in the here and now if folks would simply receive Him. "Believe and be healed. Believe and be saved. Believe and be delivered."

- Paul had no hang ups about not finishing a sermon that may have taken him hours to prepare. The goal was not, "Have I finished my sermon?" but, "Have I imparted faith?" The aim was not to have the satisfaction of a sermon delivered, but the joy of people believing to the changing of their entire life. The purpose was achieved with this crippled man before he had even finished speaking. Paul's vision was the manifestation of Christ, not the full unburdening of his long prepared sermon. In other words, to manage the miraculous, one must deliver sermons that sows the heart of the listeners with miracle seeds.

- Paul must have been attentive to his listeners more than his sermon notes. The entire objective of preaching is the eternal, long term and permanent benefit of all those listening, not to add another notch to one's sermon gun. It's all about the faith and life of the recipient of the ministry, not the achievement of a great sermon by the minister.

- The fact that he noticed the crippled man whilst in full flight and concentration of preaching, suggests that his mind was in two places at once. He was concentrating on what was said, as well as what the hearers were doing. He was mindful of his responsibility to deliver the word of God, whilst also keeping the ears of his understanding open to what the Spirit of God was saying.

- The manifestation of the Holy Spirit followed Paul's thoughts. I am assuming that there was something positive in the crippled man's posture or expression that drew Paul's attention. That's natural, not supernatural. Paul, then, saw that the man had faith to be healed; that's supernatural, not natural. In the midst of the address, by awareness and keeping his spiritual ears open while he spoke, he saw the crippled man and received quickly and vividly, "This man has faith to be healed."

- Courage and boldness were then of the highest order. For Paul to act on what he saw in the natural and heard from heaven in the supernatural, in the midst of a full blown evangelistic meeting where people are listening to one's every word, takes great courage. What if he was wrong? What if nothing happened after he spoke? It is always scary stuff. But it is also fantastically exciting stuff. What was going to happen to the crippled man would instil a strong and robust faith in not only the man who was about to walk for the first time ever, but also those in the crowd that were listening to the same address as this man had. They would see that the truth of Paul's words impacts in the physical world. The kingdom of God had come and was amongst them. That's what New Testament ministry brings.

- Paul did not pray for the man's healing. Oh! How important is this issue! He commanded the man to stand up and walk. He gave an order! The words were birthed by the Holy Spirit in Paul, carried by the Holy Spirit as he gave the shout, and received in the Holy Spirit by the crippled man listening and obeying the word of God spoken. Whosoever says to this crippling disease, "Be removed," and be cast into the sea, and shall not doubt in his heart, but believe that those things he has said shall come to pass, he shall have whatsoever he says." Paul told the man to rise to his feet and to leave the sickness behind. Paul spoke in faith. But the crippled man received what was spoken as God's word for him, and jumped up. With those ingredients Paul could not fail. Disease or malformation was defeated.

- Paul looked straight at the crippled man. When Paul wrote to the Corinthians explaining how he had come to them in the "power and demonstration of the Holy Spirit" (1 Corinthians 2:4), the Greek word used for "demonstration" means literally, "the pointing out of the Holy Spirit." As it was in Corinth, so it was here in Lystra. Paul pointed out the man, if not literally by pointing with the finger (and he may have done just that), it was by the act of Paul looking directly at him. In plain language, he stopped the meeting for the manifestation of the miraculous. That is courageous. That is Godly. That is New Testament ministry.

- Paul must have desired such a manifestation in order to be prepared to hear God, see the man, and give the word for him to rise and walk. It simply has to be part of the New Testament minister's mindset to be prepared to manage the miraculous acts of God as they accompany the ministry, as he declares the word that gives birth to faith for the miraculous in the hearts of those that are listening.

- The contents of what Paul was talking about must have encouraged an expectation for the miraculous. I cannot accept any other idea of the message Paul preached.

- Paul had a sermon that contradicted the experience of the crippled man. The word of the gospel took the man into a new vision, a new life, a new understanding, and into, what was for him, a new God.

- Note also that the miracle that God wrought in the man's body was instant and total. He jumped to his feet from a seated position having never walked in his life. No booking of appointments with a physiotherapist for this man. The Holy Spirit that inspired the address, was the same Holy Spirit that allowed Paul to know that the man was crippled (how can one naturally know such a thing when people are seated). The exact same Holy Spirit that facilitates such knowledge, was not going to leave the man in his crippled state. By the Spirit, Paul sees, Paul knows, and Paul addresses the man by pointing him out of the crowd and looking directly at him. By that same source of understanding, Paul knows the man has faith to receive the Rhema word of God, the "now" word for that moment. The same Holy Spirit, having made the very atmosphere pregnant with faith for the miraculous through the preaching of the gospel, speaks the miracle into being. From faith, to faith. From the Spirit, to the spirit. From Paul to the crippled man. God manifested through the preaching of the word (Titus 1:3 King James Version).

- Note that even though the man had faith to be healed, the healing would not have taken place if the word hadn't been forcefully spoken. The preacher had to be sent. Having arrived he had to speak. In retrospect the predestined miracle is quite straightforward. Previous to its occurrence it needed wisdom and sharp management of how to handle and minister the miraculous.

- When the Spirit born word of God is spoken, demons, circumstances and all things outside the will of God jump to obey what God has said. Paul spoke it, because God said it. The word is always true, no matter who delivers it. But the word needs the Holy Spirit. There is deep, deeper and deepest when it comes to understanding the word, and having and maintaining an anointing.

- The power of God exploded in the midst of the Lystran audience, creating an absolute furore among the heathen population. The details of the text suggest that the crowd was very large. The whole city wanted to worship Paul and Barnabas. It created opposition and divided the people. There were those who came to Christ. There were those who came to stone him. There were those who loved Paul. There were those that hated him.

- Not only is there a price that Paul paid in time past to minister in the miraculous, but there was a price also to pay in the present, because he moved in the miraculous. His own country men were on their way to Lystra to stone him and leave him for dead. They that live Godly in Christ Jesus shall suffer persecution.

It is a plain fact that Holy Spirit initiated healings, deliverance and prophetic words cause faith levels to soar. Faith brings salvation. There is nothing wrong, of course, when the sick, the demonised, or the confused come asking for healing. But when, "out of the blue," people are pointed out and ministered to, the minister is moving in the same dimension as God. It is incontestable.

The expectation of such manifestations must be part of the mindset that precipitates a sustained and regular ministry of the miraculous.

19 E.

MINDSETS THAT PRECIPITATE THE MIRACULOUS.

NUMBER FIVE: IF IT IS IN THE ATONEMENT, IT IS FOR EVERYBODY, AND IT IS FOR NOW.

The entire fullness of Christianity is conceived, gestated and birthed in an ever growing understanding of all that Christ's death and resurrection brings to the believer. According to Paul's letter to the Ephesians, in the first chapter, he spends the first fourteen verses of the twenty-three explaining how we have, "every blessing," that heaven can afford, simply because as a believer we are "in Christ," and then he spends the latter half of the chapter praying that we understand and see, with ever increasing clarity, what he has explained in the first half of the chapter we already have in Christ's death and resurrection. In a nutshell, the first half of the chapter would be simply static, non-moving truth if it was not for the fact that the Holy Spirit makes those truths dynamic, alive, moving and growing with infinite power within us. We have all that heaven can give us, but we will spend eternity getting to the bottom of what those blessings fully comprise.

In modern street language, talking in parabolic type description: God has deposited an infinite amount of heavenly currency in each believer's divine bank account, effective on earth, in this life, in the "now". It is us, we ourselves that write the cheques and make the withdrawals that are living currency in our time space world. The overall graphic that Ephesians 1 draws for us is a kind of image of Heavenly Father challenging the believer; "Go ahead! Spend what I have given you! Make my day and see if you can ever spend it all! "What we have is beyond all measure and human comprehension.

Everything a Christian has comes from the atoning work of Jesus Christ on the cross, and communicated by the resurrection life that is ours - and we receive it by faith. Our faith is our connection. And it is a firm, grip like connection. There is more power in the faith we possess than 99.9% of all Christians realise. Read the whole of Ephesians 1 again and see this as truth. The lives of many Christians is like driving a Formula 1 vehicle, designed to cruise at well over 100 miles per hour, while we drive not exceeding the 5 miles per hour we use to reverse down our driveway. Heaven has been opened to the person who has faith in Christ.

Preachers and theologians refer to all things to do with salvation as being, "In the atonement." That is healthy terminology, because it is true. It is "Christianese" language for saying that Christ bought it on the cross, and that when He cried "It is finished," the full price had been paid for all the resources that save us and set us free.

Salvation is all about forgiveness, healing, deliverance, resurrection life, raising the dead, prosperity, power and grace all being poured into the life of whosoever believes, and being sustained by that same power and life continually. The same electricity that turns a light on is the same flow of power that keeps it on.

My absolute conviction of life is based on the belief system that I have just outlined skeletally above. The huge, earth convulsing extrapolation that follows concerning whatever flows to humanity from the atoning work of Christ, is that it is for absolutely anybody who believes, and it is always for the here and the now. That's God speaking. For this writer, any statement that suggests that there is anybody outside the pale of the provision of the gospel message of Christ is not only mistaken, it is downright heresy. As well as covering every soul on the globe, the scripture screams loud and clear, "Now is the accepted time. Now is the day of salvation."

These statements above are the very reason why the people of the first century, and Christ Himself, referred to this message as, "The

Gospel,"- "The Evangel," - the meaning of which, in the Greek, means, "The almost too good to be true News."

In English we talk about somebody being saved, healed, delivered, brought back to life, prospered, sustained and/or kept in God. There is one bible word that covers all that. The word that's used in the original Greek of the New Testament is Soteria (salvation) and or Sozo (to be saved, healed, or delivered etc.). It's all in the atonement, and it's all for the now.

It is a firm swallowing of these truths that creates a mental and spiritual platform that grasps the relevance of these facts, and uses them in the management of the miraculous, while considering what I refer to as mandatory mindsets that go towards precipitating a sustained ministry of the miraculous. This needs to be seen as a practical reality and something to do, rather than a theological concept to somehow get our mind around.

Believing this fact will precipitate the miraculous in anybody's ministry. Acts 19 oozes with this presupposition in ministry.

19 F.

MINDSETS THAT PRECIPITATE THE MIRACULOUS.

NUMBER SIX: BE COURAGEOUS AND SPEAK OUT THE RHEMA PROPHETIC WORD.

There are seven miracles in John's gospel, the gospel of the Word that was God and was with God. This is the same Word that became flesh. And these seven miracles were brought into being by the spoken word of Him who is the Word. In John 2 He changed the water to wine. In John 4 He healed the nobleman's son. In John 5 He healed the man at the pool of Bethesda. In John 6 He fed the five thousand. In John 9 He healed the man born blind. In John 11 He raised Lazarus from the dead, and in John 21 He told the disciples to throw their net on the other side of the boat. Seven glorious miracles! And each one was instigated by nothing more than a word being spoken by the Saviour. These are the seven miracles that brought healing and salvation to people. I am deliberately missing out Jesus walking on the water (John 6:16-24) for another day.

"Fill the water pots with water" (John 2:7), seems so mundane, but the faith of the Saviour brought a supply of the best wine ever, without uttering the matter out loud. "Go your way. Your son lives" (John 4:50), sounds almost as if Jesus was shooing the man away. The fact was that He was probably encouraging the man to go home quickly to enter into the joy of his healed son. "Rise take up your bed and walk" (John 5:8), was undoubtedly spoken as a solemn, yet joyful command to a sick man who seems to have lost all his motivation prior to Christ's arrival at his side. Chapter 6 does not even tell us what the Master prayed over the bread and fish. It simply says that Jesus "took the loaves; and when he had given thanks, he distributed to the disciples" (John 6:11) and the provision for the thousands was complete. How I wish I could have a transcript of how Jesus prayed over His food that day. In John 9, having placed the mud created with His own saliva on the blind man's eyes the miraculous was manifested with a simple, "Go and wash in the pool of Siloam" (John 9:7). The man must have had to ask for help as to how to find the pool of Siloam, but Christ's spoken word broke the blindness that shrouded the beggar. "Lazarus come forth" (John 11:43), could not have been simpler. And in chapter 21, the disciples realised that the risen Christ was watching them when they heard Him shout, ""Cast the net on the right side of the boat and you will find some" (John21:6).

Jesus never actually "prayed" for the sick to be healed, or the demons to leave as we normally perceive and conceive prayer to be. He either spoke it into being or just touched the people concerned. In some cases the person requiring healing initiated the move and touched Him, as per the woman with the issue of blood. To be pedantic is normally to be legalistic. But when I say, "To be pedantic, Jesus never prayed for the sick or the demonised, and neither did he command His disciples to pray in that respect," I am trying to release and unleash a principle into the heart of my reader. "Lay hands on the sick and they shall recover" (Mark 16:18). That is what Jesus said. No remark concerning prayer, or even the spoken word was made there.

To add to the case I am making, there is only one little line in the middle of a sentence in Acts that suggest any of the apostle's prayed for anybody (Acts 28:8), in the manner that we normally conceive of prayer. What I mean by that is, that there is no record of anybody asking, "Dear Lord Jesus please heal this person," type prayers. Everywhere else the healing of the sick, the casting out of devils, and the raising of the dead were all performed by the spoken word, or the unspoken touch, even if it was a shadow or even one of Paul's handkerchiefs. It's a biblical principle. It is the anointing that breaks the yoke of sickness, demonisation or demonic bondage. The anointing is the verification of the man or woman of God that carries it. The anointing is the divine seal of ministry. It is the proof of being called and sent by Jesus Christ Himself. Oh for the anointing! The anointing on Paul was such that even cloths and garments that were his carried the same anointing that was upon him. Meditate on the logic of that phenomena and see if you dare to come to the conclusion that self-evident extrapolation cannot miss.

Just to add. The only model of a New Testament church prayer meeting that we have in the book of Acts, is a prayer for the anointing to heal, and the anointing to preach the word boldly (Acts 4:29-31).

The prophetic, rhema word of God, when received by whoever is ministering to people, needs to be spoken out in order for that word to be manifested. Not spoken and declared? No healing nor deliverance according to whatever the word was that was received. Not wanting to insult the intelligence of my readers: The word received needs to be spoken out loud – otherwise it is not a word but a thought that was aborted before it travelled through the birth canal of the mouth.

I believe I first heard of the spoken word being utilised in the realm of the miraculous in one of Watchman Nee's early publications. Nee's early books of course were many sermon notes gleaned from his listeners, collated together and compiled into book form. Though released in English, they were originally preached in Chinese as early as the 1920's. He pointed out that there were two words in Greek for the word, "word." There was the word "logos" and the word, "rhema." Logos, he explained, when referring to the word of God is referencing a general word, or even the entire scripture. The logos is applicable to everybody that takes the trouble to expose themselves to that word. For instance, "You shall love the Lord your God with all your heart and all your soul and all your mind," is a logos word for the whole world. "Rhema," however is for when a word is particular and personal. An example of a "rhema" word would be Jesus telling the nobleman in John 4, "Go your way. Your son lives." That was a personal word, applicable only to the nobleman. It was a rhema word.

By taking what I have just written as an overall explanatory principle of scripture, which is therefore a principle of ministry, whole movements of charismatic and Pentecostal theologies have been birthed. Whenever I have encountered accredited academic theologians in my life I have queried them on the accuracy of this mode of interpreting the Greek New Testament texts concerning "logos" and "rhema." I have no documented proof of such spontaneous and private times of discussion, but I would say that in my own research in this manner there is an 80/20 majority of academics that support what Nee stated above, which is indeed what I believe to be true. Those that disagree with the proposition are almost unanimously, those in non-Pentecostal non-charismatic frames of reference, who claim that the meanings of the two Greek words are synonymous. Methinks it is a case of settled theology impacting and ruling biblical exegesis rather than, as it should be, the other way round.

My personal steamroller that cracks this nut, even if I have an audience that disagrees with my biblical exposition of "logos" and "rhema", is the obvious and self-evident fact that there are indeed general words and personal words throughout the whole of the Bible as well as in daily living experiences. So the principle is indeed true, even if there are a few academics that reject the difference betwixt the two Greek words.

The exposition of the meaning of logos and rhema, as presented originally in the early twentieth century by Watchman Nee qualifies the Pentecostal and Charismatic explanation as to the how and why God speaks today and gives people prophetic words in the here and now in "extra biblical" times. That very statement is utterly anathema to non-charismatics, non-Pentecostals and indeed all Cessationists in general. It is my opinion that those that hold to Cessationist theological beliefs would not contemplate such an exegesis as propositioned above as it would cause them to have to move their position on what they see as an absolute, i.e. "There are no such things as miracles today." Forgive me if I sound harsh with those words, but to have preached and believed for many years, as many Reform Theology pastors have, as well as other frames of reference, with a stance that declares, "Miracles ceased with the death of the original apostles, therefore healing, deliverance and the baptism of the Holy Spirit are null and void today," have a traumatic alteration of mindset to negotiate if the prophetic rhema word was conceded to.

Then again, there are those within the charismatic and Pentecostal stable, who will insist that they are neither anointed to heal the sick, nor to speak the word in the manner here stated. I would counter that thought with what I believe to be sound biblical grounds that the call to preach and minister is a call to save, heal and deliver. The manifestation of rhema words, i.e. prophetic words that are redemptive and salvific to the body, soul or spirit are in the atmosphere for them to take hold of by faith. God is always speaking. God is always active. It is vital that we set ourselves to hear what the Spirit is saying when a person stands to minister the word. No matter how much wonderful sound "logos" is prepared and delivered, there must be a forum prepared in the midst of the "logos" for the Rhema to be brought to birth. The "surprise" rhema words are the most glorious expression of the divine presence in the ministry of the word. I believe God is always wanting to speak prophetically in the ministry of the word. God always has something to say.

I add that to the fact that I do not believe in my 40 years as a Christian that I have ever stood before an audience where there were *no* sick people amongst them. Christians have been pounded by the non-performance, or in some cases the rare performance of the biblical promises of healing and wholeness, that they neither ask nor pray for healing any more. Yet, they love God just the same. This book is a full frontal attack against the non-highlighted, and therefore non-performed promises of God amongst His people.

It takes courage, faith, and a spiritual mind for a preacher of any stature to hear God nudging them with stuff like, "That lady in the third row with the green coat has just been diagnosed with a terminal disease. Tell her I have healed her." That is scary, and incredibly challenging when it happens. It's a giant step the first time it is heard and acted upon. The goal of New Testament ministry is for such phenomenon to become the norm. The more one hears and speaks, the easier such ministry becomes, and the more details those words contain.

This manifestation is clearly part of the "pointing out" and "demonstration" of the Holy Spirit that Paul referred to in his Corinthian letters. The demons were aware that Paul carried such manifestations of the Spirit of God in his back pocket (as it were) as he ministered, that is why they knew him and feared him.

This truth is part of the New Testament minister's armoury. It was foundational, I believe in Paul's ministry of piercing the darkness in people's lives. To believe in such a spiritual weapon is clearly a mindset that precipitates the miraculous manifestation.

19 G.

MINDSETS THAT PRECIPITATE THE MIRACULOUS.

NUMBER SEVEN: HOLINESS AND PURITY OF LIFE IS NOT OPTIONAL.

This generation of high profile and celebrity preachers has, to a degree, lost the skill of presenting the New Testament call to purity and personal holiness without being legalistic and pedantic about practice and lifestyle. It simply cannot be argued against that God wants His people to live pure and wholesome lives in every dimension of living. It cannot be argued against, but it can be buried under mountainous presentations of grace, grace and more grace, at the expense of holiness, purity and personal responsibility.

I have no doubt whatsoever that the ministers and friends that flocked around Paul were won to him by the purity of his life. However, I also have no doubt whatsoever that the Judaising Christians that persecuted Paul did so because, in their concept of things, he did not teach holiness and purity in the same manner that they understood it to mean.

"For the grace of God that brings salvation has appeared to all men, teaching us that, denying ungodliness and worldly lusts, we should live soberly, righteously, and godly in the present age." **(Titus 2:11-12)**

Personal holiness for a Christian that is built solely on what a person does or does not do externally is superficial and not the way Christ presented the challenge to emulate Him. To be sure what a person does or does not do is important, but...

I was converted in a day when some churches were still defining holiness by, "No going to the cinema! No make-up on the ladies! No smoking! No drinking!" etc. (I hasten to add that I have never enjoyed membership in any church with such a paradigm) It was rules and regulations that one could maintain without having the inner man changed in the slightest. In fact one did not need to have a relationship with God at all, but could hide under the shelter of their good conduct and be a member of the church. The more exterior and superficial the criteria for a presentation of holiness, the less effective is the work of the Spirit in a person's heart. Why? Because it is human nature to want to justify ourselves before people.

Holiness is a matter of the heart, the processes of the mind, and the maintenance of an attitude. When those aspects of our existence are immersed in Christ, the outward conduct falls into line. The biblical paradigm of being holy and "attaining" and stature of holiness is embed in the logic of Jesus referring to adultery as having been committed by a person simply by thinking, dwelling and desiring the act. One cannot go any deeper than that. The full depth of human depravity has been fathomed and properly diagnosed. The call is to repent and walk in the full force of genuine repentance. The renewing of the mind as presented and explained by Paul, headlined in those first few verses of Romans 12, are all about the changing of mind, heart and attitude after one has immersed themselves in the full process of practical salvation as explained in his first eight chapters of that letter.

A holy man or woman cannot be anything but feared by the powers of darkness in the world. Holiness when fully expressed in a person's actions, thoughts and deeds pierces the darkness that binds them, and adds to the power when one begins to step into the miraculous. Holiness creates confidence. The righteous are as bold as a Lion. The holy man of faith is famous in both heaven and hell. The demons said it themselves. Jesus they knew and Paul they were acquainted with. "But who are you sons of Sceva?" Holiness is aligning oneself with thoughts, practices, attitudes and goals that are consistent with Christ's attitude and will. By being fully aligned with the heart of God both heaven and hell respond to the rhema word. Because of deep and intimate alignment with the Spirit and heart of God one can decree, "Be healed," and angelic forces will jump, the Spirit will complete His will and healing will be rampant. Alignment with Christ in the deepest meaning of the word means that, "Come out in the name of Jesus" is a divine decree that is backed by heaven and famously noted in hell.

The world has too many ministers calling out "Be healed" and "Come out you unclean spirit!" purely on the grounds that they are being true to the word without much thought of being relationally aligned with the Spirit. Holiness is a fundamental and vital ingredient to the management of the miraculous. It is God and God alone that does the miraculous. In the context of the whole process of salvation by relationship with Christ, the Saviour Himself commanded us to heal the sick, cleanse the lepers and raise the dead. But to disassociate the dynamic of healing and deliverance from the development of a pure heart and clean hands is absolute folly.

Unholy ministers not only shame the body of Christ in the eyes of the human audience, but cause a withdrawal of the blessing of God and precipitate further demonic strongholds to be built. Lack of holiness needs repentance faith and a long obedience in the same direction prolonged through all the stages of life.

How happy is this writer that the gospel has embedded in its presentation a "From now on," caveat. It is never what one was or is. It is never finalised with what one has done, or indeed what one is doing as the gospel is heard. The call of God is to rise in holiness. God's call to a person is never cancelled by one's hideous past, or self-identity as a criminal, thief or even a murderer. Whatever a person's status is as the word of God is encountered, the subliminal hard core good-news is, "From now on it is going to be different if you repent and believe."

Self-denial, the way Jesus presented it, robs us of the privilege of holding grudges, picking favourites, loving some and not others, and generally doing what "self" craves to do. Eh! Is that not why it is called "self-denial?" But it is not primarily the denial of external things. It is majorly all about denying the evil thoughts, attitudes and inner responses which – if neglected – rot the whole of humanity.

Jesus Christ was sinless. Yet He still practised self-denial. Meaning that self-denial is not only about stopping sinful practices – although it certainly includes that. If Jesus, who had no sins to break off and repent of, practiced self-denial it must mean also denying ourselves from some legitimate and righteous aspects of life that are not the best for us.

Susannah Wesley was the youngest of 27 children. No! That is not a misprint or a typo. One of twenty seven. She herself had nineteen children. One of which was John Wesley. I would not have liked to wash the dishes or iron the clothes in that household. Susannah, undoubtedly, had the grace and power working in her life as she seeded all her children with the word of God and the love of Christ throughout all her days. The regular devotional input she gave to each of her children individually was profound and led John, known within his family as "Jack," to ask: "Mother! What exactly is sin? Could you please define it for me?" Know this, that when a person is aligned with God in the deepest recesses of their being, and is feeding that alignment and relationship as if one's life depends on it (and it does), one will say things that could shock the world and radicalise the church into deeper love and grace. She said (and I quote): "John, whatever weakens your reasoning, impairs the tenderness of your conscience, obscures your sense of God or takes away your relish for spiritual things – in short, whatever increases the authority and the power of the flesh over the spirit, that to you becomes sin no matter how good it is in itself."

Personal purity, holiness and alignment with the heart of the Father could be rationally said to be the most important weapon in the armoury of the man or woman of God.

20.

BURNING THEIR BRIDGES AS WELL AS THEIR BOOKS.
ACTS 19:13-20

There is deliverance; and then there is deliverance!

There is deliverance as executed in the west that normally takes some considerable time, and for that reason is shied away from in public meetings. After all, one cannot have the entire congregation watching for an hour, the sermon suspended while people command the demon spirit out many times over a prolonged period before it finally leaves, only to discover that half the congregation have gone home. Because of those kind of dynamics, most pastors that I know would ask the person concerned to see them "afterwards," or make an appointment during the week. It's untidy, tiring, and often times embarrassing when freedom has not come to the person being prayed for. I have not only, many years ago I might add, been there, worn the Tee-shirt and starred in the DVD, I have seen the impact on other friends and colleagues in ministry.

But then there is deliverance in overwhelming power and authority, where one word is spoken, and the demon leaves screaming almost instantly. It is all over, powerfully, authoritatively and deftly in a matter of moments. When effected on those terms, deliverance is clean, impressive to watching unbelievers, faith building for Christians, and utterly glorifying God as it reveals the power that resides in the name of the Lord Jesus Christ. When I have seen deliverance ministered in that manner, it has always made my hair stand on end with the impact it has had on my own personal faith. I almost tremble with awe at making the assertions that the word of God leads us to in Acts 19:13-20. Jesus Christ has been exalted by God the Father far above all. And here, in these verses, is the practical proof of that truth as seen amongst the Ephesian people. When Paul expelled demons from people's lives, it was undoubtedly in the latter manner as described immediately above

The fact that the account in Acts is nearly 2,000 years ago impacts not one iota on the truths that are explicit as well as implicit in the text of scripture. Truth is always truth. Apart from those things that have stepped out of eternity and impacted on time, truth has always been relevant as well as simultaneously ancient and modern. It may be true that Christ died and was resurrected circa 2,000 years ago, but the impact of that eternally effective act of God Himself was being felt before the foundation of the world (1 Peter 1:20. Ephesians 1:4. Revelation 13:8. Matthew 25:34. Hebrews 4:3. Matthew 13:35. John 17:24. Revelation 17:8.). Election, as was set before the world was made, is God's responsibility. Our responsibility is to believe. We always have a role to play when it comes to faith. It was faith that brought Abel into relationship with God in Genesis 4. It was faith that caused Enoch to walk with God in Genesis 5, and it was faith that saved Noah and his family in Genesis 6:8. It was faith that that made Abraham a friend of God, and it was always faith all the way through the Old Testament right up to the arrival of Christ that brought grace and forgiveness to people. Thereafter it was faith that justified John, Peter and Paul. It was faith, also, that saved and sanctified the witches, wizards, warlocks, mediums, witch doctors here in Ephesus in Acts 19.

The account of what took place is, as is typical of the entire Bible, brevity in the extreme, as well as informative to the utmost. From verse 13-20 we are talking of confrontation with demonic forces, effected by those who are joined by faith to the resurrection power and authority of Jesus Christ. What is generally a Cinderella and whispered activity of the twenty-first century church, was obviously part of the staple diet that was on the open table when Paul was ministering. Deliverance in public, with both saved and unsaved people spectating, and with or without the consent and desire of those infested. Follow my logic and see if you agree with me as we go through the relevant verses.

In Acts 19:11-12 we have that little paragraph explaining the so called, "extraordinary miracles." The extraordinary nature of these miracles, according to Luke, comprised of the fact that cloths, aprons, and pieces of material in general, were taken, after Paul had worn them, used them or touched them, and when placed on people who were both sick and/or demonised, were immediately set free.

The fact that in the category of "extraordinary miracles," healing and exorcism (or deliverance) was effected, I suggest it is only logical that the, "ordinary miracles," were much more frequently seen, i.e. healing and exorcism effected in Paul's presence by the laying on of his hands, or the speaking of the word by the apostle.

Because of what we read in Christ's commissioning of the twelve (Matthew 10, Luke 9:1-9), the seventy (two) (Luke 10:1-15), and Paul (Acts26:16-18), we shamefully have to conclude that freeing people from demonic bondage was much more common than it is in the church generally in the twenty-first century. The ignorance of this kind of ministry is so widespread and dominating, that I have myself met many evangelical (and even one or two Pentecostal ministers) that believe it is a ministry hardly relevant today. This point of view is commonly seen by the ostracising of those ministers who, "specialise," in deliverance and who are therefore labelled as "extremists".

My assumption that both healings and deliverances were commonly seen during Paul's ministry in Ephesus is supported by the fact that, "some Jews," went around emulating Paul's manner of ministry. Verse 13 states, "Some Jews were saying, "In the name of Jesus, whom Paul preaches, I command you to come out." Verse 14 zooms in on a certain party of the, "Some Jews," who were utilising Paul's modus operandi, namely, seven travelling sons of a Jewish chief priest called Sceva. These seven encountered a slight catastrophe of ministry in their course of work as they tried to emulate the apostle. They entered a house to free someone from demonization, approaching the situation, not with the normal Jewish prayers, incantations and the quoting of certain Old Testament scriptures, as was commonly done in those days, but by commanding the evil spirits out of the man in the same manner that they had seen when watching Paul. This serious, but obviously slightly superstitious branch of Judaism was more widespread than commonly acknowledged, according to Josephus. The scattered Jews that followed this kind of work, attributed the creation and source of their exorcism ministry, believe it or not, to King Solomon. Josephus writes (Antiquities 8.45-46) that Jews of this kind of persuasion and ministry, believed that David's son Solomon had composed charms through which diseases were healed, and evil spirits cast out so as never to return; and that these operations continued to be commonly utilised among the Jews right up to his time. The Lord Jesus Himself seems to refer to this practice in Matthew 12:27, when He asks, "By whom do your children cast them out?"

This conviction that deliverance ministry was frequent and common place in Paul's ministry is even more strongly corroborated by the fact that what finally happened to these travelling sons of Sceva became widespread knowledge in the great metropolis, and did not lead to the ridicule of the seven sons, nor the exaltation of Paul, but precipitated "all" being seized with fear, and the name of the Lord Jesus being held in great honour. The incredible response of an evil spirit declaring, "Jesus I know, and Paul I know, but who are you?" and then violently tearing the clothes off all seven, shocked the general population of all Ephesus. The story of this drama was reported throughout the city in both Jewish and Greek circles, and the phrase, "They were all..." suggests that the entire city were coming to a unified opinion on the issue. All these facts combine to make a statement concerning how Paul's teaching and preaching was understood, especially those adherents of Judaism who wanted, of themselves, to work in the area of exorcism. They knew that it was

Christ who was the key element in the ministry of deliverance far above the participation of Paul. This, "Jesus that Paul preached," was clearly not to be taken lightly.

What makes the saga of the seven sons even more remarkable, is that these men, attempting to cast out demons by calling over them, "In the name of Jesus, whom Paul preaches, I command you to come out," must have, for a time, been successful. Why do I say that? It says in verse 15, "One day" (NIV. NLT: "One time"), it plainly suggests that their mimicry of Paul hitherto had been fruitful. For a time, who knows how long, this "fakery" of using the name of Jesus as some sort of charm or war cry over the demons actually seems to have worked. And there were clearly others who were doing the same. The great lesson is, of course, that to interfere with, and to try to deal with the demonic in ignorance is dangerous. To use the name and the person of Jesus Christ as a charm or an incantation is highly dangerous. To emulate men of God by emulating some outward trait, or visual expression is simply not wise. And to effect all of the above at one and the same time could even be fatal. The story is captivating in its revelation of things of the spirit. There are many who hide in the skirts of, "the church," who dangerously use the name of Jesus, without faith in Him. The demon actually said, "Jesus I know (Greek: ginosko), Paul I know (epistamai)." A stricter English, translation is closer to, "Jesus I know fully and am totally conversant with who and what He is, Paul I understand, inasmuch as, he is relational to Jesus, and therefore has authority." The fact that remote demons, i.e. geographically apart from Paul, were acquainted with him and the authority and power he carried, suggests that communication in the demonic, "Corridors of power," made sure that their minions were informed of those Christians, or in this particular case, Christian, whose power, authority and manner of life was injurious to the kingdom of darkness.

We have therefore, by clear understanding of the biblical text, the picture of "all" Jews and Greeks living in Ephesus (and by the context of the whole of chapter 19, the entire population of Asia), honouring the name of Jesus, while freely discussing the issue of demons and deliverance. Imagine! So many people who knew about and believed in the power of the occult and evil spirits, were in reverential fear, honouring the name of this, "Jesus whom Paul preached," because this "Jesus" obviously had evil spirits under His feet. They were all obviously subject to the Jesus that Paul referred to as, "Messiah."

We cannot move on without observing that even though there was an obvious volcanic explosion of the power of Christ in Ephesus, the preaching, the teaching, the lifestyle and overall presentation of the apostle did not lead to anybody referring to him as, "The man of faith," or, "The man of power for this hour." The, "White Suit Mentality," and the dark, but subtle, "Look to me because I am a man of God above you" club, was somehow not in the people's mentality even after listening to and emulating the man from Tarsus. According to the text, after having been exposed to Paul's sessions at the School of Tyrannus, converted and unconverted alike deferred all things that took place to the power of Christ, not the power of Paul. I do not say this as a prescribed law of course, people respond how they want to. However, something in Paul's doctrine and manner of life did not even suggest that he had any greatness. By the stated responses of the masses who had heard the story of the sons of Sceva, Paul Was ignored, and Jesus was honoured, even amongst those who chose not to be converted. No doubt every Jewish exorcist that had been calling demons out in the same way as Paul ceased forthwith when the sons of Sceva had repeated their story to them. They knew not to, "mess" with this Jesus, and that they had to know this "Jesus that Paul preached," as intimately as Paul did in order to see the ever glorious results that Paul saw.

Note also that even the response of the unsaved referred to the fact that Paul preached Jesus. What an incredible testimony to the trumpet like clarity of Paul's presentation.

Verse 17 carries on in the progression of thought concerning Christ conquering hell, Satan and demons in general. It moves on to one of the ramifications of the widespread fear, and reverence of Christ. Many of the converts, now walking in faith, came forward to confess their evil deeds. Note that public confession voluntarily and freely followed conversion, as opposed to preceding conversion. This informs us that in the content of the presentation of Christ that Paul was making every day, together with the manifestation of the Holy Spirit that was being seen and experienced every day, purity of body, soul and spirit, and transparency of relationship towards God and people was negotiated by confession of those sins that people were leaving behind in the ashes of their old lives.

I personally find it incredible to read that many who had believed, still wanted to confess, even after their justification. We do not hear of Paul forbidding or restricting the action, and we certainly read that he did not require it of them. In the midst of this widespread, open, and therefore public series of confessions came the ex-witches, wizards, warlocks and the like. Jesus conquering the devil was on Luke's agenda in Acts 19:17-20, just as it always has been. "Stand fast in the liberty with which Christ makes us free," is what Paul wrote in Galatians 5:1. How many Christians are there who do not know this freedom of which Paul talks?

Note also: It was deeds that were confessed, not thoughts or inclinations. Of their own accord, by open public declaration, they confessed their past iniquities. One 19th century writer perceptively states, "The efficacy of God's word, penetrating the inmost recesses of their soul, wrought that free and open confession to which perhaps even the torment of hell would not have compelled them."

"A number who had practiced sorcery..." (19:19). This writer has had some experience of deliverance ministry, but nothing at all to write home about in comparison to the man of God that I worked with for some considerable time. I refer to the senior pastor in Ikotun Egbe in Nigeria. I have witnessed and sat at the feet of what is probably the most prophetic, intelligent, authoritative and powerful deliverance ministry on the planet. It was an education. I preface my remarks here with that statement lest any should think that I am talking above myself with some of the observations I make immediately below. After witnessing many deliverances of witches, wizards and warlocks of all grades and types, I have evolved an understanding of the dynamics of what I perceive is universally consistent in the realm of the spirit, when demons come under the influence of the anointing of a man of God.

Sorcerers and wizards do not come to Christian meetings in order to get converted. They come to kill, steal and destroy. They come to disturb Christians and Church leaders. They come to pray in demonic tongues in churches where tongues are heard regularly, and to curse the proceedings. They come to infect others with their evil. They even come to kill anointed ministers of God who are making inroads and destroying the kingdom of darkness locally, or even nationally, depending on the weight of the anointing on the man or woman of God concerned. This is serious and very real. They never attend with a passive frame of mind. They attend on hell's business.

They do not come forward in appeals to be saved, or to come to faith. They stay secreted in the body of church meetings and revel in the ignorance of those around them who claim to be Christians, but have no knowledge of who they are. They particularly enjoy things when ministers do not even know that they are present. They are used to not being discovered by the vast majority of churches.

The weight of the anointing on the leader of any church they attend is what will find them out, or not find them out – nothing else works.

While moving in the prophetic, the majority of the demon possessed that I saw delivered, were actually "seen" by the senior pastor/prophet beforehand. By "seen," I mean that he as a prophet could clearly take note of where they were in the context of the thousands that were present. What he saw, I am not conversant with. I have heard him state one time, that he saw some darkness, like a mist, in certain areas of the congregation, hovering around a particular person and so strode closer to them, only to have a manifestation of screaming, or something similar, before he confronted them. I have also, on missions in other countries, as well as in his own church, witnessed him walk into a mass of standing, waiting people and go directly to those who needed deliverance. My point is that the anointing, when it is heavy enough, breaks the strongest and darkest of yokes on people's lives.

Even though I have witnessed some of the greatest manifestations of the power of God, New Testament ministry and management of the miraculous in the life of the pastor in Lagos, something inside me prohibits me from thinking that he moves in a dimension that is higher than Paul. What I have been taught from the start of my Christian life makes me wary of thinking that I in my lifetime have met somebody who moves in the power of God to a greater degree than Peter, John or Paul. Because of that *a priori* presupposition, I am left in a state of awe to imagine how Paul moved in the issues of deliverance, healing and prophecy. The response, for instance, of all the witch-doctors and the major demonic forces in Lagos to my African mentor's full frontal attack on the kingdom of darkness I still find incredible, years after my first discovery of what was happening. Many seriously demonised men and women, who were so deeply infested with demons and remarkable evil power, that they were angry and distressed at losing their covens and chapters to Christ through the pastor, came in dreadful earnest to pull him down and shame him. Young witches came to seduce him. Men and women came to kill him. I have seen him prophetically reveal to the church that certain people were present with knives, guns, and sometimes with wire that was to be used in an attempt to strangle him. Those people of this evil calibre who live in Lagos were delivered and gloriously converted, becoming strong and Godly members. Some of the loudest and seemingly violent people who were witches and wizards, once delivered, came to faith in Christ, and became some of the gentlest and most lovely Christian people. Oh the pernicious evil of the devil! Oh the incredible grace of Christ! I have always been struck by the tangible serenity and peace that rested on those delivered from the darkest of bondages.

One man contrived a meeting to get face to face with the African pastor with whom I served whilst carrying a bottle of acid. He had been commissioned to destroy the ministry that was doing so much damage to Satan's kingdom. The prophet confronted him prophetically before the acid was even seen. The man, I believe, is now a strong member in the church and a lovely Christian man.

The only other qualifying reason I have seen witch doctors and the like come willingly into the presence of the word and power of God is when they themselves are ill, or even dying. They always hide by using nice Christian sounding names, and then join the prayer line claiming to be Christians. I have seen many of such a kind, revealed by a prophetic word. The pastor/prophet in Lagos still delivered them in the name of Jesus, of course, and led them to Christ.

My point in these observations is that if this happens in the twenty-first century to a man like my friend in Lagos, why should I think it was any different for Paul in Ephesus. In fact, logic suggests to me that it must have been similarly worse for Paul. A Christian minister, even of apostolic stature like Paul does not get to be famous amongst Jewish unbelievers, gentile heathens, demons, and a whole Roman province, by preaching nice three point sermons climaxed with a verse or two of "Just as I Am," followed by the so called, "sinners prayer." We are talking of a holy, powerful, devil stirring presentation of Christ, interspersed with healings, deliverance and prophetic pronouncements in the demonstration (i.e. "the pointing out") of the Holy Spirit. The message that Paul presented, rose to such an incredibly high profile across Ephesus and Asia because of his self-effacing, Christ glorifying, battle against the devil. He was so successful that even the Asian people that did not believe, honoured the name of Christ, and not Paul. Oh that we knew his secret!

These converted sorcerers brought their books. Their books, scrolls and writings were worth a lot of money because they were either filled with many years of learning of the occult arts and practices that they themselves had learned and written, or they had purchased them at great price containing spells and incantations that others had created or discovered. Make no mistake about it that writings and documents in those days (scrolls as they were) were much more precious than we would esteem them today. One could lose a book today and buy a replacement tomorrow in the twenty-first century. Their books, however, were written by hand, and once burnt were lost forever. The dark knowledge that they contained were no doubt considered by the sorcerer's fraternity of Asia as priceless.

Burning these books revealed a remarkable degree of contempt for the occultist sins they had erstwhile been part of. Like the idolaters coming to repentance in Isaiah 30:22, they were saying, "Get you hence." There were others who even threw their silver and gold to the moles and to the bats" (Isaiah 2:20). They were taking, if you will, a violently godly revenge on those things that had been the instruments of sin to them. They were proclaiming, with all the force of their faith and conviction, the evil of it, and that those very things that were once treasures, were now utterly detestable to them. And they were burnt of their own volition, not by required precept.

This holiest of bonfires plainly revealed their resolve never to return to the use of those dark machinations that their books referred to. They were so fully convinced of the evil and danger of them that they would not just put them in their cellars or attics to gather dust, having them within reach, but, being steadfastly resolved never to make use of them, they gladly celebrated Christ and burnt them. The public burning inferno shows clearly how that those that truly repent of sin will keep themselves as far as possible from returning to it.

By burning them, of course, they prevented these hideous documents from doing mischief to others. If Judas had been nearby he would have said, "Sell them, and give the money to the poor;" or,

"Auction them! We can buy Bibles and good books with it." But then, what mischief might be done by them that owned them? It was therefore, the only safe course to take, to commit them all to the flames. Their monetary worth is noted by Luke, showing all that witnessed the burning the new found contempt of the wealth of this world in the converts. I cannot help but wonder if the price of the books was estimated by those that were trying to talk them out of destroying them?

By this action, however, they publicly testified their utter joy in their conversion from such wickedness. These converts joined together, freely and happily in making this bonfire. They did it in a public place. They done it privately, everyone in his own house. However, they chose to do it together, by consent, that Christ and his grace in them might be the more magnified, and all about them the more edified.

This account in Acts 19:19-20 is recounted for its impact on the newly founded church in Ephesus and the statement it makes of Christ the mighty conqueror over all the powers of the devil and his hordes. From the end of verse 12 through to the end of verse 20 in Acts 19, the subject is the power of Christ over the devil, the public awe at the demonstration of the power of God, and the preaching of Christ that gave the revelatory grounds for the miracles of changed lives that Ephesus and Asia was seeing more and more in the three years that Paul was there.

The ceremony was done in public, for all to see. This was freedom being violently seized and entered into. The public spectators would have obviously asked, "Why?" By word of mouth, the word of the Lord spread widely. If we desire to be in earnest partaking in the fruits of such a mission, every pursuit and enjoyment must be given up which hinders the effect of the gospel upon the mind, or loosens its hold upon the heart. And that is exactly what this bonfire signified.

It has to be added also, that items to which people were emotionally committed to, or treasured in the heart more than is proper, could also have psychic or spiritual ties that inhibit growth in Christ and overall freedom. In a church I once visited there were three Sri Lankan men, all brothers who were strong and committed members of the church, but, by their own testimony, as well as the testimony of the church as a whole, were always overly serious and grave. None of them had ever displayed joy or even smiled over the years of their Christian experience. The visiting evangelist went to pray for them but stopped and said," I see pieces of string that hold you in chains! What does this mean to you?" The three brothers all raised their shirts to reveal a piece of string that had varied colours and the odd bead attached. These strings were tied around their waist in childhood by their parents as a sign to their family idol that they were committed to the idol. The evangelist asked for a pair of scissors and asked the brothers to cut the ties off their bodies. The three of them suddenly manifested with agonising screams and cries. The string was cut on each of them, resulting in a final loud cry as each of them found peace and freedom immediately the string was cut. They each stood up, smiling, laughing and even dancing. They had each been committed Christians for twenty years or so, but never free. Just as those strings, linked and connected to demonic powers held those three brothers, some of these books, if not all, would have undoubtedly contributed to the freedom of the offerers as the flames consumed them.

Preachers of the gospel are sent forth to wage war against Satan. They are intended to be the protagonists – the aggressors, if you will, not the defenders, in this holiest of holy wars. On the rock of the revelation of who Christ is, Christ builds His church, and the gates of hell will not prevail against it. The minister of God is to take the battle to the gates of hell. By this means, Christ goes forth conquering and to conquer. The deliverance of sorcerers is a wonderful thing for the kingdom of God, but the removal of demonic infestation sublimely puts Jesus Christ in a proper and appropriate perspective. He is the

Mighty Conqueror. And we need to state that the casting out of evil spirits from those that were demonised is only one aspect of Christ's victory over Satan. There was grace in the deliverance of these sorcerers, but there was more grace in the fact that as they burnt their precious books of spells and incantations, they were affirming that they were "ex-sorcerers," and new creations in Christ.

This freedom to burn the books, and fully, publicly confess their previous evils that Paul allowed without constraining or restraining the converts, and he simply stepping into the background while they declared their faith, is equally a valid and conscious aspect of his management of the miraculous. The entire proceedings needed to be a complete and thorough work of the Holy Spirit without any human intervention in its manifestation. And it needed to be seen by the masses to be so.

21.

FOLLOWING IN THE TRAIN OF HIS TRIUMPH.

"After all this had happened..."

Acts 19:21

New Testament gospel ministry as defined by the apostle Paul, and seen in Ephesus, is a conjoining of the word and the Spirit, as well as manifesting tangible authority and power, that all melds into a prophetic presentation of the reality of Christ. It is delivered and released through a person that has been dealt with by the Holy Spirit for that very function.

When both word and Spirit have a high degree of release, fullness, weight, authority and power, it convicts and converts and merges into accompanying miraculous manifestations amongst the listeners, and prophetic inspiration in the one ministering. In its strongest and most concentrated mixture it sits on the life of the man or woman of God preaching, impacting all that he or she says or thinks. When these dynamics are persistently and consistently exercised, it becomes, sometimes immediately- sometimes developing over time, an almost permanent abiding anointing upon the minister's life. He ministers to others, even while "not ministering." There are several phenomena in this syndrome. One of them is the way in which it divides people with the deftness of a cleaver. The heavier the anointing, the more it tends to divide the believer from the unbeliever, as well as believer from believer. It causes the rise as well as the fall of many (Luke 1:34). It is these dynamics, amongst others, that are all essential ingredients that cause the activity to qualify as, New Testament ministry.

If the parameters of New Testament ministry, as given to us in Acts, are there as a model for us to emulate, we cannot soundly expect anything less than what we read about in the sacred text. Anything short of what we read, cannot be classified as New Testament ministry. The soundness of New Testament ministry is the very foundation of any kind of management of the miraculous.

THE PROPHECY AND THE PROMISE.

Prophecy and promise are sourced from the heart of God the Father, and proceeded by the Spirit of God, and then uttered through the word of God via the Son of God. The spirit of prophecy, after all, is the testimony of Jesus (Revelation 19:10). God reveals His plans and purposes to us so that we can come into a place of agreement and alignment with Him, and thereby bring into reality whatever has been promised.

Any time in scripture where God speaks prophetically to a person with a promise of their destiny (i.e. Abraham, Joseph, Moses etc.), they are never ready for the fulfilment at the point of time when the promise is given. To fulfil the prophecy, and/or promise, they have to grow up into the character that is ready for the blessing. Joseph dreamed that people, as well as his own family would bow down to him in servitude. But when he received the dream he was in servitude and submission to all. He had to grow in wisdom, as well as years, before he would be the man he dreamed of in the prophetic promise. Paul received a prophetic word, he agreed with it and the promised outcome. He then needed to commit himself to the divine process of fulfilment.

Jesus Christ spoke this prophetic word to Paul at the very point of his conversion, radically and deeply challenging his entire character. It does not seem so, however, as we read through the book of Acts at first mention. It is in Acts 9 where we have the moment of change for the apostle, told in what is, "real time," in the narrative. The words of Christ were: "Saul, Saul, why do you persecute me?"(9:4 NIV). "I am Jesus, whom you are persecuting... Now get up and go into the city and you will be told what you must do." (9:5b & 6 NIV). That hardly seems prophetic in the chapter 9 account. However, it seems Luke was saving having to repeat himself, because that very moment is recounted twice again before we finish the full read of Acts, and each time we gain a little more intelligence as to what Christ actually said to Saul of Tarsus, "Apostle elect." At the end of Acts 21, and throughout Acts 22, we have a picture of Paul standing on the steps that led up to the Roman barracks, waving his hand for silence, and telling his story to a vast crowd in Jerusalem. He tells us a little more of the revelation that Christ spoke to him whilst he lay blinded in the dust of the Damascus Road. Once again, we quote only the words that the Lord Jesus spoke. "Saul, Saul, why do you persecute me?"(22:7 NIV). "I am Jesus of Nazareth, whom you are persecuting." (22:8 NIV) "Get up ...and go into Damascus. There you will be told all that you have been assigned to do" (22:10 NIV). We have a little more data that he was to learn about his God given assignment in Damascus. But we still do not have the full force and depth of Christ's challenge to his person, *per se*.

In Acts 26, however, he tells the story again to King Agrippa. Focussing on the words of Jesus alone, we have a more extensive text. "Saul, Saul, why do you persecute me? It is hard for you to kick against the goads" (26:14 NIV). "I am Jesus, whom you are persecuting, Now get up and stand on your feet. I have appeared to you to appoint you as a servant and as a witness of what you have seen of me and what I will show you. I will rescue you from your own people and from the Gentiles. I am sending you to them to open their eyes and turn them from darkness to light, and from the power of Satan to God, so that they may receive forgiveness of sins and a place among those who are sanctified by faith in me."

Now we have it. Prophecy and promise. His full assignment, as well as the promise of deliverance from persecution of both Jews and Gentiles, all of which will take the rest of his life to fulfil. Note the following:

1. Saul of Tarsus had received the prophetic promise, from the Father, by the Spirit, through the Son.

2. He was to be Christ's servant, i.e.: Doulos, i.e. an Apostle (26:16).

3. There was the promise of more revelation ("What I will show you" 26:16b). Revelation is what would sustain Paul throughout the rest of his life.

4. There was the predicted horror of the need of divine rescues and deliverance from both Jew and Gentile (26:17). This is what demanded strength of character, and a sanctified will. How many would choose to continue with Christ if, at the point of conversion, God revealed the suffering and persecution that was coming their way. It was going to be so severe that it would require God Himself to rescue Paul.

5. There was also the divine confirmation of a coming ministry of deliverance, and scripture teaching in opening people's eyes from darkness to light (26:17).

6. And the power of God was to rest upon him for demonic deliverance in turning people from Satan to God (26:18).

7. And this would all take place so that those who were thus ministered to would receive forgiveness of sins and a place among those who were made holy by faith in Christ. It must, in those first moments after conversion blinded his heart as well as his eyes.

That is all very wonderful, challenging, good news for Saul, apart from the persecution section of the list of assigned destinies. God had set a series of predetermined appointments to bring to pass His promise in Paul's life. Paul was going to require rescuing from time to time. Through the many tempestuous winds that blew against his life, God was letting Paul know that He had already prepared a way of escape. To hear God Himself promise that he would rescue him must have been simultaneously wonderful to know that he had a perpetual divine Lifeguard, yet, incredibly intimidating to know that there were going to be times when He would need rescuing. When this writer attempts to put his own feet in Saul's sandals, the courage it must have taken to receive that promise, to align himself with it, and to walk in it, is seriously staggering.

It was Clive Staples Lewis that wrote, "Courage is not simply one of the virtues, but the form of every virtue at its testing point." It is a remarkable truth, and one that sketches a portrait of the Apostle Paul like no other. Courage of a precious calibre was demanded to receive Christ's words, and then to spend his life placing himself in line with those words, giving thanks to Him who had loved him and had given Himself for him.

All through Paul's life and ministry he encountered fierce life threatening persecution, yet he had always been rescued from it. His freedom in Ephesus for the majority of the time, excluding the Christ rejecters of the Ephesian Jewish Synagogue, was a wide open door. We are not told of any animosity towards him in Ephesus until he was making plans to leave (Acts 19:21 and 19:23). 1 Corinthians 15:32 suggests that Paul finally came face to face with animalistic opposition in some kind of physical, as well as spiritual collision. Whether or not that refers to the oncoming tsunami of a riot that Acts 19:23-41 tells us about, we are not certain. The "great and effectual door of ministry," was opened to him, and was finally beginning to close as Paul was entertaining thoughts of moving on. But that was after, nearly three years in the great metropolis.

POWER AND AUTHORITY

Three years is a considerably long period of time to be confined (or released – depending on how one looks at it) with daily public ministry to groups of people in the same place. The sustaining of a man's health, strength and inspiration to consistently minister at the level Paul ministered was surely a supernatural phenomenon. The sustenance of such high level giving of self was, and is greatly connected with the infusion of divine power and authority that was his in abundance. In Luke 9:1-3, When Jesus had called the Twelve together, he gave each of them power and authority to drive out all demons and to cure diseases, and he sent them out to proclaim the kingdom of God and to heal the sick. Which means their preaching and their ministry to sick people were all accompanied by the same power and authority that Christ Himself carried. They might not have had the character, the understanding, the knowledge, or exercised at the exact same level that Christ carried (the scripture says Jesus had the Holy Spirit without measure), but the authority and power they went with was indeed the same authority and power that was intrinsic to Christ's being, that exuded from His person.

Jesus sent His disciples out to confront and act against demonic activity, sickness and disease. He literally and factually gave them power and authority to get the job done. They used that power and authority, and were extremely exultant in that fact. The authority and power they were given, was given by the voice of Christ Himself in a face to face commissioning. Paul moved in this power and authority to a remarkable level throughout his life as an apostolic minister, and it was also given him in a face to face dialogue with Christ on the Damascus Road (See Acts 9, and 26:16-18). It took years before that power and authority was seen to surface and manifest in his life, but it was placed there from the word go, at his conversion. As far as I read and understand from scripture, I would strongly suggest that this moving in the power of God reached a peak while he was at Ephesus, as recorded in Acts 19.

While the tide of faith rose, and the impact of his ministry increased in Ephesus and Asia, there were two extreme results concurrently coming to the boil. There were ever increasing numbers of those that had come to faith in Christ, together with an ever increasing spread of the gospel by word of mouth all over the Roman province. The whole of Asia heard the word (Acts 19:10. 19:20). And, simultaneous to this rise of faith, was the negative impact on those who had heard and yet chosen not to be converted, or to have faith in Christ. The seeds that were saving some, were synchronically damning others. This was by no means a passive rejection. The Equinox High Tide of unbelief was about to surface in Ephesus. Animosity was rising from beneath the surface of Ephesian society, to show itself in a volcanic explosion. The heathen culture was about to reject both Christ and his bond-slave Paul. Acts 19 tells us it was after the burning of the books by the ex-sorcerers, and after Paul's decision to leave Ephesus had been made.

In the midst of this dual build-up of faith with some, and unbelief and antagonism with others, Paul ploughed on with a deep and ruler straight furrow, ministering with the afore mentioned power and authority of Christ day after day. Authority is meaningless without power behind it. Power is dangerous if there is no authority to manage it. People today, often preach with authority, yet without power, excepting that power that is intrinsic in the message of the gospel. There is such a thing as a "powerful word," and an "authoritative word," yet without the accompanying manifestation of that power or the fulfilment of the promises of the word. That is low level authority. That, sadly, is a common phenomenon, especially in Western Christianity. On the other side of the fence, church history of the last century or so has revealed quite a few men and women of God that moved in the power of God to heal and deliver, but seemingly were authority-less when it came to preaching. I do acknowledge, however, that a minister can have great authority, and move in manifestations of power, and yet still be a weak preacher. Carrying the authority of Christ, and moving in the power of the Spirit is from a completely internal root that must, somewhere, have external fruit. Great power does not always mean a great preacher, however. Power without authority is strikingly dangerous.

Authority and power, when moving as conjoined twins in a person's life cannot be mistaken. Such a thing is uncommon. There is a "common message" in some churches, and there is an "uncommon message" in others. A common message may be true, but does not impact the listener, because of lack of power, or authority, or both. An uncommon message is what is desired in these uncommon times. By this, I refer to preaching which, because of the power and the authority that is present in the declaration of truth, strikes the listening soul causing awe and amazement, and ultimately a manifestation of those things declared, i.e. repentance, faith in Christ, and a desire to be holy, and the manifestation of the miraculous.

Paul had both power and authority in abundance. Both power and authority are given of God, honed, sharpened and deepened by attention to an ever deepening relationship with Him. It cannot be faked. It is part and parcel of the overflow of a deep intimacy with the Master. I believe it is true to say that even with power and authority there is deep, deeper and deepest, that is, a gradation of manifestation. However, I believe strongly that, "no power" in ministry, overflows from "no relationship." I do not mean that such ministers are not saved, sanctified or living a right life. God forbid! What I am saying is that the level of relationship that is fundamentally required for New Testament ministry is lacking when power and authority is not present. Because one believes in the call of God, and has taken to the public platform to manifest that ministry to which he or she believes they were called, that minister must have been dealt with to the degree that his relationship with God has placed an overflow in the human spirit that results in New Testament ministry. Jesus Christ never commissioned anybody to preach without also commissioning them to heal the sick, cleanse the lepers and raise the dead. When that occurs, it is simply an overflow for no other reason than to bless others.

The minister must have conquered satan not only to the security of his own soul, but for the empowering and releasing of those to whom he ministers, that is the sheep to whom he is called to lead. The minister must be walking on ahead of those that are ministered to (Luke 19:28). To walk in the ministry, with the claim of being called of God, demands a deeper relationship than what is commonly seen in "normal" Christians. Real relationship with God cannot but impart His power. The words promised to Paul at his conversion, as stated in Acts 26:16-18, are words that cover all true ministers of the gospel.

The real fruit that flows out of a deep intimacy with God, and profound relationship with Him, is power. To know God in this way is to know His power. That is what Paul enjoyed. Knowing awesome facts about God does not change one's relationship with Him. One must gain a knowledge that flows out of actually knowing and continually relating with Him in holiness and purity. From that "knowing", within the relationship with God Himself, there blossoms a manifestation of power and authority. Thus we have the saying that, an effective witness not only knows his faith but shows his faith. Robert Murray M'Cheyne said, "A holy minister in the hands of God is a fearful weapon of righteousness."

THE WORD AND THE SPIRIT.

It is God's power working through His Word and His Spirit that brings about power to heal and deliver. This is the only dynamic with which to manage the miraculous. It is, indeed, part and parcel of the miraculous. Having the word alone can be incredibly frustrating. Knowing the biblical teaching concerning God's promise to heal and deliver is a wonderful thing, but without the presence of the Holy Spirit to carry the preached word and the prayed words, there is much less of an impact, than when the word is carried by the unleashed power of the Holy Spirit.

God's word refreshes our mind. We experience this as we read God's word. That is, indeed, a function of the Holy Spirit, yet that in itself is not knowing the Holy Spirit per se. God's Spirit renews our strength. His actions, and one's relationship with Him has a tangible effect in the physical, time space world. Not only must we have God's Word but we must have God's Spirit.

Many preach, thoroughly knowing the written word of God, but not knowing the Holy Spirit in the same comprehensive manner. This is how Paul knew both the word and the Spirit. We need to receive the Holy Spirit in the same way that the human heart relates to Christ. There are gifts of the Holy Spirit, and there are the gifts of Christ.

There is the voice of the Holy Spirit, and there is the voice of Christ. The Holy Spirit needs to be received and allowed entrance into one's life and body to dwell there. The entrance to such a life is via the baptism in the Holy Spirit. When the Holy Spirit takes residence within us He does so with the thought of aiding us in developing a holy character. Faith in the word, while relating intimately with the Spirit of God breaks the powers that, when allowed to run wild, ruins us all, as stated in Romans 7:15 (I do not understand what I do. For what I want to do I do not do, but what I hate I do).

God's Spirit makes God's word work. Without God's Spirit, God's word will not work. It is static. Without God's Spirit the word remains on our lips. God's Spirit is given us from above. The Spirit is required to renew our strength, the Word is needed to refresh our minds. The load of life - financial life, emotional life, marital life - should never be bigger than one's spiritual life. One's spiritual life carries the entire load of life. If the load of life is bigger than one's spiritual life, reality becomes haywire, and chaotic. In that situation one may even have dreams without meaning, or worse still, no dreams at all. No dreams? Then something is very wrong.

We conclude, therefore, that authority and power in New Testament ministry really must go hand in hand. Authority without power is useless. Luke 4:36 lets us know that, "All the people were amazed and said to each other, "What words these are! With authority and power He (Jesus) gives orders to impure spirits and they come out!" What sort of word was this that amazed the people? Jesus did not only have authority over demons, but power to force them to come out. To those who have received the Holy Spirit, as Paul had, not only do they have authority over disease and demonic activities just like Jesus had, but they also have the power of God to actually control them and tell them where to go. And they obey. They have no choice. This is vital to managing the miraculous.

GOD'S WORDS AND GOD'S ACTIONS

A person who has the friendship of, and enjoys intimacy with the Holy Spirit can move in the same dimension as Christ did. Luke 20:2 says, "Tell us by what authority you are doing these things," they said. "Who gave you this authority?" The world wonders at those who move in such power, and so do many in the church. I have heard Christians, and indeed ministers, malign those men and women of God who move in great power and authority. I have heard of some being labelled as "witch doctors," simply because of the level of power and authority they move in. Such criticism is, I believe, commonly rooted in cheap and rampant jealousy. David's, "Touch not the Lord's anointed. Do His prophets no harm." Rings my bell when I hear of such things.

The whole point of where we are going is: Jesus Christ did not give us powerless authority. We need to realise this and speak in keeping with and according to that power. "The kingdom of God is not in word, but in power" (1 Corinthians 4:20). If I want to speak, "In the name of Jesus" it must be done according to and in line with the power of the Holy Spirit. If this does not take place, the ministry will be full of empty talk, and there will be some in the huge danger of uttering wasted prayers as well as muttering useless sermons, that is, prayer and preaching that does not end up with any result, and often times causes destruction. Remember the seven sons of Sceva and beware! They had the word of power (even if it was only a single sentence), but no personal authority or power.

When prayer is not in line with this power that is so freely given by God, it is superficial. One may hear oneself, as would the people around them, but God will not. If our prayer is not according to the truth of God's word, it will be idle, meaningless and often times destructive. We have to see as biblical logic, as well as common sense, that the idea of God talking, without God acting, is just outrageously nonsensical. The very idea of God telling you He is the Saviour and Healer, without moving to save and heal is preposterous. Just as it is nonsense to claim that Jesus is Lord and then to behave in a contrary manner, it is equally unhelpful when ministers of the word claim that Jesus is the healer, without manifesting that very power to heal.

RECEIVING AND MAINTAINING

In all we have written above, we are enlarging upon the anointing of the Holy Spirit in order to minister as did the preachers of Acts, as well as the Lord Jesus Himself. An anointing must be stepped into and received. To receive something from God is always comparatively easy. The difficult thing always is to maintain the gift, or anointing once it has been received. When ministers don't have an anointing it is the most important thing to get. But once you have it, maintenance is the biggest priority in the universe.

It is the anointing of the Spirit that attracts persecution, condemnation and intimidation, as well as miracles, deliverance and prophecy. Make no mistake about it, the anointing of God divides (Acts 19:9). It divides between faith and unbelief, and often attracts persecution as well as praise. The only thing that can maintain the anointing is character, and by that I am referring to Christ-like characteristics embedded into the believing man or woman of God. It is Christ-like character that is always hailed posthumously as great, yet commonly persecuted as disruptive in a person's own lifetime. Great men simply have great habits. Those habits are the scaffolding framework that helps construct the image of Christ in their person. Human praise rubbishes the anointing when that praise is inappropriately received. It leads to dependence on works instead of anointing. Human praise needs to be inwardly rejected, even if it is responded to with kindness. If not, the anointing is in danger of being lost. It is better not to receive the anointing at all, than to receive it and lose it. Ask King Saul and he will tell you all about that freak of the spiritual dimension: the lost anointing. Lack of character and the reception of human praise makes one nothing but a normal human being, as opposed to a mighty man of God. The New Testament minister, when operating within the parameters that Christ Himself laid down, is definitely not merely human. The New Testament minister has great treasure in his earthen vessel

Paul's anointing led to the salvation and freedom of many thousands of people. It also led to the utter chagrin and hatred of many more. Paul was consistent in acting with God all through his time in Ephesus. Any minister that does not act in concert with God conceivably needs deliverance. It was Paul's consistency that shook the whole of the province of Asia. The sowing of the seed had brought out fruit of 100, 200 or even 300 fold in some lives. In others it had revealed that the word could not enter, thus allowing the devil to steal it, or the thorns and thistles to thwart it, or the rocks and stones to stop the seed from taking root. Ephesus, and indeed the whole of Asia had become two spiritual camps, those that submitted to the gospel, and those that were roused up against that same gospel.

What would that division lead to?

22.

THE LABOUR PAINS OF THE TRANSFORMATION OF A NATIONAL CULTURE. ACTS 19:23-41

It was Paul's management of the miraculous that brought about a change of lifestyle for the city of Ephesus, and the population of Asia as a whole. Nowhere is it seen in Acts 19 that Paul asserted himself into the psyche or general consciousness of the people of Ephesus. His strategy was to get on with the job as a daily routine of 5 hour meetings, visiting and praying with people in the evenings and keeping his profile in those contexts only. The extraordinary miracles were done without his presence, as was the much repeated story of the sons of Sceva. It all raised Paul's profile around the whole of Asia, yet nowhere are we told that he even attempted to present himself as a celebrity. The name of Jesus Christ and Paul were conjoined in the Ephesian world. His life was such that he could say to them, follow me as I follow Christ. He would have seen the "white suit" syndrome as obscene.

It was the truth of the whole gospel, with signs and wonders accompanying the preaching and teaching of the word. Healing, deliverance and prophetic demonstration of the Spirit was the norm. It changed the culture of Asia. Paul was simultaneously self-deprecating, yet extravagantly Christ exalting. This was the secret of managing the miraculous. The secret of the Lord is with those that fear Him.

Martin Luther changed the world with only half the message of the gospel. The emphasis of "Justification by faith alone" is a truth of incredible power. By itself, because of its own intrinsic power in the concept of saving faith, Luther left the world a much better place because of the light he saw in the scriptures that declare, "The just shall live by faith." I will not say that those words are all he ever taught. God forbid. He preached much truth, but that emphasis, that vein of truth that built the Reformation, is how he is remembered. And that is only half the message, if not, less than half.

His grasp of that truth when planted into the hearts of men and women by his forceful preaching brought about something that can only be referred to as a sovereign move of God as truth became embedded in the hearts of millions of people. Life was changed in Europe. Societys and cultures were changed. Where the word of God grows and prevails People's lives and habits are transformed, and when that happens in great numbers nations are literally transformed.

A nation's culture is what that nation considers to be a normal way of living. Conversion to Christ, and development in that knowledge of Christ, places in the human heart and mind a whole new outlook on life, and a new conviction of what is normal and good. Lifelong liars, converted, feel the imperative call to speak truth. Adulterers and fornicators now feel the call of God to live in purity and integrity. The new creation in Christ starts a new culture. In my life I have not seen anything quite so beautiful as an entire family of Grandparents, parents and several children all getting converted on the same evening. I remember it being eight or nine people all together in a family that was, up to that evening, living together but fragmented and divided. The impact of the gospel was astonishing. Several years later that family were powerful in evangelism and setting a model for other families to follow. Their new family culture impacted all around. It brings societal change.

Wherever there is a sovereign move of God amongst men, there are tangible changes in that society that reflect that move. It may be ever so slight, it may be seismic and change the entire lifestyle of the locale, but when the gospel of Jesus Christ bites and becomes embedded and engrafted in the hearts of people, it impacts circles of friends and colleagues, and those people together change things right where they are. I am not only referring to what goes on in the subjective hearts of people, but what goes on there is actually what motivates and creates the resulting changes in their lifestyle and thus, their external society. There are times when one person who is already influential in the lives of people before conversion, comes to faith and thereafter changes the modus operandi of his large circle of friends, or his business, or the circles in which he moves, or even the very nature of the product he makes and sells.

In historic revivals in Britain over the last couple of centuries there were amazing social shifts. The Pubs (bars) and clubs would mostly close. Sales of alcoholic drinks would drop through the floor. Numbers of police on the streets were reduced because of the drop in crime. The volume of sickness and the inability to work in society drops also. All kinds of things change in a society simply because people become Christians and start changing things where they are. Such a social shift took place in Ephesus while the volume and depth of conversions changed the cultural skyline.

To understand this kind of thing, it is necessary to note that those that have come to know Christ wilfully and very happily change lifestyle, motivated by their faith and desire to follow Christ. But businesses that deal with issues and products that are generally considered not helpful to the person of faith, suffer greatly. People who have been pub owners all their lives lose lots of custom when a society turns to Christ. Tobacco dealers suffer lack. Betting shops close. In some society's I have read about in the midst of revival, the dance halls have closed and been taken over by churches in exactly the same way that a spiritual decline causes church buildings to become factories and dance halls today.

It is when faith in the hearts of people dominates and becomes robust, informed and intelligent, that society changes. I read one academic book on demographics that stated that if 14% of a population become activists in a certain lifestyle or cause, that 14% is enough to create critical mass and major seismic changes in that society. Acts tells us that "all of Asia heard the word." Picture the scene. Three years of daily preaching, teaching, healing and deliverance by Paul and his team, and the scripture quietly states that the whole of Asia (of which Ephesus was only one city) heard the word. It does not say that the whole of Asia was converted, but it does say that great fear fell on many because of the power of the name of Jesus and the authority that Paul moved in. So; Paul had lit the blue "touch paper" of the gospel firework. It was simply a matter of standing back and waiting for the explosion.

The explosion came from that part of Ephesian society that suffered most from the backwash of people turning to Christ. One of the most lucrative industries in Ephesus, if not in the entirety of Asia was the worship of Diana/Artemis and everything to do with that occult sect (Artemis was the Greek name for the Roman goddess Diana.). From the cult grew "Diana/Artemis" parasitical industries. Creating clay statues of the image of, "Artemis," and of the Temple that dominated the city, was a lucrative line of business. The temple itself was considered the glory of Ephesus: 425 feet long and 220 feet wide, having 127 white marble columns 62 feet high and less than 4 feet apart. In the inner sanctuary was the many-breasted image supposedly dropped from heaven. It had the city of Ephesus and the province of Asia utterly bewitched and captivated.

Making money out of people, places or things that were remarkably popular was not thought up in the last 100 years or so as we often think, but it was heavily rampant in Ephesus in the days of Paul, circa 54 AD.

The people turned away from Artemis, simply because it was widely known by all people in Asia that this, "Jesus whom Paul preaches" was more powerful and authoritative than any other divinity that they knew of. So attendance to the temple, with its religious prostitutes, idol worship and sacrifices had drastically diminished – as had all the parasitical industries that rode on the back of the movement. The sale of statuettes and models of the "Ephesian letters" which was obviously a mighty wealth creating industry had died overnight - at least over the nights of three years.

Even though the historians refer to clay casts of Artemis and the temple, I have no doubt at all that there would have been clothes that the priests and priestesses of Artemis wore, and items of the temple, be it altars, incense holders, sacrificial knives and any kind of paraphernalia that could be cheaply copied and sold. While the masses of Ephesus and Asia were devoted to Artemis, the money flow and the industrial balance was maintained to a degree where the economy of Asia was healthy.

However, along had come this man Paul. Between two to three years later any business that was associated with products or productions that were not consistent with Jesus Christ, or the lifestyle of following Christ and His teachings, had taken a dive. Things had changed. The Christians would have given thanks for such a phenomenon. The business owners would have thought very heatedly against the man responsible for the loss of business and many a business man's investment money.

So! What happened?

"About that time there arose no little disturbance concerning the Way. For a man named Demetrius, a silversmith, who made silver shrines of Artemis, brought no little business to the craftsmen" (19:23-24). Demetrius, it seems, was not a cheapskate dealer in clay shrines or models, but a high class dealer in silver shrines for the "glory of Artemis." Each trade seems to have had its own guild, or Trade Union. Perhaps Demetrius was a responsible leader of the guild for the manufacture of silver shrines and images. We do not have the details. However, we do discover that Demetrius was a man of great influence. His despair at what had happened to his business was contagious to all that heard him whinge about his losses.

Demetrius had come to the end of his tether. He had to blame somebody. The only tangible person was this man, Paul. He brought together people of the trade who made their incomes in a similar fashion. *"These he gathered together, with the workmen in similar trades, and said, "Men, you know that from this business we have our wealth"* (Acts 19:25). Since the temple of Artemis was considered one of the Seven Wonders of the World at that time, and must have been a remarkably spectacular sight, people came from far and wide to view it. People made pilgrimages similar to those made to Lourdes, St Peters in Rome, or Mecca. Their purchase of silver shrines and images produced great wealth and a sustainable lucrative business for the craftsmen.

I do not mean to be trite, but a cursory read of Acts 19 will cause you to note that Demetrius wasn't primarily upset because his goddess was being disrespected or neglected. Not at all. He was upset because Christianity was beginning to affect his pocket and his bank balance! However, not wanting to sound as mercenary as he definitely was, he added a little religiosity to his address, knowing fully that if the ignorant masses didn't feel anything at all to his loss, they would create a furore if he faked grief for the dear old stone idol Goddess who had made him rich. Master of manipulation, he plays on the religious feelings of others toward Artemis. We must not show so much naiveté as to think his motives were anything but financially motivated. He had bills to pay, and it was "all Paul's fault" that his income had diminished.

Demetrius continued addressing the growing crowd. *"You see and hear that not only in Ephesus but in almost all of Asia this Paul has persuaded and turned away a great many people, saying that gods made with hands are not gods. And there is danger not only that this trade of ours may come into disrepute but also that the temple of the great goddess Artemis may be counted as nothing, and that she may even be deposed from her magnificence, she whom all Asia and the world worship"* (Acts 19:26-27). That is some kind of plea. I can sense his crocodile tears and his passionate entreaty. What a wonderful, dear, devoted follower of the goddess was Demetrius. So concerned for her welfare and progress amongst the hearts of the masses. Not! The man was a total sham in his declared motives for the obscene statuette of Artemis.

Perhaps Demetrius thought that if they shouted and screamed loud enough those who had come to faith in Christ would shake their heads, come to themselves and declare, "Oh yes! How could I have been set free from sin, degradation and demonization by Jesus Christ? How could I have left a ridiculous piece of stone that looked like an egg shaped woman surrounded with lots of breasts? How could I have left the demonised worship and prostitute priestesses of Artemis for the purity and love and grace of knowing Christ?" How ignorant could Demetrius have been about Paul, his message, and what was going on in Ephesian and Asian society?

The temple Paul would have seen as he entered Ephesus was built, we believe, around 333 BC. The day he first caught sight of the place, it must have been heavily populated with a preponderance of people inside and around in its environs. As Paul was considering leaving Ephesus, the temple still stood but was far short of its previous multi-million shekel turnover. As a by the way, Christianity conquered Ephesus and the temple. By the time the great Temple was razed to the ground during a raid by the Goths in 262 AD, both the city and the religion of Artemis were in terminal decline ready to breathe their last. When the Roman Emperor Constantine rebuilt much of Ephesus 60 years or so later, he utterly refused to restore the temple. Constantine claimed to be a Christian and had no interest at all in pagan temples. Today the site of the temple is a boggy wilderness of a field. A handful of columns are still erect to remind visitors that once there stood in that place one of the wonders of the ancient world. While Demetrius spoke he had no conception at all of how the world could go on without the wonder of the world that, hitherto, had made Ephesus so attractive to so many.

The crowd were as vulnerable as could be and succumbed one hundred per cent to the guiles of the Union leader. *"When they heard this they were enraged and were crying out, "Great is Artemis of the*

Ephesians!"' (Acts 19:28). Oops! Something had backfired. The speech of Demetrius, wanting to raise custom for his silver shrines, had turned into a desperate last ditch religious meeting for the cult. Tied up with this religious fervour was a very human pride in their goddess and the thought of someone "disrespecting" her made many of the Ephesians angry. It was all religious mob mentality now, and the basic reason for Demetrius wanting to get rid of Christianity was somewhat diminished as a demonic worship service for Artemis commenced.

The cries that were exalting the great Artemis of the Ephesians upped the ante, and the evil mentality that followed the demonic adoration wrought its malicious work.

Wherever Demetrius was when he started the speech, the audience had turned into a demonstration, and the demonstration had turned into a mob. And where there is a mob, there is an inclination towards violence. Mob violence loses its human faculties and assumes the demonic violence that was at the heart of the whole furore. And "furore" is what it was. The main cause of such a spectacle as a violent mob is confusion. And sure enough, the whole scenario was out of the hands of Demetrius now. The man is only once referred to at the end of it all, and that was because the town clerk wanted to know who to blame if or when the Roman authorities asked him as to the whys and wherefores of the riot.

The crowd quickly grew because of the noise. Wherever it had geographically started wasn't big enough to cope with the crowd. So what did they do? *"The city was filled with the confusion, and they rushed together into the theatre, dragging with them Gaius and Aristarchus, Macedonians who were Paul's companions in travel"* (Acts 19:29). This is humanity turned animalistic. The crowd started moving. This was very dangerous for spectators who may have been stood in the pathway of the rush. Passive spectatorism is quickly interpreted as opposition of the "valiant cause" of the mob. It was a sort of, "If you aren't for us and running with us, you must be against us!" mentality. The psychological dynamics of mob-rule are seriously frightening. We are almost sure that the Gaius that was "press ganged" by the now raging mob, was the same Gaius of Corinth that Paul baptized, as mentioned in 1 Corinthians 1:14. Aristarchus, we know from other scriptures, and was from Thessalonica (which is in Macedonia). He travelled with Paul on other occasions into Greece, and later to Rome (Acts 27:2). Paul had a wide variety of companions that shared ministry with him. He was definitely not a "one-man-show".

The word picture that Acts 19 creates is such that one cannot but see that friends and associates of Paul were known by the non-converted people of Ephesus. Paul's mission had seriously elevated the profile of his team as well as himself. In their confused insanity, and the mob psychosis, anybody that was known to be friendly with, or part of Paul's team, was obviously a prime target for abuse, if not for murder. Gaius and Aristarchus were in seriously deep trouble. The most violently extrovert of the mob had grabbed the two of them and they were caught in the Tsunami wave of violent thought and footsteps into the Ephesian theatre – a venue that, remarkably, still stands today.

The volume of sound, as well as the volume of people, swept in to the semi-circular auditorium. The theatre has a potential seat for 24,000 people. We are not told if it was full or not, but whenever I read chapter 19 of Acts, I envisage the entire Christian population praying for peace as they stood back and watched out of sight of the general melee and the entire unsaved population in the auditorium who were in a raucous demonically inspired frenzy.

Paul was watching, out of sight. However, he was not content to remain hidden. *"When Paul wished to go in among the crowd, the disciples would not let him. And even some of the Asiarchs, who were friends of his, sent to him and were urging him not to venture into the theatre"* (Acts 19:30-3). The disciples were of the twelve or so that Paul had "recruited" into his team in Acts 19:1-6, and were those disciple he took with him when he left the synagogue to commence meetings at the school of Tyrannus. It is clear that these twelve disciples knew that if Paul were to appear before the crowd, the animalistic horror of their temper would not hesitate to tear him to pieces. It was an incredibly ugly and terrifying scene. The apostle, after all, did write, "I fought with wild beats at Ephesus."

The demonised mindlessness of the whole rose to a Vesuvian volcanic peak. *"Some cried out one thing, some another, for the assembly was in confusion, and most of them did not know why they had come together"* (Acts 19:32).

Oh the clarity of insight that the scripture feeds us with concerning that thing from hell called, "the mob." They walk the streets shouting their cause in a "sound-byte" sort of way that does not clearly define their goal. The interested masses join in, not wanting to miss something that may be important. This means that the more people they pick up on the way, the less intelligence there is amongst the people as to why they are there. It was so rough that the "Asiarchs" spoke up. The Asiarchs were the leaders of society and local government in Ephesus. They saw it as it was and refused themselves to try to stop the phenomena. They did send messages to Paul telling him that it was unwise for him to enter the auditorium at all. I have a mental picture of several of the disciples holding Paul back as he was wanting to enter the fray and preach the sermon of his life, which, if he had been allowed to, may have been his last.

Then surfaced all the shouters, screamers, speech makers and extremists. The manic chaos was complete. Some said one thing, and some another. The confusion was very dark. Then the bible tells us how dark it was: *"Most of them did not know why they had come together."* The blind had led the blind. The stupid had led the vulnerable.

Paul had seen all this before, though perhaps not on this scale. Some of the Jews in Thessalonica had used a similar tactic to get rid of him (Acts 17:5-9). And if one wants to get to the worst possibilities of mob rule, even earlier, during Jesus' trial, the chief priests manipulated the crowd to get them to force Pilate to crucify Jesus (Mark 15:9-15). These biblical examples, as well as this awesome display of evil machination in the great theatre at Ephesus show us how dangerous a mob can be, easily misled, and having the capability to mislead more, and be manipulated to meet someone else's evil goal.

"Some of the crowd prompted Alexander, whom the Jews had put forward. And Alexander, motioning with his hand, wanted to make a defence to the crowd" (Acts 19:33). The Jewish contribution to the debacle was definitely not in support of Paul. We don't know who this Alexander is apart from the fact that he was a Jew. This single Jewish personality was very brave and attempted to quiet the crowd in order to address them. I would have loved to know what it was he wanted to say, but Luke does not indulge us, even if he knew. Perhaps the Jewish contingent were worried in case it became an "anti-Jewish" rally. Perhaps they just wanted to say that, "we have nothing to do with this Jewish man called Paul." Perhaps this Alexander wanted to speak against, "The Way," to incite the crowd to more violence. Who knows?

But the lemmings just continued to walk over the edge of the cliff and follow the mob. *"When they recognized that he was a Jew, for about two hours they all cried out with one voice, "Great is Artemis of the Ephesians!"* (Acts 19:34). But the crowd doesn't let Alexander speak at all, because they recognized that he was a Jew, and therefore not a follower of Artemis either. The frenzied mob is so hyped up, high, stoned and energized in their pointless fury that they shout "Great is Artemis of the Ephesians!" for two full hours! Can you imagine! Picture the incredible hypnotic effect of the scream of the crowd. It takes 5 seconds to shout out once, "Great is Artemis of the Ephesians." That means it was cried out twelve times every minute. That is 720 times in an hour; 1,440 times in two hours. What a great way to get a headache. How much more could the human mind take. Few knew why they were there, and so they cry out the religious inanity: "Great is Artemis of the Ephesians." Once would be ridiculous. Two hours is simply short circuiting any system of mental logic.

We are not told what happened to Gaius and Aristarchus during this two hours of the cries of the damned.

Two hours later, "When the town clerk had quieted the crowd, he said, *"Men of Ephesus, who is there who does not know that the city of the Ephesians is temple keeper of the great Artemis, and of the sacred stone that fell from the sky?"* (Acts 19:35). The town clerk, is known to have been the secretary of the city who published the decisions of the Ephesian civic assembly. He was the most important local official and the chief executive officer of that assembly, acting as go-between for Ephesus and the Roman authorities. This man must have been very well-known and respected within Ephesian culture and was therefore able to get the crowd to silence themselves long enough for them to listen to him. He mentions in his recorded remarks in Acts 19 that Artemis' image actually fell from heaven. It is supposed by many that the monstrous shaped piece of rock was associated with a meteorite in some way.

The town clerk continued: *"Seeing then that these things cannot be denied, you ought to be quiet and do nothing rash. For you have brought these men here who are neither sacrilegious nor blasphemers of our goddess."* (Acts 19:36-37). Whatever had happened to Gaius and Aristarchus, they were still alive and in the midst of the mob and their shouting. In essence the clerk tells the masses something, like a father telling off a little child. In modern street language he tells them, "Everyone knows that Ephesus is the city of Artemis. There is no need to continually shout and repeat it over and over!" He calms them and says that doing any sort of harm to Gaius and Aristarchus would be endangering the city's standing with Rome. On top of all this going on, he also told them straight that there was not any proof that these two men had done anything criminal or even spoken disrespectfully of Artemis. I feel all the Christian people who were watching and listening give a deep sigh of relief at that moment.

He finishes with, *"If therefore Demetrius and the craftsmen with him have a complaint against anyone, the courts are open, and there are proconsuls. Let them bring charges against one another"* (Acts 19:38). He knew who had started the riot for he specifically names Demetrius. He makes it clear who is responsible for starting the riot. He makes it clear that there are legal procedures that Demetrius can follow if he has a true case of being wronged by Paul or his followers. All very logical, all very legal, and calm. On top of that, if the representatives of Rome want to deal with somebody for the riot. Demetrius is the number one person to talk to, not the town clerk.

One senses the entire madness being resolved in a moment. The crowd had come to itself. Demetrius, hearing his name mentioned by the town clerk in the same breath as proconsuls and courts, I feel assured to say, quickly hid amongst the crowd. *"But if you seek anything further, it shall be settled in the regular assembly"* (Acts 19:39). It is known as a fact through archaeological findings that there was a regular civil legal assembly that was held three times a month in Ephesus. *"For we really are in danger of being charged with rioting today, since there is no cause that we can give to justify this commotion"* (Acts 19:40).

When the clerk says "we are in danger of being charged with rioting" he means they are in danger of being charged by the Romans, since Ephesus was part of the Roman Empire, in the Roman province of Asia. There must have been some sort of financial charge involved or some strict penalty that the Romans could exact from the city if the riot had been proven to have become violent. The town clerk's job was to stand between the Ephesian and the Roman authorities.

"And when he had said these things, he dismissed the assembly" (Acts 19:41). Phew! The crowd was silenced and calmed, Aristarchus and Gaius were released, seemingly alive and well, and all went home

peacefully. I wonder what happened to Demetrius and his business thereafter.

It was a scary business that day. And one cannot but think about things that Doctor Luke has not told us in the book of Acts. Paul says in 1 Corinthians 15:32 that he had fought with wild beasts at Ephesus. Was this the debacle in which that fight took place? Did the apostle Paul really fight with wild beasts at Ephesus? Or was he merely referring to the mindless animalistic ranting of the Ephesian crowd that day?

The riot of Acts 19 is intended, I believe, to help us understand the workings of the gospel when widely received in any society. Godless businesses will begin to fail. The spirit that now works in the children of disobedience is not passive in its opposition to the gospel of Jesus Christ. The impact of the preaching goes far beyond the character of the preacher. Some of the things that shook the city were things that happened in Paul's absence. The faulty deliverance ministry of the sons of Sceva, the cloths and handkerchiefs that healed in Paul's absence, the riot that started in Paul's absence, even if we know he was present at the hub of the mission, reveal that Paul was not present for all the breakthroughs. Paul was the stone in the water, the extraordinary miracles, the sons of Sceva incident, the other exorcists emulating Paul and the riot, were all ripples caused by the dropping of that stone.

The love of money is the root of all evil. It was money that motivated Demetrius. Satan uses mindless mob activity to confront Christians. That is still true today. Demetrius and the mob never gave a thought to the substance of Paul's message. It was not an issue of Paul's mind. It was an issue of the business run by Demetrius, and mindless sheep who followed the crowd. There is a worldly mindset that argues with pragmatism and self-interest against truth. The case of Demetrius was not even for Artemis. The cry of the people of, "Great is Artemis of the Ephesians," was actually a digression from the original point, as often happens when the Christless are confronted with the glorious person of Christ.

Christ Himself was not considered by Demetrius or the mob. A common phenomenon in gospel opposition. Notice how, under the control of their passions, intelligent people quickly become ridiculous. Strong emotions are not evil per se. Paul himself was moved for Christ in wanting to speak to the crowd. But Paul's emotions were in Christ, in the Spirit and righteously motivated.

We have, sadly, no record of a single sermon that Paul preached in Ephesus. However, since he gave public lectures every day for three years, it is certain that he had often expressed his view that there is only one God. The gospel was, and ever will be unfriendly to the gods of paganism. Notice that what the Town Clerk said about the Christians was very different from what Demetrius said when he agitated against Paul. He said that Paul did belittle Diana (v. 26). It is possibly the only line of the speech of Demetrius that was absolutely true.

The town clerk was a politician. He was merely manipulating the mob in an effort to keep it under control. But we need not suppose that he even attempted to speak the exact truth. He was, after all, a politician seeking to save himself and the city from serious trouble from the Romans. He would not have been the first politician who had bent truth to end a crisis.

Wherever the gospel is preached in power, authority and purity there is always "no small stir about the way." Those most similar to Paul are mostly considered extremists today. As if Christ Himself was not extreme.

The world is transporting itself downriver to hell. The gospel of Christ is like salmon swimming, not only upriver, but up the Niagara. Riots are the norm for the normal Christian minister and life.

Judaism with both Pharasaism and Sadduceeism, heathen philosophers, and demonic idolaters in Ephesus, hitherto had got on comparatively well enough together. However, no sooner had the gospel made its appearance in the power of the Holy Spirit, than the kingdom of Satan begin to be in danger, and his hordes raised a disturbance in the world. There were riots simply because a reputedly small Jewish man came with practical presentations of the person of Jesus Christ.

Paul was faithful in all his dealings with the word of God. He was a sower that went forth to sow. The results of the seeds that he had sown impacted many people long after he had gone. Here in Acts 19, people were rioting who had never met him. The antagonism of the old rejected culture will always fight to the death. The management of the miraculous, both subjectively in Paul's heart and mind, and objectively, as his quiet humility was seen by the masses, was the secret to his sustained ever increasing impact over three years.

23.

PAUL'S PERSECUTION, PRISON AND PRESSURE IN EPHESUS?

"... I fought with wild beasts at Ephesus..."

1 Corinthians 15:32

"... We do not want you to be uninformed, brothers, about the hardships we suffered in the province of Asia. We were under great pressure, far beyond our ability to endure, so that we despaired even of life."

2 Corinthians 1:8.

If, like Paul, we live in such a manner as to stand the test of the glare of the Judgement Seat of Christ, we can depend upon it that the world will not speak well of us. It is so, and it has always been so. If the Tiber rises too high, or the Nile too low, the remedy is always feeding Christians to the lions," said Tertullian. His point was that people persecuted and hated Christianity irrationally, and then looked for reasons to justify that persecution. Paul was walking along a new road, unknown to many. He was challenging definitions of normalcy everywhere he went, and his most impacting period and location was during the three year mission in Ephesus and Asia. As it was with the Lord Christ, so it was with Paul. The servant is not above the master. Our species, under the tyranny of its fallen nature has become so constituted that those who walk on the well-trodden common path always throw stones, or something worse, at those who are treading a new and uncommon road. Dietrich Bonhoeffer wrote in his book, "The Cost of Discipleship;" "When Christ calls a man, he bids him come and die." That was something Paul knew from the first day he was converted (Acts 26:16-17).

Paul wrote in his last days a statement that our modern generation of western cosseted Christians struggle with. *"They that will live Godly in Christ Jesus shall suffer persecution"* (2 Timothy 3:12). Ouch! Why oh why couldn't Paul have written, "They that live Godly in Christ Jesus may, possibly, if the circumstances contain such a thing, suffer a little trouble, but, don't worry... it might not really happen?" Why does he have to be so black and white? Why does he have to be so clear and unequivocal? However, the, "Ouch!" becomes louder, longer and more heartfelt when we get to grips with the fact that it wasn't Paul talking, but Christ through Paul. We are talking Holy Scripture when we speak that verse. There are precious few Christians that pray for 2 Timothy 3:12 to be fulfilled in them. If we are not receiving some type of ridicule for our beliefs as New Testament believers, we are undoubtedly doing something wrong, or falling short somewhere in our commitment. 2 Timothy 3:12 is an absolute. Great minds possessed of great concepts, ideas and vision, usually share those ideas and concepts in the midst of their persecution. Paul had enough persecution for ten thousand Christians of the modern west. The verse is so striking in its terrible starkness that I notice many modern translations soften the blow. It is "Those who want to...," or, "those that desire to live godly." Too soft! "Not true to the Greek text," my Greek speaking friends tell me. "Those who choose to live Godly?" That will do! But the point is, that the persecution does not come to beat down the desire, or the hunger, or the want to live Godly. The Devil can handle that by ignoring it. It is the doing of it that makes hell tremble and the devil loose his hordes to get you killed. Period! End of story!

If you have ever read Richard Wurmbrand's book, "Tortured for Christ," you possibly, like me, paused and wept for a moment when one comes to a section that was written so plainly and without melodrama: "It was strictly forbidden to preach to other prisoners. It was understood that whoever was caught doing this received a severe beating. A number of us decided to pay the price for the privilege of preaching, so we accepted their [the communists] terms. It was a deal;

we preached and they beat us. We were happy preaching. They were happy beating us, so everyone was happy." I read it and thought of the twelve apostles rejoicing because they had been considered worthy to suffer for Christ when they were beaten in a manner somewhat similar to Wurmbrand (Acts 5:41).

If external and social forces and culture were the reasons behind declining and non-influential Christianity in the west, there would be no churches in existence today. The greatest periods of church growth, geographic and numeric expansion, and carrying weight in society, particularly the first-century, occurred in viciously adversarial and confrontational cultures. Christians, and ministers are not hindered by external forces. History tells us that this is a fact. Christians and leaders are hindered only by their own lack of commitment and selflessness. Paul was owned and completely subject to Jesus Christ. This man was utterly selfless in his care and love for those he brought to Christ. Paul could say, like so few could or can, "Follow me, as I follow Christ."

"But!" you may say, "Paul wasn't persecuted in Ephesus! It's true there was a riot, yet he did not enter the fray and was stopped by the disciples from going into the furore in Acts 19 in the great Theatre of Ephesus. No persecution there!" Really?

In order to hit straight on with this issue, and what happens when a man gloriously moves in the miraculous we will have to do some straight talking. And, I do not use the word, "gloriously" lightly. 1 Peter 4:14 says, *"If you are reviled for the name of Christ, you are blessed, because the Spirit of glory and of God rests on you."* Paul was clearly reviled in most of the places where he ministered, and especially so in Ephesus. (Just a note to say that many modern translators dilute the word, "reviled" to a mere, "insulted." That is how the western scholars of Christianity see things. "Pink and fluffy" is what I call it.). Paul's experience of being reviled in Ephesus, caused him at one point, to give up on life and any expectation of revival.

So, how do I break the news? Where do I start?

Here's something that many students may consider outrageous for me to assert. It is my strongly held opinion, almost a conviction that Philippians, Philemon and Colossians were not written from Rome at all, but from Ephesus.

Now of course, you want my rationale behind that statement. And you will ask, of course, how prison could bring Paul to a "near death experience?" After all, we read that Paul was free to socialise whenever he was writing from prison.

Let me start by saying that there are a few highly ranked scholars, some alive and some gone home to their eternal reward, who said this first. I cannot claim originality to this insight.

However, let's not lose track of why I am making the point. We are talking of the secrets of character while managing and maintaining a ministry of the miraculous. Christ-like attitudes to persecution and injustices perpetrated against one's person are important for maintaining an open spirit towards God, an unwaxed ear to the Spirit, and a clear eye to the word of God. I live in the UK where it is comfortable to talk about persecution (at least at the moment). I have just had a large meal prior to writing these notes, I am free to attend my church prayer meeting and I can talk to anybody on the street about Christ, and still remain free and contented. So I am painfully aware that where I am coming from is purely theoretical when I talk of persecution. But Paul was in a tight situation in Ephesus. In fact, Paul was in an Ephesian furnace.

If gold must be gold, it must pass through fire. Imagine the scenario. Paul is lucratively making tents every morning (Acts 20:18 and 24), ministering at the school of Tyrannus for five hours every day in the early afternoon (Acts 19: 9-10 in the Amplified), and visiting house to house, both Jewish and Greek night and day (Acts 20:20). Then he has letters to write to resolve issues in churches that he has founded, as well as posting his ministering assistants to various churches at various times as needs arose. On top of all that, the effective door of ministry that had been opened to him had finally resulted in a street riot. Paul was rooted, firmly, in the power, authority and energy of God, and was now considering leaving Ephesus (Acts 19:21).

Whatever is not rooted in God cannot stand the test of time. And what Paul was achieving in the three years in Ephesus would impact the world for eternity. The letters he wrote in those days has fed and guided the church for two millennia. In the face of life's trials and troubles, it is only when one's decision to serve the Lord is born of faith and commitment that one will overcome. Faith when ministered with a pure heart is infectious. Uncommon blessings attract uncommon challenges. Satanic forces were receding from Ephesian culture. Paul had gone where no man had ever been before in Ephesus. He had impacted the whole of Asian society, the scripture says so (Acts 19:10. Acts 19:20). If one decides to do what no one has ever done before, one must be ready to experience trials that no one has ever experienced before. And Paul hit those trials head on. We should, like Paul, see our trials as an opportunity for us to honour God before men.

As a Christian, affliction may have been testing Paul, but it could not destroy him. Hard times could not break him as a Christian, just as fire cannot destroy gold. The more fire gold receives, the purer and more expensive and uncommon it becomes. The more hard times he experienced, the better equipped he was for where he was going. So, as a child of God, when we continue to experience trying situations, we must not lose heart. The higher Hand that is leading us is leading us all to something higher (1 Corinthians 10:13).

Where was the Apostle Paul situated when he wrote to the Philippians to thank them for their financial gift? Where was he when he sent the runaway slave Onesimus back to Philemon in Colossae, bearing the scrap of papyrus that contained the appeal to his master in behalf of the newly converted slave of Christ? Which prison was he in when he wrote to the church he had never met in Colossae (Colossians 4:10)?

Plainly enough, as has been preached and taught for almost two millennia, he was somewhere in prison (Philemon 1; Philippians 1:13. Colossians 4:10). It has been usual to assume that he was writing from Rome (Acts 28:30). I have heard preachers, only once or twice in my life, teach that they were written from the prison at Ceasarea (Acts 24:27). My conviction, however, is that they were written from prison in Ephesus. While there is no direct statement in the New Testament that Paul was ever in prison at Ephesus, there is much indirect testimony which, collectively, is incredibly cogent.

Paul was imprisoned more than twice, or even three times. This is plainly inferred by his expression "in prison more abundantly" (2 Corinthians 11:23). In the same Epistle (2 Corinthians1:8), which was definitely written soon after Paul's three-year residence in Ephesus, he speaks of being in a situation in Asia, which pressed him down exceedingly, in which he despaired even of life. The only place that could have been, was Ephesus. In the "real-time" of the Acts narrative, that means it must have occurred in Acts 19. And in the First Epistle to the Corinthians, written while at Ephesus (1 Corinthians 16:8), Paul mentions a circumstance not elsewhere alluded to, namely, that he "fought with wild beasts at Ephesus" (1 Corinthians 15:32).

There is more! In Paul's letter to the Romans it is stated that Aquila and Priscilla had laid down their own necks for Paul's life (16:4). It is only biblically explained by concluding that that they were at Rome at the time Paul wrote his letter to the Roman church, and that this unexplained act of devotion to Paul was activated at a crucial hour in Ephesus, for that is the place where they spent most time with him during his peak of ministry. It is a biblical fact that this couple left Rome before 50 AD at the edict of Claudius, and went to Corinth, from where they went with Paul to Ephesus (Acts 18:2,18, 26). Contributing to my arguement that Paul was imprisoned at Ephesus, the expression "Andronicus and Junia ....my fellow-prisoners "(Rom. 16:7) becomes noteworthy.

A reading of the letter to Philemon also reveals evidence to support my presupposition of an Ephesian imprisonment. Paul tells Philemon that he would soon visit him. He asks Philemon to prepare a lodging place for him when he gets there (Philemon 22). Had Paul been at Rome in prison at that time, he could not have expected to reach Colossae in the near future, for his plan was to push on toward Spain (Romans 15:24-28), and it is this writers opinion that he doubtless fulfilled that plan. How could Paul write one letter saying that after he left Rome he would go to Spain (Romans 15:24.15:28) and then write another from the same venue saying he was going to see Philemon in Colossae. One is west from Rome - one is East from Rome. It could not be done. Conclusion? Paul was indeed planning to go to Spain when he was freed from his Roman "open prison," and was also planning to go to see Philemon after his Ephesian stay. I do not believe he got to see Philemon, however, for reasons we will discuss in our next chapter.

On top of the above logistics, an internet study of travel conditions in the first century makes the case sure that Onesimus, when he ran away from Philemon, would go to Ephesus, just 100 miles away, rather than undertake the arduous and highly expensive journey to Rome. Onesimus was a penniless slave. Note the difficulty and danger that attended Paul's own journey there. Rome, as a geographic source for the slip of a letter to Philemon, must be out of the question on this occasion. Piecing the whole saga together, it seems that Philemon probably visited Ephesus with his slave Onesimus and heard Paul, whereupon the both of them became Christians and returned home to Colossae. Soon after, Onesimus flitted from Philemon probably wanting to become a disciple in Paul's team. The letter to Philemon was intended to have been carried by Onesimus who was sent home by Paul.

There exists a ruin in Ephesus whose masonry dates from' a period preceding Paul's day, which bears the local name of "Paul's Prison." Photographs and artefacts from the ruin were taken by Professor Deissmann of Berlin (circa 1914). This professor certainly believed that he had evidence to support the view of Paul's Ephesian imprisonment.

If the letter to Philemon was written from Ephesus, it is likely that the affectionate epistle to the church at Philippi was also written from the same place. Why? Timothy is included in the address of Philippians (1:1), and it is known that he was Paul's helper during the early part of the Ephesian ministry (Acts 19:22; 2 Cor. 1:1). However, Timothy was probably *not* with Paul in Rome. Luke and Aristarchus were the Apostle's fellow travellers on his voyage (Acts 27:1, 2), and it is quite certain that Timothy was ministering elsewhere when Paul was enduring his last imprisonment in the empire's capital city, as the two Epistles to Timothy witness. He could not be writing an Epistle with Timothy, if he was also writing two epistles to Timothy.

There's more even to add to this train of thought. While imprisoned at Rome, Paul was at liberty to preach the gospel (Acts 28:30), for he lived in his own hired house. But while undergoing the severe trial to which he refers in his letter to the Philippians, he himself is not free to preach, although others, some with a good attitude and spirit and some with a not so good motive, are preaching the Word (Philippians 1:12 and on). Philippians, therefore, could not have been written from Rome.

There might have been a good reason why he did not go into any kind of detail in Philippians concerning his distress at Ephesus. The Philippians evidently knew the details of "the things which happened" to him (1:12). How do we know that? A regular exchange of letters and personnel was taking place, as was the case when Paul was in Thessalonica (Philippians 4:16). At least one other letter is assumed in Philippians 3:1. Epaphroditus had been sent to them and had returned (Philippians 4:18). Timothy is shortly to follow (2:19). Paul expects to hear again from them soon, to know how they responded to his instruction. It is clear that without DHL or UPS deliveries in Paul's time, from such a distance as Rome, this regular exchange of correspondence and messengers could hardly be maintained. I believe the phrase is: "logistically impossible!" It's just common sense, really. In Philippians 2:24 the apostle expresses his intention, if God allowed him the privilege, to see the church at Philippi himself "shortly." However, on the presupposition that he was at this time in Rome writing Philippians we have the contradictory clash with his announced plan to visit Spain, already highlighted above. It doesn't make sense to think of Rome as the place from where it was written. An Ephesian imprisonment makes the entire geographic logic of it all, straight forward.

We do not read that, during his first imprisonment at Rome, Paul entertained any fear of an adverse decision. His appeal to Caesar was taken with the confidence that he had done nothing worthy of death. Even the Roman officials agreed on this point (Acts 26:32). But when he writes the Epistle to the Philippians he is in prison (Phil. 1:13), and is apparently facing a crisis which may result in his death (1:21 on). So, again I say, Paul could not have been writing Philippians from Rome where he weighs the advantages of living or dying. He is "in a strait betwixt two." But he hopes to live, believing that he is needed still in the development of the Macedonian churches. In this "strait" the Christians at Philippi are following his course sympathetically (1:7; 4:14), and send him a present to help him in his time of trial. I cannot understand the situation any other way. Paul was in prison at Ephesus.

It is true that this thesis (or rather hypothesis) of an imprisonment at Ephesus may be rubbished and denied by the fact that nothing of a specific statement of it appears in the New Testament. But it must be recalled that there is very little related of the events that attended Paul's three-year ministry at Ephesus.

On top of that there is a key observation that few writers of all academic stature refer to; namely that:

THERE ARE EVENTS IN PAUL'S LIFE THAT ARE JUST NOT IN THE BOOK OF ACTS.

I fully realise that to say this makes it easy to imaginatively invent all sorts of things with the P.S saying, "Ah well! This is just one of those things that Luke decided to omit," but it is absolutely true. I qualify myself by asserting that I believe in the absolute accuracy of the book of Acts and its complete veracity in the account that it gives us. One does not, however, need to have a Master's Degree in Bible to get hold of the fact that Paul talks of some high profile experiences in his life, throughout his epistles that Acts does not even hint at. It is simply impossible to accurately discern where Paul was, or what parts of the Acts narrative are leaps of time jumping forward, missing various dramatic moments. To keep it brief, I simply list a few of these obvious omissions in the text of Acts:

- Christians receiving the Spirit in Galatia (Galatians 3:2). This is not mentioned anywhere in Acts(Acts 16:6. Acts 18:23).

- Miracles in Galatia (Gal 3:5). None are mentioned at all in Acts (Acts 16:6. Acts 18:23).

- In prison more frequently (2 Cor 11:23). Only once in the story of Acts prior to Acts 20:3 where we believe 2 Corinthians was written are we told of an imprisonment of Paul. (Acts 16: 23-31).

- Five times received 39 lashes (2 Corinthians 11:24). We have no account in the Acts of the Apostles, or elsewhere, of any one of these five scourgings, which the apostle underwent from the Jews. The flogging in Acts 16:32 is not to be confused with the lashings.

- Three times beaten by rods (2 Cor 11:25). Acts has only one note of such a Roman punishment before 2 Corinthians was written (Acts 16:22-23).

- Danger from rivers and bandits (2 Cor11:26). There is no such accounts given in Acts.

- Cold and naked (2 Cor 11:27). No story in Acts refers to cold or nakedness. Surely an apostle reduced to nakedness must be seen as a major event in his life. Nevertheless it is not mentioned in Luke's account.

- Three shipwrecks (2 Cor 11:25). Only one is mentioned in Acts, and that was several years after 2 Corinthians was written, so Luke omitted three shipwrecks from Paul's biography in Acts.

- A day and a night adrift in the open sea (2 Cor 11:25). Not so much as even hinted at in Acts.

- Fully preached in Illyricum (Illyricum is modern day Albania) (Romans 15:19). Acts does not tell us Paul preached in Illyricum at all.

- Facing death in Asia (Ephesus) (2 Corinthians 1:8-10). These pages are focussing on all that took place in Ephesus, and "facing death" is not even highlighted in Acts (Acts 19 -20).

- Fought with wild beats at Ephesus (1 Corinthians 15:32). Whether the "beasts" that Paul refers to were animal or human, there is definitely no such account given to us in Acts. We are negotiating this issue in these pages at this moment.

- The vision of heaven and the thorn in the flesh (2 Cor 12: 1- 6). Nowhere else in scripture is this experience mentioned, and definitely not in Acts. We are forced to guess when it was, and many expositors have different theories.

- We have no account in Acts of Paul confronting Peter at Antioch (Galatians 2:11-21).

- Paul's visit to Crete (Titus 1:5). In Acts, he seems to never go to Crete. Where do we fit that one?

- Paul states in 2 Corinthians that he was going to visit Corinth for the third time (2 Corinthians 12:13. 13:1). In Acts he only makes two visits, and one of them is deduced by all to be Corinth, even though it mentions a generic "Greece." (Acts 18. Acts 20)

This makes it clear that Luke was not attempting to write an exhaustive biography of Paul at all. It was a purposeful, intended story, with episodes deliberately inserted or omitted in order to tell the story how he or perhaps Paul himself wanted.

I make this point to say that no matter how astutely we put together the biblical statements that we have concerning Paul's travels after leaving Ephesus, we cannot ever be sure of facts, dates and incidents that are simply not there for us to make conclusions about. Paul's desperate attempts to explain why he didn't visit the Corinthian church after leaving Ephesus (2 Corinthians) can only be properly explained by suggesting that there were letters he had sent and a visit to Corinth that he must have made that Acts does not tell us of. Of course, most bible readers will exclaim, "What are you saying? There are only 2 Corinthian letters! We have them both in the Bible!" But do we have all of Paul's correspondence with the Christians at Corinth in the canon of scripture? It is plainly inferred that we do not.

I utterly disagree with any idea that the Corinthian letters in the scriptures are a "hotch-potch" of several letters stitched together by later scribes and writers. What absolute tosh! That suggestion is another of the imaginative machinations of the higher critics that I contemn utterly. There is not as much as a hint of disunity in any of the ancient Greek manuscripts. Check that out with all the academics. There are no variations of the literary units. In all the many manuscripts there is none that does not contain all thirteen chapters of 2 Corinthians (Although chapter 13 "seems" to have been unknown to Clement of Rome in 96 AD, it is clearly quoted by Polycarp in 105 AD). The Corinthian letters in scripture are both understandable as fully self-contained and self-explained units. There also seem to be certain themes which show its unity, i.e. suffering. The internal evidence is, as always with the modernists, utterly too invented and undecipherable to the vast majority of readers, and clearly subjectively made by the imaginative meanderings of the minds of some so called scholars attempting to shock their professors into giving them their Phd's.

There is, of course, the encounter with the seven sons of Sceva, who tried to imitate Paul's ministry of deliverance (Acts 19:13 on), but this cannot be what Paul refers to in his speech to the elders at Miletus (20:19), namely, "trials which befell me by the plots of the Jews." Nor can the uproar caused by Demetrius the silversmith be thought of as the cause of "many tears"; for Acts 19:30 leads one to believe that Paul was not in the midst of that disturbance at all. On the supposition that it was necessary for Paul to use discretion in referring to his imprisonment at Ephesus, may it not be that there is a veiled reference to it in the remark to the Ephesian elders, as he leaves them at Miletus, "Now I go bound in the spirit unto Jerusalem"? That is a weak remark, but possibly cryptically made, if everybody present knew what he was referring to.

The reference in Philippians 1:13 to the "Praetorium" has been supposed to point conclusively to Rome. But the word is constantly used to designate royal residences. See that it is so in Matt. 27:27; John 18:28, 33; 19:9; Acts 23:35. These "Praetoria" are palaces of Roman governors around the empire. The Praetorium of Phil 1:13 may easily have been at Ephesus. Ephesus was, after all, the capital city of a Roman province.

The expression "those of Caesar's household" also offers a slight objection to the Ephesian imprisonment idea. But it is possible that the term includes slaves and freedmen of the royal family who lived elsewhere than at Rome. Very likely such persons formed special groups in the Christian communities' at large centres of Roman authority.

Sorting out the chronology of Paul's life is one of the most difficult problems of all New Testament study. Results attained or stated, including my own, stand constantly in need of revision. In this essay of mine only two of Paul's letters have been considered; but if the above argument be sustained by further investigation, it is likely that the accepted dates of some other Epistles may be revised also. If the above attempt at explanation does not convince, it at least offers something to tax the brain and meditations of my readers. The presupposition of an imprisonment suffered by Paul at Ephesus when cross referenced with his remarks in 2 Corinthians leads me to say that Paul suffered greatly whilst in Ephesus.

Whether or not my thesis here has any real gravitas is irrelevant to my point that if we are seeking God to flow in the miraculous, the serendipity of Persecution must be included in the package. Paul knew what near death experiences in the pursuit of evangelism was all about.

24.

PAUL THE PROPHET.

"Afterward Paul felt compelled by the Spirit to go over to Macedonia and Achaia before going to Jerusalem. "And after that," he said, "I must go on to Rome!"

Acts 19:21 (NLT)

It is argued by some that Paul is never referred to as a prophet in scripture. But whether his prophetic anointing was subservient to his anointing as an apostle or just another anointing alongside that of his apostolic authority, it cannot be gainsaid that Paul was a prophet. On top of that I think that there is a lot of credibility in those that teach that Paul and the original twelve apostles were all intrinsically gifted with the entire five-fold ministry package and were each an apostle, a prophet, an evangelist, a pastor and a teacher. But we are camping on Paul the prophet in the context of managing his ministry of the miraculous.

What is a prophet? A prophet is a human interface between the invisible world and the visible. A prophet is a human being that hears and knows and hears God in a way that most Christian people do not. A prophet, by the very nature of who and what he is in the sight of God, seems incredibly uncommon and abnormal in the sight of men. A prophet has had communicated to him what theologians say is incommunicable, that is he touches, no matter how lightly, no matter how little, a sliver of God's omniscience. He has seen and knows what would otherwise be unseeable and unknowable to human kind. A prophet can be a Seer. All Seers are prophets. Not all prophets are Seers. A Seer can see things future, things past, or even present things that are out of natural sight and knowledge. It is the explanation of what is seen that is the miraculous and leads to healing and deliverance. A prophet can hear from God and reveal a person's root problem that is the one major issue that transcends any problem that a person thinks they have. A prophet can see what God is doing. A prophet can hear what God is saying. A prophet senses God's intimate thoughts.

Prophets generally do not speak orthodox "Christianese" language. Not only are their words not commonly used in Christian circles, but often, when they are moving in Christ, the issues that they are dealing with in the Spirit are utterly unknown and inconceivable to the vast majority of believers. Prophets can be so "unorthodox" in their language and perspective on things that most Christians want to deny them, decry them and defame them – or all three. When prophets confront the voices of orthodoxy, the "orthodox" hold their hands up in horror and say, "That's not God!" or, "He has a demon!" The polite upper class English Christians say, "Oh! He has another spirit!" as if their gentle English would be more acceptable to God's ears as they deprecate what God is doing in the prophet's heart, life and ministry. Unfortunately dry orthodoxy is the plague of modern western Christianity. The "Dry Orthodox" contingent are in the vast majority. It was dry orthodoxy that shouted, "Blessed be He who comes in the name of the Lord" on a Sunday, and "Crucify Him," the following Friday.

Murdering, a prophet never silences him. Prophets seem to speak more powerfully and more influentially from posthumous notes made into books than they did when alive and heard in the flesh. The likes of Maria Woodworth Etter, Smith Wigglesworth, and George Jeffreys were all vilified by the majority in their life time to some degree, yet declared to be almost Haloed faultless saints after they were gone. A prophet needs to be wild, giant and dangerous to impact a nation or, as in the case of Acts 19, a sub-continent. In God's sight they are living the normal life. In the sight of man, they seem extreme, intimidating and even unsound.

Millions of Christians are sure they have never seen or heard a prophet in their life time, and for that reason believe that there are none today. But they are here, alive on the planet and fulfilling God's call. The prophetic ministry is the nearest thing to God's heart. The prophet has always been God's verbal contact with his chosen people. Note how many times in scriptural accounts where God did not speak to the king or the people, but to the prophet. God speaks prophetically before He does a thing. Amos 3:7 reveals to us that, *"Indeed, the Sovereign LORD never does anything until he reveals his plans to his servants the prophets"* (NLT). So it is clear that some prophets, somewhere in the earth are key ears and hearts in all of God's intentions and actions. God shares Himself with his prophets, even today. Prophets were key, along with the apostles, in laying the teaching and prophetic foundations on which the church of Christ is built (Ephesians 2:19, 3:5, Acts 3:21).

The very first New Testament sermon was a rationale for those that spoke in tongues with licks of fire on their heads, and gave the impression that they were drunk. When explaining what was happening, Peter quoted from the prophet Joel. He stated that the tongues and seeming drunkenness amongst the 120 from the upper room, were exemplars of part of what the prophet Joel predicted (Joel 2:28-32). It was God beginning to pour out His Spirit on all flesh. But it wasn't the full story on that day of Pentecost in Acts 2. This outpouring of the Spirit would bring people's sons and daughters to full blown prophecy. The young would see prophetic visions, and the old men would dream prophetic dreams. Men and women together would prophesy, said Joel. Prophecy and the supernatural release of the kingdom of God in people's lives that exudes from prophecy would be the normal way of life the more God's Holy Spirit was poured out. The church age should be as much, if not more, "The age of the prophet," as it was in the days of the writing prophets. Joel said so.

No! I do not believe there are to be additions to the canon of scripture. New Testament prophets preach the Rhema word of the Lord. The Rhema is the word for the moment that comes from the Spirit of the Lord. It is my conviction that the Bible sanctions prophets in the New Testament without the slightest interference with the completion of the canon. There are times when things cannot be proven to be consistent or otherwise with the Bible. Agabus prophesied and predicted a famine (Acts 11:28). There is no chapter and verse to justify such a prediction. But it occurred just as he said in 45 AD in the fourth year of the reign of Emperor Claudius. Again he prophesied over somebody's belt. He tied his hands and feet with this strap and pronounced , "In this way the Jews of Jerusalem will bind the owner of this belt and will hand him over to the gentiles" (Acts 21:10). The belt belonged to the apostle Paul, and it happened exactly how Agabus prophesied. There was no scripture verse to validate or invalidate such a prophetic statement. The only thing that could validate or invalidate the drama of the prophecy was whether or not what he said came to pass. And it did.

The prophetic word is a vital requirement to the health and prosperity of the true church of Jesus Christ world-wide.

A prophet is particularly protected and looked after by God, the One who chose them to be a prophet. There are five ministries that Christ has given to His church; apostles, prophets, evangelists, pastors and teachers. Yet He says things about prophets that He does not say of the other four. For instance, "Touch not the Lord's anointed, and do His prophets no harm" (Psalm 105:15). There is a lot of meat packed into that little carcase of words. Speaking against prophets is a dangerous business. Prophets are anointed by the Spirit of God. It may be that everybody who is anointed are not necessarily prophets, but know this, that every prophet is anointed by God. Anointed means that God has poured something of Himself over that person and you cannot speak against, touch or harm a prophet without first speaking against and touching God Himself. And that is the finality of it. And don't think for one little moment that because one hears of a moral fall of a prophet that he is fair game to criticise. Prophets know how to repent. That is one of the reasons they are prophets. The rule is that whether they walk in grace and power, or whether it seems from the human point of view that they have lost their anointing, do not touch them negatively by word or deed. You will pay for it if you do.

The importance of these words are seen in Samuel and David (both of whom were prophets) who were not wanting to do any harm to King Saul who was also known to be "among the prophets." Saul treated David despicably and pursued him with a demonic lust to murder him. However, because of the anointing that was at one time placed on Saul's life, David knew how dangerous it was to reciprocate the violent thoughts of the first king of Israel.

Another verse of scripture states; "Have faith in the Lord your God and you will be upheld; have faith in His prophets and you will be successful" (2 Chronicles 20:20). And somehow, that Old Testament king of Judah who spoke those words has, by that statement, elevated the function and office of the prophet to an almost impregnable level. It is as if he is equating trusting God's word, to trusting the prophet. That is the crux of the matter exactly. Have faith in what the prophets say, and you will succeed. That is a promise of scripture. When a prophet does what he is called to do, hang on to that word, it may literally save your life.

There is deep, deeper and deepest in the realms of prophecy as well as in the world of prophets. They are all in the call of God. Those that are "Deep," may speak things that seem not so important to many, but they are the lifeblood to that prophet. Receive it. The "Deeper" prophet may declare things that the "Deep" prophet cannot see, and so people may consider the "Deep" prophet is wrong and the "Deeper" prophet is correct, or vica verca. The fact will be that if they have both spoken the word of the Lord, no matter how different the words may seem, they will both come to pass. The "Deepest" prophet may declare words that both the "Deep" and the "Deeper," cannot relate to receive or even understand. This is how criticism and unrest occurs within the body of Christ world-wide. Let them prophesy according to their measure of faith. God give us all the wisdom to hear what the Spirit is saying to the churches.

With all the above said (and I could say much more), I declare that the apostle Paul was indeed a prophet. He fits all of the criteria mentioned above, especially the criteria of the "Deepest." The prophet that moves in the "Deepest," of the prophetic realms finds it difficult to be understood by many, even of his peers. It seems to me that Peter gently tells us that he himself did not always understand what Paul was saying (2 Peter 3:15-16). The greatest minds that have ever lived have been meditating on Paul's prophetic writings for two millennia and we still have not fathomed some of his thinking.

Most Christians, unfortunately, live in the lowland plains of the Spiritual. There are those that climb God's mountains in the Spiritual realm, and thereby gain a view of life and an understanding of ministry and sickness, deliverance and suffering, fallen human nature and those that have a new nature given to them by Christ. Prophets see things that the vast majority do not think of, see, or experience. They are deepest simply because they have climbed to the highest peaks. Where they need to walk is narrow, and it is like that only because their vision is so wide.

It is neither helpful, nor appropriate for a prophet to have pet hang ups, or special hates, or particular preferences of subjects to denounce. If he has a particular hatred of a particular kind of sin, it biases his heart when God gives him a word for people who indulge in that particular evil. A prophet is honed by God to feel what He is saying when he or she utters the message, to cry when God cries, to laugh when God laughs and to be able to relate to God as friend with friend. Paul cried for the sin of one young man in Corinth, and wrote with tears about the issue (2 Corinthians 2:4). Paul wept and felt desperate for Jewish people to become Christians (Romans 9:1-2). These are character traits of a prophet of God. He doesn't just pass on a message from God, like smiling while he delivers a letter, the contents of which he knows nothing. The prophet carries God's heart as well as God's words. The prophet is God's interface with man.

A prophet of God is precious to the Almighty. Those who hold the perspective that theologians refer to as "Cessationists," that is that all miraculous acts of God such as healing, deliverance, the baptism in the Holy Spirit, tongues and prophecy have ceased, talk falsely and incredulously of such things. "They must have ceased!" they cry. But God never changes. People and the church of Jesus Christ ebb and flow in their understanding and zeal, but God Himself never changes. Jesus Christ is the same, yesterday, today and forever. God always has his prophets in every generation. Paul was one of them in the generation in which he served, though known more popularly and pedantically accurately, as an apostle.

Prophecy, whether it be on a national, local, church or personal scale is an essential and vital weapon in the ministry and management of the miraculous. What I mean by that is that even though prophecy is intrinsically supernatural and miraculous in itself, when personal prophecies reveal the secrets of a person's heart, sickness or bondage, it prepares the way for healing and salvation in every dimension. It is all part of the management of the ministry of the miraculous. Personal prophecy can be a key that opens incredibly large doors. Even the largest of doors swing on little hinges, and one little word from God can often swing the door of the human spirit wide open, facilitating deliverance and healing like nothing else can.

Acts 19:21 tells us that it was revealed by the prophetic Spirit that rested on Paul, that he must go to Macedonia, Achaia and then Jerusalem. Then he solemnly added the postscript, "And after that, I must go on to Rome." This was all by revelation and the voice of the Spirit.

There are those who prophecy by the gift of the Holy Spirit. There are those who prophesy as moving in the gift of Christ. There are those who prophesy in the church body in that gift of the Holy Spirit as referred to in 1 Corinthians 12 and 14. There are those who are prophets as a gift of Christ to the body of Christ, as explained in Ephesians 4. In this verse Paul heard from God concerning his personal itinerary and ministry. This was prophecy cum direction of a very personal and far reaching kind. In a unique and very powerful way that has impacted the world for two thousand years, Paul spoke for God and had received communications from God which, even though he is not specifically and directly referred to as a prophet in the scriptures, definitely qualify him as one. His entire life speaks prophetically to the church still.

My own relationship with prophets of various depths and character has led me to conclude that true prophets, quite often, do not have a choice in some of the things they do, just like Paul here in Acts 19:21. He was compelled to go to Macedonia, Achaia and Jerusalem. He seems to have no choice in the matter. He has heard from God. Most ominously, however, was his latter statement of how he must see Rome also. The Spirit of God compels prophets, in the same way that Paul was here compelled about his own life. They do not hear God with loud claps of thunder or a voice from heaven that shakes the building where everybody hears. They hear God, silently yet clearly, and when they do, to the uninitiated it is overwhelmingly powerful and bohemian as to the weight they give those words. To those that know and understand, they learn as they watch and listen. There are times when it seems by cursory observation that a prophet picks the word out of the air, and in a moment he has seen something that when spoken out, changes the entire world for the one who was the recipient of that particular prophetic word. It is so spontaneous and easy that it seems to some that he or she invented his "prophetic" word. Yet it impacts so much, so powerfully and benefits people so incredibly that it couldn't be anything else but God speaking. The whole exercise is vindicated as being a "God thing." I used to say that "a prophet carries God around with him." Silly me! It is God that carries them around.

We are told in Acts 13:1 that *"there were in the church at Antioch certain prophets and teachers; as Barnabas, and Simeon that was called Niger, and Lucius of Cyrene, and Manaen, which had been brought up with Herod the tetrarch, and Saul."* We could all discuss whether or not it means that some of those five men were teachers and others were prophets, or whether all five of them were both teachers and prophets, but this writer is content to affirm that Paul was a prophet as well as a teacher.

A prophet is a spokesman from God and for God, and thus is incredibly vulnerable to abuse from those that do not like the word from God to be so personal, so direct, and so "In your face." Those that live on the plains of spirituality cannot at all cope or tolerate those that live in the mountain tops seeing in the Spirit more than others do. A prophet (or prophetess) speaks in God's name and by His authority and power (Exodus 7:1). He, or she, is the mouth by which God speaks to men (Jeremiah 1:9; Isaiah 51:16), and hence what the prophet says is not of man but of God (2 Peter 1:20, 21; compare Hebrews 3:7; Acts 4:25; 28:25). Prophets are the immediate organs of God for the communication of his mind and will to men (Deuteronomy 18:18, 19). The whole Word of God, in this sense, is prophetic, inasmuch as it was written by men who received the revelation they communicated from God, no matter what its nature might be.

The Apostle Paul wrote more than one half of the books of the New Testament. To be a true prophet Paul must evidence some of the characteristics that are required of a prophet. Paul was sent by God and was always conscious and mindful of his being sent. One of the fundamental bases of the validity of Paul's commissioning is centred upon the divine visitations he experienced.

Christ-like character, and the manifest fruit of the Spirit is undoubtedly more precious in God's sight than any manifestation, no matter how miraculous. The manifestations of Christ to Paul, however, speak not only of his receiving apostolic authority, but his prophetic anointing also.

As many of the Old Testament prophets were divinely appointed into their ministry and calling by means of a literal visitation, and their seeing something of the manifestation of the God of heaven, sometimes even with personal appearances of God, so Paul, likewise, had such validating manifestations that confirm his high calling as an apostle and prophet.

Scripture actually records ten visitations which Paul experienced, all of which had a remarkable bearing on his ministry and his consciousness of being sent, as well as the certainty of his salvation. We note these visitations as a preface to commenting on the weight of the words and decisions he made as expressed in Acts 19:21.

25.

PAUL WAS ACTUALLY CONVERTED BY A VISION OF A DIVINE VISITATION. (ACTS 9:1-9; 22:5-11; 26:12-20).

The Apostle Paul received several direct words from Christ Himself as recorded in the scriptures, the first precipitating his own salvation experience on the road to Damascus. There are three versions of this call in the book of Acts. In one of the accounts given by Paul himself in Acts chapter 26, it is clearly stated that he was aware of his calling from the moment that he first heard Christ speak to Him. I do not believe he could have understood all the implications and ramifications what Christ said in those first moments of confrontation with God and his destiny, but they were clearly made plain as a statement as per Acts 26:12-20, and he received this predictive, prophetic information via a face to face meeting with Jesus Christ Himself.

It was not merely an impression that Paul received, nor was it "just" a voice. Saul of Tarsus actually saw the Lord Jesus. He says so in I Corinthians 9:1. Paul informs us also, in 1 Corinthians 15:9 that he was the last in a long line of many people that saw the resurrected Saviour. The word "appeared" in I Corinthians 15:8 is the same word used by Paul in depicting the appearance of Christ to the Apostles and others after the resurrection. Make no mistake about it, Paul met Jesus Christ in a visible and audible manifestation. Most people would call that a visitation, if not, a vision.

All three accounts of Paul's conversion state that he heard Christ's voice saying "I am Jesus." How far this voice was externally audible to the others is again uncertain. In the contradiction between hearing the voice (Acts 9:7) and not hearing the voice (Acts 22:9) the difference in the case (hearing the sound with the genitive, and understanding the sense with the accusative) is in harmony with ancient Greek usage. All that were present saw the light, but Jesus spoke only and directly to Saul (Acts 22:9). The claims of mass hysteria are laughable in the picture given by scripture. The whole thing was objectively seen, heard and experienced. For Paul to have seen the Saviour in the same manner as the other apostles did, as Paul claims, he would have had to have seen an objective tangible vision of Christ. The confrontation was utterly objective and external. Paul's personal response was another thing.

Barnabas set forth fully the story of Saul's conversion to the twelve apostles, including the description of how he had met with Jesus and talked with Him, and he also recounted Paul's entire identification with Christ in Damascus through his full testimony in preaching. The apostles received him and recommended him to the disciples. If it doesn't satisfy some scholars in the twenty first century, it certainly satisfied the apostles whose life could have been in danger by receiving a murderer claiming he was changed.

1. **During those first three days after Paul's first visitation, Paul was also directed in his newly given faith and understanding by a prophetic vision.**

Paul says in Acts 26, that the call to follow Christ and the commission that would demand his entire life, was given by Jesus Himself: "To this end have I appeared unto you to appoint you as a minister and a witness (26:16)."

Ananias, however, the second Christian man who went by that name in the book of Acts, had a revelation from God. Not wanting to be humourously quaint, the revelation to Ananias is very revealing. God told Ananias in Acts 9:11-12, that Saul was praying. Paul had been blinded by the visitation on the Damascus Road, but even though he was *blind* as he prayed, he *saw* in a vision, as plain as day, a man called Ananias placing his hands on him and restoring his sight. God told Ananias that Paul was a chosen instrument, and that he would show him the things that he must suffer for Christ. Ananias prayed for Paul and sure enough he was healed. So within 72 hours of that initial sight of Christ on the Damascus Road, Saul of Tarsus was again immersed into revelatory dealings with God. Paul must have been aware that he was saved, a particularly chosen instrument in God's hands, and that he had a high calling from God, in Christ Jesus.

All this knowledge and understanding was by vision, and revelation. The viciousness and violence of his life prior to the Damascus Road experience was so famously (or infamously) high profile amongst Christians that they had trouble in believing what had happened to him straight off. But it was all by the initiative taken by God to reveal Himself to Paul that brought the situation about.

2. **Paul (although he was still known as Saul) was also personally established in his faith and doctrine, if not by a vision, per se, it was definitely by supernatural revelation of the Holy Spirit.**

Paul encountered the Almighty and All-knowing in an even more intimate way during his stay in Damascus which is recorded by Luke in Acts 9:23 when he speaks of "many days." "Many days" means literally a considerable number of days. The epistle to the Galatians sheds more light on the stay annotated in that one single verse of Acts 9:23. In Paul's angry letter to the Galatians, Paul is arguing that his apostleship and his doctrine are God-given, and that he was taught what he knows not from Bible School or book learning, but by direct revelation from God. He could not possibly say it in any clearer way. *"Nor was I taught it except by revelation from Jesus Christ"* (Galatians 1:12). The understanding that we gain, as we survey the entire New Testament, is that Paul knew everything the twelve apostles knew. Peter and the others could add nothing to Paul's faith and doctrine. It is as if Christ from heaven had communed with him as He did on earth in the days of His flesh with the other apostles. It was at this time that the revelation of the Son of God was increasingly being revealed *in* him, whereas on the road to Damascus the vision was revealed *to* him.

We cannot escape the fact that the entire spiritual status of Paul at this time was supernaturally achieved by God's initiative. His establishment in the faith was a God driven thing without the normal human helps of a pastor, a lecturer, an academic master or a college course. There was no middle man to dilute or alter the revelation as it landed into Paul's spirit (I Corinthians 11:23; 15:3; I Thessalonians 4:15). The revelation was as pure in its reception as it was in God who revealed Himself. Thus Paul is truly a completely independent witness to the Gospel. He received no instruction from the apostles in any way whatsoever, only direct from the Holy Spirit, which meant that, eventually, when he met the twelve, his gospel agreed exactly with what they knew.

Paul was later in Jerusalem. Perhaps his life was in danger while he was there. It would have been understandable for people to be angry with him. Firstly there would have been a large Jewish contingent who would have been enraged that their former hero of Judaism, had now "changed sides," as it were. They would not have approved of his presence in Jerusalem. Then there would have been many, Christian or otherwise, who would have had loved ones or relatives who were Christians whom Paul had erstwhile killed, or had imprisoned before his conversion, i.e. Stephen's family (Acts 8:3 and 9:1).

3. **Paul has a heavenly vision, and an insight from God Himself on what was happening with other people who were remote from him.**

As a staunch Jew still, Paul was praying in the Temple one day when he fell into a trance. Paul's own words are that he, "saw the Lord speaking." We are left to extrapolate and conjecture that this happened on that visit where he first met Peter. Christ's first word was, "Quick!" Be assured that when God says, "Quick!" He means, "Now!" "Leave

Jerusalem immediately, because they will not accept your testimony about me." In plain English, it infers that Jesus was telling Paul to run for his life, for some were on the cusp of coming to look for him. This is all recorded in Acts 22:17–21. Paul was told to make haste and leave Jerusalem. Leaving Jerusalem was a present imperative, but Jesus also committed Himself, saying that at some future point, He would direct and send him to the gentiles.

The actual fulfilment of Jesus' words here did not occur until Acts 13:1 – 3, where Paul was prophetically set aside to travel abroad with Barnabas. Thereafter, we do not here of Paul turning to the gentiles until his first visit to Pisidian Antioch (Acts 13:42–46). Acts 13:46-48 records a major historic event. The complete rejection of Paul and his preaching by the Jews was the practical situation that gave Paul a revelatory understanding of his mission from God. The fact that he had spent three years in Arabia and Damascus (Galatians 1:17) and later not less than five years in Syria and Cilicia (Galatians 1:21; cf. Acts 9:30), as well as the circumstance that during these years his preaching was almost if not quite, exclusively to Jews and Hellenists indicate that Paul had not yet come to the full consciousness of his distinctive mission, but that it was made increasingly manifest to him in the course of his missionary labours. And he had only arrived at all this profound understanding of God, the gospel, and mission to the gentiles, through direct revelation from heaven.

I am recounting these experiences in the chronology that I understand is there in the scriptures. Based on my understood chronology,

4. Paul's next major divine visitation was the substance of what is recorded in 2 Corinthians 12:2.

Paul received remarkable revelation and profound understanding by being translated to the third heaven. In 2 Corinthians 12:2 the apostle is obviously talking about himself. Again as in Acts 22:17 the apostle speaks of falling into a trance, although the word "trance" is not used. However, the language of being somewhere, yet not knowing if he had gone to that place in the body or out of the body, suggests very much a trance like state. He states that this occurred about fourteen years prior to the writing of this particular epistle. The writing of the epistle may be fixed, without much risk of error in 57 AD. The vision, "fourteen years before" (2 Corinthians 12:1) was in 43 AD, six years after his conversion

The book of Acts does not record this incident. Scholars are left to deduce and extrapolate that Paul was in Tarsus or possibly Antioch during this window of chronology. Opinions differ greatly. Some think it was near the time that Barnabas came seeking Saul for the work in Antioch (Acts 11:25). Some insist it was more than likely during Paul and Barnabas' second visit to Jerusalem which occurred just prior to Paul's being set apart by the church of Antioch for missionary service (Acts 12:25). Probably this vision and revelation were vouchsafed to him then, because he was going for the first time to incur shame and suffering for Christ.

Paul does not give us the details of what he heard in the third heaven. In fact he says it was unlawful, or, not allowed by God, to be repeated. Whatever happened, and whatever was revealed to Paul, was designed only for him, and for the purpose of establishing him more fully in Christ.

5. Paul went to Jerusalem by vision (Galatians 2:2)

Paul went to Jerusalem at one point, simply because a revelation compelled him to go. He did not go to argue his beliefs. He went by revelation to resolve the issue of circumcision with the apostles first. There was a huge and heated debate by some insisting that all Christians should be circumcised. Paul believed that those who spoke against him were, "false brothers" (Galatians 2:4). The fact that Paul went up by revelation was mentioned in Galatians to remove even the remotest doubt that Paul may have been summoned by the apostles of Jerusalem in order to be disciplined or corrected.

Again the force of their testimony in conjunction with Peter's testimony of the gospel being revealed to the gentiles resulted in total acceptance of non-Jewish people into full recognition by the church. Thus, Paul was again assured that his call was valid and that his being sent forth was in the will of God. All these occurrences that contributed to Paul's experience were revealed to him by divine visitations and/or revelation.

6. "Where not to go" given by revelation (Acts 16:6-7)

Later we read that Paul received expansion of vision and active ministry by divine revelation. He was guided where not to go, and where to go, by pure revelation. The Holy Spirit gave them negative as well as positive direction. The Spirit of Jesus had restrained them from preaching the Word of God in the province of Asia (Acts 16:6). They were restrained in the same manner in Bithynia (Acts 16:7). Not sure of where to go to next, Paul had a vision of a man calling him over to Macedonia. Paul went to Macedonia fully knowing that God was planting the pathway for his steps before he even got there.

Macedonia in effect was a signal and emblem for Paul's access to the whole western empire of Rome. All these revelatory visitations, and supernatural occurrences were nailing God's word and will firmly into Paul's psyche. The point that we are making is that supernatural revelation was given to him concerning the nature and reality of his call, and that supernatural revelation was used to assist him in the communication of the message that was embedded in his call. The message itself was supernaturally communicated to Paul, and was to be supernaturally communicated to those to whom he was to minister. It was all divinely given tuition for Paul's overall management of the miraculous. As many preachers love to say, "It was a complete set up!"

7. Told to remain in Corinth by divine visitation (Acts 18:9-11)

The length of Paul's visits to the many places he visited and ministered in is almost an irrelevance to Luke, until Thessalonica, and then Corinth. Paul had a riot formed against him at the front end of his first visit to Corinth. Although we are not told anything in Acts or the Corinthian letters, it seems Paul might have been thinking of leaving. "One night the Lord spoke to Paul in a vision." It's all there in Acts 18:9-11. Jesus told Paul to keep on speaking for there were many people in Corinth who were to become Christians. He then stayed there for 18 months. The field was ripe and ready for a harvest of a large crop of Gentile souls and so it was that Christ appeared and spoke to Paul so that the divinely ordained apostle would fulfil God's purpose in Corinth.

This little moment in Paul's life is really wonderful, and the revelation from the Master profound. Paul received first, the promise that he should be divinely protected against the hostility and ill treatment of Christ's enemies, and on the other hand, it was revealed to him that Christ knew of a large number that would believe in the city. A revelation of facts not yet apparent is glorious. He knows the beginning from the end. This must have been exhilarating in the midst of any trouble Paul was going through at that moment.

8. A revelation of comfort and assurance as Christ stand with Paul (Acts 23:11)

A ninth vision came to Paul while he was in Jerusalem for what scripture tells us was his third visit as a minister of Christ. He had been violently taken by the worst of the Jews and brought to the Sanhedrin where such disorder had resulted that Paul's life was in danger. The commander of the Jewish Guard withdrew Paul for safety. It was on that very night wherever Paul was kept that the Lord actually stood near Paul. Acts 23:11 is a remarkable moment. "Be of good cheer: I am satisfied with your testimony; you have done what you could; the results do not depend on you." The importance of the message was incredibly uplifting for the apostle. Christ's word was concerning Paul's thoroughness, "…for as you have thoroughly testified the things concerning Me in Jerusalem, so you must also testify in exactly the same way in Rome."

Paul was ready to fight with wild beasts whether they were at Rome or anywhere else. He was aware that he had divine approval.

9. A revelation in the midst of the storm (Acts 27:23)

The tenth and last vision that I am aware of came when Paul was in the midst of the long storm while being taken to Rome by ship. As recorded in Acts 27:23, an angel of the Lord stood by the apostle. It is a piece of logic that Paul must have embraced and fastened to his soul in the midst of the dreadful and prolonged storm. If the promise made to him in Acts 23:11 was to be fulfilled, then he must have had the assurance of his life being sustained so that he could personally testify in Rome. Added to that logical string of thought, according to Acts 9:15 Paul was to testify to "kings", i.e. plural. As of that date, according to the records we have, he had appeared before only one king, that being Agrippa. The fellow travellers of the apostle would escape with their lives, along with all the sailors that manned the ship. They would all be saved from death, simply for the sake of Paul, in as much as God assured Paul of their safety as an act of grace to him. Or, at least, that is how it reads to this writer.

The ongoing validity of Paul's mission and ministry, did not depend upon one divine vision, glorious though that was. As much as is recorded in the scripture Paul had many visitations and revelations. These regular supernatural key inputs that fed Paul's understanding of the cosmos were key to who and what he was. It helped confirm the world-view that he taught. The continuity, the ongoing repetition, as well as the direct bearing which they had on Paul's life must have compelled him to accept the presence of the divine Planner of his entire life.

The fulfilments of each revelation and promise must have also demonstrated to Paul that he was being sent by God. The validity of Paul's vision concerning Ananias was complemented by Ananias also receiving exact divine direction. The desert and or Damascus revelation, was validated by the agreement and completeness of Paul's message and that of the Apostles in Jerusalem. The success of the advice at Jerusalem from the twelve apostles again assured Paul that he was purposefully called. The harvest for the kingdom of God in Macedonia and Corinth also proved those instructions to be of divine origin. The commission to testify in Rome was also completed and the saving of the lives at sea set in Paul's heart as firm as rock that he was, yet again, on a truly divine mission. Paul knew he was sent of God and was constantly objectively conscious of God's call.

It is these ten visitations and visions that were undoubtedly the foundational platform upon which Paul's ministry of the miraculous was built. Visions and supernatural manifestations are not necessary to faith, but I have noticed in all the people that I have met who have had such visitations that their faith was more vital. And consciously exercised in all of their activities.

But what did this prepare Paul for?

Because he was converted, confirmed, established and continually guided by what we would refer to as supernatural means, it educated Paul in the manner and means of the supernatural power of God, and how to move in that divine power and authority. It facilitated a more intelligent management of the miraculous in his life.

Strangely enough, just as I find a Decalogue of instances where God entrenched Paul in his faith by manifestations of the supernatural, I find also a Decalogue of instances where his education in the Spirit allowed and facilitated Paul to minister to others in the miraculous.

As I feel confident to suggest that throughout Paul's life there was actually much more than ten visions and/or visitations that established and built his faith up (2 Corinthians 12:7), I am also certain that there was much more than ten miraculous events in Paul's ministry for Christ. But the ten that are highlighted in scripture as instructive.

1. Ministry of the Miraculous in Cyprus.

On his first stop, in his second city, on his first missionary journey, Paul was at Paphos in Cyprus. The proconsul had a sorcerer as one of his personal attendants, and Sergius Paulus, the proconsul, actually asked for Paul and Barnabas to explain what they were teaching. The sorcerer opposed them before the proconsul and tried to turn him away from the faith. The first launch of the miraculous that we hear of in Paul's ministry was here at this moment. Think of the faith, the courage, the understanding of God, and the ear to what God was saying, as well as the eye to see what God was doing, when Paul says to the sorcerer's face, *"You son of the devil, full of every sort of deceit and fraud, and enemy of all that is good! Will you never stop perverting the true ways of the Lord? Watch now, for the Lord has laid his hand of punishment upon you, and you will be struck blind. You will not see the sunlight for some time"* (Acts 13:11). Consider the deep grasp of the character and the ways of God for a man to jump into such a pronouncement. Many modern theologies keep clear of this exposition as some find it difficult to connect "God is Love," with such a judgement. My answer to such people is that the Bible must define or definition of God's love. God is just as well as holy. The God who, in the Old Testament, commanded a man and his family to be stoned to death for picking up sticks (Numbers 15:32-36) is the same God that died on the cross of Calvary. Such facts have to teach us the construct of God's unfathomable love, in the light of His perfect judgement. What is more, scripture tells us that what Paul said came immediately into effect, and the sorcerer needed someone to take his hand and lead him around (Acts 13:4-12).

What Paul said was prophetic. In and of itself this does not confirm his status as a prophet, but the rhema word of God was in his mouth. In the name of Christ the sorcerer was blinded, but just for a season. This demonstration of the word of power, as well as the power of the word, caused the proconsul to believe. As it was, so it is today. If millions of this generation are to believe, they must see proof that Jesus Christ is the same yesterday, today and forever.

The point is that a true prophet speaks words that redirect and change lives not only of the righteous, but also of the unrighteous.

2. Ministry of the Miraculous at Iconium

Still in Paul's first journey he had crossed from Cyprus to what we would today call Southern Turkey, and was at a place called Iconium. In this place he started, as was normal for Paul, to start at the Jewish Synagogue. Acts 14:1 says that they preached so well that a large number of both Jews and gentiles believed, but a Jewish contingent had both Paul and Barnabas, together with John Mark derided. However, in the midst of the persecution, the scripture says that they spoke so boldly for the Lord that He confirmed the message of grace by enabling them to do miraculous signs and wonders. This manifestation of the miraculous brought out persecution that was life threatening. They left the town to move on to other pastures. Knowing when to stay in the midst of life threatening persecution and when to leave was also an integral part of Paul's management of the miraculous.

It is noteworthy that even though in the earlier part of Paul's missionary trips he fled when his life was threatened, later in life he stayed and fought against the persecution with grace, character and prayer.

The point must be seen that when the full word is preached with the anointing of the Spirit, with great boldness and sincerity, with no thought to one's own safety, that attitude is a constituent part of the overall strategy that manages, savours and sustains the management of the ministry of the miraculous.

3. & 4. Ministry of the Miraculous at Lystra

Having left Iconium, Paul went to Lystra where he engaged with a man who had never walked before in one of his public declarations of the gospel. Paul spiritual character and comfort when mixing with the gentile cultures, had grown to the point where he was now being referred to by a gentile name - Paul, and the scripture, from this point on, says it was Paul and Barnabas, as opposed to Barnabas and Saul. It clearly infers that Paul was now the leader of the duo. Again in a circumstance that demanded faith, boldness, insight, a prophetic word of knowledge from heaven, and eyes to see what God was doing, Paul shouted at the crippled man to stand up on his feet – and he made the call in the midst of a public gathering. The crippled man was healed immediately. The town was in such uproar that they concluded Paul and Barnabas were two of the Greek Gods come down to earth. The response of the apostolic pair was, of course, to insist that they were two very ordinary men simply doing what Christ had told them to do. No "white suit" attitude here.

The acute point in this example is that Paul was ready for, and looking for, an opportunity to move in the miraculous, and was listening to God as he preached. The miraculous, though absolutely accomplished by faith in the word of God, has to be made room for in the ministry of the word. Also, it is a mind stretcher to consider what it was that Paul said that convinced a man who had never walked that he could walk, and that he had faith to do so (Acts 14: 8-18).

So having disabused the people of thinking that they were deities, the Jews from previous towns came to Lystra and convinced the people that they were devils. They then stoned Paul and crudely dragged him out of the city thinking that he was dead. Such is life for those that live godly in Christ; Gods on Monday, devils on Tuesday and stoned and left for dead on Wednesday (Acts 14:19-20). Though Paul had been left for dead, the disciples gathered around him. Perhaps they prayed. We are not told. But after they encircled him, Paul got up onto his feet. Did he run? Did he say, "Take me away from this place?" Not at all, he walked straight back into the city.

The point of the episode is that the miraculous recovery of Paul was a demonstration of the power of what God had put into the man. The scripture talks of some people in the future, and it says of them, *"They overcame by the word of their testimony, the blood of the lamb, and they loved not their lives unto the death"* (Revelation 12:10). Those words weren't actually talking about Paul, but they might as well have. And loving Christ over his own life was yet another key factor in Paul's management of the miraculous. Paul said in Philippians 3:10 that he yearned that he might know the power of Christ's resurrection in his life. This stoning happened quite some time prior to Paul even being at Philippi, but resurrection power was surely present in the healing of the crippled man who had never walked as well as Paul's own recovery from being stoned and left for dead.

5. Ministry of the Miraculous at Philippi.

Then in Acts 16:16-18 there is the deliverance of the demon possessed girl in Philippi. This account is a sure and clear statement of Paul's power and authority that he knew he had in Christ and exercised it when necessary. He did not ask for the compliance of the girl or her mentors. He didn't check whether she had faith in Christ or not. She interrupted Paul's preaching and talks with the people over several days. She declared that Paul and Silas were servants of the most high God who had come to show them all how to be saved. "What's wrong with that?" I hear you ask. The point is that Paul discerned that these words of affirmation were mockingly spoken by fortune telling demons who were trying to assume authority over Paul. He cast the demon out of the girl which upset the money making business men who had the girl under their control, and thus, to cut the story short, caused a furore that and Paul and Silas imprisoned.

The overall lesson is that the power and authority of Christ does not need acquiescence by the human subject to be delivered. Deliverance is not necessarily done with a person's approval. Deliverance is God's word spoken against the devil. It does not need a democratic vote of approval first.

6. Ministry of the Miraculous at Ephesus

The sixth example of Paul moving in the miraculous is the very examples we have read of in Acts 19 while Paul was in Ephesus. These healings with the aprons and cloths were prophetic in as much as the miracle was manifested through inanimate items that were not even items of clothing. Cloths and aprons carried the anointing that was on Paul and carried a statement of faith that had impregnated them whether or not Paul prayed over them, said anything over them, or even if they were taken without Paul's knowledge. It was the ultimate in prophetic action.

This was similar to the woman who touched the hem of Christ's garment. Why? Because it was an inanimate object that had touched the Lord's body. Jesus had not prayed over his garments, neither had he prepared them as a healing tool or weapon. The woman came in an action that Jesus was not watching and did not know of. In a sense, the woman was healed in a "remote" healing, as were those who were delivered and healed by touching the apron or cloth that was taken from Paul.

I believe that the Spirit of God can work in this way when He is completely at home and comfortable with the lifestyle and attitude of the one with whom He is living. As it was with Jesus, so it was with Paul. So it was with Peter and his shadow also. Healings that are manifested remotely from the mind and will of the ministering person are extraordinary. These are wonderful examples of a prophetic person's influence stretching beyond what is "normal" in the realm of the supernatural. The miracle is done by the Spirit without the knowledge of the carrier. The Spirit works according to His will. There are other examples of this kind of thing. Ezekiel, seeing what was going on in the temple of Jerusalem whilst sitting in Babylon (Ezekiel 8). Elisha knowing exactly what and where the King of Aram (Syria) was doing with his army when fighting Israel. Whatever the king of Aram said, even in secret, was divinely whispered to Elisha (2 Kings 6:8-12). Jesus healing the nobleman's son in John 4, and delivering the Canaanite woman's daughter (Mark 7:24-30). The anointing of the prophet means that distance is never a barrier.

7. Ministry of the Miraculous at Troas

Moving ahead of our real time study in Ephesus, the next prophetic action we read of that was extraordinary was the raising of Eutychus as recorded in Acts 20:9-11. Eutychus fell asleep on the window ledge of a house with many candles or torches burning brightly. It was a time before glass windows were invented. The heat and fumes of the inside sent Eutychus to sleep, whereupon he fell out of the third storey windowsill. The fall killed him. But it is what happened next that wreaks of the prophetic. Did Paul pray? No! Did he command Eutychus to come forth from the realms of the dead? Not at all! He did not even take his hand to whisper, "Young man I say to you arise." Did he not simply look at the dead body and shout, "In the mighty name of Jesus Christ?" No! Any of those responses would have been prophetic. But the prophet merely lay on top of Eutychus's cadaver and embraced him. He then simply announced, "Don't be alarmed! He's well!" Job done. There is a huge difference from being prophetic, and being a prophet.

I remember once in Lagos, that when chatting to a group of pastors from South Africa I was held to account for the pastor/prophet's conduct. I was accosted by the group as to how they could possibly be invited to join a prayer line where they were not actually prayed for (as if it was anything to do with me at all). I had to laugh. My laughter made them more furious. I wasn't trying to infuriate them. I simply thought that their thought processes were ludicrous. Their point was that man of God, who was the senior minister, merely touched most of them, and did not say a word. With others, he simply stretched out his hand to them – and silently so. My answer to the South African pastors was simple: "The pastor's prophetic anointing transcends the ordinary. He merely stretches out his hand – prophetically – as per Acts 4:30. The prophet is speaking by hand gesticulation, without a spoken word." The group was stunned into silence. I do not know whether they were silenced because of agreement with my answer, or disagreement. But I left the group with nothing more to add.

A true prophet's anointing has a weight to it that brings some trivial words or actions into play for a mighty deliverance or healing. The healing of Eutychus speaks to me that not only was Paul a prophet, but that he was a well-seasoned and greatly experienced prophet of God.

8. 9. & 10. Ministry of the Miraculous at Malta

The eighth sighting of Paul the minister of the miraculous was the snakebite on the beach at Malta. Having just been saved from "death by shipwreck," when most people would be happy to sit by a fire and be nursed and ministered to, Paul was out picking sticks and twigs with which to light a fire. Snuggled up between some of the sticks Paul had unknowingly picked up a viper. And vipers are poisonous. There may be some silly people who argue against the validity of the latter sections of Mark 16, however, Paul firmly believed verse 18 which fed his faith by saying, "They shall pick up snakes...and it will not hurt them at all."

The scene is almost humourous. It seems that as he threw the wood on to the fire, the viper was left hanging on to Paul's hand by its teeth. The locals that were watching went off into a fantasy heathen world of empty thought. *"This man must be a murderer. For even though he escaped death at sea, Justice will not allow him to live."* They watched as Paul shook of the viper and carried on as if nothing had happened. The locals were extremely macabre and stared at Paul waiting for him to swell up, or simply drop dead. But Paul did not even know what was going on. When nothing happened, the locals ceased calling him a murderer and called him a god. The truth was that he was neither murderer (he was in actuality an ex accomplice to murder), nor was he a god. He was a prophet of Christ. The consciousness of the man was so buried in his ownership of an intimate relationship with Christ that he was, by an active, stubborn faith, impervious to the snapping of a poisonous viper. From that instance, the head man who ruled Malta at that time had a sick father whom Paul laid hands on. He was healed. After that more people on Malta were brought to him and were healed.

To this writer, these accounts, when seen in their combination, scream at me that Paul was a prophet, even though his prophetic gift was seemingly submerged with his apostolic gifting. Unknown to us today as a motive, it is absolutely clear that Luke had a logic and rational for what he both included, as well as excluded from the book of Acts. I say this because of things like the table immediately below:

Peter	Paul
"...many wonders and miraculous signs were done by the apostles" (2:43)	Paul and Barnabas (the apostles) did many miracles and signs in Iconium (14:3–4)
Lame Man from birth (3:1–10)	Lame Man from birth (14:8–11)
Earthquake ends a Prayer meeting (4:31)	Earthquake ends prayers sung to God (16:26)
Curses Ananias and Sapphira (5:1–11)	Curses Elymas (13:8–12)
Healing with a shadow (5:15)	Healing with a handkerchief (19:12)
Peter grants miraculous gifts through hands (8:17)	Paul grants miraculous gifts through hands (19:6)
Raises Tabitha from the dead (9:40)	Raises Eutychus from the dead (20:9–12)
Peters chains loosed (12:7)	Paul's chains fell off (16:26)

Paralleling Paul and Peter's ministry was obviously done for a reason. Analysis of Acts and comparing it with Luke's gospel is to be an area of fruitful study sometime in the future.

Although the role and function of prophet was undoubtedly submerged in the more authoritative apostolic gift that rested on Paul, without any shadow of a doubt the three pronged ministry of healing, deliverance and prophecy – especially of personal prophecy, is the key to a sustained and consistent attack on sin, sickness and the devil in people's lives. Paul's management of the miraculous was tied up in not only sustain, but improving the manifestation of these gifts, by bringing his body soul and spirit into captivity to Christ.

26.

"OF MICE AND MEN!" "OF PAUL AND PERSECUTION"! WHAT'S THE DIFFERENCE?

"Afterward Paul felt compelled by the Spirit to go over to Macedonia and Achaia before going to Jerusalem. "And after that, " he said, "I must go on to Rome!"."

Acts 19:21 (NLT)

"When the uproar was over, Paul sent for the believers and encouraged them. Then he said good-bye and left for Macedonia."

Acts 20:1 (NLT).

2 *"When I came to the city of Troas to preach the Good News of Christ, the Lord opened a door of opportunity for me. But I had no peace of mind because my dear brother Titus hadn't yet arrived with a report from you. So I said good-bye and went on to Macedonia to find him."*

2 Corinthians 2:12-13 (NLT)

In a deep desire to know more of Christ, we are trawling through a period of time in which this writer considers Paul to have been moving in such grace and power as to be the ultimate peak of New Testament ministry. The Apostle Paul's mission to Ephesus, and his impact on the whole Roman province of Asia is one of the hardest challenges of scripture to emulate. I do not believe that any church, denomination or evangelist has ever matched Paul's "Mission to Ephesus and Asia" in any way whatsoever. Ephesus was taken for Christ. The whole of Asia heard the word of God. Churches were founded in many places and we know of at least 14 that were founded around this time throughout Asia. Those I am aware of are listed below in the context of these pages. It was such a God sanctioned mission that when Jesus Christ Himself wanted to speak to the church as a whole in the text of the Apocalypse, He did not tell John to write to Jerusalem, Antioch, Rome or Alexandria. It was the most established churches and divinely significant churches that came into being as a result of Paul's mission in Asia while he was based at Ephesus.

Paul did not leave Ephesus sedately, or in a planned way. He certainly was in the process of planning to leave (Acts 19:21), but he was to be there through the winter at least until Pentecost (1 Corinthians 16:8). He left in a state of pressure and discomfort. Because of the importance and huge impact of the campaign in Asia, and the seemingly smaller issues that caused Paul to leave the great city of Artemis, we intend in these pages to state what this writer believes to be the reasons why he finally left Ephesus at the time and in the manner that he did. It may surprise you. It is an incredible statement concerning the management of the miraculous in a minister's life.

After this statement today, our next chapter will be an attempt to fathom the motives and principles of Paul's responses to the situation that compelled him to leave three years of the most successful ministry that any man, and the church universal has ever known.

To facilitate a full statement of it all, we will look at:

1. **THE FRIGHTFUL CIRCUMSTANCES THAT COMPELLED PAUL TO LEAVE EPHESUS.**

2. **THE TROUBLESOME CHURCH THAT COMPELLED PAUL AWAY FROM EPHESUS.**

3. **THE PROBLEMATIC SERIES OF LETTERS THAT COMPELLED PAUL TO LEAVE EPHESUS.**

1. THE FRIGHTFUL CIRCUMSTANCES THAT COMPELLED PAUL TO LEAVE EPHESUS.

Paul left Ephesus at the time, and in the way he did, because of deep personal unease with possibly physical as well as mental discomfort. After suddenly, if not hastily leaving Ephesus he went straight to Troas with the same great motive by which he was always driven, i.e. that of preaching the gospel of Christ (2 Corinthians 2:12-13). He was, as he originally planned, on the way to Macedonia, but the opportunity was providentially given, and the apostle seized it. However, on this particular occasion, did he have another motive as well for stopping there? I ask this question because he then left Troas for what this writer believes to be exactly the same reason he left Ephesus.

We have no clue as to the length of time he stopped over at Troas. Paul was preaching there so successfully and freely that he referred to it as "an open door." And yet, he did not continue. He was anxious, so he says, to see Titus and for news of where the Corinthian church was in sorting out the issues for which, not only had he written his advice and commands, but had fully imparted his whole mind to Titus to speak on his behalf. He was so anxious – and this is huge – he actually left his preaching for the lost at Troas, and moved to Macedonia, eager to meet his own personal ambassador to Corinth with any news he might have.

Grasp the picture. The apostle to the gentiles, left the mother of all revivals and the ultimate of all evangelistic efforts for lack of news from the troublesome Christian people of Corinth. And even though another door of ministry had divinely opened to him, he could not rest while waiting for news, in fact – the impression is given that he could not focus on what he was doing. So after a hasty exit from Ephesus, Troas also was left behind. The man was plainly suffering. Whatever we know or don't know as to the causes, Paul was, as we say, "in a state," about Corinth. I clearly remember the principal of the Bible College I attended four decades ago, Rev. George Wesley Gilpin teaching us that, "We are not only called to be, "fishers of men," but we have to also be "keepers of the aquarium."" How wise! How prudent! How evident, here in Paul's mentality and actions, that the great apostle was in agreement with the great Wesley Gilpin.

When I read the whole text of Acts 19, it seems to me that as early as Acts 19:21 he was calmly coming to the conclusion that his intense campaign of ministry in the metropolis of Ephesus, and his sending of teams all around Asia, founding churches wherever they went, was coming to completion and conclusion. He had received it, "in the Spirit," (Acts 19:21) that he needed to go to Macedonia, Achaia and then Jerusalem, post scripted with, "I must go on to Rome." I read these remarks as being made in the routine of his life at Ephesus. It was of God's design that he was to leave - but not yet! He planned to leave after winter, after Pentecost (1 Corinthians 16:8). This statement substantiates that he was writing First Corinthians from Ephesus long before the winter months. It also presupposes that he wrote 1 Corinthians after the instance of Acts 19:21, that is, after he had decided to leave Ephesus. We surmise from this that First Corinthians was written 5-6 months before he had, at this time, planned to leave. This decision was made strategically and calmly. Paul was planning his itinerary and diary.

Then we read in Acts 19 of the riot that was started by Demetrius the silver smith. In the text, as Luke wrote it, it is clear that no pain or physical hurt was done to the apostle in the context of that particular riot (Acts 19:23-41). However, as soon as the uproar was concluded, Acts 20:1 informs us that he called the disciples around him (that is the, "about 12," that he met in Acts 19:1-6 who had been ministering both to him, with him). Paul spoke words of encouragement to them, and then said "Good-bye." Finito! He then left Ephesus. "He said Good-bye and set off..." The entire tone of the sentence suggests a sudden change of attitude, even, a spontaneous decision to leave.

What changed Paul's plans?

The apostle was anxious and in pain over a few issues with the church he had founded in Corinth, and his discomfort over this issue caused him to change his plans a couple of times. At this point, it would seem that he left Ephesus suddenly, thus cancelling the thought of staying over winter, creating accusations in the hearts of some at troublesome Corinth that, "Paul does not keep his word." And this was happening at the very moment that some travelling, "false apostles," were utterly undermining his authority and teaching in the Corinthian church. But Paul did not seem to know this at the time he left Ephesus.

Some time prior to leaving the Ephesian "revival," he had sent the big guns in to deal with Corinth. Apollos was too much of a novice. Timothy was seen too much as Paul's favourite youthful protégé. Titus, however, was Greek, mature and perceived to be his own man, and one of, if not the most senior and sober associate of Paul. Titus was Paul's best means of communication, next to going himself to Corinth. He had chosen not to go to Corinth until certain matters were placated. His plans were, therefore, on hold, until the return and the news of Titus (2 Corinthians 2:1-4).

Contemplating the necessity that precipitated the changing of Paul's plans reminds me: It was the Scottish bard Robbie Burns who created the phrase, "Of Mice and Men." It is only four words out of a very long sentence in one of his poems. The poem is humorously entitled, "To a Mouse," and was actually written in 1786. I clearly remember, in my youth, my English Literature teacher attempting to read the poem to a small class of four of us, using as broad a Scottish accent as he possibly could, pretending to be the great poet. For my none-UK readers, Robbie Burns is to the Scottish people what Shakespeare is to the English, or Goethe to the Germans. For those who are not au fait with any of the writings of Burns, it is a remarkable truth (at least to the English) that he wrote, quite literally, in his broad Scottish accent. Although they are hailed as the work of an utter genius, some of his writings are almost unintelligible to the contemporary conformist English eye and ear. Being an old English

Etonian from the South of England, my English Literature Teacher's accent was even funnier than the poem.

I am not rambling, I have a point to make. The creative need for Burns to write the poem, "To a Mouse," came from his incidental destruction of a mouse's winter nest whilst ploughing a field. The poem is a verbal apology written to the poor mouse made both homeless and vulnerable because of: 1. its "dream home" being dissipated by an earthquake that was an astronomical 122 on the Richter scale (i.e. Burns' deep plough), as well as: 2. The agenda that the mouse had planned for hibernating in the cold, long, dark nights of Scotland's winter, being shattered in a single moment of time by the poet. The poem describes how the, "Wee, cowering, timorous beastie," plotted and planned to stay warm in the snow, making his nest in this field, only to have the whole idea overturned by Burns himself. To express it in, "English English" (as opposed to Burns' "Scottish English"), Burns states, "The best laid plans of mice and men often go awry and leave us nought but grief and pain." The grief and pain that came to this "wee beastie," came also to the mighty apostle in great severity. He also made his plans for winter, and, oh, how the apostle was left with grief and pain! It was an emotional plough that overturned Paul's winter plans. The apostle's plans were for a safe house throughout the cold period, but ... The anxiety of what was happening at Corinth caused him to change his plans again and again.

So what happened next?

It was, I believe, extreme anxiety that caused him to drop everything and leave Ephesus, and that same anxiety (although undoubtedly increased with time) was what took him from Troas. He had no rest in his spirit, in Troas, because he did not find Titus his brother. It is logical to deduce and extrapolate that if he left the two places hurriedly, in quick succession, and he plainly states why one of the departures was made, that the template for leaving the second port of call (Troas) was the same motive for which he left the first port of call (Ephesus). His mental anguish was grounded in his eager anticipation of for news from Corinth via Titus, his delegated mouthpiece to Corinth (2 Corinthians 2:12-13).

The entire, "Saga of the church at Corinth," must have been mammoth to Paul. Try to imagine what the Corinthians were doing to Paul's patience, troubling his soul in such a way. Their attitude and correspondence, together with the news from the ministers that Paul had delegated to visit Corinth must have tortured his heart as well as his mind. As Paul brooded over the scenario, so the issue grew in its importance both to the apostle, as well as to God. It seems the more Paul communicated with Corinth, the worst things were getting. He would, seemingly, resolve some issues, and thereafter hear of other issues raising their ugly head over the parapet, matters that were even more complex and damaging to the overall work of God. What is more, it had transcended issues of principle and had now degenerated into personal abuse of the Paul. He was being accused of ungodly conduct and misleading the people. Paul grew more and more disquieted and uneasy until, in a remarkable intolerable oppression of spirit, he felt that he could no longer continue to preach to the lost in Troas, and so he left for Macedonia, so desperate was he for knowledge of the response from Corinth. This is amazing to my mind!

This writer finds Paul's actions and priorities at this point of time utterly revelatory. I see Paul as the ultimate role model for all Christians, and especially ministers. This priority choice, this value judgement, as far as this writer is concerned, is a game changer, if not a total paradigm transformer. He left the huge move of God in Ephesus hastily and "in a fragile state," for the same reason he left Troas hastily and "in a fragile state." I understand how it is to some people almost unforgiveable to even suggest Paul was beaten down with any issue, but the scriptures explain it so plainly. Anxiety concerning the church in Corinth had him utterly distracted.

There is a need to state what we know, and what is conjecture concerning Paul's condition as he left Ephesus for Troas, and Troas for Macedonia. The book of Acts informs us that Paul had three years in Ephesus, he decided that he was going to leave, and then after a riot by the silversmiths – a riot in which Paul himself was not harmed or manhandled – he suddenly decided to leave. We would be left to conclude that he decided to leave because of the riot where he was neither physically involved nor harmed, if it wasn't for the letter that we refer to as Second Corinthians. We are there informed that something terrible happened to Paul in Asia (2 Corinthians 1:8-9). 2 Corinthians 1 does not refer to anywhere else but Asia, i.e. Ephesus. What took place was so terrible that it nearly killed him, and it was so prolonged that he actually concluded that he would not survive the situation. He says exactly that. What was it? Scholars generally assume it was harsh physical manhandling, torture even, as well as chained imprisonment in Ephesus. We also have intelligence from Second Corinthians that tells us that simultaneous to whatever was threatening his life, the church in Corinth was, to put it in blunt twenty first century street language, "driving him nuts."

Some psychologists interpret the language that Paul uses in Second Corinthians as evidence of a breakdown. Was that what Corinth did to him? Was it the hardship and affliction of persecution? Or was it the imprisonment that we believe he endured in Ephesus? An imprisonment not mentioned in Acts or Corinthians, but is concluded by closer examination of some of the "prison epistles" of Paul that are not consistent with his prison experience in Rome? Or was it a compendium of Corinth, persecution and prison that nearly broke the great apostle? I believe this latter thought is more than likely.

From Ephesus to Troas! From Troas to Macedonia! And we are not told how many other cities, towns or villages Paul alighted on in Macedonia, only to anxiously move on while he was looking for Titus. In what town Paul actually met his loyal and greatly trusted friend, we are not told, but somewhere in Macedonia, Paul turned a corner – and there he was. Titus was happily greeted and Paul was greatly relieved of his painful tension of mind by news and intelligence from the

Corinthian Christians, news which, although chequered, was, in the main, favourable. We know it was chequered, because of what he wrote in 2 Corinthians. From Titus, Paul learnt that his change of plan about visiting the troublesome group of saints had given them grounds for unfavourable criticism, and injurious remarks about his character (2 Corinthians 1:17). Titus had been well received on the whole, yet even with his experience, he was filled with fear and trembling with the church there (2 Corinthians 7:13-15). Titus was to return to Corinth, leaving Paul yet again, carrying the scroll of what we refer to as Paul's Second Letter to the Corinthians (2 Corinthians 8:6).

From this letter we learn that, whatever may have been the nature of his condition when he left Asia, whether it was grievous injury from beatings and violence against his person, or external persecution and inward anxiety caused by his persecutors, as well as the issues with the Corinthian church, or all of these three – his stay in Macedonia had suffered from the same overwhelming distress which had marked the close of his residence in Ephesus, and the brevity of his stay in Troas (2 Corinthians 7:5-7). Paul himself describes his condition as one of mental and physical prostration. *"Our flesh had no rest, but we are troubled on every side, from fightings without, and fears within"* (2 Corinthians 7:5). This was a long trip, the details of which we are not told. As a by the way, we can only conjecture that it is during this trip that Paul went up to Illyricum – modern Albania (Romans 15:19).

We have no idea of how many days, weeks or months, Paul's ministry trip around the churches of Macedonia claimed. Luke passes over the whole trip with extreme brevity. It was not Luke's intention to give what every bible lover and scholar in the world craves for i.e. an exhaustive biography of all that Paul said and did. He does not even mention the stories and the sagas that must have been going on in the churches of Macedonia keeping Paul back from his intended, planned and promised visit to Corinth. He must surely have preached again at Philippi the capital of Macedonia Prima, Thessalonica the capital of Macedonia Secunda, and Berea, the capital of Macedonia Tertia.

As he went, I cannot help but think what a challenge to Paul's grace and character it was to be pleading for money from each Christian fellowship that he visited, the majority of whom were plunged into poverty, who had already given in his first visit towards the offering to help the poor in the church in Jerusalem, the very church who had sent emissaries with letters of commendation to Corinth, and who were now bad mouthing the apostle and undermining his teaching. Corinth had believed these emissaries that Paul refers to as "false apostles," and were backbiting the father of their faith. Talk about, "Biting the hand that feeds you!" It was a wrestle, and a pain to Paul, relief from which could only come to him when he remembered that the leaders of the twelve apostles at Jerusalem had bound him by a special injunction, or was it a commitment, to take care of the poor (Galatians 2:10).

I can only surmise that somewhere along the line he considered his usefulness to Macedonia (and Illyricum?) completed, and so, the apostle finally set his direction on the road to Corinth.

Of the utmost importance to our delving into Paul's management of the miraculous, we take note again that somewhere after meeting Titus, while Titus was still with him, while ministering around Macedonia, Paul wrote Second Corinthians. This was the letter that accompanied Titus back to Corinth, and preceded Paul's arrival there.

We hear not one word as to what went on during the three months of Paul's visit to Corinth apart from what he wrote there. Yet Paul was surrounded by friends, colleagues, co-workers and those that loved him, and during those three months he seems to have placated the troubled waters of the Corinthian church and composed the letter to the Galatians, and the missive to the Romans. Something wonderful and restoring must have been going on while he was in Corinth.

2. THE TROUBLESOME CHURCH THAT COMPELLED PAUL TO LEAVE EPHESUS.

What can we say about the church at Corinth and what they did to the mind and emotions of the apostle Paul? Let's start from the beginning of their story.

Paul's first visit to the city of Corinth (Act 18:1-28) extended over eighteen months. This was, of course, prior to the Ephesus campaign. He left Corinth happily, had a brief stopover in Ephesus, and went on to Antioch. It is remarkably significant that, on this occasion he did not go at all to Jerusalem. (That is a story there for another time.) Paul left Antioch ministering throughout Galatia and Phrygia, before he arrived at Ephesus. That arrival to the city of Diana brings us to Acts 19:1. Paul must have had many communications with Corinth throughout the three or four years after he had left them in Acts 18:28. He touched base with them humanly, through the deputies and colleagues in ministry whom he would have commissioned to go and minister whilst he was travelling elsewhere. 2 Corinthians 12:17 tells us this is true (*"... Did any of the men I sent to you take advantage of you?"*). It is only after his mission to Ephesus, in the ongoing course of what is commonly referred to as Paul's third missionary journey, that actual personal interaction with Corinth could have been geographically possible again. However during his stay at Ephesus there were Corinthian visitors, as well as letters, passing both to and fro, that kept Paul informed of things.

Along with Alexandria in Egypt, and Antioch in Syria, Ephesus was one of the three major cosmopolitan ports in the eastern geography of the Roman Empire. What made Ephesus so ideal for Paul's major push for Christ in Asia was the fact that from the famous and well used port, there were ships facilitating correspondence and visitors to and from the other churches around the Aegean, aiding Paul's care of all the churches (2 Corinthians 11:28). There were roads that ran eastward through the long wide valleys to other major cities in the province. It is a geography vaguely similar to the valleys in the south of Wales in the UK, yet on a much larger scale. Paul made use of this geography by sending his assistants and protégés up the valleys to evangelise Asia while he carried on the work in Ephesus. (Who knows, Paul may have visited Colossae and Philemon, while Luke, for some reason, did not feel free to tell us (Philemon 22)).Thus we have the example of Epaphras going to Colossae, Laodicea and Hierapolis (Colossians 1:6-8. 4:13 and 16.). Academics and archaeologists believe that after Paul's three year church planting mission, there were churches all over Asia, evidence being found as well as written documents that substantiates churches in Miletus, Troas, Assos, Cyzicus, Magnesia, Tralles, Metropolis, and Hierapolis as well as Colossae and the so called, "Seven Churches of Asia." I have no doubt whatsoever that the, "Seven Churches of Asia," as referred to in the book of Revelation, were founded during these incredibly productive years while Paul was based in Ephesus sending his travelling team of protégés out to emulate what they had seen their mentor do in Ephesus. Smyrna was only 35 miles north of Ephesus, Pergamos 80 miles in the same direction. These were the distances that Epaphras and others would have had to have travelled in order to plant satellite church bases encircling Ephesus and permeating Asia. Thyatira was 90 miles away, Sardis 55, Philadelphia just short of 100 and Laodicea only 40 miles away. These seven churches were all within a couple of day's journey from Ephesus, and therefore easily accessible by Paul's roaming team of evangelists. Paul himself had never seen the people of the churches in Colossae, Hieropolis or Laodicea (and undoubtedly many of the other newly birthed congregations in Asia), yet he obviously considered them as part of his "flock" (Colossians 1:24). The imminence of the ports facilitating the sea lanes being used to dispatch both letters and personnel to churches all around the Aegean, rendered Ephesus as a central Headquarters for "Apostle Paul Ministries Incorporated," at least for the period he was ministering there. Ephesus was taken for Christ. The whole of Asia heard the word of God. Asia's culture was changed.

As we have been slowly walking with Paul for this historical period of 2-3 years, we have seen how he ploughed the furrow for Christ in the midst of a heathen, gentile Roman province, with all kinds of pressures and buffettings. He describes one period of his experience in Ephesus as "fighting with wild beasts" (1 Corinthians 15:32), confronting physically as well as spiritually, violent people in the city of Diana. Added to this he expresses how there was the "pressure" weighing heavily upon him, of his anxiety for the churches (2 Corinthians 11:28). He had obvious concerns with the legalistic faction that was considerable in both size and influence that was still based at the church in Jerusalem. There was the impact of these legalists wherever Paul had been - Galatia, Cappadocia, Macedonia and Achaia, and the problems they caused needed constant attention all the while on this, his third journey. And in the midst of all these contemporaneous problems, Christians in Corinth seemed to have gone to the extreme in anarchy. The freedom that Christ had brought them was now being exhibited in sheer licence.

It is in the first chapter of First Corinthians where we are introduced to Chloe (1 Corinthians 1:11). We know nothing about her, apart from gleaning from various scriptures a vague outline of her situation in life. The fact that Paul recognized a group of people as belonging to "the house of Chloe," suggests she was a high profile Christian woman of some acceptance within the Corinthian church. I would even suggest she was a leader. From what the historians tell us, at this period of time the name of a husband, or father would have been commonly used in order to identify her, not the female's name, unless she was widowed, or had some startlingly strong character that made her a force to be reckoned with. Stephanas, Fortunatus, and Achaicus were from Corinth and either related to, or close to Chloe. They turned up on Paul's doorstep in Ephesus with, "a few church problems," while he was hard at work. It seems, from what we deduce from Paul's writings that these three, quite literally, came with a list of issues for Paul to resolve. It is also highly probable that these three returned to Corinth to deliver Paul's letter to the Christians there that would probably be the letter we refer to as First Corinthians. I carry no truck at all with those that propose that First Corinthians is a cobbled quilt of bits and pieces from a number of letters.

What brought them to their father in the Lord was every pastor's worst nightmare.

Because of the raw material that Paul had to work with in Corinth, it must have been plain to see that, like the children of Israel coming out of slavery with Moses, it took a single day to get Israel out of Egypt, but a generation to get Egypt out of Israel. The Corinthian church, like Israel, was in a bit of a self-inflicted mess. They were paradoxically free in Christ, yet utterly sold into bondage with the old heathen life clinging tightly to them. After 18 months of ministry in the huge city, where one cannot but believe that Paul poured out his heart, his theology, his attitude to God, life and people; in what was, at that point of time, the longest stay Paul had made in any single place on mission, this trio came with a metre long scroll of parchment with questions and problems for their "good old Paul" to look into and resolve.

What were these problems?

There were cliques and factions in the church, using different minister's names as rallying points. This was majorly divisive and no small issue. How were they to deal with it? (1 Corinthians 1:10 – 31)

There were accusations concerning Paul's authority, integrity and character (1 Corinthians 9). This festering malignant growth was to increase in its virulence and was absolutely why Titus had to go to Corinth after Timothy and Apollos had been, as a diplomat to speak up for Paul. This would have been painful for the trio from Chloe's house to explain to Paul, just as it would have been painful for Paul to receive. What should the apostle do in order to respond properly?

Sexual immorality, to the point of a male sleeping with his step mother had taken place within the church. This seems to have been committed with people who were high profile within the fellowship at Corinth, and was therefore influencing many. What were Paul's instructions on this? (1 Corinthians 5:1-12)

Lawsuits were being taken out by Christians against Christians, believers taking believers to court. Imagine the ill feeling and relationship problems spawned by such a thing within the church. What were Paul's instructions on how to handle such a divisive series of events? (1 Corinthians 6:1-11)

Marriage issues for singles were being asked about. Sexuality and the conduct of pre-marital relationships needed to be explained from a Christ-like perspective (1 Corinthians 6:12–7:40).

Food that was cheap at the market, even though it had been sacrificed to idols, was being bought and eaten by Christians. Should a Christian eat such fare? The answer would impact the financial budgets of the poor, as well as the spiritual life of all. What would the apostle advise? (1 Corinthians 8)

Conduct at the Lord's Supper seems to be described as chaotic. One gets the impression that the gatherings and church services at Corinth were anything but religious, but in a way that was not God directed. Surely Paul knew how to correct these deficiencies! (1 Corinthians 11:17-34)

Issues concerning the conduct of women in the church meeting were being asked about. I cannot but think that somehow there were Jewish influences in the church at work with this matter. (1 Corinthians 11:2-16)

The use of supernatural charismata effected by the Holy Spirit in the lives of the members, which seemed to be commonly used, were being abused and discredited within the church get togethers and in the presence of unbelievers. What was Paul's mind on this? (1 Corinthians 12, 13 and 14)

The doctrine of the resurrection and some false extrapolations from the understanding of Paul's teaching were being spread around. Not only was there abuse of the teaching, but some were suggesting that the teaching was irrelevant, others that the resurrection had passed. (1 Corinthians 15)

Collecting money to help poor Christians in other parts of the world where Paul travelled seems to have been queried. Was his integrity being maligned also? (1 Corinthians 16:1-4)

It is such an incredible list that one has to wonder about the mental, never mind the spiritual capability of the Christians in Corinth. Was it because there were a huge number of converts added to the church since Paul left Corinth, and that the newcomers had not had these things explained to them properly? I find it difficult to believe that Paul could hear of any of these queries and think, "Oh yes! I never mentioned this, or that!" The list was enormous, and horrific. Every aspect of the issues that were seemingly rampant in the Corinthian church are, I would suggest, considered basic fundamental Christian teachings in today's church, and I feel certain they were elementary in the context of Paul's preaching. Not that the twenty first century church is free of all these problems and their modern equivalents cum parallels, but they are issues that many basic courses in Christianity would cover.

And these issues exploded upon him in the midst of a remarkably intense mission in Ephesus. What a barrel full of rubbish it was, tipped into Paul's thought processes, consuming his waking hours. The three visitors must have broken Paul's heart when it was all finally explained, or read out.

It is a challenge to comprehend the trials and anxieties that beset Paul during his stay at Ephesus, without mentally perceiving the gravity of the causes for concern that he was carrying. He must have been tortured by what can only be referred to as surreal aberrations of the thinking of those people he himself had brought to Christ and taught in Corinth. Let anybody with a heart for, or experience in pastoring, grasp the state of things that must have torn Paul's heart in two. Imagine if you can, how punch upon punch must have buffeted his mind and thrown him into a deep morass of wonderment as from time to time he had news of darkness added to bleakness, as rumour and fact, verbal report then written epistle informed him how thickly and tenaciously the demonic tares of false concepts, ungodly living together with a growing mistrust of Paul himself, were growing together with the wonderful seed he had planted in Galatia as well as Corinth. He must have thought at times that his battle to keep Christians worldwide free from Jewish legalism was a lost war. This must have been a greater suffering than any prison or stoning he ever encountered.

Apollos, novice as he was, must have returned from Corinth with news that introduced Paul to the trouble spots amongst the Christians. Or was the rhetorician so flattered with his warm reception as a speaker that he didn't see what was going on? Timothy had been and would also have kept his "Father in the Lord," abreast of the situation. Titus now had finally made ground with them. Paul had, at the end of his stay in Ephesus, been away from Corinth for about 4 years. Perhaps their longing for him, his words and his fatherly character, were so strong it led them to speak of him unjustly in his prolonged absence – a sort of inverted expression of love for the apostle, a kind of spoilt child response to Mum and Dad not giving them what they wanted. Quintessential immaturity! "Why? Oh why can't you, dear Paul, come again and stay with us? You must be bad because you are staying away!"

So serious was this infestation of wild misconduct and misunderstanding in the Corinthian church that these associate ministers and leaders, men of God had been sent by Paul to resolve issues, and bring reconciliation in all the relationships concerned. Apollos went of his own desire (Acts does not tell us that it was Paul that sent him), and by all reports was greatly received as some kind of master of the preached word. He was a new and clearly expressive teacher of the scriptures. Timothy and then later Titus were also sent to not only pour oil on the troubled waters at Corinth, but to also set broken limbs of fellowship, as well as amputate cancerous teachings and practices. Ultimately – he must have realised - Paul would have to go himself. I believe he knew this all along. But he was set not to visit them until certain of these issues had been resolved amongst them.

From everything we read of Paul's life, and within every extrapolation we can make from his letters, the church at Corinth was the most labour intensive, high maintenance, problematic group of people that the apostle ever came in contact with. If he did have a physical, mental or emotional infirmity around this period, as I think, and some academics suggest, it would be absolutely understandable. Corinth would have been a graveyard to most pastors. And then to read 2 Corinthians 1 where he tells us that at one point he had given up on the chance of living through the hardships that Ephesus brought upon him, we cannot but wonder how he did not suffer a complete emotional collapse. Perhaps he did.

This was clearly some of, if not, the darkest hours in the Apostle's history since the days he spent in blindness at Damascus (2 Corinthians 7:5). Corinth must have appeared to Paul, to be in full revolt against him. I have pastored with two or three separate yet simultaneous dissidents in a church, and as pastor, thought I was ready for the mental hospital with the stories that were told of me and the abuse that was thrown at me. But the letter we refer to as First Corinthians answers a whole truckload of issues that if they were contemporaneous with the churches of the majority of pastors in the world today, would surely lead to ministerial resignations or emotional breakdowns around the globe. Paul writes of this period that he was, "pressed out of measure, above strength." Paul – I understand my brother -howbeit in the very slightest and minute degree - what you must have gone through.

It was because Paul was under this continued strain of excitement in Ephesus and anxiety from Galatia and especially from Corinth that many academics even conclude that his strength totally succumbed and fled. Some even suggest that he was seized with an attack of sickness, which threatened to terminate his life (2 Corinthians 1:8-9; 4:7-18; 5:1-4). I really am not sure where to go with that one. I simply do not accept it. However, altogether with what we know, it can be clearly seen from our wise and lofty lookout post of the twenty first century that the fate of his mission and of Gentile Christianity as a whole, trembled in the balance at various times, and possibly this was the moment that would break the power of Judaistic thoughts, or be broken by them once and for all. Never had he felt himself so helpless, so beaten down and discomfited as on that melancholy journey from Ephesus to Troas, and if he was physically debilitated (at least we know for sure that he must have been greatly weakened), he did not know whether Titus or the angel of death would reach him first. It's all there in Second Corinthians for us to read and study, pondering in awe and wonder as to how Paul overcame it, maintaining his integrity, his relationship with God, his friends and his sanity. On top if all this, his ministry of the miraculous continued.

3. THE PROBLEMATIC SERIES OF LETTERS THAT COMPELLED PAUL TO LEAVE EPHESUS.

Before we look at the manifestation of Christ in the heart of Paul while all this was going on (that's in the next chapter), we shall just highlight a little more of the deep complexity of the Corinthian problem to clearly show the pressure that had been put on the apostle at this time.

First of all, to start at the beginning, I utterly disagree with any idea that the Corinthian letters, especially Second Corinthians in the scriptures are a hotch-potch collection of several letters stitched together by later scribes and writers. What absolute tosh! That suggestion is another of the imaginative machinations of the higher critics that I contemn utterly. There is not so much as a hint of disunity in any of the ancient Greek manuscripts. Check that out with all the academics. There are no variations of the literary units. In all the many manuscripts there is none that does not contain all thirteen chapters (Although 2 Corinthians 13 "seems" to have been unknown to Clement of Rome in 96 AD, it is clearly quoted by Polycarp in 105 AD). Both the Corinthian letters in scripture are understandable as fully self-contained and self-explained units. There also seems to be certain themes which speak for their unity. The internal evidence is, as always with the modernists, utterly too invented and unbelievable to the vast majority of readers, and clearly, subjectively made by the imaginative meanderings of the minds of some so called scholars attempting to shock their professors into giving them their PhD's.

But given my assertion that the biblical Corinthian letters are two complete wholes, we have to ask some questions:

What do we do with 1 Corinthians 5:9, *"I wrote to you in my letter not to associate with sexually immoral people?"* (English Standard Version) This statement of Paul's clearly says that there was another letter sent before the one we refer to as 1 Corinthians.

Where are we supposed to fit this first missive in the chronology of Acts? Was the initial letter (we shall call it "Letter A") sent from Ephesus? Or, did an earlier Corinthian group of representatives come with other queries before Paul arrived in Ephesus? Was it written while he was on his way to Ephesus, perhaps? We are, without any doubt, logically forced to accept the idea of a first letter to Corinth before the one we refer to as First Corinthians. As there was no postal system in Paul's day, and as the only way Paul could have known about what was going on in Corinth was by somebody turning up with news, or perhaps with a letter, we have to understand that there had been a continuous flow of intelligence to and from Paul since he left Corinth. Following this line of thought, it looks like we should be considering three letters, even though we only have two in our possession. If there were any more, none are extant, so we are merely presupposing a "Letter A." We therefore understand that there was at the very least:

> **Letter A** being sent to Corinth from Paul. When and from where, unknown!
>
> **First Corinthians,** being sent, presumably, about six or seven months before Paul first intended to leave Ephesus (1 Corinthians 16:8).
>
> **Second Corinthians,** sent after the event of Paul leaving Ephesus, leaving Troas and going through Macedonia southwards, and up to somewhere in the real-time of Luke's account around Acts 20:3.

There is more, however.

What about statements in 2 Corinthians that suggest, even, a fourth letter? :

"And I wrote this same to you, lest, when I came, I should have sorrow from them of whom I ought to rejoice; having confidence in you all, that my joy is the joy of you all. For out of much affliction and anguish of heart I wrote to you with many tears; not that you should be grieved, but that you might know the love which I have more abundantly to you. But if any have caused grief, he has not grieved me, but in part: that I may not overcharge you all." (2 Corinthians 2: 3-5)

Again:

"Another reason I wrote you was to see if you would stand the test and be obedient in everything" (2 Corinthians 2:9).

And again:

"Even if I caused you sorrow by my letter, I do not regret it. Though I did regret it - I see that my letter hurt you, but only for a little while." (2 Corinthians 7:8)

And yet, again:

"So even though I wrote to you, it was neither on account of the one who did the wrong nor on account of the injured party, but rather that before God you could see for yourselves how devoted to us you are." (2 Corinthians 7:12)

Are these remarks referring to Letter A? First Corinthians? Or is there a fourth letter in the reality of things? Does 1 Corinthians 5 read as though it was written with tears? Is it possible that when the Corinthians first read what we refer to as 1 Corinthians 5, that they would have all been smitten with grief and sorrow? Is there anything that suggests that Paul was in a spasm of much affliction and anguish when we read 1 Corinthians at all, especially the fifth chapter? Absolutely not!

Without doubt there are issues in 2 Corinthians that refer to what was written in 1 Corinthians. But it is the tears, the grief and the emotional references that cause this writer to say that it must be referring to yet another letter. But there are other factors that add to the issue.

It simply could not have been First Corinthians that it was only referring to, because in that epistle it says in chapter 16:5-7 that Paul wanted to have a long stay with the church at Corinth and so would not see them until after Pentecost the following year. So there was between 6 and 8 months planned between Paul writing First Corinthians and the original plan to leave Ephesus. I do not believe Paul could have waited that long for a reply, or at least for the intelligence of how the Corinthians had responded to his instructions in First Corinthians 5. If he was anxious for the news from Titus as he left both Ephesus and Troas, there must have been another issue, and/or another letter that created that anxiety.

Paul was desperately waiting for Titus to return with the news, and it is logical to assume that Stephanas, Fortunatus and Achaicus, being Corinthians themselves, and being the ones that brought the questions to Paul, would have returned with First Corinthians under their arm. There must have been another letter that Titus was sent to deliver. It is feasible to see that Titus went to correct whatever problems were newly current in Corinth, and that in order to add to his authority in dealing with the issues, he carried a letter from Paul stating what he had arrived to implement.

All this put together means that there must have been a fourth letter, that was third in chronological order from Paul to the Corinthian church. We shall refer to it as Letter B. The sequence would then have been:

> **Letter A** being sent to Corinth. Is it possible that there was more than one group of Corinthian visitors to Paul while he was in Ephesus? Whatever, 1 Cor 5:9 demands that a first letter was sent.
>
> **First Corinthians** being sent, presumably, about six or seven months before Paul had originally planned to leave Ephesus (1 Corinthians 16:8), and carried by Stephanas, Fortunatus and Achaicus who were of the house of Chloe in Corinth.
>
> **Letter B.** Sent with Titus, an obvious dearly beloved and greatly trusted Christian friend of Paul. If my conjecture is correct, it is this letter that was written with deep tears and emotion by Paul, and received with similar emotions in Corinth.

Thereafter there would have been:

> **Second Corinthians** sent after Paul had left Ephesus and Troas, and while he was in Macedonia.

Having explained the complexity and intensity of the progressing correspondence between Paul and the Corinthian church, we also need to grasp how extraordinarily introverted and directionless was the situation in Corinth. We have to see that no matter how thankful we are to God for the Corinthian letters in scripture, there are some things in life that will simply not be corrected by a letter or letters, no matter how inspired and anointed those letters may be. Human interaction and face to face relationship is a secret of the kingdom. That is why Christ came and dwelt amongst us. We are saved and kept by relationship with Jesus. The church is sustained and progressed by warm relationships within with each other, and Christ-like relationships reaching to those without, as well as an ever growing relationship with God.

Corinth was a city that was rampant with evil. It is a well-known fact that in New Testament times, to "live like a Corinthian," was a euphemism for bad living in all streams of sin and evil. Paul spent eighteen months amongst the people there, missioning for Jesus Christ. Some professors of New Testament history reckon that the Corinthian church was numerically one of, if not the largest city church of all, spread all over the metropolis in many and various homes. Remember that Paul's mission in Ephesus impacted a whole province, and although there might have been more converts, they were not all based in the city of Ephesus. The Corinthian campaign was "merely" city wide.

I believe this whole story about Corinth is an issue of incredible importance in aiding us to understand Paul at the peak of his ministry. What we are about to discuss in our next chapter shows us the humanity, the sensitivity, the vulnerability and the utter fragility of

Paul's human nature. The revelation of his human openness and weakness was not only concurrent with the awesome demonstration of power and authority that he ministered with whilst at Ephesus, but it is seen to be one of the very constituent ingredients of that manifestation of power. We are searching for the secrets of a ministry of the miraculous. What we negotiate here is unpalatable to many, but an absolute requirement I believe in getting to grips with the nature and practice of this Christ-like apostle. We need to make this part of our grasp of what we know to be one of the mightiest men of God that ever lived.

What's the ultimate point of all this story about Corinth, and its impact in respect of Paul's ministry in Ephesus? Simple! No matter how big, how important, how powerful and how Godly a man or woman may be, it is fundamental to relate to all people as equal to one's self, in fact to defer to others as better than one's self (Ephesians 5:21. Philippians 2:3), and to strive to maintain loving, warm relationships based on reality and motivated by a desire to be Christ-like. This is why Corinth and its problems troubled Paul's sense of peace. It is absolutely imperative to not talk down to anybody, and, if anything, it is more helpful to talk up to people, which is what Paul does in Second Corinthians in particular. The troublesome, nastiness of all the things that went on in the Corinthian church could have been castigated by Paul, and even cast them away as having received the grace of God in vain, and thus to let them wallow in their own mire, "handing them over to Satan." But Paul saw them as Christ saw them. Love does not keep records of wrongs committed against it. Paul's defence of his character and integrity was made by mimicking the foolishness of false apostles who considered themselves, and convinced the church at Corinth that they were even "super-apostles." We will go further with this in our next chapter.

The fact that Paul gave them so very much of his time, his prayers, the man hours of his team, and his tears as he wrote to them, says so much about his paradigm, his mindsets and principles on the issues of pastoring people - and relationships in general.

In the next pages we will go into the detail of Paul's responses to being maligned and verbally assassinated by those he had brought to faith. The Christ-likeness and sensitivity of him whom we consider to be one of the greatest men who ever lived, humiliating himself by giving them explanations of his personal actions and motives is a phenomena and one of the greatest manifestations of Christ in the apostle.

27.

THE PEAK OF TRANSPARENCY AND SUFFERING.

Second Corinthians

In this chapter we look at something that very few of us in the western world, by experience, know anything about. I have never suffered in the way that we are about to look at in the life of Paul. But I find that Christians of all flavours and colours in the UK when discussing "Suffering," as well as, "Persecution," always add the word ..."yet." We have not suffered . . . yet." "We are not persecuted ...yet." But the changes in western society, especially in the UK seem to be bringing a wind of change that may turn into a tsunami of death for some. How soon? Take a guess! As I write it is total theory, but theory that I have learned from the few people that I have known who have gone through persecution and attempts on their life for no other reason apart from their faith. I know some who have had assassins break into their house to kill their children and not they themselves. I lean most on the words of a man I once was close to who jokingly says he has a "PhD in Persecution." And he has the physical scars to show for it.

There is suffering that comes just because we are alive and relating with people and the world. It doesn't matter who you are, it ebbs and flows with the circumstances of life, accidents and/or the people in our lives. Next, there is the suffering that comes from sickness, whether it is with yourself or somebody you love. The source is utterly different in as much as sickness is something God has promised to rid us of if we come to him as Healer. Sickness is something God wants to heal. But while it is present the suffering it causes is just the same as any other source of suffering. After that, there is suffering for Christ from the malice of others –i.e. persecution. We are talking of plain, straight forward malevolent hurt or restraint with no other reason than the fact that one is aligning themselves with the person of Christ. I am talking of mental, if not physical torture. These three general headings cover everything and everybody in the world. Suffering is a universal pain! Pardon the pun.

Paul suffered for Christ. I mean seriously suffered. I do not mean that he missed promotion at work because of his faith. I sympathise with those who have been there and worn that Tee-shirt, but Paul entered into something so much worse. I do not mean that his neighbours refused to talk to him because he was a Christian. I empathise with those that have borne such loneliness and perhaps even social harassment in that way. However, when I talk of Paul, I mean incredibly much more. I mean that Paul suffered as in being stoned by a mob and dragged outside a city and left for dead. I mean he was flogged for causing a riot because of the message of Christ that he carried. What I really mean is that he suffered because lots of people, many of them Christians, turned against him, and some even rented mobs to do him hurt. There were very few places where he wasn't pursued by people intent on doing him harm, and some even vowing to kill him. Trust me when I tell you, that when a group of men take a vow together that they are never going to eat again until they have killed a certain person, we are talking of a man being enmeshed as victim in the deepest dynamics and the darkest shroud of persecution (Acts 23:12-15). Paul had the entire satanic catalogue of stealing, killing and destroying thrown at him over a prolonged period of time (John 10:10a). Demonic powers were intent on stealing the results of his labours, killing him outright and destroying all that he stood for and all he had built. The Lord Jesus Himself told Ananias that He was to show Paul, *"How great things he would suffer,"* for His sake (Acts 9:16). And, oh how great were the things he suffered!

Suffering in this life is the heritage of the bad person, of the remorseful and penitent person, and was, most importantly, the heritage and raison d'être of the Son of God while he tabernacled amongst us. In plain English, suffering comes to us all in one way or another. The suffering of the Godless should lead them to the cross of

Christ. The suffering of the Godly should be because they have been to the cross of Christ. The eternal purpose of God for mankind is hinged and pivoted in the very cross of Christ and what Jesus accomplished whilst He was there at the place called Golgotha, suffering. The bad thief is crucified, the penitent thief is crucified, and the Son of God is crucified. Each one ended the days of their mortal coil, on a cross.

By this biblical fact and symbol we see and understand the widespread heritage of suffering that is ubiquitous to the existence of mankind. Whoever you are, wherever you have been in life, if you can tell me that you have never suffered in anyway, I would be bold enough to call you a liar. Some of us have suffered to near death, some of us have suffered by merely experiencing some unjust judgement or accusation, but life is a forum for suffering somewhere along the line, Christian or not. Jesus Christ did not suffer because it was the godly thing to do. It was fallen mankind that made him suffer. He suffered because there was no other way the rampage of suffering and sin could be halted. Because of what He suffered, a day is definitely coming, right here on planet earth when there will be no more suffering at all. We live in a world where pain and suffering are commonplace and, "normal." Any discussion of how pain and suffering fit into God's scheme ultimately leads back to the cross where Jesus Christ died. That was the most vital moment of history, revealing what life and indeed the cosmos is all about. The evil of men's hearts brings suffering. That same evil brings death. That is the ultimate suffering for those bereaved. But we can never lose sight of the fact that Christ conquered sin, sickness, death, the devil and the grave, and all the suffering that goes with those things – and then He rose again. We cannot lose our grasp on the fact that He now lives in the power of an indestructible life, a life that we are partakers of through faith in Him. Our faith is our connection.

However, having said all this, and believing it with all our hearts, still, the biggest challenge to faith and understanding, of course, is when the meek, the mild and the godly, seem to suffer horrendously more than the wicked and evil manipulators of this world do. How perplexing! People of the world struggle and kill to be "top dog" and the "innocent" get trampled on and starved in the process of their ascent, suffering as they are trodden on. Oh the challenge to the human understanding of the realities of this fallen world!

Take note of this, also: When we are talking of "suffering" *per se*, we are definitely not talking about sickness and the accompanying pain and suffering that accompanies it. Don't get me wrong. I fully acknowledge that some would argue that the pain caused by sickness is the largest source of suffering on the planet – and those that say such things may very well be correct. Sickness, after all, is nothing but insipient death, whether the sickness is terminal or not. The challenge that the scripture makes to the commonly held status quo of millions of Christian believers, however, has more obviously stated factual material to assist us with the required paradigm change, than the spiky issue of, "Why do the righteous suffer?." God heals the sick, Christ commanded the apostles to lay hands on people allowing Him to remove that kind of suffering. But he actually promised them suffering by persecution that could not be removed.

Let me explain by shocking some. When Paul writes things like, "You know how through infirmity of the flesh I preached the gospel to you," Paul was not stating that he was sick whilst preaching. When he says, "My grace is sufficient for you: for my strength is made perfect in weakness," He was not telling us that his thorn in the flesh, his weakness, was a sickness. The case for "proving" Paul was ill is made by the Cessationists combining all the similar scriptures of Paul concerning his personal state, piling on other verses such as, "Most gladly therefore will I glory in my infirmities," and, "I take pleasure in infirmities." Then they conclude their interpretation by explaining the modern English word that we often use for being ill, i.e. "infirmity." Voile! There you have it. Their conclusion is that Paul was ill most of his adult life. This writer believes that this is error of the most deceptive kind.

This word, "infirmity," is translated from the same Greek word (Asthenia – mostly translated as infirmity, or weakness) that Paul used when he wrote: *"Likewise the Spirit also helps our infirmities: for we know not what we should pray for as we ought: but the Spirit itself makes intercession for us."* It is also the same word used in the letter to the Hebrews which says that the prophets, *"Out of weakness were made strong."* It is even used to clarify the manner in which Christ was crucified: *"For though he was crucified through weakness, yet he lives by the power of God."* The word weak (or weakness) in these scriptures is always the same word used when Paul said: *"When I am weak, then am I strong."* If the word weak meant he was sick, then the word strong would logically mean that he was well. To use the word, thinking it refers to sickness, strains the straightforward obvious meaning. These words translated "infirmities" and "weakness," with reference to Paul's life, were never intended to mean sickness or disease. When Paul speaks of his weakness before the church, he is expressing his nothingness in his own strength and his dependence upon the Spirit and power of God: That your faith should not stand in the wisdom of people, but in the power of God.

Paul was specifically promised suffering from the moment he was converted (Acts 9:16). We also are promised sufferings – probably to a different degree than Paul's, but the book says clearly that, *"They that live godly in Christ Jesus shall suffer persecution"* (2 Timothy 3:12). The entire tenor of scripture teaches Christians to literally expect the suffering of persecution. It is also true that the entire gist and timbre of God's promises in scripture is that God wants to heal people who are ill. Suffering because of persecution is actually promised. Healing from the suffering of illness is also promised. In any human suffering, whether from sickness, or persecution for Christ's sake, we are taught to be resilient and glad that Christ has suffered for us. The apostles rejoiced that they were considered worthy to suffer for Christ – that was suffering through persecution. Yet they were commanded by the Lord Himself to lay hands on the sick that they would recover. Suffering through sickness has a mandate from heaven for Christians to remove.

We must all be prepared for some degree of pain and suffering if we are following Christ, simply because we are living and breathing. Pain and suffering are part of the programme. We are even told by Him who suffered more than anybody has ever suffered, and for everyone who has ever suffered, *'Blessed are they that mourn.'* Somebody has written "God had one Son on earth without sin, but never one without suffering." How true! How utterly thankful we are for the sufferings of Christ! How blessed we are because of His resurrection also! Blessed be He, Who came into the world for no other purpose than to suffer, and in so doing took away the sins of the whole world.

However, we must not forget something else as well. We all know somebody, somewhere who has been made nastier, more irritable and more intolerable to be with simply because of their outrageously undeserved suffering. It is not correct, nor is it even true to say that all suffering perfects people. What utter Tosh! Suffering only perfects one sort of person, and that is the one who accepts the call of God in Christ Jesus, and sees the purpose of God through their experience of suffering, no matter from what direction that suffering comes. That is the wisdom of the Bible. There is no growth or development of Christ-like character without change. There can be no change or transformation without the continuous progression of dying to sin and living to righteousness. That means losing some things and gaining others. This logically means that there is no change without fear or loss. And, not wanting to be too simplistic; there is no loss without pain. That is a sound definition of the Christian life. The sufferings of Jesus Christ were many even before He entered into what we refer to as, "The Passion."

Paul suffered because of his love and passion for Jesus Christ. He loved Christ, but only because Christ loved him first. He did not choose Christ. Christ chose him and ordained him to bring forth fruit.

Because Paul was utterly sold out in his love for Christ, he loved people. He loved those who did not love God. He lived to bring them to the place of love where he was. That is the reason Paul loved deeply and passionately the people who came to know Christ through his own declaration of those things that he believed. Paul loved the people who were converted out of the evils of the city of Corinth. Paul loved them and was utterly pained and made to inwardly suffer when they turned on him. We are never so defenceless against suffering as when we love. Love, by its very nature, renders the one doing the loving vulnerable. If the one that loves is not loved in return by those that are loved, we have what poets call "unrequited love." Unrequited love may make wonderful poetry, song lyrics and novels, but it is conceivably the most painful state to be in for any human being. And Paul was constrained by the love of Christ, the greatest most powerful love in the entire cosmos, to love the Christians in Corinth. His pain from the rejection and disparagement of the church of Corinth was excruciating.

The history of all nations and cultures teach us that out of suffering have emerged the strongest souls who overcome and make progress for the betterment of their people, and sometimes, even for the whole world. All of the most massive characters in world history were and are seared with scars – scars physical, emotional, mental and spiritual. It is the dying larvae which produces the soaring butterfly. It is the crushed grape that yields the wine. Some cryptic prophet, profound in his inspiration said, "The wound is the place where the light enters." Generally speaking, people are not prepared or able to rejoice in their suffering unless they experience in their thought processes and belief system, a huge biblical revolution of how they think and feel about the meaning of life. Human nature and Western culture make it well-nigh impossible to rejoice in suffering in any circumstance. To rejoice in suffering is a miracle in the human soul wrought by God Himself through His Word being engrafted into the spirit and the psyche of man. The apostles had been scourged and whipped in their flogging, and then the Bible makes us shudder when it tells us that the twelve came out, *"rejoicing because they had been counted worthy of suffering disgrace for the Name"* (Acts 5:41). What on earth has happened to the thinking processes of men who respond like that to the worst kind of suffering?

To be the master over life's sufferings is to be a skilled and crafted overcomer. Mind management is the first priority of the overcomer. Smooth seas do not make skilful sailors. A peaceful quiet life does not create good fighting soldiers. Christians need to be prepared to suffer. To choose to suffer cannot be healthy in and of itself; in fact, to make such a choice must mean that there is something wrong in a person's life. However, to choose God's will even if it means deep suffering, is a very different thing. No biblically minded, Christ-like Christian ever chooses suffering. Never! He or she chooses God's will, as Jesus did, whether it means suffering or not. Paul chose the will of God. And how much did he suffer for that choice!

In Second Corinthians we have a comprehensive revelation of Paul's interminable suffering. The letter is filled with insights and revelation as to the whys and wherefores of his ongoing state. Our first brief observation is to see –

1. THE REVELATION OF SUFFERING FROM PAUL'S GEOGRAPHIC ITINERARY.

Paul clearly links his progression of suffering with the places he visited. He seems to remember places by what sufferings were perpetrated against him there. The whole of 2 Corinthians tells of his most recent itinerary over the previous 3 years plus, interwoven with awesomely heavenly insights concerning where he was in God while he was suffering. For analytical purposes he gives us four places, each of which had caused him deep suffering. His character was being denigrated by visiting preachers to the Corinthian church, and the fact that he hadn't fulfilled a commitment to have been there at the time promised brought Paul to the place of a needful response. His explanation has details of his sufferings scattered throughout the letter. It is as if he boasts of the sufferings, using them to validate his appointment as an apostle by Christ Himself. He must have realised that while sharing moments in his life that would have brought tears to his eyes each time he recalled them, he was talking to people, some of whom might be laughing, or at least remaining unmoved by his words. Paul was not writing and looking for an emotional, "Poor boy! There there!" come back at all, however, what he shares is incredibly personal. I have heard people who were tortured for Christ decades previous, who still wept as they recalled what they went through. And all this stuff that Paul shares in Second Corinthians was still very recent to him. Paul was dicing with death, and all the Corinthian church could get upset about was the fact that he hadn't turned up as he promised he would. I cannot see this as anything but excruciatingly painful for the apostle.

TROUBLE IN ASIA

The troubles that enveloped the apostle at Ephesus (Asia) are explained in 2 Cor 1: 9-11. Paul was so harassed and suffering that he despaired of life while he was there. Some writers think he was talking of things that happened in Acts 13 and 14, but the obvious reason for this explanation of what happened in Asia in 2 Corinthians 1 is that it is part of the reason for his non arrival at Corinth. Otherwise, why on earth would Paul want to start off the defence of his very apostleship and non-arrival by referring to something that happened many years before? There have been moments in my life when I thought I was about to die. All of these separate moments occurred while in a car as a passenger and foreseeing momentarily either potential collisions or too narrow gaps between vehicles while overtaking. For one split nano-second in each of these experiences I had the presentiment of dying. For each of those moments I surrendered myself to Christ in death. They are all graphic moments implanted deeply in my psyche. I remember the fear, the adrenalin rush and the shock. Several times, for fleeting moments is one thing, but to wake in the morning and live through a whole day (or days) while expecting to die any minute is something I find hard to imagine. He gave up the expectation to survive in Asia. For Asia, read Ephesus. The cold wintry harassment and persecution of Ephesus held him back from travelling. The Corinthians were upset he did not turn up. But Paul had other issues to contend with. Grace grows best in winter. Paul was facing death for the same message that had saved the souls of the Corinthian church. Yet they were complaining of his late arrival.

Even though he talks about his suffering on their behalf, and that his life is their life, we cannot but come to the conclusion that the Corinthians knew about his persecution in Asia, yet don't seem to have cared one way or the other about it. I find it impossible to believe that Timothy and Titus both being sent to Corinth at separate times to minister there did not let the Christians know what Paul was going through. I say this, even though, Paul explains it as if they would not know about it until they read the letter. These Corinthian people seemed to have fickleness added to their list of character flaws and failings.

TROUBLE IN TROAS

Then there was the anxiety whilst Paul was in Troas (2 Cor. 2:12). Paul was seemingly leaving Ephesus later than expected because of the afore mentioned negotiating with death there. He left Ephesus for Troas. He arrived at Troas and started preaching. But, the mighty apostle could not focus on his preaching whilst he was eager for Titus bringing news from Corinth. This was obviously a more subjective form of suffering caused by objective confrontations from letters and personnel from Corinth, but suffering it definitely was. Paul was just not himself during that visit to Troas, exactly as it seems he was not himself when he left Ephesus. His imprisonment, the details of suffering (and possibly even torture) - neither of which are we given a clue as to what particularly happened in the book of Acts - as well as the problematic unjust statements being made about him from Corinth, all contributed to the pressure on the apostle's mind that caused him to suffer. And remember also the trouble brewing in the Galatian churches which precipitated the biblical epistle. That furore was all beginning to take place at this very moment in Paul's history. It was all pressure, howbeit subjective, that caused mental suffering for Paul. Because Titus did not arrive, he left Troas, together with all his worries, and headed for Macedonia.

TROUBLE IN MACEDONIA

The trauma within Macedonia was also acute (2 Corinthians 7:5). Paul left Troas, and sailed to Macedonia along with his anxiety and a few friends. We have no idea where he landed, but from what we are told, it seems he started in the north, possibly from Thessalonica or Philippi, and travelled southward addressing both the churches as well as the unsaved as he travelled. It is somewhere around this period that some scholars suspect Paul entered Illyricum (modern day Albania), but that is only conjecture.

Whilst in Macedonia, Paul's sufferings continued. No details are given in the book of Acts. Again, we do not know the nature of his reception throughout his journey. Whatever had caused his deep suffering in Ephesus had led him to be travelling with a large party of helpers more than are mentioned anywhere else in Acts. It seems Paul needed the fellowship, and perhaps some sort of care, as a result of whatever it was that had taken place in Ephesus. Weymouth has it as, *"For even after our arrival in Macedonia we could get no relief such as human nature craves. We were greatly harassed; there were conflicts without and fears within"* (2 Corinthians 7:5). Darby has the same verse as, *"For indeed, when we came into Macedonia, our flesh had no rest, but we were afflicted in every way; without combats, within fears."* Of the nature of his fears were we have some sort of clue. He was feared concerning the church at Corinth and the direction it could take at that moment. There must have been concerns about being harassed and pursued by the Jewish contingent that always seemed to be at his heels no matter where he went. Paul was infamous in Jewish circles almost everywhere. The seeds of intelligence concerning the judaisers in the Galatian churches must also have been a concurrent torturous burden on his shoulders.

These recollections and lists of times of suffering in 2 Corinthians are the words, not of a neurotic hypochondriac, nor a cosseted man who had never known pain, pressure or suffering. This was the apostle of Christ to the gentiles who had experienced suffering of the cruellest and most evil kind. He was an expert on the subject of suffering, and yet whilst in Macedonia he tells us that his body had no rest and that he was afflicted in every way. Combats (i.e. fights) on the outside, and fears on the inside was how he explains his visit to Macedonia, while moving towards Achaia (Southern Greece). I cannot in anyway assume violence from the apostle himself when he says, "combats without," but I am sure that there were many who treated him violently. This period in Macedonia was obviously fraught with incredible hardship. The intense suffering that Paul went through had become merely a normal day at the office. There was no end to his personal pain.

Enter Titus, stage left. The relief derived from the "meet-up" with Titus was welcomed and embraced in while Paul was in Macedonia. (2 Corinthians 7:5) Imagine how huge the situation had been to Paul when he tells us in one breath that although he was afflicted in every way, he was profoundly comforted and consoled by the coming of Titus. We do not know how long Titus was with Paul in Macedonia, but it was long enough for the apostle to write the whole of 2 Corinthians. The relief seems to have been great. The news was, to some degree, welcome. But there was still enough problematic stuff that needed what to us, is twelve chapters of precious scripture.

Titus is sent to address Corinth one more time before Paul gets there. (2 Corinthians 8:16-17). In one of the most open-hearted sections of Paul's writings, "The Second Epistle of Paul the Apostle to the Corinthians," is more tender than any other in the New Testament. Paul is happy to say that he thinks Titus loved the Corinthian people even more than he did. Having read 2 Corinthians many times, I am always left with the feeling that Paul is so nervous about going to the city of Corinth with unresolved issues. He does explain it all of course within the letter, but the sufferings of rejection left him feeling that any visit he made may cause more suffering if he did not get some colliding viewpoints into harmony with where he stood.

THE ATTEMPT TO AVOID TROUBLE AT CORINTH

Paul had to address any plan for a future visit to Corinth (2 Corinthians 1:16). It had to come sooner or later. Paul obviously considered that the letter going with Titus to Corinth would be sufficient to open up the way for him to go to Corinth and have a successful visit that would be beneficial both to the church and himself. But there is an addition to our intelligence here that is not given to us in Acts. In Acts, his plan was clearly to cross to Macedonia and then travel southwards, finishing up with a stay in Corinth. But here he explains a plan that was totally different. He states that his original plan was to cross from Ephesus to Corinth directly. Then travel northwards through Macedonia in a round trip, returning to Corinth for a longer stay. Meaning that Corinth would have had two visits. This meant that not only were the Corinthians deprecating Paul for not arriving, but also for having changed his itinerary leaving Corinth just one visit and not two. Like little children crying for Daddy, they were upset about the surprise change of plan.

This leaves us with a major question in attempting to sort out the chronology of Paul's decision making. At what point of time did Paul plan to go to Corinth first? And, what point of time did he change his plans and decide to go to Macedonia first?

My own thoughts are that by reading over and over Acts 18-20, and then the whole of 2 Corinthians several times in quick succession, the plan to visit Corinth first thing after leaving Ephesus must have been made early on in his Ephesian stay. Perhaps it was promised through the three Corinthian visitors early in the mission in Ephesus. Perhaps that was the plan that he referred to in 1 Corinthians. But with the heat of persecution in Asia, then the false teaching that was being promulgated in Galatia, as well as the damaging relational troubles in

Corinth, Paul's plans were turned on their head. With no telephone, radio, mobile phone or email, if Paul changed his mind one day on the direction he was to take, it could be weeks and possibly months before some could discover that things had been altered. But it is there in the letter – he was committed to visit Corinth again.

We have to assimilate the hard truth, that Character cannot be developed in ease and quiet. Character is built by the joint efforts of a will that wants to achieve a goal, then working to achieve that mission and the negotiation of all the people, demons and circumstances that seek to thwart that goal and/or vision on the way. Only through experiences of trial and suffering can the human soul be truly and practically strengthened, ambition inspired and success achieved. There definitely is no other way. Out of suffering have emerged the world's strongest souls throughout all of history. The most massive characters have been seared with scars, simply because of confronting their opposition head on. That confrontation meant that there had been suffering - even when conjoined to overcoming. The entire world is full of those that have suffered and those that are suffering. It has also a huge number of those who have overcome and those that are in the process of overcoming. As an overcomer, Paul was one of Christ's greatest trophies of grace. The bigger the mission, and Paul's mission was to win the entire gentile world, the bigger the opposition! The bigger the opposition, and Paul was continually confronted with vicious and powerful opposers, the deeper the scars! The deeper the scars, the more acute the suffering! Suffering becomes beautiful when anyone bears great calamities and injustice (especially personal injustice) with cheerfulness, not through insensibility but through greatness of mind, and Christ-likeness of attitude. Paul's second letter to the Corinthians, and his attitude to rejection is deeply sensitive and gracious.

We need to be sure to instruct our own hearts that the fear of suffering is always worse than the suffering itself. It is this writer's commitment never to be silent whenever and wherever he sees human beings enduring suffering and humiliation within my own circle of influence. We must always take sides. Neutrality in this is wrong. Neutrality helps the oppressor, never the victim. Silence encourages the tormentor, never the tormented. Passivity of spirit is rarely righteous.

Paul postponed death by living the way he did, by suffering the way he did, by errors – and he made a few, by risking, by giving and sometimes, even by losing. If one tries to exclude the possibility of suffering which the order of nature and the existence of free-will involves, one will find that they have excluded life itself. When life draws to a close, people never regret having suffered; rather they regret having suffered so little, and suffered that little so badly.

Power, no matter how well-intentioned, tends, nearly always, to cause suffering. Those that gain power often abuse its use. Love, being vulnerable, absorbs the suffering under the jackboot of power. In a point of convergence on a hill called Calvary, God renounced the one (i.e. power) for the sake of the other (i.e. love). You may suffer and yet be un-Christ-like, but no man can be Christ-like and fail to suffer. Paul was a model of Christ-likeness, and a veteran sufferer. If a person, by the grace of God, becomes a partaker of the divine nature, that person must also inevitably become a partaker of His sufferings.

Job's three friends simply assumed that sin and suffering are always inexorably bound together in a sort of "cause and effect" bonding. The presupposed mindset was that whenever and wherever there is one, there is the other. Notwithstanding what they knew to be true about Job's character, they refused to budge from their hideous philosophical stance. They refused to allow the possibility that on occasion, as mysterious as it might seem, a righteous man might suffer greatly, hideously. But here we have an example more striking than Job. Paul the righteous was pursued to the end.

2. THE REVELATION OF SUFFERING IN PAUL'S MOTIVATIONAL MINDSET

Paul's inner sufferings were also linked with the misunderstanding, and criticisms concerning his motives for doing things. There is definitely a profound connection between Paul's sufferings and the barrage of what was being said about his raison d'etre, in Corinth. He was being badly thought of, and character weaknesses were being laid against him that we in the twenty-first century see as his strengths. Paul needed to respond to this.

It is remarkable how excruciatingly vulnerable Paul makes himself to the people at Corinth. Second Corinthians is a deep revelation of the heart and mind, the affection and tenderness that Paul felt towards these people. It would have been so human to shout at them, or even ignore them, but Paul condescends with true grace to explain himself to a group of people who were hardly worthy of such a response in most people's eyes. I often think he was casting his precious pearls of wisdom and experience before swine.

The first critical accusation that he addresses in 2 Corinthians was concerning his non arrival in Corinth, that is, up to the moment in time in which he wrote the letter. We referred to this situation above. In the book of Acts he says plainly that he was intending to go to Macedonia and work his way down south to Greece and Corinth, which is exactly what he did (Acts 19:21. Acts 20:1-3). However, 2 Corinthians reveals to us the commitment he personally made to the Corinthians which was to leave Asia and sail firstly to Corinth. From Corinth he would travel northwards through Macedonia, and then return southwards stopping at Corinth for another visit. The Corinthians were eagerly looking forward to two visits. They had heard however about his change of plan and did not know what to make of it. At the time this occurred there was a visiting preacher (or preachers) in Corinth who had authorisation by letters from the apostles at Jerusalem. This man, or group of men, were obviously Judaisers who negated Paul, his character and his message with every chance they were given. Paul's change of itinerary they said was obvious proof of Paul's total lack of integrity. The Corinthians were deferring to the man (or men) with "letters from Jerusalem," and were now believing that Paul was inferior to other preachers, despite the fact of what he had accomplished in their city. Indeed Paul was the father in the faith to a huge number of Corinthian believers. The infestation of such thoughts escalated to suggest that Paul wasn't even a true apostle of Christ. The anguish and agony of heart that this situation brought to Paul must have been a momentous burden.

The visiting minister (or ministers) also made an issue of how Paul's correspondence to Corinth sounded so authoritative and powerful, so opposite to what his physical presence and his vocal speech suggested. It is almost as if they were accusing him of having some kind of "Ghost Writer," who was writing the letters for him. The whole thing was extremely hurtful to Paul.

Then there was the group within the Corinthian church who said that they were, "Of Peter." Nearly all the academics today, still insist that Peter definitely had not set foot in Corinth up to this point of time, if he ever went there at all. So what was the, "I am of Peter," group about. One can only surmise that by repeated stories of the like of which we are told in the early chapters of Acts, they held a kind of doctrinal Petrine slant at best, or at worst they were a sort of "cult" or "deviation" within the church. It could only have been a romanticised view of the Big Fisherman that had grown through the stories of Peter's own management of the miraculous. When there was trouble in Jerusalem, Peter just spoke and people dropped dead, as with Ananias and Saphira in Acts chapter 5. Paul had been in prison several times, but had never been released by angels, as Peter was. Paul was, however, released by an earthquake. Peter had spent three years in the physical presence of Jesus, in fact t2here were men and women who were not even apostles who had spent more time with Jesus than Paul had. Paul's so called "inferiority" to the twelve, and others was plain for all to see. If this wasn't the mentality of those who claimed to be of Peter, it must have been a line fed them by the visiting ministry at

Corinth. Paul was simply not one of the twelve, and the ministry that was at that time in Corinth sat under the words and influence of the twelve continually. "We've been sent by, and have letters from Peter, James and John in Jerusalem," must have seemed to carry much more weight than, "Paul sent me!" "Oh yes? You mean the converted killer of Stephen that the Jewish Christians in Jerusalem disparage?"

Paul's answer to these "accusations" and the derisive logic pitted against his character and person was unique. His answer was, in a way that we understand from the twenty-first century perspective, looking back, even more impressive than the twelve. Paul leaned on the fact of the direct divine revelation and authority that he had been given. His authority was direct from heaven, and was not shown by letters written by apostles, like the visiting ministry to Corinth had proudly shown. Paul's letters of authority he cleverly claims were the changed lives and the living faith that was beginning to dominate the lives of the Corinthian converts. As far as Paul was concerned there were so many who had a glorious testimony of meeting with Christ in the gospel message, that no other letter from any earthly man was required, not even from the twelve in Jerusalem. The twelve "apostles of the lamb" were indeed the final authority to the vast and ever growing number of Christians in the world, but Paul had seen things, heard things and learned things that we have no indication that the twelve had. And he had been educated by his adventures and research in "prayer in the Holy Spirit," as opposed to talking face to face with Jesus in the days of His flesh.

Jesus told the twelve that the Holy Spirit would teach them "all things," and that there were actually things that Jesus could not tell them until they had received the Holy Spirit, and thereafter it would be the Spirit Himself who would reveal things to them. Paul might not have had three years walking around Judaea with Jesus, but he had, since his conversion had an incredibly inspired ear in listening to what the Spirit was saying. And with this in mind, Paul asserts in 2 Corinthians how he learnt directly via the revelation of the Holy Spirit.

The visiting ministry from Jerusalem had been financed from Jerusalem, and undoubtedly had received some kind of financial ministry gift from Corinth. It was all official and business like. "Inferior" Paul, however, worked for himself in secular work making tents. He doesn't even get paid for his labours. Paul's ingenuity in self-funding was not seen as "proper" by the Corinthians, undoubtedly yet another idea fed into the Corinthian Church psyche by the men, from Jerusalem.

How was Paul supposed to defend himself, apart from sarcastically apologising for not having been a burden to them, which is exactly what he did! It is phenomenal to this writer that the mighty apostle Paul should even attempt to answer such a ridiculous accusation. This proves to this writer how huge an issue it was to Paul to assert his integrity, and in so doing facilitate the Corinthians maintaining their faith and any integrity they had. Churches are filled with disillusioned and disappointed Christians around the world who have lost faith and/or become cynical because of the discovery of a church leaders lack of integrity. Paul was striving to make the faith of the Corinthians a sustained reality of life in the Spirit just as he had taught them, and not to allow them to sink into negative thoughts and diminished faith, thinking that Paul was a villain with bad motives and had "tricked" them all along.

Seemingly, some at Corinth wanted one of the twelve to have a permanent base there. Perhaps that was another reason why there was a "Peter" party in Corinth, even though we are almost certain Peter never went there. Paul was "unofficial" and "non-ministerial" by his self-help skill of tent making. Again I ask; how was Paul supposed to defend himself without insulting the visiting ministry?

It was obvious that he was being accused of misrepresenting Christ's message as he hadn't been with Christ in the days of his flesh. His entire teaching was to be brushed under the carpet if the Jewish visitors had their way. The charge was: "How could this man know more than the twelve who lived with him for three and a half years?" Because that is exactly how it seemed.

Paul's response was simply to say he had heard from God. It was divine and heavenly revelation that saved him, called him, and fed him. The proof of the reality of those revelations, the call and the gift of his understanding was they themselves, i.e. the church in Corinth. However, that was too pure and straight for the visitors who were claiming that Paul was demented and not to be trusted. They said he was a fool. Paul plays up to their accusation and says he is talking like a fool in the latter chapters of the epistle.

The pain and anguish of all this character assassination must have sorely grieved the apostle and created suffering of a kind few of us will ever know. Paul was in seriously deep water that had eternal consequences for the Corinthian Christians. Their entire integrity of faith was in the balance. That faith had, as part of its constituent ingredients, trust in the character and integrity of Paul. That is why it was so torturous to him. It was necessary to defend himself in order to maintain the foundation of the faith of the Corinthian church. It really was water that a man could drown in. I have met pastors, now ex-pastors, who drowned in scenarios similar to this one, losing their faith in the rising tide of character assassination.

God brings men into deep waters not to drown them, but to cleanse them. A believer can never be the same after passing through humiliating suffering when responded to correctly. It is important to receive God's arrangement in all circumstances, whatever. Paul did not bid us to give thanks *for* everything, but he did say to give thanks *in* everything. Submitting to this arrangement is always the discipline of the Holy Spirit. To escape God's arrangement just one time is to lose an opportunity to have our capacity for faith and character enlarged. Make no mistake about it, Paul was fighting for the life of the Corinthian church – a much bigger issue than just fighting to save his own face.

If we bear the cross unwillingly, we make it a burden, and load ourselves more heavily; but we must bear it. And bearing it willingly lightens the load. "We are born helpless. As soon as we are fully conscious we discover loneliness," said Clive Staples Lewis. The same man said, "It is by human avarice or human stupidity, not by the churlishness of nature, that we have poverty and overwork." Wilfully, determinedly taking up the cross to follow Christ relieves the burden. Burdens must be carried, but in Christ the burden becomes light (Matthew 11:28)

THE REVELATION OF SUFFERING IN PAUL'S RELATIONAL CIRCLE

As well as his long history of persecution and pain, and as well as his very motivation being disparaged, there was, finally, a very hurtful connection between Paul's relationships with the people in Corinth and the sufferings that these relationships caused him. Paul related quite openly and intimately with the folks in Corinth, and as the church is reckoned to be numerically only second to the size of the church in Ephesus and Asia, it means the apostle was sharing his heart with a huge number of people via his Corinthian letters. This was like the Sunday papers' scandal sheet in downtown Corinth. The apostle was stripping his heart naked for the church to see. Paul leaned on and lived in open heart relationships, as opposed to "closed" and "private" authority from "The Oval Office of the Apostle Paul." Paul's opponents had handmade letters of authenticity, and claimed the delegated authority of the twelve apostles and Jerusalem. This was something that Paul could not and would not ask for. His authority was not derived by any human authority, no matter how legitimate, but given direct from heaven. If the twelve ever offered to give him letters of authorisation I have no doubt whatsoever he refused to accept them. Paul and his message are indivisible. Paul was so open that he could confidently encourage his converts to follow him and emulate his example. I have known many men of God, and have followed and emulated those who set an example. But I confess I have never known any man of God so well that I could follow and copy them without qualification. Paul's life was an open book to all that knew him and walked with him.

The apostle insists that he had been entirely open and honest with them in every dimension of relating (2 Corinthians 1:12-14). He was utterly and sincerely transparent with them. This was his assurance. And even though he was fully aware that the visiting preacher(s) from Jerusalem would obviously get to hear of the letter, if not to read it altogether, he talks plainly and in a robust manner. These assertions were to be read by anybody who was bothered to read them or had an interest in the troubles between Corinth and Paul. They had accused him of being double minded, two faced, and downright lying. His answer was of a singular mind, a bare faced statement of integrity and a claim for sheer and unadulterated truth in his words and motives.

Then there was the issue of money. These ministers from central office in Jerusalem were questioning Paul's integrity with money. Paul had been collecting for the poor people in Jerusalem, as suggested by the Eldership in Jerusalem in their meetings with Paul years previously. His trustworthiness with money was obviously under attack. For that reason we have Titus returning to Corinth to ensure that the money promised was received, and that he himself would send others to verify the honest handling of the package. Paul did not even want to see the money, all he wanted to ensure is that it would go to Jerusalem and be used for the intended purpose of the givers. In this respect, sending the Greek Titus was so wise, he was one of their own countrymen.

In all these relational issues Paul was not afraid to assert that he had direct divine authority and guidance. It is astounding how that Paul literally makes himself personally accountable to those who, themselves are proving to be unaccountable. The grace upon him to do such a thing is, to this writer, deep and wide

THE REVELATION OF SUFFERING IN PAUL'S AUTHORITY BEING CHALLENGED

Last of all, Paul was not ashamed to open the diary of his thoughts and even to let people know things about him that were unnecessary for them to know. Paul's authority, having come directly from vision and revelation from heaven was, for that very reason, intensely personal. He could not refer to "studying" under Jesus's tuition, or the years I spent with the twelve. It happened to him privately in prayer. There was no "Certificate of Degree," or "Badge of membership." It was not something he would discuss lightly. To explain his knowledge of Christ and the supernatural visions and revelation that he had absorbed was something he refers to as "foolish". I have found that people who talk about experiences like what Paul had lightly, have failed to grasp all the grace that was embedded in the revelation that was given.

Paul discusses such things here because his authority was being thoroughly undermined and his very apostleship brought into question. It can be quite intimidating to hear the way some people share heavenly visitations. Paul did not want to intimidate, but definitely to assure his readers of his authority in Christ. He approaches it in this manner so as not to lord it over their faith.

The two things Paul appeals to are incontrovertible. 1. Visions and revelations that gave him his understanding of God and the gospel message. 2. The miracles and the spiritual power that proved supernatural approval to his unparalleled ministry (2 Corinthians 1:14. 3:2. 9:21-28. 1 Corinthians 9:1. 15:10.). His sole irresistible weapon in this was the sword of the Spirit, which was the word of God in his heart.

The humility and the condescension of the apostle is the secret to his character and the manner in which he was receiving and moving in the miraculous. We need learn to regard people less in light of what they do or omit to do, and more in the light of what they have suffered and the character they carry. A man that studies revenge keeps his own wounds green. Paul was here attacked maliciously, yet answered in a grudgeless manner. They gave our Master a crown of thorns. Why should Paul, or we ourselves, hope for a crown of thornless roses? Suffering in the path of following Christ is the clearest display of the worth of God in our lives. Faith-filled and even joyful suffering is necessary in this world for formulation of the most intense, authentic worship. When we are most satisfied with God in the midst of suffering, Christ will be most glorified in us in worship. When we embrace more persecution and suffering for the value of Christ, there will be more fruit in our worship of Christ. The man that wrote Second Corinthians is guileless in the midst of being hated and rejected. In God's sight, such character is priceless. It is too similar to the character of Christ for Heavenly Father to ignore.

When a minister of the gospel moves in the miraculous, especially when it happens on a regular basis, most Christian people assume that he, or she, must be walking in a degree of holiness that most people know nothing about. Is this a solid biblical conclusion? It should be … but …the down to earth experiential truth is that the ministry of the miraculous does not necessarily presuppose a correspondingly high degree of holiness proportionate to the signs and wonders made manifest.

Jonah had some shocking motivational thoughts when he was sent to Nineveh. The last verses of the last chapter of the book of Jonah reveal the reason why he ran westward when God had sent him eastward. Jonah was sent to Nineveh to preach a message that was very short; "In forty days Nineveh will be destroyed! Repent!" Could it be any simpler? But Jonah knew all about God's grace. He was aware that if they repented that God would forgive the Ninevites, and in so doing, to Jonah's way of thinking, that would be some kind of disappointment in the light of the incredibly dramatic message, no matter how brief it was. He sat outside Nineveh and pouted in a sort of depression simply because God forgave the population of Nineveh.

Jonah and true holiness in motivation and thought did not go hand in hand. Nevertheless Jonah was a true prophet of God.

Judas Iscariot also moved in the realm of the miraculous. I do not think that anybody would ever assume that he walked in absolute holiness at any time in his life. On top of that any of the twelve disciples who had anything that exhibits wrong attitudes or action in the gospels, must be also included in the qualifying list of, "Those that moved in the miraculous with shortcomings in their walk of holiness." In Galatians we read of how Paul actually confronted Peter concerning hypocritical conduct that was inclusive when there were no Jews about, but exclusive when there were. Yet people were still healed when his anointing even permeated his shadow.

Paul's claim was absolute transparency and holiness. But note, he quotes the miracles and the heavenly visitations as a proof of his authority, not his holiness.

Second Corinthians, I believe gives us revelation and insight into Paul's character in great depth, and it is all inclusive in the package of mindsets and worldview integral to managing the miraculous. The letter opens a window into the very emotions of his heart. It is the agitated self-defence of a wounded yet loving spirit to an ungrateful and erring yet not completely lost and incorrigible group of human souls. The apostle pours out the essence of his character to them and begs them, in return, not for a dry, cold, critical appreciation of his eloquence, or a comparison with other doctrines, but with the sympathy of brothers, if not the affection of children.

Parts of this letter are painfully personal. We may think that the ambassador for Christ had dropped his anointed mantel and had taken on the nature of a mere man. But when we realise that essentially the human being and the ambassador for Christ are inseparable, then the folly of the boasting and the shame are not mere revelations of his character but revelations of how the mighty man of God generally related to his God as well as to people. This letter was written with extreme tension of mind, and in the midst of a constant struggle between the deep emotions of thankfulness, and violent indignation. This missive is utterly striking because it shows a new philosophy of life poured out not through systematic doctrines, treatises or dissertations, but through occasional bursts of human feeling and a naked exhibition of his heart. He explains his fearful tribulations, excessive and beyond his strength, whether caused by outward enemies, or physical injury, that he has just gone through in As0ia, i.e. Ephesus. These things, whatever they were, brought him to the very edge of despair as well as the grave. But it happened so that he would trust God who raises the dead. He offers himself to the Corinthians as a faithful loving father of the faith. In this letter Paul is no longer occupied with the rectification of practical disorders and theoretical heresies. He is contrasting his own claims with those of his opponents and maintaining an authority which had been most violently attacked.

Paul has more to say re suffering in Acts 20, words we have to negotiate in another chapter.

My meditations on Second Corinthians here stated are seen by this writer to be very necessary contribution to understanding the sustainable ministry of the miraculous. Character and integrity is absolutely the most desperately needed attribute of Christ in the paradigm of all Christian people, especially those who move in the miraculous and by doing so become high profile personalities in a "celebrity obsessed culture." If one wishes to do like Jesus Christ, one must be like Jesus Christ. I spit on legalism and pour contempt on rules and regulations, but purity of heart and mind I desire above all things. The heart that wrote this letter lived in the fountain source that sprayed the miraculous wherever he went.

28.

FULLY PREACHED THE GOSPEL WHERE NO ONE HAD PREACHED BEFORE.

"Therefore in Christ Jesus I have found reason for boasting in things pertaining to God. For I will not presume to speak of anything except what Christ has accomplished through me, resulting in the obedience of the Gentiles by word and deed, in the power of signs and wonders, in the power of the Spirit; so that from Jerusalem and round about as far as Illyricum I have fully preached the gospel of Christ. And thus I aspired to preach the gospel, not where Christ was already named, so that I would not build on another man's foundation; but as it is written, "They who had no news of Him shall see, and they who have not heard shall understand."

Romans 15: 17-21 (NASB)

Paul's language as well as his phrases of expression are fantastic. They are fantastic because at times he says some things that we do not understand fully. Preachers, teachers and professors of Theology, however, all try to explain what he meant especially in his difficult statements – and Paul has lots of t0hem. The true nature of this confusion defying struggle is to read the Bible as comprehensively as possible in the valiant skirmish to get into the writer's head and heart and to authoritatively say, "This is what this person said, and this is what he meant." This writer spent three glorious years of his life living within the constraints of a man who moved in the miraculous like most of us move in the kitchen, i.e. Freely, easily and seemingly self-indulgent for his own purposeful delight. It was easy and powerful and Christ glorifying every step of the way watching this man, hearing what he said, and seeing what he did. It was because of where he stood in Christ that he made statements and throw away one liners that were often mystifyingly cryptic, mystically and deeply perceptive, as well as breathtakingly prophetic. His relaxed asides were all revelatory to me. And in the same way, this little section of Romans has always intrigued me. It lets us into Paul's motives and rationale as to where he went and why. He is talking about his preaching and his ministry of the miraculous.

We are looking at these thoughts because he wrote these after Ephesus (Acts 20:1) and before he addressed the elders on the beach at Miletus (Acts 20:17). These thoughts reveal some of the motives behind the man and the way he managed his agency in the supernatural.

After writing 2 Corinthians, Paul finally arrived in Corinth and spent three months there (Acts 20:2-3). I have no doubt that his state of being became healthier in body, soul and spirit than he had enjoyed for a good few years. Why do I say such a thing? Simply because it seems he healed all his broken relationships and differences of opinion with people in the church at Corinth (and how he was pained with all that furore), and he had also written Romans and Galatians while he was there. However, and most of all, he was continually surrounded by eight brothers – colleagues – assistants or whatever title we need to give them, to keep him company and minister to Paul just as he undoubtedly ministered to them. The conversation with the eight, and Paul's ministry in Corinth must have been stimulating to say the least.

Acts 19:20 talks about the word of God growing. How can the word grow? It grows by its repetition in the mouths of many people. It grows in the hearts of people so that it creates faith in Christ. It grows inasmuch as a new generation becomes the torchbearer for the following generation of people. The word of God grew in its social and spiritual influence throughout Asia, "so mightily grew the Word of the Lord and prevailed." It is truly an all prevailing word. When delivered in faith, received by faith, and kept by faith it changes the world. It was not a mere dragging of its feet, it didn't seek to conquer by being whispered and tantalisingly dropped when people were embarrassed to discuss it. It marched and fought with people's consciences and prevailed. The word of God ran amuck amongst people's hearts, lives and families wherever Paul went. It was, wherever Paul declared the unsearchable riches of Christ, a mighty forcible and victorious power. It was, to be sure, a growth, a development and manifestation of the Word of God in the earth. It was a mighty weapon in the hand of Paul. He had fought it out in all its depth and detail with God Himself, and when he preached the word a great battle was being fought between the power of truth and the power of error. God was so manifested in the preaching of the word (Titus 1:3 KJV). That is what preaching is all about.

"Therefore in Christ Jesus I have found reason for boasting in things pertaining to God." I cannot really see this "boasting" he was talking about as if he was indulging in braggadocio, attempting to pridefully talk of what he has done for God. However, he is indeed talking about what he has done and why. The next sentence says, *"For I will not presume to speak of anything except what Christ has accomplished through me."* He can assert the principles on which he has worked for Christ. He was called to address the gentiles. No other apostle made such a claim. So Paul has a reason for boasting in what God has done through him because of the uniqueness of his call.

Paul then explains how he can make such assertions. What did Christ do through him? Because of what Christ did through him he could show the world that it was, *"resulting in the obedience of the Gentiles by word and deed."* In plain English it was proven to be of God because of the changed lives. He did not simply get people to speak like him and use the words he used, but their deeds also altered. This was his pride and joy; the masses of changed lives that he left behind him as he followed on in the train of Christ's triumph.

How else did Christ show Himself through Paul? *"In the power of signs and wonders, in the power of the Spirit!"* Ah! We have it! Signs and wonders in the power of the Holy Spirit. Wherever he went he preached, and the Lord worked with him, accompanying the word that was declared. Paul carried himself in the power and demonstration of the Spirit." He spoke so plainly and directly to ensure that their faith would stand in the power of God and not in the wisdom of man. This was Paul's boast. He was called of God, anointed by God, sent by God and made fruitful by God.

Then he makes the statement that astonishes me. Gentiles turning to God! Signs and wonders in the Spirit of God! Where did all this take place? He explains, *"so that from Jerusalem and round about as far as Illyricum I have fully preached the gospel of Christ."*

Just what did Paul mean when he wrote, *"I have fully preached the gospel of Christ"* (Romans 15:19)? Did he mean that he preached all the doctrines of scripture? Tosh to that! Of course that could not be what he meant. Does it mean that he fully reached every single person in the places he launched himself into? The answer to that, again, must be an emphatic "No!" simply because he wrote to people whom he had never met who had become Christians. Did he mean he preached it with the extreme fullness of the anointing of the Spirit? Does it mean there was nothing else to be preached after he had declared his message?

Let's get more basic. Is it ever possible to preach the gospel, but not preach it "fully"? Now we are really talking turkey. The rubber has hit the road when preachers and teachers set themselves to be honest with this question. The knife may puncture a boil with some of us when we get to grips with this issue. Can one preach only a part of the gospel? Such a thing, of course, is definitely possible. It is completely self-evident that many churches today do not fully preach the gospel as Paul is explaining here. The "fully preached gospel" is embedded in something else that he said, as far removed from theological truths being counted and listed as the East is from the West. He has just stated that the summation of all his achievement is wrapped up in gentile people being obedient in word and in deed, and their transformation being aided and assisted with mighty signs and wonders in the power of the Holy Spirit. The fully preached gospel is words and signs, lives changed by the miracle healing power of God and the righteous deeds thereafter lived by an obedience to the faith.

So here we have the man that wrote half of the New Testament declaring that his words, and his sermons and teachings, were, by themselves, just not enough. That is not how Jesus did it! Even the words of Christ were not enough! Jesus went about doing good and healing all that were oppressed by the devil (Acts 10:38). This is the master church builder Paul talking, not myself. Paul did not invent this idea, the idea comes from simply doing what Jesus did. Aren't we also supposed to live like Jesus? Whoever wants to do like Jesus, has to live like Jesus.

The point is that words, even good words, yes, even words of power and perception, do not drive the demons and the demon inspired habits and lifestyles out of people. The word of God washes the mind and the soul, but it is the power of God brooding over the preached word that is the power of God to salvation. The gospel message, when properly declared saves people from hell itself. Faith comes by the preaching of that word – the full word.

So, it cannot be intelligently concluded that "fully preached," means anything else other than speaking the word of God with miracles accompanying alongside. It was the signs and wonders, the healing and the deliverance following the word, the prophetic insights that brought out the revelation of the secrets of men's hearts that made the address the "full preach."

It was in this form of "fully preaching," that Paul saw and delivered "from Jerusalem and round about to Illyricum." That is, as far east as Jerusalem, and as far west as north-west Greece and Albania. Everywhere in scripture where we know Paul went, according to what he wrote here, the signs and wonders proliferated. It cannot mean anything else.

Have we let the penny drop into our thinking "one arm bandit" of a brain? The statement according to what Jesus said in the Great Commission, and what Paul is saying here, is that no matter how thankful we are to God for the fabulous and wonderful preachers in the world, without the following signs and wonders, the gospel has not been fully preached. The gospel gives us something to see as we;; as something to hear.

Let's take it further. It suggests that no matter how many people have been brought to Christ, no matter how fabulous and unforgettable the address was, no matter how many doctrinal truths were grasped by the audience, if there was no signs and wonders accompanying it, the gospel has not been fully preached. Preachers – all preachers I am sure - want to preach the full message. Anybody that would, in any context, only give half the message that they were sent to deliver can honestly be called a bit of a misnomer. Wouldn't you agree? In fact half a message is downright disobedience.

When Paul wrote in 2 Corinthians 12:12 that *"Truly the signs of an apostle were accomplished among you in all patience, in signs, and wonders, and mighty deeds,"* many church leaders justify the none-seeking of the miraculous because it is only granted to those of an apostolic calling – a statement founded solely on that verse. However, what about Philip in Samaria? He was no apostle. What about Stephen in Jerusalem? He was a deacon who preached and saw the miraculous in his off duty moments. On top of that I would like to suggest that there was a little more than the signs and wonders, there was the patience (translated by some as perseverance) and the mighty deeds.

The world-wide problem is, and always has been, that people examine the man who is declaring the truth in a more imperative light than they should. Truth has been lost, and ground given to Satan because of preachers and teachers who do not present themselves in a godly light. Prosperity, divine healing, deliverance, even the baptism in the Holy Spirit, as well as other sacred truths of scripture are all, to a degree, disparaged and often rejected by huge sections of the church world-wide because of the misgivings that the Christian world has about the high profile proponents of those individual truths and emphases. Immature it may be, but the fact of the matter is plainly stated. "I don't like preacher X because of things I hear about him (or her), and for that reason I doubt their motives and reject their message." So tradition sets in, and truth becomes lost to a generation or even generations. It is my opinion that this is why many leaders in the church do not declare or believe in a "fully preached" gospel as Paul declares.

If millions of this generation are to believe, they simply must see proof that Jesus Christ is the same yesterday, today and forever. I believe the gospel message when properly declared should be accompanied by the power and demonstration of the Holy Ghost proving the hard solid tangible truth that the gospel is absolutely rock sure true!

Paul boldly stated that, *"My speech and my preaching were not with persuasive words of human wisdom, but in demonstration of the Spirit and of power"* (1 Corinthians 2:4). The Greek here means to truthfully "point out" or "with proof." Paul was saying in plainest language; "I preach the gospel with proof. God and the Holy Spirit are backing me up with signs and wonders!"

A person really needs help to misunderstand these utterly plain statements. Hebrews 2:4 says that God confirmed the preaching of the writer, who was anybody but Paul, with *"Signs and wonders, with various miracles, and gifts of the Holy Spirit, according to His own will."*

The only New Testament prayer we have in a church prayer meeting is where the body of believers pleaded, *"That signs and wonders may be done through the name of Your holy Servant Jesus"* (Acts 4:30). What system of logic is it that stops us praying the same? "I believe the bible, BUT..."

The scripture says that they went out preaching everywhere, *"The Lord working with them and confirming the word through the accompanying signs"* (Mark 16:20). "Accompanying," literally means, "running alongside."

Paul finishes this little paragraph of scripture by saying, *"And thus I aspired to preach the gospel, not where Christ was already named, so that I would not build on another man's foundation."* This was his boast. He boldly went with Christ where none other had been before. Such a goal might be a little more difficult in this age as many have already heard in many quarters of the planet.

What is my point? We need to hunger for and submit ourselves so fully to Christ that we preach and or believe in a gospel that needs to be "Fully preached."

29.

THE LONELY WALK FROM TROAS TO ASSOS.

"We went on ahead to the ship and sailed for Assos, where we were going to take Paul aboard. He had made this arrangement because he was going there on foot. When he met us at Assos, we took him aboard and went on to Mitylene."

Acts 20:13-14 (NIV)

The biblical experience of Paul, as well as other giants of the faith in scripture, is very plain. The higher the peak is in God, the darker the satanic confrontation is from hell. The brighter the revelation is of the Spirit, the blacker the shroud that satan throws over life in an attempt to blanket out the impact of the brightness of that revelation. The more like Christ a person becomes in this life, the more hell and its powers remove the gloves to get down and dirty and wipe out the, "Little Christs," that bring loss to the kingdom of darkness ("Little Christ" is a loose translation of the word "Christian."). Make no mistake about it; In Ephesus Paul had martialled a campaign that was so comprehensive in what it presented, and so strategically brilliant, that it had overturned an entire subcontinent for Christ in a period of time that amounts to about three years. Hell had been shaken. The power of God had been seen in the earth in a manner that had only previously been seen in the life of Christ and in those opening days of the church after Acts 2. Hell shook when this man Paul rose up every morning and walked the streets.

Some have asked me, "What about the scripture that says, 'Resist the devil and he will flee from you? (James 4:7)'" No problem! James is talking about what goes on in the mind and heart of the believer. In that mode, as you submit to God, the devil fleas from you. However, always see Christ's experiences as the model. No one could be more submissive to God than Christ was to His heavenly Father. On the cross, internal to his thought patterns and responses, the devil had fled. Externally however, the forces of hell had never been so concentrated or active throughout the whole history of mankind. In the same principle, Paul was submitted to God, and internally, even though in 2 Corinthians 1 he had given up on living and expected the angel of death to take him, neither his faith, nor his confidence in God was even scratched – in fact it had increased. The more he submitted to God, the more the devil fled from him - internally. Concurrent to this, and in the same yet paradoxical way, the more Paul submitted to God, the more active were the powers of hell in their external attempts to shipwreck his faith and distract him from his goals and aspirations. That is why the scripture promises that, "They that live godly in Christ Jesus shall suffer persecution."

The whole Ephesian workload of letters, maintaining relationships with troublesome churches, preaching, teaching, ministering deliverance regularly, and praying for healing, as well as being the General, the chief advisor, the head strategist and father to his team of workers, including conducting a five hour service every day, and not forgetting his tent making business and his pastoral visits which were also on a daily basis – *all* these things in combination must have taken its toll on Paul's physical frame. On top of all that, he had "fought with wild beasts at Ephesus," however that is to be interpreted, and been persecuted so viciously that he had resigned himself to death (2 Corinthians 1).

As well as being to heaven and beyond in his ministry, he had definitely been to hell and back in the thrust and parry of severe torturous persecution. He was never again (as far as scriptures tell us) to conduct a straightforward mission, in the normal understanding of that word. Of course, he was still on a mission; he was still intending to witness to Caesar himself. The visionary gift that was within him, however, began to see a little more than the issue of witnessing for Christ in the presence of Caesar.

Because of all the above, and before we get to the hugely revelatory "Goodbye on the Miletus Beach," there is one more moment I want to highlight that is relevant to our understanding of Paul's management of the miraculous. Well, actually, it is more than a moment, it is what was probably one single whole day, possibly two. We are talking about a thirty plus mile walk.

Very strangely, Paul left his eight friends on board the ship that was to take them to Assos while he went to the same place by foot. Even Luke was absent from Paul on the ship. Because this part of Acts tells us that Luke himself was present to witness Paul make the decision to leave his companions for a while (It is one of the famous, "we," sections), and because Luke was making notes on all the huge things that took place in Paul's life, the fact that this "utter non-event" is mentioned suggests that to Luke's perception of things, and undoubtedly to Paul's, to set off across land alone, leaving all his "carers" on board ship was of huge significance. We are talking about one single hike – a thirty-three mile walk where Paul had insisted on being alone.

How and why did Paul push for this to happen? It does suggest also that if I am correct in theorising that the doctor and the rather large party of helpers were present because of Paul's physical fragility, or emotional vulnerability, Paul's state of being must have been greatly improved.

To set the scene fully, after having finally arrived in Corinth and spent 3 months there, Paul was about to leave Greece for Jerusalem (Acts 20:3). The impression is given that at a point of time *after* Paul had gone aboard ship, he discovered a plot to kill him. Perhaps the prospective murderers were on-board the same ship and were overheard plotting. If Paul had not boarded the ship, perhaps he had heard that the "would be" assassins were planning to board the ship and get rid of him at open sea. Whatever the details are, having heard of the plot, Paul spontaneously decided that he would not sail from Greece in order to cross the Aegean, but travel northwards again through Greece and into Macedonia. His plans had been seriously messed up yet again. It meant that he would not be in Jerusalem for Passover. Such is the life of the persecuted. They have to make it up as they go along in order to stay one step ahead of the demonic and the murderous.

At this time, Paul was still in the company of his eight companions; Sopater of Berea, the son of Pyrrhus, Aristarchus and Secundus of the Thessalonians, Gaius of Derbe, Timothy, Tychicus and Trophimus of Asia, and of course the beloved Physician, Luke (Acts 20:4). All Paul's letters reveal to us that he loved people, and he loved to be in their company. These eight men must have not only been greatly enriched by being with Paul over so long a period, but Paul was undoubtedly blessed and enriched by their company. My thesis is that Paul left Ephesus deeply shaken and in need of "carers". Perhaps it would be better expressed that Paul needed mature Christian company through the convalescence of whatever it was that had happened in Ephesus (2 Corinthians 1).

He had been alone with Luke in the few days of his ministry in Macedonia, having sent the seven ahead to Troas (Acts 20:5). The implication of the biblical text is that from Ephesus to Macedonia (perhaps also to Illyricum) and then on to Greece and Corinth for three months, and including his journey from the quayside in Greece, these eight companions were together with him all the way. If one jumps, however, from Acts 20:3 to verse 5 in order to maintain the story line, it is not clear whether Paul sent the seven ahead from the time of crossing the border into Macedonia, or further north along the Macedonian south east seaboard. What is clear is that somewhere on the way northward, while in Macedonia, seven of the colleagues were encouraged to go on ahead and wait for the other two at Troas. Paul and Luke continued together until they met the team at Troas, where they all spent a week together, undoubtedly ministering.

After the all-night meeting in the city of Troas in north western Asia Minor (Modern Turkey) where years before the apostle had heeded the Macedonian Call (cf. Acts 20:7–12), Paul's party proceeded to the port of Troas to embark southwards. Luke reports, *"We went before to ship, and sailed unto Assos, there intending to take in Paul: for so had he appointed, minding himself to go on foot"* (Acts 20:13).

Why on earth would Paul do such a thing? Here is this writer's opinion.

In the midst of all the activity, travel, persecution and ministry from Acts 20:1 to Acts 20:12, Paul had issues to sort out with God as well as himself. In Paul's prophetic spirit, he had received a vision about his future. It is not stated here, but later on, especially after we read what was said at Miletus, and then what Christian people were saying to Paul, *"in the Spirit,"* as he travelled on to Jerusalem, and seen in the light of his unnecessary "Appeal to Caesar," I personally believe that he himself had received in the Holy Spirit, pictures from God of what was going to happen to him and where.

Paul was strong and mature enough in Christ, I believe, that if he was to die in Rome, the Lord Himself would have revealed something of that reality to him. We will never know how much, of course, till we ask him in glory.

Heaven was moved to reveal to him that he would not see many more years in this life, and although he had stated in Romans that he fully intended to go to Jerusalem, to Rome, and then to Spain (a letter that he had written during his three months in Corinth), it seems to me that Heaven had other plans that were revealed to Paul whilst on his journey back up north through Macedonia. What were those plans? Jerusalem? Yes! Danger and life threatening circumstances in Jerusalem? Very much so! (I do not believe that God would have revealed all this to various prophets and/or prophetic type of Christians on his trip to Jerusalem without having revealed it first to Paul.) Then what? To Rome? Yes! To witness for Christ before Caesar himself? Yes! And afterwards? Blank! I believe the mists that enshroud mankind's vision of the future were by the grace of God slightly dissipated and cleared for Paul to have a glimpse of what he could prepare himself for.

I believe all this because:

- He had a sense of destiny for being in Jerusalem for Pentecost. (Acts 20:16). He was *"compelled"* to be in Jerusalem when the largest crowds would be there. For him to say that he was, *"not knowing what will happen to me there,"* suggests he knew something untoward was to cross his path there (Acts 20:22).

- In every city he had attended to that point, the Holy Spirit warned him that "prison and hardships" would be facing him (Acts 20:23). The fact that mentions "every city," tells us that it was not his internal communion with God that told him this, but the prophetic gift on the churches he attended that all predicted the same.

- He had clearly seen that he would never see the Ephesian elders again (Acts 20:25). This means that he had a sensible and true understanding that he was soon to die. There is a revelation to wrestle with if ever there was one.

- Through the Spirit, the people of God encouraged Paul not to go on to Jerusalem (Acts 21:4). This remarkable statement opens up avenues of thought concerning the prophetic gift that books could be written about. It also confirmed the huge step that it was for Paul to go to Jerusalem as he did.

- Another emotional farewell on a beach (Acts 21:5) tells us plainly that it was understood by all that his death was imminent. Although Paul did not know clearly what was to beset him, the inference of it all was that he was going to meet death. What would each of us do if we knew the date of our time to die?

- Agabus did not help to assuage the trepidation of what Jerusalem would bring to Paul (Acts 21:10-11). Paul was aware of this expectation I believe as he entered Macedonia (20:5), and that was the reason he sent seven of his party ahead to Troas. Perhaps he needed Luke for care and attention. It was a weight to Jesus in those days before the Passion, just as it was a weight on Paul at this time.

- The trouble it caused in the relationship between the present team and Paul had built to a climax where they confronted the apostle with a plea for him to keep away from Jerusalem (Acts 21:12-14). I cannot accept that so many people had insight to what was happening to Paul, and he not knowing it by revelation first. The only time to fit the revelation in is after he had written Romans where he is planning to go to Spain, and before the strange behaviour of wanting to be alone with Luke, and then alone for a day or two walking by himself from Troas to Assos. A weight from heaven had fallen on him.

- There is confirmation by Christ himself that Paul would testify of Christ in Rome (Acts23:11). Paul had seen this in the Spirit already (Acts 19:21). This weight was on him as he walked alone from Troas to Assos.

Wrongful and unjust execution - just as His Lord had experienced, was on its way to meet Paul. Stepping into eternity faced with the defining choice to curse his maltreats or to bless them as he died – exactly as Christ had endured, had set a rendezvous with Saul of Tarsus. Knowing how he was to be maltreated and suffer ahead of its occurrence – the same as Jesus went through, Paul was carrying the news in his consciousness. The man was fully informed of the pain that was on its way to him – again, just as Jesus encountered. And, possibly the worst agony of all, the insight that he was to be rejected by friends and those around him, and be left to die alone. All these circumstances were so similar to how the Lord of Life Himself stepped through the curtain of life's departure zone into the realm of the dead. It was at that point, i.e. death,that their experiences would have differed. At His death, Christ descended into Sheol to release the innumerable righteous dead and then to take them captive to heaven and the presence of God. Paul, however, would have immediately entered into the presence of Christ in the glory of heaven at his death.

Getting into Paul's humanity and personal experience of life, all this, of course, meant that there were many good-byes to be said, many attitudes and responses to be made before God. To Paul it meant that suddenly he was faced with deep emotional words to be spoken to those he knew and loved, and to those who had loved him in his pastoral and Christ-like role in their lives.

It is my strongly held opinion that Paul had all this running around in his thoughts and was not having time alone enough to file them in his memory banks and to order his thoughts, his feelings, and his relationship with Christ about it. Indeed, with such weighty thoughts burdening him, he needed to get hold of the reality of what was from God, and what were his own fears or anticipations surfacing and mingling with the revelation. In short, he needed time alone. Why else would Paul do such a thing, seemingly, so suddenly, as to walk off and leave his team on board? My rationale is the only reason there could have been for such a sudden gesture of spiritual impulse on the apostle's part. It was simply nothing less than a blatant desire to be alone with God. It could not have been because these deep and grave visions of his destiny had suddenly hit him as he was boarding the ship. It was the same reason that had caused him to send the seven ahead while he was still in Macedonia.

And so, here we are. Paul alone! Walking alone! Thinking alone! Praying alone! Paul had exactly thirty three and a third miles to walk by himself. Paul would not have risked missing the boat at its next port (Assos) if he had not been certain he could reach that city ahead of the vessel. He surely could not outstrip the ship on foot over those 33 miles, even though the highway then was probably considerably better than the same route is today.

One day, this writer will take the same walk from Troas to Assos as Paul did. It is part of my bucket list. And when I take that walk, it will not be alone, I will take some friends with me who will know and understand my desires in life.

I Googled, "Troas." Actually, one has to Google "Alexandria Troas," to find the geographical site today. ("Alexandria Troas, Turkey, Ezine") All the Bible dictionaries and commentaries assure me that the Troas of scripture is definitely the Alexandria Troas of today. There is no site change at all. Assos is also present and correct, as was in Paul's day. I confess that I do have a problem with the fact that most commentaries and Christian "experts" talk about it only being a, "Twenty mile walk," whilst Google maps assure me that it is a thirty three and a third mile walk on the shortest route. Google Maps also assures me that the walk would take me 11 hours and 11 minutes. I have no idea how fast I would have to walk to make that prescribed time. We are not told how long it took Paul to make that walk. The fact that Google reckons I could walk it in 11 hours and 11 minutes makes it more than probable that Paul set off in the early morning and arrived at Assos in the mid evening. We are talking of a single day.

Most Christian travellers I know who have done such a walk seem to take Turkey's main north-south highway (number E 24) paralleling the Aegean in order to escape the horrendous road continuing south to Assos, which the weathered locals seem to suggest is "definitely" the route that would have been Paul's, two millennia since.

We do not know how long a stay Paul had in Assos before boarding the ship his colleagues had taken from Troas on this, the first leg of the trip back to Judea. Perhaps the lone figure that strolled into Assos that day was not recognised by his solitariness. His name would undoubtedly have been known there. His face perhaps was not known. Assos had already been evangelized! Paul did not plant the churches of Mysia. The Asians themselves did! It doubtless happened during the first two to three years of Paul's earlier residence in Ephesus, during which period, Luke reports, *"all they which dwelt in Asia heard the word of the Lord Jesus, both Jews and Greeks"* (Acts 19:10). Most of Mysia, including Assos and Troas, had by 52 AD become part of the Roman Proconsular province of Asia. Paul's travelling evangelistic team, as well as the converts from Ephesus must have fanned out over that entire landmass, spreading the good news of life in Christ. I am more than convinced that it must have been the most extensive and comprehensive evangelistic outreach of all time!

The New Testament tells us nothing of the church at Assos, but archaeology attests its prominence in later times. It is definitely known that Christians were eventually able to take over the property of the pagan temple in the agora. They made so many changes in its architecture, to suit it for Christian worship that excavators have been able to learn very little about its original layout.

I have considered all this because of the weight that was in Paul's heart to influence his words to the Ephesian elders as a farewell address.

Assos doesn't look much at all today, and the city that was Troas is in complete ruins. But in these lines we have highlighted the most significant event in all the history of this once-prominent place. The brief visit of a Christian missionary who walked here for reasons we can only conjecture about (which I have done above) was enough to earn its place in history.

How I would so love to make that same walk.

31.

THE MILETUS GOOD-BYE
(ACTS 20:17-21)

Paul must have had the presentiment that he was living in his last days. How long he had to live, and where death would happen was seemingly unknown to him. He was planning to go to Jerusalem, then to Rome, and then to Spain, at least that was his plan as he wrote his glorious letter to the church at Rome (Romans 1:11.Romans 15:23-25). Since the plot to kill him at the Greek harbour, however, some sort of insight, heavenly revelation, or vision seemed to have struck him, and struck him hard. On beginning to move north through Macedonia he sent all his protective and caring friends ahead of him, all except the doctor that is (Luke) (Acts 20:3b-6). On reaching Troas where the seven friends had been waiting for him, he spent seven days there (Acts 20:7a), and on the Sunday service seems to have ministered all through the night, right up to daybreak the following day (Acts 20:7b-12). Very strange! Whether Paul was preaching all that time or just lost in discussion is difficult to discern with the Greek text. It is safer to suggest it was a bit of both all through the long dark hours.

With a man like Paul whose blood was oozing with revelation, vision, understanding and power – if he did suspect his death was near and approaching - wouldn't it have been "normal" for him to want to share all he could before he goes to be with Christ? He raised Eutychus from the dead in the middle of the particular night we are referring to and then, afterwards, just carried on with the ministry and/or the discussions.

After the group had separated another strange thing happened (at least, as far as all the information we have about Paul in the book of Acts, it seems strange to me). Paul packs his whole team, including

Luke, on to a ship that was doing the trip from Troas to a little place called Assos, around the promontory of land in between those two places (about 60 miles or so), while he himself, utterly alone, walks over thirty miles cross country to the very same harbour with the intention of meeting his team on the ship when he got there (Acts 20:13-14). How strange!

We have already thought it through as to why he made such a trek. This all sounds to me like a man with a lot on his mind. Was it stress? Or was he merely adjusting himself to facing death, and preparing his spirit to walk in grace no matter what was going to happen to him? Or was it just that he wanted to be alone? If he did, this is the only time we are aware of while on mission that he preferred to be alone.

With his team of eight friends, Paul sailed down the western coast of Asia Minor (Turkey, to us today) (Acts 20:13-17). From Assos, Paul boarded the afore mentioned ship carrying Luke and the other seven. They then headed for Mitylene on the southeast coast of the island of Lesbos. Mitylene was a day's boat journey from Assos and they spent the night there. From what Paul says in Acts 20:23, in Troas, Assos and Mitylene respectively he met some Christian people who were either prophets, or at least of a prophetic inclination, who declared to him that prison and hardships were ahead of him, especially in Jerusalem. The town of Mitylene ("mutilated") is on Lesbos, the third largest of the Greek islands and just 9 miles off the Asian coast (Acts 20:14). To hear such heavy prediction from heaven, while standing on an island called, "Mutilated," must have been sobering to say the least.

The next day it took several hours from Mitylene to sail to Kios (Acts 20:15). I am told that Kios means "Snowy." It is a rugged island situated between Samos and Lesbos. And without doubt, no matter how brief his stay there, somehow, someway, somebody gave Paul the same prophetic word about suffering at Jerusalem. Prophets, prophecy and the prophetic must have been much more common than it generally is today. Paul says he heard the same in every city he entered. That's a lot of prophetic words, from a lot of unrelated Christian people – and they were all spot on, in fact they were (pardon the pun) dead accurate. God help us in the twenty-first century to hear what God is saying as well as they did in the first century. Kios is separated from the mainland by a 5 mile wide straight. Most of the island is occupied by craggy limestone hills and has impressive cliffs, particularly on the eastern side. The island's principle town and port, Chios, lies half way down its eastern coast and is obviously where Paul stopped. There was a definite "snowy blizzard" approaching Paul in terms of his circumstances and ministry.

The next day, the third day since leaving Troas, they crossed the mouth of the bay leading to Ephesus and came to the island of Samos. Again the almost boring, scary, engaging prophecy was repeated to the apostle. How on earth did Paul cope with such consistency of messages from people who were conceivably all unknown to each other, yet all hearing the same word from the Holy Spirit? Stunning and almost traumatic is how I would describe it. Samos is a small island, only 27 miles long. It is located south of Chios, where they were the previous day, north of Patmos and about a mile off the Turkish coast. The name Samos is from Phoenician meaning, "rise by the shore." Paul was having to rise in faith on the shores of death by the sounds of things.

After leaving Samos the ship sailed for Miletus, a major city about 35 miles south of Ephesus (Acts 20:15) on the main land. Miletus means "pure white fine wool". It is on the coast of western Asia Minor and was one of the most important cities in the ancient Greek world. It was situated at the mouth of the Meander River. The city's main export was wool, which is once said to have been marketed in every corner of the ancient world. By the time of Paul's visit, however, the city was living on past glories. The remains of this once great economic, cultural and political centre were now isolated and sunken in an alluvial plain. But there was no soft woollen reception for Paul in Miletus.

Four days after raising Eutychus from the dead and speaking all night at Troas, Paul is about a twelve hour walk from Ephesus, only slightly more than the walk he took from Troas to Assos.

Acts records no incidents or preaching stopovers at Mitylene, Kios or Samos. Paul even decided to sail past Ephesus to *"avoid spending time in Asia, because he was in a hurry to reach Jerusalem by the Passover."* But Why?

Why didn't Paul drop in at Ephesus? If he had, surely it would have saved him time not lost it. From Miletus it would have taken a day to send messages to the church elders there, and another day for them to get to where Paul was. So, when Acts 20:16 tells us that he didn't want to spend time in Asia because he was in a hurry to get to Jerusalem for the feast of Pentecost (Acts 20:16), I cannot but scratch my head at the statement given. Some think he didn't touch base with the church pastors at Ephesus because he might not have been able to leave in time because of the response of the populace, whether it was Christians who appreciated him and would want him to stay longer, or the anti-Christian people who demonised Paul and wanted him imprisoned, tried, persecuted and/or dead. The scripture does not tell us one way or the other.

I have no idea at all how long the operation would have taken, but, according to Acts 20:17 it was from Miletus that Paul sent the messengers (discreetly, quietly and dare I say secretly) to bring the leaders of the church at Ephesus to see him. Messengers sent to Ephesus, over 35 miles away, would have taken round about a 12 hour trek, or much less, of course, on horseback. Add to that the time it took for those leaders to reach Miletus, it was perhaps a whole day waiting for the arrival of the Ephesian pastors, bishops and elders.

If my assumptions, and the assumptions and findings of archaeologists and theologians are correct, the elders of Ephesus would have created a very large and substantial group of people. Certainly hundreds! They arrived, and without any small talk, or minor details being given, Luke jumps into what they had arrived for. Paul addressed them all. I am alliterating his address into six sections.

- **YOU KNOW ALL ABOUT ME – THE MESSENGER (20:18-19)**

- **YOU KNOW ALL ABOUT THE MESSAGE – THE GOSPEL (20:20-21)**

- **I KNOW SUFFERING IS ON THE WAY (20:22-24)**

- **I KNOW THIS IS GOOD-BYE (20:25-28)**

- **I KNOW THAT TROUBLE AMONGST YOU IS ON THE WAY (20:29-31)**

- **I COMMIT YOU TO GOD AND HIS WORD. (20:32-35)**

YOU KNOW ALL ABOUT ME – THE MESSENGER (20:18-19)

Paul starts with: *"You know how I lived the whole time I was with you, from the first day I came into the province of Asia"* (Acts 20:18). What a wonderful opening line for a man to be able to make.

Paul wanted to briefly review his ministry among them. This is a review of what is past. (He will later, in this address, talk about what was present as well as what would be in their future.) He wanted all accounts of human relations settled before he leaves them for the last time, or before he dies. This is undoubtedly the speech and language of a man who is expecting to die shortly. It has a deep sense of drama and destiny permeating the whole.

The whole purpose of the three years in Ephesus was to bring people to a saving faith in Christ, and thereafter build them up in that faith so that they could respond to life's issues by the practice of that living faith in the Living God without requiring Paul's help. The goal of Christian ministry is to bring people to that point of full independence within their own faith and total dependence on Christ.

"You know..." Happy is the man whose life has been so manifestly consecrated to Christ, that he can begin his address with so confident a statement as this. How profound is this remark! We have no record that anybody contradicted his opening word. Paul was a man with a free and clear conscience.

"You know how I lived ... with you." The people knew Paul and how he lived. His life was utterly an open book. Their faith was not only the theological concepts embedded in the preaching of the gospel message, not only in the establishing of that faith by seeing the miracles Paul ministered, but their life had been ministered to by studying a life modelled on Christ, as was Paul's. Their model was not only standing on the anecdotal facts of Christ's life, what He said and what He did (None of the gospel's would have been written at this point of time), but the fleshed out model in the life of the apostle from Tarsus. He had lived where they lived. He had worked among them and showed himself friendly and godly. He that would have friends must show himself friendly. Teaching godliness, if unsupported by the life, carries but a faint and doubtful impression, if any at all.

"You know how I lived the whole time I was with you." There was not a time when he was not in plain view. It would seem that he did not even have a day off to be by himself. This means that Paul's ministry to the people of Ephesus was not just at, "Church Service," time. They were invited to emulate him when they saw him out of the church gathering. He set the example in his work, his relationships, his responses both to praise and criticism. His response whilst in persecution and hardship would have been studied by all. Paul, *"fought with wild beasts at Ephesus,"* and I have no doubt whatsoever that whatever happened to Paul in the meaning of those words, that it spoke volumes to the Ephesian and Asian believers, and the leaders to whom he was addressing himself at this point of time. This man was

the nearest thing to Jesus Christ they would ever meet perhaps, not counting the Apostle John.

This was a man talking from the platform of a hard earned privilege. We are reading the transcript of the words of a man who could look his old friends in the face (20:17). There was not a man in Ephesus who could make him hang his head. He could fearlessly refer to his past (20:18). Do not read negatives between the lines. There is no braggadocio air in his attitude. It is the honest confidence of a man content to have his record scrutinised, in the full belief that it will be his ample vindication. This man, since his conversion, was like the prophet Samuel who also asked people to point out any fault he may have had, or sin he may have committed. On that occasion also, the entire nation of Israel was still and silent. So these elders of the Ephesian church were silent as Paul made equally bold assertions similar to those of Samuel.

One translation interprets Paul's words as, *"The whole time I was with you all."* Paul lived his life freely and in the Spirit before everybody (Act 18:4; Rom 1:14; 1Co 1:23). He had no favourites, no special ministry for special people. He lived and interacted with all he met, modelling Christ with every acquaintance.

"From the first day I came." Surely this means that some of the "about twelve," that we read of in Acts 19:1-6 were there, present before him, in the group he was addressing. Those first disciples surely could say that they had studied, watched and made observations on life style and practice, as well as doctrine, from the first day Paul stepped across the city limits of Ephesus. This man did not have a honeymoon settling in period. Paul did not wait for a few days so that he could reconnoitre Ephesus and its culture. He didn't spend a fortune in an attempt to get hold of the demographics of the city. He got down and dirty from the day he arrived. Wise is that person who shows his true colours just as soon as he comes among strangers. It took less than one day for some Ephesians to find out that Paul was a man of God and the purpose for which he had come to Ephesus.

Paul's farewell address to the Ephesian elders is the nearest thing to Paul's letters that we have in the book of Acts. In Paul's three missionary sermons (13:16-41; 14:15-17; 17:22-31) and five defences (Acts 22-26), Paul was addressing non-Christian audiences. But he speaks here to Christians. The reader can see that in a situation similar to those he faced in many of his letters, this farewell to the Ephesian elders reads like a miniature letter of his style and language. Heading each section is an introductory formula: *"You know"* at verse 18. *"Now behold"* at verse 22. *"Now behold I know"* at verse 25, and finally *"And now"* at verse 32.

"I served the Lord with great humility and with tears and in the midst of severe testing by the plots of my Jewish opponents." (Acts 20:19).

"I served the Lord..." He served God in everything he did. What an incredibly basic biblical philosophy. He is still referring to, *"the whole time I was with you"* (20:18). Yes! He served his team. Yes! He served the Ephesians. Yes! He served the whole of Asia. Yet, in the midst of all those priorities clamouring for first place in his life, they all had to stand in line to his priority in serving Christ alone. Paul served God faithfully (Act 20:19).

"I served the Lord with great humility." One is not serving God if one is proud. At the Judgement seat of Christ (2 Corinthians 5:10) any pride present in the Christians heart will be seen to be "wood, hay and stubble" and not "gold, silver or precious stones." I suppose one could carry on with the preaching, teaching and praying in that state – but pride dulls the blade, clouds the heart, blinds the eyes of the understanding, and kills the flow of the divine life within. Oh for a greater understanding of the very nature of humility and the practice of it. It could easily be pride to say, *"I served the Lord with humility,"* but not in this case. Paul has no axe to grind, no case to make, no position to vie for. Those that stood before him had all a great deal to thank God for in the person of the apostle, and knew that as a model of Christ, Paul was Christ's ambassador par excellence. Paul indeed

served with humility (Romans 7:13; 1 Corinthians 15:9; Ephesians 3:8; Philippians 4:12; 1Timothy 1:15). The chief of apostles and the greatest of preachers, thought so much of Christ that he thought very little of himself.

"...and with tears." Oh dear! Let me hide at this point. How many men could cry for the sake of others when in the midst of great trouble themselves. Paul served the Lord with tears. I have certainly served myself with tears. I have definitely served my own sins and shame with my tears. But, as I write, I cannot honestly say that I have ever, knowingly, served the Lord with my tears.

I believe that the Lord is served when tears are shed while meditating on other people and the world at large, as God sees them. God is served when tears are shed for the lost masses in need of salvation. I do not mean mechanical or theatrical tears. I heard in Britain many years ago, an American preacher addressing considerably large crowds. I heard him speak on three different occasions in three different locations. He preached the same sermon each time. That was bad enough. But when I tell you that he wept at the same point of the sermon each time he delivered the address, you will understand me when I say that those kinds of tears do not impress God, nor should they impress man. I am seriously talking about those moments when our hearts break in tune with God's heart for the lost masses of humanity. These are issues that enable the Holy Spirit to locate us and manifest his miracle working power within us, flowing out towards those in need. Paul served the Lord with tears. That means Paul served with tenderness. Paul's masculinity and authority was not challenged by his tears. The bravest of apostles wept. The Son of God wept. To weep then, need be no sign of weakness. Tears are not fears, nor should they be feared. These tears undoubtedly fed and increased the healing anointing that was on Paul's life. This manifestation of the heart of Christ, this softness of Spirit, was part of the fuel and engine of what sustained Paul's wise and discerning management of the miraculous.

Tears are mentioned three times in this episode of scripture. His tears were consistent with his energy and courage, and a mark of the true greatness of Paul. His tears are a revelation of him having a conscience and sensitivity of nature surpassing the tenderness of any women. So he speaks of the tears that were (a) occasioned by his trials, and especially by the deadly hatred of the Jews. (b) The tears of his pastoral anxiety, and, (c) His tears mingled with the tears of the elders of Ephesus, once they had heard the prophetic word of the apostle that he was now leaving them for good, and they would see each other no more. Lord, help us to weep in a godly manner.

"And in the midst of severe testing by the plots of my Jewish opponents." Paul served God with humility and tears in the presence of deep suffering and opposition (Act 9:23; Act 23:11; 2Co 11:26). One translation puts it as, *"With trials."* When we think we have a monopoly of Christian sufferings, let us pause and consider what lay behind these two words of Paul's (2 Co 11:23-33). We are not talking of him comfortably sitting in a detached house in the peace and quiet of the English country-side discussing suffering. This is a man who was being constantly harassed and persecuted by both believers and unbelievers wherever he went. How incredibly difficult it seems from our western perspective to conceive of how a man would maintain faith, clarity of vision and self-esteem when having such attacks from so many quarters. The overall focussing of vision set on Christ, come hell or high water, is s deep secret of a ministry of the miraculous, in fact it is the deep secret of the entire Christian life.

All this is still under the umbrella of those opening phrases that said, *"You knew how I lived among you the whole time."* The whole time! This means that in the eyes of the Ephesians to whom Paul ministered, Paul was faithful in life and teaching (Acts 20:21). He was consistent in doctrine and manner of life. He was unchanging in his moment by moment conduct the whole time he was there in Ephesus. What glorious work of grace was this in an ex-murderers life!

This address of Paul to a considerable group of pastors and church leaders is a clear testimony of guiltlessness. How heavenly is that. It is by having lived a life of huge responsibility amongst them, he is, in another sense, freed from all responsibility.

YOU KNOW ALL ABOUT THE MESSAGE – THE GOSPEL (20:20-21)

"You know that I have not hesitated to preach anything that would be helpful to you but have taught you publicly and from house to house. I have declared to both Jews and Greeks that they must turn to God in repentance and have faith in our Lord Jesus" (Acts 20:20-21).

Paul's statements concerning his character, life and ministry are seriously profound. We err if we separate his character from his management of the miraculous. We seriously enter a Slough of Despond if we cannot see the strong unbreakable link between his character and the miraculous in his life and ministry. We see the tension in the following paradoxical couplets that come to mind as we analyse Paul's address.

Faith and action go together in Paul's life. Faith believes as if only God could do something. But when man acts, he must act as if all depends on him. For three years Paul confronted the idolatry and rage of Ephesian cults, religions and demons, and turned the city upside down. His faith was as vital as his action. James wrote that *"faith if it has not works is dead, being alone."* This is sometimes quoted as if he and Paul were not agreed. But look at this restless, ceaseless, mighty worker at Ephesus, Corinth, Athens, Rome, and Jerusalem. Paul spent his entire life as a Christian harnessing his "works" to his faith. It was against those who believed their good works would get them to heaven that Paul argued with, but never with James.

Humility and courage are conjoined twins as far as Paul is concerned (verse 19). When humility is at its best it most magnifies God. When courage is at its best it most magnifies God. That is the Divine secret of their harmony. They come together at the foot of the cross. Humility is seeing oneself as completely subject to and a servant of God. Courage is continuing in that servant hood while being threatened with death and/or torture. Humility suggests human weakness. Courage suggests divine strength.

Tenderness and severe conscientiousness are mutually impacting in the life of Paul. There was a deep pathos in the apostle's nature. He has been utterly misjudged and misunderstood by the sentimentalists who count him cold and harsh because he speaks the whole unadulterated truth. But how did he tell it? Like his Master, *"with many tears."* And yet his conscience kept his tenderness from wimp like weakness, and restrained him from mutilating truth through mistaken notions of love. He told men, even while he was weeping, *"that they were the enemies of the Cross of Christ."*

Some things must be active and living inside a person before they can go down on that person's record. The quality of a person's doing depends on the quality of being. Every man is the artificer of his own fortune, because every man is the builder of his own character. Apostolic character does not just happen, it is built. To have our life story as something worth looking at, and for it to be a joy in anybody's memory (especially our own), it needs to be embedded in the life and nature of Christ. We need to have our entire manner of life and doctrine scarred with the chains that bind us wilfully to Christ, to truth, and to people, all three. Treachery to any of this trio is treachery to all.

"You know that I have not hesitated to preach anything that would be helpful to you." This almost suggests that he shared his philosophy of ministry with the people whom he was addressing – which of course is something that Paul must have done. *"You know ..."* is a good phrase to use when addressing the leadership teams that you yourself had led to Christ and nurtured into mature leadership characters. They had grown to love and know the man. Why else would they have left their homes and trades to hear what he had to say?

"I have not hesitated..." The point is that if Paul saw a need for a concept of godliness to be declared and taught, he did not dawdle or hesitate. He preached about whatever he saw the need for. "Not hesitated to preach anything that would be helpful to you." Preaching must be helpful for the listeners. And for that to take place, the preacher needs to be divinely discerning about what his listeners need help about.

"...But have taught you publicly and from house to house." This is yet another important factor in the context of Paul's management of the miraculous. There are some issues that can be spoken from the pulpit or the soapbox and declared even from the roof tops to the largest crowds. But there are other points of truth and God's word that need to be quietly shared across the dinner table, that apply differently, and specifically to different cultures, different families and even different individuals. Paul's ministry was so wonderfully comprehensive to every person he ever came into contact with.

Added to that, it is more than inspirational for the body of the church to see their pastor in the context of normal life and not in the status of celebrity. No white suit. No celebrity mystique. No maintained distance to prevent people from seeing Paul close up. None of the, "Don't talk to me I am important," brigade. The entire mindset behind "white suit evangelism," or, "celebrity status ministers," is something that may occur in the mind of the masses, but it is not to be encouraged by the actions or words of Paul. He saw the people daily, went from house to house and wept and discussed with them. He was a man, not just a famed preacher.

The minister of God needs to both preach and teach. Both need to be made plain publicly and in the home. *"I have declared to both Jews and Greeks that they must turn to God in repentance and have faith in our Lord Jesus."* The preaching of the gospel reaches across all cultures, both genders, all ethnic groups, both public and private audiences. That gospel message, in essence, is never different or changed in one iota. Repentance towards God and faith towards our

Lord Jesus Christ are both at the foundation as well as the superstructure of Christianity. What Paul is saying is that they must continue with the same universal flavour that is at the crux of the gospel message.

What Paul is stating hitherto in summary is that for three years he has been an extremely high profile character in Ephesus and its surrounds, and that he has maintained a pure conscience not only through not having committed any wrongs, but that in doing good things, he did them excellently. A spirit of excellence was upon his life. The point of these words is in the assertion that he had laid a solid and firm foundation in the lives of all the Christians in Ephesus and in Asia. The ministry of the miraculous was built co-existing with a ministry of deep integrity.

I KNOW SUFFERING IS ON THE WAY (20:22-24)

"And now, behold, I am going to Jerusalem, constrained by the Spirit, not knowing what will happen to me there, except that the Holy Spirit testifies to me in every city that imprisonment and afflictions await me. But I do not account my life of any value nor as precious to myself, if only I may finish my course and the ministry that I received from the Lord Jesus, to testify to the gospel of the grace of God." Acts 20:22-24 (ESV)

A sublimely inspired ministry of truth and miracles will never be beyond persecution and tribulation. If the perfect Son of God, who did all things well and walked under the anointing of the Holy Spirit for the miracles and truth He delivered, was shamed, persecuted and crucified by the world, make no mistake that those who walk with God will sooner or later experience the same sort of thing. They that live godly in Christ Jesus shall suffer persecution.

He knows from God that persecution, prison and personal hardship is on the way. How do human beings live with this sort of revelation? The answer is, of course, that God does not share this kind of revelation to those who couldn't cope with it. Paul here confidently forecasts his own near future of *"prison and hardship"* (verse 22). His crystal clear words of retrospection now change gear and focus on a clear view of the immediate future. His past is indeed prophetic of his future. The deeper he delved into God and ministry, the deeper the response of persecution and hardship would return energised by the very powers of hell.

This is the language of courage and fearlessness. This is courage surfacing in the consciousness and the will of the apostle. This is the desperately brave determination that comes from the absolute conviction that God has a purpose, a destiny and an achievement for Paul to make in the world – no matter what the cost.

Jerusalem just cannot be avoided (verse 22). Whatever was to happen after Jerusalem – if there was an "after Jerusalem" - something was to start in the holy city that would define his future thereafter. Paul had no idea what was to happen excepting that it was to be, *"prison and hardship."* The apostle, however had a different response to many other times previous to this when hardship was known to be in the offing. There were times when he allowed himself the luxury of escaping the trouble that was threatening him. He escaped from Damascus in a basket (Acts 9:25. 2 Cor 11:33). He left Thessalonica by the encouragement of the converts and moved on (Acts 17:10). This, however, was different. There was the inner vision of destiny and righteousness about this oncoming horror. He was ready to meet it and he says so.

Despite the danger that was obviously prepared for him, Paul was set like concrete, just as Christ himself was when the time of His Passion drew near. This is important to our understanding of Paul's management of the miraculous. We need to make a note of the apostle's conformity to the sufferings of his Lord (Luke 9:51. Philippians 3:10. Acts 20:23-24). The Master Himself did not consult even His most intimate friends, but simply assured them *"that He must go to Jerusalem"* (Mat 16:21). The disciples were most unwilling that He should put Himself into the environs of such danger.

But Jesus replied by a prompt rebuke, Nothing could shake His purpose (Mar 10:32). In the same manner also, Christ's chosen bond servant Paul, went *"bound in the spirit"* (Acts 20:22) and only revealed to his closest colleagues and brothers his settled purpose. Many tried to dissuade him, but in vain. Such intrepid persistence as this was made possible to the apostle simply through his intense devotion. All that he wished for was to accomplish his course and to fulfil that ministry which he had received, not from man, but from the Lord Jesus. His entire philosophy was to live to Christ and for Christ. Anything short of that was not blessing him at all.

Paul was bound in the spirit to go to Jerusalem, knowing that he was to be bound in the body after he got there. He knew, and yet he did not know. He knew that dangers were before him, but he did not know, or care, exactly what they were. *"Prison and hardship"* – but he was still going. The apostle preached faith, and had faith. It was for that reason Paul went on to Jerusalem without any doubts concerning what would happen. Most people would believe in God as long as they were looked over and protected from harm. Paul, however, to a different degree knew that he was being looked over no matter what was to befall him. He was not expecting to be saved *from* harm, but *in* whatever harm came to him. Being looked over was not in the saving of his life, or keeping him from harm. Being divinely looked over was wrapped up in his own commitment to do exactly what God had asked of him. No matter how risky, or dangerous that was, Paul conceived of no other way to stay in the love of God apart from knowing what God wanted, and then doing it no matter what. He knew he was to suffer. He may even die. But he was absolutely certain that he was looked after by his divine Lord. Paul doubtless loved life and the mission the Saviour had given him to fulfil, but he loved the Lord Jesus Christ Himself a great deal more. He would obey what was given to him as a commission with and embrace all the consequences. It was an inescapable assignment from God. What on earth could the prospect of death do to deter him? If he lives he serves Christ, if he dies he is with Christ. Paul taught by word and deed, by doctrine and manner of life, that life itself is good for something only as it is put to some good use. He knew that he who loses his mortal life for Christ's sake finds thereby life immortal.

"But I do not account my life of any value nor as precious to myself, if only I may finish my course and the ministry that I received from the Lord Jesus, to testify to the gospel of the grace of God" (Acts 20:24). Somehow, the more I read these lines, the more conscious I become that I am ignorant of this kind of commitment. I do not mean by that, that I do not consider myself committed to Christ. What I do mean is that I could honestly repeat Paul's words here and thoroughly mean it. However, I have never been in any situation that has threatened my life for the sake of Christ. I have been rejected for Christ. I have been told that some jobs, and even promotions had been deferred because of my Christian convictions, but I have never been threatened with, "Deny Christ or die!"- Yet!

The sentiments expressed in this moment of Paul's address set a new bench-mark for the definition of, "committed Christian." Let's just call the spade what it exactly is. Paul was utterly selfless, totally Christ filled and had no latent sense of intuitive self-defence. The apostle was homed in on Christ's will and the divine purpose. 99% of all Christians would claim that, "God would not ask me to be a doormat to be walked upon. I must stay away from wicked people. Why should I go when the Holy Spirit testifies everywhere I go that I shall suffer in Jerusalem? I have a free will. I shall not go to Jerusalem!" But Paul refused to even parley with any such self-justifying escapism. He knew what Christ wanted of him, and in no way whatsoever would he even consider withdrawing from the commission given. Whatever was to happen to him, he would be a witness of Christ's saving grace.

I KNOW THIS IS GOOD-BYE (20:25-28)

"And now, behold, I know that none of you among whom I have gone about proclaiming the kingdom will see my face again.

Therefore I testify to you this day that I am innocent of the blood of all, for I did not shrink from declaring to you the whole counsel of God. Pay careful attention to yourselves and to all the flock, in which the Holy Spirit has made you overseers, to care for the church of God, which he obtained with his own blood." Acts 20:25-28 (ESV)

Now Paul jumps into the mystic and prophetic. *"I know that none of you ... will see my face again."* Without trying, Paul has just put this address and these men into a scenario that none of them will forget till their dying day, and one that they would be repeating over and over again to many people until their last day. Undoubtedly for several generations children, then grandchildren and even great grandchildren would hear about how their elderly or deceased forefather was present when Paul said his good-bye to the Ephesian pastors.

This was prophecy - intensely personal prophecy. He was prophesying not only that he would never see them again. That in itself was personal to him, as well as earth shattering to them. I do not believe, however, that this was the reason he had called them all to him. He called them because he had a personal word of prophecy for them. It is my contention that, as a prophet and apostle, Paul would have often ministered in this way in a whole raft of circumstances. His track record had the audience gripped by every word and nuance of inflection as he spoke.

Paul, as a minister of Jesus Christ considered himself bound to be absolutely faithful to all who came under his charge. There are parts of God's word that are pleasant to utter. There are phases of truth adapted to win the attention of unbelievers without disturbing their consciences or mugging their indifference. But there are other parts of the "counsel of God" that arouse violent opposition and forbid any kind of admiration. There are truths that enter the soul like sharp irons, and the impenitent hardened souls of people regard them often as the "personal opinions" of the preacher, or they shrug them off as the antiquated forms of a dead theology from earlier ignorant days in history. It is so easy to say that we have outgrown the teachings of previous generations! The temptation assails the Christian teacher to slur over or suppress the parts of the message that are in their own day unpopular. But nowhere did any such temptation touch Paul. He had to tell them a very unpleasant truth. Trouble and twisting of the word was to rise from within their ranks. *"None of you will see me again!"* At least, not in this life. *"I am innocent of the blood of all!"* The lies, deceits and heresies would not be rooted in anything he has said or modelled to them. *"Pay attention to the care of the flock!"* Make the care of other people your priority. Straight, true, forceful and yet gentle. Wonderful! And in the same breath; horrific!

He had gone about the lives of these men proclaiming the kingdom of God. He had declared as fully as he knew how. He had prayed, wept, visited, loved, befriended and given them all he had to give. From this point on they had to take what he had given them and run with it, yet without him. The master builder was confident about the teaching he had imparted. He was satisfied of the doctrinal, spiritual and social infrastructure he had shared and built into the psyche of believers in Ephesus.

"Pay careful attention!" They were hitherto under-shepherds to Paul, and now, from this moment they were promoted to be shepherds without Paul to consult or even ask. They needed to pay careful attention to how they were leading the flock.

It is important to embrace the truth that no matter how good the pastor, no matter how solid the teaching, no matter how experienced a group are in handling and dividing the word of truth, even the fruits of such a wise master builder as the apostle Paul could go astray once his hands were removed from the Ephesian operation. Paul was prophetically letting them know the imperative need of care, wisdom and good pastoring. Doctrinal chaos was in the offing.

The Holy Spirit Himself had appointed them as pastors of the church of God, and that holy calling demanded care, diligence and persistence in walking in the ways of truth. Take hold of the truth that no matter which of them were to later turn from the truth, they were all appointed by the Holy Spirit to be shepherds of the flock. That they were ministers of the word was God's choice. How well they handled, or mishandled their position was their choice. Even a man called Judas Iscariot was appointed by Christ in the power of the Holy Spirit to be a mighty deliverer. Iscariot's end was his choice, not God's.

Without any doubt whatsoever, at this point of Paul's address there would have been absolute silence. Perhaps there were slight whimpers here and there at the thought of never seeing Paul ever again, but the hungry hearts of these, the leaders of the huge group of believers in Ephesus and its surrounds, were aware that they were hearing the Rhema word of God for them at that moment. They did not live by bread alone, but these were men who knew that they lived by every Rhema word that proceeded from the mouth of God. It was a solemn moment.

Paul reminded them assertively that the same Holy Spirit whose guidance he was wilfully locked in to obey had the appointment, confirmation and direction of their ministry also (20:28). Such was the clear mandate of pastor, elder, and/or bishop in the early Church, and so it is today. The elders are only in authority to the same degree that they are under the authority of God. No authority, not even Paul's, allowed those elders to lord it over God's people. They were also given various commissions and callings to equip the church of Christ, but no pastor, elder, bishop or apostle is to ever forget that Christ said *He* would build His church. He never gave His church away to another.

"Take heed to yourselves!" Note that the shepherding of one's self is the first requirement for a Christ-like shepherding of others. Pastors are not to allow their position, post or calling to tempt them to take their spiritual health for granted, or to relax that vigilance over their own hearts, an issue which the word bids all Christians to keep. They are exhorted – and it could actually be read *as a command* – to take heed to themselves. If they were, by any means, to neglect their devotional self-examination while still performing a public ministry, they would get caught in the syndrome of becoming nothing but religious hacks, pedlars of the word and grow more and more unfit to be the real channels of spiritual guidance to others. They would have failed to take heed that their walk with Christ was in the Spirit. Because of the ministry and responsibilities of church leaders, any coldness, inconsistency, or walking in the flesh will do double injury to the cause of Christ.

I KNOW THAT TROUBLE AMONGST YOU IS ON THE WAY (20:29-31)

"I know that after my departure fierce wolves will come in among you, not sparing the flock; and from among your own selves will arise men speaking twisted things, to draw away the disciples after them. Therefore be alert, remembering that for three years I did not cease night or day to admonish every one with tears." (Acts 20:29-31 ESV)

Finally, he gives them the real reason why he had to see them and leave with them the word he had received from heaven. This was not something he felt, or sensed. This was something that he absolutely knew from God. *"Fierce wolves!"* That is using the analogy of the church being a flock of sheep. Embellishing that parabolic language with false teachers being wolves that come to feed on the lambs as well as the unguarded adults among the flock, Paul states flatly that fierce wolves are on their way with attitudes and mindsets that are to destroy and corrupt the church of Christ.

But what is worse, is that some of these fierce and gruesome wolves will arise from their own ranks. They will twist God's word and draw people after them. Some of those fierce "wolves to be," were in the very audience he was addressing. The call of Paul is for them to be alert to what is coming and ensure that none of them will be caught in the satanic net of error. They are besought to remember the tears with which he admonished them all over the period of time he was with them. The prophetic word was stark and sternly rooted in their spirits. The unspoken message was, "Beware you strong shepherds, that none of you morph into fierce wolves!" The politics, the interaction, the character clashes, the jealousies that trick spiritual people into a trance of carnality and fleshliness can be absolutely tragic.

This is the message for which he called them together. It was the last statement of his ministry among them that was to close Paul's personal "hands on" ministry to Ephesus.

In the same way that the shedding of tears is mentioned three times in Paul's discourse on the beach at Miletus, so is "blood," or the laying down of life, mentioned three times.

o   Paul was willing to yield up his life at Jerusalem if it was required for Christ. (Acts 20:24)

o   The apostle was free from the blood of all men. He kept himself pure by so preaching the gospel, that if any heard and refused it, their blood would be on their own heads. (Acts 20:26).

o   The Church of God has been purchased by Christ's blood. (Acts 20:28)

Who said Christianity is light? This is heavy duty, "blood, sweat and tears," living for the very glory of Christ. There must have been a sense of imminent grief amongst the Ephesian elders. *"After my departure shall grievous wolves enter in among you, not sparing the flock. Also of your own selves shall men arise speaking perverse things."* Although he and the disciples, along with these elders had laboured three years in Ephesus, and though they might strive ever so faithfully in the future to feed the flock of God, yet all that care, labour, ministry and prayer could not ensure perfect loyalty to the truth of God's word.

The ever uncertain variable in the calculus of this equation is, as always, the instability of the human heart. No apostle was ever able to keep an entire Church true to the faith. Even Christ Himself lost Judas

(John 17:12). The most devoted and faithful worker will always find a shrinkage in his results. It is a fact of life. Peter already had foreseen *"false teachers among you...denying the Lord that bought them."* John later, warned Christians against *"the Antichrist, who has already come."* Jude wrote to Christians exhorting them, *"to earnestly contend for the faith which was once delivered unto the saints. For there are certain men crept in unawares ... denying ... our Lord Jesus Christ."* This is a universally common phenomena of satanic interference in people's hearts and minds. We are all exposed to things that are not consistent with God's word. This is because we live in the midst of a generation that is without faith and hope. Trusting in Christ is not a mere intellectual acknowledgement of His person, but adherence and commitment to trusting Him and being dependant on Him for everything. Many try to get acquainted with God by their feelings. But feelings rise and fall like the weather. Feelings are influenced by what we read and see. If exterior, ungodly things in life affect our feelings (and they do), and our feelings control our faith, it clearly means that one can be a Christian, yet, sadly, controlled by satanic devices.

I COMMIT YOU TO GOD AND HIS WORD. (20:32-35)

"And now I commend you to God and to the word of his grace, which is able to build you up and to give you the inheritance among all those who are sanctified. I coveted no one's silver or gold or apparel. You yourselves know that these hands ministered to my necessities and to those who were with me. In all things I have shown you that by working hard in this way we must help the weak and remember the words of the Lord Jesus, how he himself said, 'It is more blessed to give than to receive.'" (Acts 20:32-35. ESV)

Salvation is received and developed through God and the word of His grace. Our affections and emotions must be set to receive the word of God without questioning. The word of God needs to be engrafted, embedded and absorbed into our entire lifestyle and thinking. It is the word of His grace that builds Christ's nature into us. The final spiritual ministration of the apostle to the elders at Ephesus was to commend them to Heavenly Father and the word of His grace. This was not a perfunctory and meaningless bit of religious jargon, but a practical and real application of prayer and speaking to the future mountain of heresy and a twisting of that word of grace. It is the word of grace that builds, and finally will bring the inheritance of the kingdom to all those who are separated to that word.

The apostle brings his remarks to a close by referring to the lifestyle and habits which were plainly seen and easy to follow by all the Ephesians who daily studied his every move and hung on to every word he spoke. He strikingly counselled his audience to follow his own example as to self-support as well as supporting others. At Ephesus, where it had been so common to practise occult as well as pseudo-spiritual arts for the gain of filthy lucre, it was eminently advisable that the elders and pastors of the Christian community should prove themselves utterly disinterested in thoughts of financial gain. It was healthy too that they should show an example to others in practicing something that Christ said (that is not recorded in scripture anywhere else), "It is better to give than to receive." (20:35).

It is necessary to note that when Paul dropped the word of warning, which undoubtedly must have added alarm to the sorrow of the assembled elders, he foresaw that teachers of error would appear at Ephesus even in their own ranks. He did not expand on the subject, but sounded an incredibly solemn alarm; *"Watch!"* From the message spoken by the Lord Jesus in later years, we learn that the evil here spoken of did indeed arise (Rev 2:1-7). We also gather that Paul's warning had not been without good effect.

The closing statements of Paul's fatherly and prophetic address display the true spirit of the faithful servant, the loving father, and the God hearing prophet. *"I have coveted no man's silver, or gold, or apparel. I have showed you all things, how that so labouring ye ought to support the weak."* He was speaking to men who lived in a commercial centre and were used to measuring values of life in terms of gold and silver. They could appreciate, therefore, the unselfishness of a man who had no regard for the precious things of trade. It is horribly possible to have a low motive even in the highest service, for there is no work of any kind on the planet which self-seeking may not spoil. A continued service for others, the helping of the weak and sinful, begets the habit of subordinating selfishness. The kind of unselfishness which the world likes to see is that which gives up the things the world prizes best. Self-assertion the world understands, but it is nonplussed before self-denial. Our influence as labourers for the kingdom must spring from the degree of our unselfishness.

We cannot get an indifferent world to accept a gospel of the cross while we are avoiding crosses in our daily living. It was because the elders knew that the cross was the centre principle in Paul's life that they regarded him with so much affection.

And so, with this all said, Paul fell to his knees in prayer, and they all followed his example. How I would dearly love to have seen the transcript of his prayer, and even more to hear the cry from his spirit for the sake of these men of God that he loved. He prayed, and they all wept. Weeping, embracing and kissing were in abundance. The book says that they were in a state of grief at the thought of never seeing him again in this life (Acts 20:36-38). They accompanied him to the ship and no doubt mournfully watched him board the vessel. Acts 21:1 baldly says, *"After we had torn ourselves away from them, we put out to sea."*

And so Paul's mission to Ephesus, at least in terms of his personal hands on ministry, ended at that very moment.

Ephesus was taken.

32.

A BACKWARD LOOK AT THE BIG PICTURE AS PAUL LEAVES EPHESUS BEHIND?

"According to the grace of God which is given unto me, as a wise master builder, I have laid the foundation, and another builds thereon. But let every man take heed how he builds thereon."

1 Corinthians 3:10

Paul moves on from Miletus to Jerusalem, and I am still in a state of awe, left with the overall vista of Acts 19 and 20 in my rear view mirror to ponder and meditate on. We can opportunistically use the opening Paragraph of Charles Dickens' novel, "A tale of Two Cities," as a commentary on Paul's time in the capital city of Asia: "It was the best of times, it was the worst of times, it was the age of wisdom, it was the age of foolishness, it was the epoch of belief, it was the epoch of incredulity, it was the season of Light, it was the season of Darkness, it was the spring of hope, it was the winter of despair, we had everything before us, we had nothing before us, we were all going direct to heaven, we were all going direct the other way." This is profoundly accurate of what went on in Acts 19, along with other insights from Second Corinthians. It was a time of striking polemics in the responses of the people. So how do we analyse an overview of Paul's greatest and final mission?

This had been undoubtedly Paul's finest hour, as well as his worst. Actually, it was 3 years, slightly more than an hour, yet, in those three years, not only does his preaching, teaching and ministry of the miraculous hit an all-time "high impact" peak, but the persecution he faced whilst he was there was worse than any that even he had encountered previously. Considering he was stoned and left for dead at Lystra (Acts 14:19-20) and then never seems to mention it anywhere else, I conclude that when Paul explains that the opposition in Asia was so intense that he gave up on life, it plainly means that what came against him in Asia (i.e. Ephesus) was beyond most normal concepts of what is nowadays termed as abuse (2 Corinthians 1:8-9). If Paul gave up on life we are seriously talking of the ultimate definition of having a rough day. He did say in First Corinthians that he fought with wild beasts during his stay at Ephesus (15:32). Obviously, he was referring to some kind of animalistic torturous attacks on his person – and I mean physical. Consider my resulting statement then, that if Paul gave up on life whilst "delivering the gospel goods" in Ephesus, one cannot but grasp that the curse of persecution was as intense as the power of God was on his mission in the whole of Asia. In the opening salvo of these pages I stated some extravagant remarks about Paul's activities in Ephesus exulting in what I consider to be the peak, or the very apex of all the New Testament definitions of apostolic ministry. Assuming my readers have read the rest of my thesis here, I believe I have explained fully why I consider Paul's mission to Asia to be the absolute pinnacle of apostolic mission and the glass case perfect model of evangelistic strategy for all time. The flaw in a modern application of whatever insight I have received is that the strategy I see needs a Paul to "General" the whole thing. Where are the Pauls? Where are the Generals and the strategic Field Marshalls for Christ?

Acts 19 was the best of times because the whole of Asia heard the word of the Lord. It was the worst of times because many put feet to the thought of wanting Paul dead while he was there. It was an age of wisdom, for every preacher and teacher under Paul's influence, who was then harnessed into the same driving mission as Paul and were all in submission to their mentor holding campaigns in other parts of Asia. It was an age of crass foolishness, for in the midst of God Almighty healing, delivering and saving huge numbers of people, there were those who wanted the gospel silenced simply because one of the offshoots of multiple numbers becoming Christians was the diminishing sale of silver shrines and idols in the province. This "stranger," Paul, had the nerve to take people away from worshipping a lifeless bit of stone that had been given the name of Artemis/Diana. So he was "obviously" perceived as a villain.

It was an epoch of faith. All through Asia the name of the Lord Jesus was held in high esteem (Acts 19:17), by both Christians and pagans. However, it was also an epoch of incredulity, for if all Asia heard the word, yet all of Asia was not converted, even in the face of some remarkable demonstrations of the power of Jesus Christ, incredulity must have matched the faith of the converts in its depth and wide sweeping influence amongst unbelievers. It was the season of Light, for Christ had visited Ephesus. It was a season of darkness because Paul, amongst others was persecuted to the point of death.

It was simultaneously a spring of hope with multitudes coming to faith in Christ, but a concurrent winter of despair for the intensity of unbelief, occultists and worldly business men wanting Paul out of the way. The anointing of God on the life of the diminutive Jewish Apostle of Christ split the population. There were those who had come to Christ and had everything before them, as well as those who flatly and violently rejected Christ leaving nothing before them. There were groups amongst the Ephesians and the Asians who could say, "We are all going to heaven." But there were still vast numbers of Christ rejecters who could laugh and say, mockingly, "We are all going the other way."

Therefore, we need to reprise the "big picture," and allow the Technicolor graphics to solidify in our mind's eye. It is an epic blockbuster of a picture. It is one of those stories that just have to be read and pondered. I believe that the personal imperative which the issues that Paul stirs up in Ephesus is to go through the biblical record and to chew on what we have in our own hands. The purists refer to this process as "meditation." The drama we are considering was between 27 months, and 3 years long. Where did it start on the timeline of history? I am asserting that it was 54 AD – that's more like a strong suggestion actually. But I won't fall out with anybody who differs with me. If anybody wants to be pedantic about it, let them do a good bit of research, the kind that anyone can find from books and the internet. One will find a whole bagful of dates and quite a few reasons why they are each, "correct." The earliest I found was 52 AD, and the latest was 56. I have read a lot of the theses as to how, what and why it must be such and such a date. I don't think knowing the exact date is vitally important to getting to grips with the biblical text of Acts 19, but obviously it helps to have your own study and meditative time around it all to have a personal opinion. I have landed on 54 AD. But that is an assumption that I cannot refer to with total conviction.

First we state the skeletal outline. Paul came to Ephesus and initially gained the following and commitment of a dozen or so disciples. Following his deeply held principle of, "To the Jew first," Paul spent three months preaching, teaching and discussing with the Synagogue adherents. The whole group of Jewish worshippers polarised listening to Paul so often, and those who wanted to stay with pregnant Judaism instead of Christianity, the very child that came from the loins of Judaism, were too vehement and obstructive to Paul and the progress of the gospel while he stayed in the Synagogue. So, Paul transferred his operation to the school of Tyrannus. It is at this point that the fireworks begin. Paul was making tents and making considerable amounts of money that allowed him to board and lodge his party. He would preach, teach and minister for five hours every day, and then go from house to house of both Jews and gentiles teaching, preaching and generally watering the seeds that he had planted in the hearts of the people. There are those that choose to believe that because Paul was talking to the elders of the Ephesian churches when he made his remarks about going from house to house every day, it was only the elders and pastors that he visited. Those Christians who have an almost cultic approach to the concept of leadership, and they are many, are welcome to their biased opinion. I flatly reject it.

With Paul mentoring his team, modelling both ministry and preaching curriculum to the group, he then sent them out (undoubtedly in two's) to various population centres around Asia. This perspective is biblically endorsed only by the account of Epaphras who founded a church at Colossae. This seems to be the soundest logic when considering how the whole of Asia got to hear the word of God. We have no other hints that Paul ever left Ephesus during the mission.

If the team that Paul sent out were moving under the same imparted anointing and biblical insights as their mentor, then we have it clearly understood that with a dozen or so of "cloned Paul's" itinerating around Asia the place would have been generally shaken by the power of the gospel.

Over the period of time that this mission was making inroads to Asian society, riots and complaints came boomeranging back on Paul's head.

With a huge number of converts resulting in people having new purchasing habits and lifestyles, the major industries that had anything to do with the occult and idol worship in general started to face decline in the new dynamics of the Asian economy. Just like any population would blame their leaders when a country seems to be mismanaged, not being able to complain against Rome without their lives being endangered, those with complaints to register concerning their failing businesses all with one accord pointed the finger at, "This man Paul," and those pesky Christians.

Even though the book of Acts merely tells us of a single riot where Paul was not injured and actually held back by his friends from exacerbating the situation by making a speech, Second Corinthians lets us know that persecution of the most terrible kind was militant against Paul and conceivably others of the team.

The writer's personal experience of observing ministry that moves in the dimension that Paul moved, is that characters like Paul are passionately supported and loved by those who have been the recipients of God's blessing through him, and equally passionately hated by atheists, witch doctors and mediums, and other Christian ministers who have the awful stench of jealousy. In my years in Lagos my anecdotal mental statistics would lead me to suggest that the majority of a 25,000 congregation were introduced to their solid faith through a simple request for healing. People healed in the name of Jesus while at the point of death tended to turn to Christ and their entire social entourage of family, neighbours, work colleagues and social acquaintances would eagerly follow. It may not be true that miracles turn everybody to Christ, but it seemed wonderfully true that simple story telling over and over again about how a crippled man came to walk, or a deaf man came to be able to hear clearly, won more for Christ than the best preaching. On top of that, with so many people who were deep into the occult having a profound awareness of all things spiritual, once converted, the understanding of the gospel of previous agents of Satan is more profound than the rank and file of millions of Christians in the west. From my perspective, in Africa, it seemed to me that the church members would die for their pastor, just as, in the same way, others – including many Pentecostal ministers – seemed to want him done away with. In the same way as with Paul, I am convinced that he was loved beyond measure by the Ephesian believers, and hated beyond reason by those that opposed him.

In the midst of all this going on in Ephesus, the huge church at Corinth had issues and arguments that had escalated to severe criticism of Paul's character. From reading both First and Second Corinthians, it seems feasible that the trouble in Corinth was more of a reason for Paul to leave Ephesus than the persecution there. That, indeed, is what I have concluded in my notes on previous pages. Notwithstanding, I am also of the opinion that whatever trauma Paul was immersed in during his Ephesian imprisonment was enough to supply a second piece of solid rationale for Paul to "leave town," and to escape from death threats in Ephesus.

Somewhere in the midst of the huge and ever-growing acrimony and persecution, Paul quickly left Ephesus. He travelled through

Macedonia, and possibly, at this time, into Illyricum, and then down into Corinth where he stayed over winter for three months.

During this period of time (i.e. from the latter days at Ephesus, through to his leaving Macedonia on the way to Jerusalem) Paul received prophetic words concerning his own future as well as the future of the church at Ephesus. He obviously received the word first himself, and thereafter heard the statements repeated time and time again from others as he travelled. These words that were first voiced while he was still in Ephesus obviously developed into more of a burden as time progressed. He knew he had to return to Jerusalem and there suffer hardship.

He earlier was convinced that he would see Rome, but the insight he received about the trouble that was to come at Jerusalem seemed to make him unsure as to whether he would live to see Rome. He also saw deep into the hearts of the people at the church in Ephesus and had to address their leaders as he passed by Ephesus on his way to Jerusalem. The prophetic word was that even though he claimed their blood was utterly off his hands, and that he had taught them all he knew, Ephesus would become a hotbed of false teachers in the not too distant future. He would not ever see any of them ever again, and he told them that they should be extremely watchful, for some of the heretics and false teachers would arise from amongst the ranks of the elders that he was addressing. And so Paul sailed on to Jerusalem.

Later Paul sent a circular letter to all the churches in Asia. I refer to the letter we refer to as "Ephesians."

It was even later that Paul sent Timothy to pastor what must have been a huge work of God in Ephesus. After Timothy, the apostle John is known to have assume the role of pastor/bishop to the whole of Asia.

When Christ appeared to the apostle John and imparted all that we refer to as "The book of the Revelation of Jesus Christ," the entire book was intended to be circulated and read in the churches of Asia.

Although there are notelets from Christ Himself to be sent to the seven most influential churches of Asia within the book of Revelation, the book was for all in Asia. John the aged last survivor of the original twelve received the apocalyptic visions of the last book of the bible while on the Isle of Patmos. It would seem, that by the time the apostle John had taken over as the head of the churches in Asia, the largest, or at least most influential churches were the seven mentioned. But Colossae, Hierapolis and several other population centres also had churches based there. Archaeologists and historians have found the evidence to back these statements.

About the Author

Meet Keith Lannon, a native of Manchester, England, whose passion for exploring the timeless wisdom of the biblical narrative has spanned over five decades. With a background in preaching, teaching, editing and writing, Keith has spent years delving into the depths of biblical relevance for twenty-first century living.

Keith is the eldest child of seven, all of whom are now in their senior years. Keith now lives in Derby, England.

Following the success of his acclaimed debut work, "Management of the Miraculous," Keith here holds his microscopic insights into the incredibly intense three-year-mission that opened up western Turkey in the real time of Acts chapter 19.

Keith's life's journey has taken him far and wide, sharing his insights and wisdom across continents. From the bustling cities of the United States to the vibrant landscapes of Africa and Europe, Keith's unique presentations have captivated audiences, earning him high-profile invitations to speak to crowds numbering at times in the thousands.

Join him as he unveils the compelling story of the growth of Christianity in the once evil and mystical occult spirituality that rotted and festered in the city of Ephesus. You will find him offering fresh perspectives and timeless lessons for readers seeking deeper understanding and spiritual enrichment in the presentation of the person of Jesus Christ.

Keith Lannon Ministries. email: keithlannon49@gmail.com

Available now on Amazon:

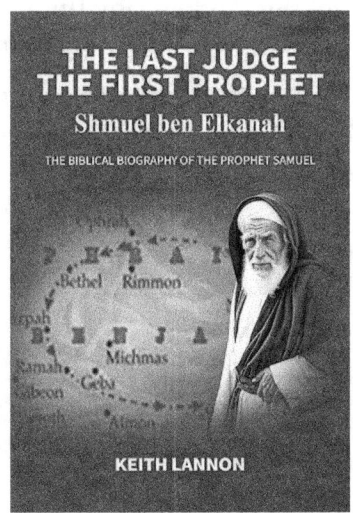

The Last Judge, The first Prophet.

Biography of the Prophet Samuel.

By *Keith Lannon*

Immerse yourself in the profound life and teachings of the revered prophet Samuel with this comprehensive volume. Meticulously crafted over years of dedicated research, it blends academic rigor with spiritual insight to offer a captivating portrayal of his journey. Seamlessly weaving historical context with devotional depth, this work presents a compelling narrative that is both accessible and enriching.

Designed to resonate with both scholars and seekers alike, its narrative style invites readers to delve into the complexities of faith while navigating the intriguing tapestry of Samuel's life. Whether you're a seasoned Bible student or a casual reader, this volume promises to captivate your imagination and deepen your understanding of biblical history.

A timeless treasure, it stands as a testament to the enduring relevance of Samuel's story and the profound impact of his teachings. Engaging, thought-provoking, and spiritually enriching, this work is destined to become a classic in the realm of biblical literature. Dive into its pages and embark on a transformative journey through the life and legacy of one of history's most influential prophets.

www.ingramcontent.com/pod-product-compliance
Lightning Source LLC
Chambersburg PA
CBHW070456120526
44590CB00013B/663